THE
ULTIMATE
BOOK OF
SPORTS
LISTS
1998

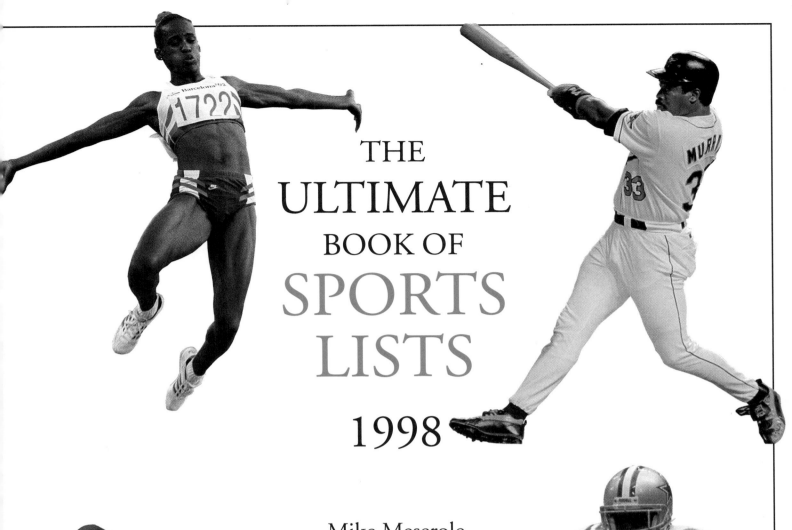

THE
ULTIMATE
BOOK OF
SPORTS
LISTS
1998

Mike Meserole

DK PUBLISHING, INC.

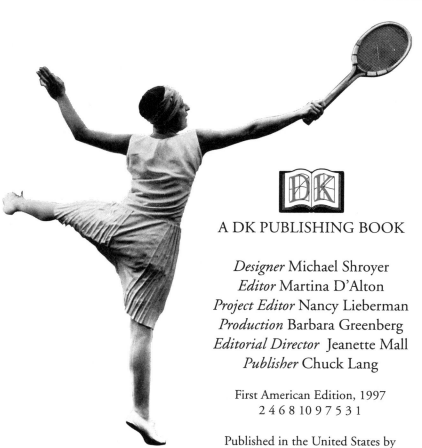

A DK PUBLISHING BOOK

Designer Michael Shroyer
Editor Martina D'Alton
Project Editor Nancy Lieberman
Production Barbara Greenberg
Editorial Director Jeanette Mall
Publisher Chuck Lang

First American Edition, 1997
2 4 6 8 10 9 7 5 3 1

Published in the United States by
DK Publishing, Inc.
95 Madison Avenue, New York, New York 10016
Visit us on the World Wide Web at
http://www.dk.com

Reproduced by Pre Press Imaging
Printed and bound in the United States by
R.R. Donnelley & Sons

Library of Congress Cataloging-in-Publication Data
Meserole, Mike.
The ultimate book of sports lists / by Mike Meserole — 1st
American ed.
p. cm.
Includes index.
ISBN 0-7894-2279-4 (hc : alk. paper)
ISBN 0-7894-2134-8 (pbk.: alk. paper)
1. Sports—Miscellanea. I. Title.
GV707 .M47 1997
796—dc21   97-20800
                                             CIP

Contents

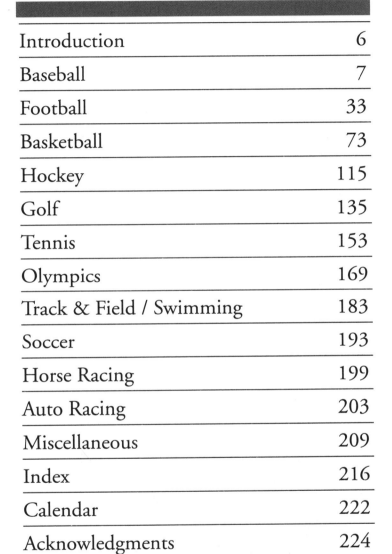

Introduction

When Tiger Woods won the Masters golf tournament in April, the 21-year-old was proclaimed "the next Jack Nicklaus" by the experts. Jack Nicklaus himself said as much a year ago at Augusta, when he and Arnold Palmer, two former champions with 10 Masters titles between them, played a practice round with Woods. "Arnold and I both agreed," said Nicklaus afterward, "that you could take his Masters and my Masters and add them together, and this kid should win more than that." Not *could* win more than 10 Masters. *Should* win more than 10. It reminded a few observers of Bobby Jones' comment about Nicklaus in 1965: "He plays a game with which I am not familiar."

And that's why, over 30 years later, Jack Nicklaus is the most familiar name in golf. He is the game's greatest champion, and he has the titles to prove it. Turn to the golf chapter on page 135, and you will see his name or picture no fewer than 54 times in 18 pages. In Grand Slam tournament history, no player has won more championships (18) or finished second more often (19) than the Golden Bear. Walter Hagen is a distant second in majors won, with 11, and the next closest runner-up is Palmer with 10. It makes you wonder if anyone will ever surpass Nicklaus.

You never know. In 1979, who figured a 5-foot-11, 165-pound, 18-year-old named Wayne Gretzky would eventually elbow the legendary Gordie Howe out of the way as the National Hockey League's all-time leading scorer and win nine Most Valuable Player awards? Or that 21-year-old guard Michael Jordan, who averaged only 17.7 points a game in college, would win nine scoring titles and overtake Wilt Chamberlain as the National Basketball Association's most prolific scorer?

The fun of being a sports fan is watching contemporary stars take on the legends, seeing how they measure up on the field and in the record books. *The Ultimate Book of Sports Lists 1998* is about measuring up. Who are the leaders and who's gaining on them? From the Super Bowl's greatest underdogs to the Iditarod's most successful sled dog drivers. From the fastest qualifiers at the Indianapolis 500 to every NHL player with 500 or more goals. From the shortest players in NBA history to the highest-grossing sports movies in Hollywood history. From the youngest winners at Wimbledon to the oldest managers in baseball.

These lists and a thousand more like them await your inspection. I hope you enjoy thumbing through the following chapters as much as I did compiling them. If you have any comments or suggestions for lists in future editions, please send them along. You can reach me care of DK, Inc., 95 Madison Avenue, New York, NY 10016.

BASEBALL

Ken Griffey Jr. of Seattle hit 56 home runs in 1997, giving him 294 homers in just nine seasons.

World Champions

Most Appearances in World Series

No.	Team	Record
34	New York Yankees	23-11
18	Los Angeles Dodgers	6-12
16	San Francisco Giants	5-11
15	St. Louis Cardinals	9-6
14	Oakland Athletics	9-5
10	Chicago Cubs	2-8
9	Boston Red Sox	5-4
9	Cincinnati Reds	5-4
9	Detroit Tigers	4-5
8	Atlanta Braves	3-5
7	Pittsburgh Pirates	5-2
7	Baltimore Orioles	3-4
6	Minnesota Twins	3-3
5	Cleveland Indians	2-3
5	Philadelphia Phillies	1-4
4	Chicago White Sox	2-2
3	New York Mets	2-1
2	Toronto Blue Jays	2-0
2	Kansas City Royals	1-1

Franchise moves and name changes: •Dodgers—9 appearances in Brooklyn and 9 in Los Angeles; •Giants—14 appearances in New York and 2 in San Francisco; •Athletics—8 appearances in Philadelphia and 6 in Oakland; •Braves—2 appearances in Boston, 2 in Milwaukee, and 4 in Atlanta; •Orioles—1 appearance as St. Louis Browns and 6 as Baltimore Orioles; •Twins—3 appearances as original Washington Senators and 3 as Minnesota Twins. Note: The Florida Marlins (1-0), Milwaukee Brewers (0-1), and San Diego Padres (0-1) have each appeared once.

All-Time Winners

Twenty franchises have won the World Series since the National and American leagues first met in 1903.

No.	Team	Championship Years	Lost World Series
23	New York Yankees	1996, 1978, 1977, 1962, 1961, 1958, 1956, 1949-53, 1947, 1943, 1941, 1936-39, 1932, 1928, 1927, 1923	1981, 1976, 1964, 1963, 1960, 1957, 1955, 1942, 1926, 1922, 1921
9	Oakland Athletics	1989, 1972-74, 1930, 1929, 1913, 1911, 1910	1990, 1988, 1931, 1914, 1905
9	St. Louis Cardinals	1982, 1967, 1964, 1946, 1944, 1942, 1934, 1931, 1926	1987, 1985, 1968, 1943, 1930, 1928
6	Los Angeles Dodgers	1988, 1981, 1965, 1963, 1959, 1955	1978, 1977, 1974, 1966, 1956, 1953, 1952, 1949, 1947, 1941, 1920, 1916
5	Boston Red Sox	1918, 1916, 1915, 1912, 1903	1986, 1975, 1967, 1946
5	Cincinnati Reds	1990, 1976, 1975, 1940, 1919	1972, 1970, 1961, 1939
5	Pittsburgh Pirates	1979, 1971, 1960, 1925, 1909	1927, 1903
5	San Francisco Giants	1954, 1933, 1922, 1921, 1905	1989, 1962, 1951, 1937, 1936, 1924, 1923, 1917, 1913, 1912, 1911
4	Detroit Tigers	1984, 1968, 1945, 1935	1940, 1934, 1907-09
3	Baltimore Orioles	1983, 1970, 1966	1979, 1971, 1969, 1944
3	Atlanta Braves	1995, 1957, 1914	1996, 1992, 1991, 1958, 1948
3	Minnesota Twins	1991, 1987, 1924	1965, 1933, 1925
2	Chicago Cubs	1908, 1907	1945, 1938, 1935, 1932, 1929, 1918, 1910, 1906
2	Chicago White Sox	1917, 1906	1959, 1919
2	Cleveland Indians	1948, 1920	1997, 1995, 1954
2	New York Mets	1986, 1969	1973
2	Toronto Blue Jays	1993, 1992	none
1	Florida Marlins	1997	none
1	Kansas City Royals	1985	1980
1	Philadelphia Phillies	1980	1993, 1983, 1950, 1915

The St. Louis "Gas House Gang" in Detroit before Game 1 of the 1934 World Series, from left: Dizzy Dean (pitcher), Leo Durocher (shortstop), Fran Orsatti (outfield), Bill DeLancey (catcher), Ripper Collins (first base), Joe Medwick (outfield), player-manager Frankie Frisch (second base), Jack Rothrock (outfield), and Pepper Martin (third base).

Best Postseason Records

Based on winning percentage, including the World Series (since 1903), League Championship Series (since 1969), League Divisional Series (since 1995), and the 1981 League Division Playoffs (between half-season champions in that strike-shortened season); through the 1997 season. Records include three tie games from the 1907, 1912, and 1922 World Series.

Pct.	Team	Games	Record	Post-seasons
.688	Florida Marlins	16	11-5	1
.600	New York Mets	40	24-16	4
.589	New York Yankees	237	139-97-1	37
.571	Baltimore Orioles	84	48-36	11
.558	Oakland Athletics	120	67-53	18
.547	Cincinnati Reds	86	47-39	12
.537	Cleveland Indians	54	29-25	6
.533	St. Louis Cardinals	122	65-57	16
.520	Atlanta Braves	102	53-49	12
.512	Toronto Blue Jays	41	21-20	5
.500	Boston Red Sox	81	40-40-1	11
.500	Montreal Expos	10	5-5	1
.482	Minnesota Twins	56	27-29	8
.471	Detroit Tigers	69	32-36-1	11
.471	Milwaukee Brewers	17	8-9	2
.455	San Francisco Giants	112	50-60-2	17
.449	Pittsburgh Pirates	89	40-49	14
.447	Los Angeles Dodgers	150	67-83	22
.444	Chicago White Sox	36	16-20	6
.419	Kansas City Royals	43	18-25	7
.400	Seattle Mariners	15	6-9	2
.386	Philadelphia Phillies	57	22-35	9
.375	Anaheim Angels	16	6-10	3
.357	Chicago Cubs	63	22-40-1	12
.316	Houston Astros	19	6-13	4
.308	San Diego Padres	13	4-9	2
.250	Colorado Rockies	4	1-3	1
.250	Texas Rangers	4	1-3	1

As a pitcher, Babe Ruth won two games in the 1918 World Series, the last time the Boston Red Sox won the title. He joined the New York Yankees before the 1920 season.

Managers with Most World Series Appearances

App.	Manager/Team	Record
10	Casey Stengel, New York (AL)	7-3
9	Joe McCarthy, Chicago (NL)/New York (AL)	7-2
9	John McGraw, New York (NL)	3-6
8	Connie Mack, Philadelphia (AL)	5-3
7	Walter Alston, Brooklyn/L.A. Dodgers	4-3
6	Miller Huggins, New York (AL)	3-3
5	Sparky Anderson, Cincinnati/Detroit	3-2
4	Frank Chance, Chicago (NL)	2-2
4	Tommy Lasorda, L.A. Dodgers	2-2
4	Dick Williams, Boston/Oakland/San Diego	2-2
4	Billy Southworth, St. Louis (NL)/Boston (NL)	2-2
4	Bobby Cox, Toronto/Atlanta	1-3
4	Earl Weaver, Baltimore	1-3

Note: Three managers have led two different teams each to World Series titles—Sparky Anderson (Cincinnati, 1975 and 1976, and Detroit, 1984); Bill McKechnie (Pittsburgh, 1925, and Cincinnati, 1940); and Bucky Harris (Washington, 1924, and N.Y. Yankees, 1947).

World Series Cancellations

The World Series between the champions of the National League (founded in 1876) and the American League (founded in 1901) has been played continuously, with two exceptions, since 1903. In 1904 John McGraw, manager of the N.L. champion New York Giants refused to play the Boston Red Sox (the surprise winner of the 1903 Series) because he did not consider them worthy opponents. In 1994 a players' strike protesting the owners' call for revenue sharing and a salary cap achieved what two world wars and a 1989 earthquake could not—it canceled the 1994 World Series. The strike was called on August 12, 1994, and did not officially end until April 2, 1995.

All-Time World Series Leaders

Asterisk (*) indicates player active in 1997 postseason.

BATTING

Whitey Ford of the New York Yankees pitching to Pittsburgh's lead-off batter Bill Virdon in Game 3 of the 1960 World Series.

Highest Batting Average
Based on at least 50 at-bats.

Avg.	Player
.418	Pepper Martin
.418	Paul Molitor
.391	Lou Brock
.390	Marquis Grissom*
.373	Thurman Munson
.373	George Brett
.364	Hank Aaron
.363	Home Run Baker
.362	Roberto Clemente
.361	Lou Gehrig

Highest Slugging Average
Based on at least 50 at-bats.

Avg.	Player
.755	Reggie Jackson
.744	Babe Ruth
.731	Lou Gehrig
.700	Lenny Dykstra
.658	Al Simmons
.655	Lou Brock
.636	Pepper Martin
.636	Paul Molitor
.624	Hank Greenberg
.611	Charlie Keller

Note: Slugging average is total bases divided by at-bats.

Most Hits

No.	Player
71	Yogi Berra
59	Mickey Mantle
58	Frankie Frisch
54	Joe DiMaggio
46	Hank Bauer
46	Pee Wee Reese
45	Gil McDougald
45	Phil Rizzuto
43	Lou Gehrig
42	Eddie Collins
42	Elston Howard
42	Babe Ruth

Most Games

No.	Player
75	Yogi Berra
65	Mickey Mantle
54	Elston Howard
53	Hank Bauer
53	Gil McDougald
52	Phil Rizzuto
51	Joe DiMaggio
50	Frankie Frisch
44	Pee Wee Reese
41	Roger Maris
41	Babe Ruth

Most Runs Scored

No.	Player
42	Mickey Mantle
41	Yogi Berra
37	Babe Ruth
30	Lou Gehrig
27	Joe DiMaggio
26	Roger Maris
25	Elston Howard
23	Gil McDougald
22	Jackie Robinson
21	Five players tied.

Most Runs Batted In

No.	Player
40	Mickey Mantle
39	Yogi Berra
35	Lou Gehrig
33	Babe Ruth
30	Joe DiMaggio
29	Moose Skowron
26	Duke Snider
24	Hank Bauer
24	Bill Dickey
24	Reggie Jackson
24	Gil McDougald
22	Hank Greenberg

Most Stolen Bases

No.	Player
14	Lou Brock
14	Eddie Collins
10	Frank Chance
10	Davey Lopes
10	Phil Rizzuto
9	Frankie Frisch
9	Honus Wagner
8	Johnny Evers
7	Five players tied.

Most Home Runs

No.	Player
18	Mickey Mantle
15	Babe Ruth
12	Yogi Berra
11	Duke Snider
10	Lou Gehrig
10	Reggie Jackson
8	Joe DiMaggio
8	Frank Robinson
8	Moose Skowron
7	Hank Bauer
7	Goose Goslin
7	Gil McDougald

Most Times Struck Out

No.	Player
54	Mickey Mantle
37	Elston Howard
33	Duke Snider
30	Babe Ruth
29	Gil McDougald
26	Moose Skowron

Most Wins

W-L	Pitcher
10-8	Whitey Ford
7-2	Bob Gibson
7-2	Allie Reynolds
7-2	Red Ruffing
6-0	Lefty Gomez
6-4	Chief Bender
6-4	Waite Hoyt
5-0	Jack Coombs
5-0	Herb Pennock
5-3	Catfish Hunter
5-3	Vic Raschi
5-4	Three Finger Brown
5-5	Christy Mathewson

Most Losses

W-L	Pitcher
10-8	Whitey Ford
2-5	Joe Bush
2-5	Rube Marquard
2-5	Eddie Plank
2-5	Schoolboy Rowe
5-5	Christy Mathewson

Most Saves

No.	Pitcher
6	Rollie Fingers
4	Johnny Murphy
4	Allie Reynolds
4	John Wetteland
3	Roy Face
3	Firpo Marberry
3	Will McEnaney
3	Tug McGraw
3	Herb Pennock
3	Kent Tekulve
3	Todd Worrell

Most Games

No.	Pitcher
22	Whitey Ford
16	Rollie Fingers
15	Allie Reynolds
15	Bob Turley
14	Clay Carroll
13	Clem Labine
13	Mark Wohlers
12	Waite Hoyt
12	Catfish Hunter
12	Art Nehf

Lowest ERA

Earned runs allowed per game; based on at least 30 innings pitched.

ERA	Pitcher
0.83	Harry Brecheen
0.87	Babe Ruth
0.89	Sherry Smith
0.95	Sandy Koufax
1.01	Monte Pearson
1.06	Christy Mathewson
1.32	Eddie Plank
1.35	Rollie Fingers
1.36	Bill Hallahan
1.58	George Earnshaw

Most Games Started

No.	Pitcher
22	Whitey Ford
11	Waite Hoyt
11	Christy Mathewson
10	Chief Bender
10	Red Ruffing
9	Bob Gibson
9	Catfish Hunter
9	Art Hehf
9	Allie Reynolds
8	Seven pitchers tied.

Most Strikeouts

No.	Pitcher
94	Whitey Ford
92	Bob Gibson
62	Allie Reynolds
61	Sandy Koufax
61	Red Ruffing
59	Chief Bender
56	George Earnshaw
49	Waite Hoyt
48	Christy Mathewson
46	Bob Turley

Most Innings Pitched

No.	Pitcher
146.0	Whitey Ford
101.2	Christy Mathewson
85.2	Red Ruffing
85.0	Chief Bender
83.2	Waite Hoyt
81.0	Bob Gibson
79.0	Art Nehf
77.1	Allie Reynolds
64.2	Jim Palmer
63.0	Catfish Hunter

Most Walks

No.	Pitcher
34	Whitey Ford
32	Art Nehf
32	Allie Reynolds
31	Jim Palmer
29	Bob Turley
27	Paul Derringer
27	Red Ruffing
26	Burleigh Grimes
26	Don Gullett
25	Vic Raschi

St. Louis Cardinals' pitcher Bob Gibson opens the 1968 World Series with a strike to Detroit's Dick McAuliffe.

All-Time Postseason Leaders

Including the World Series (since 1903), League Championship Series (since 1969), League Division Series (since 1995), and the 1981 League Divisional Playoffs (between half-season champions in that strike-shortened season). Asterisks (*) indicate players active in 1997 postseason.

BATTING

Oakland A's slugger Reggie Jackson batting against Tom Seaver of the New York Mets in Game 6 of the 1973 World Series.

Most Games

No.	Player
77	Reggie Jackson
75	Yogi Berra
67	Pete Rose
66	Terry Pendleton
65	Mickey Mantle
64	David Justice*
63	Lonnie Smith
62	Mark Lemke
55	Two players tied.

Most Hits

No.	Player
86	Pete Rose
78	Reggie Jackson
75	Steve Garvey
71	Yogi Berra
67	Marquis Grissom*
63	Mark Lemke
61	Roberto Alomar*
59	Mickey Mantle
58	Frankie Frisch
58	Terry Pendleton
57	Fred McGriff*
57	Lonnie Smith

Most Home Runs

No.	Player
18	Reggie Jackson
18	Mickey Mantle
15	Babe Ruth
12	Yogi Berra
11	Steve Garvey
11	Duke Snider
10	Johnny Bench
10	George Brett
10	Lenny Dykstra
10	Lou Gehrig
10	Fred McGriff*

Most Runs Scored

No.	Player
42	Mickey Mantle
41	Yogi Berra
41	Reggie Jackson
37	Babe Ruth
36	David Justice*
36	Fred McGriff*
35	Rickey Henderson
33	Marquis Grissom*
32	Steve Garvey
30	Three players tied.

Most Runs Batted In

No.	Player
48	Reggie Jackson
40	Mickey Mantle
39	Yogi Berra
37	Fred McGriff*
35	Lou Gehrig
33	David Justice*
33	Babe Ruth
31	Steve Garvey
29	Moose Skowron
27	Roberto Alomar*
27	Ron Cey
27	Ron Gant
27	Graig Nettles

Most Stolen Bases

No.	Player
25	Rickey Henderson
20	Davey Lopes
18	Roberto Alomar*
18	Omar Vizquel*
17	Kenny Lofton*
15	Joe Morgan
14	Lou Brock
14	Eddie Collins
13	Vince Coleman
13	Ron Gant
13	Willie Wilson

Highest Batting Average

Based on at least 70 at-bats.

Avg.	Player
.391	Lou Brock
.368	Paul Molitor
.363	Home Run Baker
.361	Lou Gehrig
.357	Thurman Munson
.338	Steve Garvey
.337	George Brett
.336	Cal Ripken*
.333	Billy Martin
.328	Marquis Grissom*

Highest Slugging Average

Based on at least 70 at-bats.

Avg.	Player
.744	Babe Ruth
.731	Lou Gehrig
.661	Lenny Dykstra
.658	Al Simmons
.655	Lou Brock
.627	George Brett
.624	Hank Greenberg
.615	Paul Molitor

Note: Slugging average is total bases divided by at-bats.

Most Times Struck Out

Based on at least 70 at-bats.

No.	Player
70	Reggie Jackson
54	Mickey Mantle
48	Devon White*
45	Jeff Blauser*
43	Willie McGee

Most Wins

W-L	Pitcher
10-3	John Smoltz*
10-6	Dave Stewart
10-8	Whitey Ford
9-6	Catfish Hunter
9-9	Tom Glavine*
8-3	Orel Hershiser*
8-3	Jim Palmer
8-7	Greg Maddux*
7-2	Bob Gibson
7-2	Allie Reynolds
7-2	Red Ruffing
7-4	Dave McNally
7-4	Jack Morris

Most Losses

W-L	Pitcher
9-9	Tom Glavine*
2-8	Jerry Reuss
10-8	Whitey Ford
1-7	Charlie Leibrandt
8-7	Greg Maddux*
6-6	Steve Carlton
9-6	Catfish Hunter
10-6	Dave Stewart

Most Games

No.	Pitcher
38	Mark Wohlers*
30	Rollie Fingers
30	Rick Honeycutt
29	Paul Assenmacher*
27	Dennis Eckersley
26	Tug McGraw
24	Jesse Orosco*
23	Alejandro Pena
22	Five pitchers tied.

Lowest ERA

Earned runs allowed per game; based on at least 70 innings pitched.

ERA	Pitcher
1.06	Christy Mathewson
1.83	Waite Hoyt
1.89	Bob Gibson
2.16	Art Nehf
2.31	Ken Holtzman
2.35	John Smoltz*
2.44	Chief Bender
2.50	Dave McNally
2.61	Jim Palmer
2.65	Tommy John
2.70	Orel Hershiser

Most Games Started

No.	Pitcher
22	Whitey Ford
20	Tom Glavine*
20	John Smoltz*
19	Catfish Hunter
18	Orel Hershiser*
18	Dave Stewart
17	Greg Maddux*
15	Jim Palmer
14	Steve Carlton
14	Don Sutton

Most Strikeouts

No.	Pitcher
132	John Smoltz*
94	Whitey Ford
92	Bob Gibson
91	Orel Hershiser*
90	Tom Glavine*
90	Jim Palmer
84	Steve Carlton
79	Greg Maddux*
73	Dave Stewart
70	Catfish Hunter
65	Dave McNally

John Smoltz of the Atlanta Braves has won 10 postseason games in 20 starts since 1991.

Most Innings Pitched

No.	Pitcher
146.0	Whitey Ford
137.2	John Smoltz*
133.0	Dave Stewart
132.2	Tom Glavine*
132.1	Catfish Hunter
126.2	Orel Hershiser*
124.0	Jim Palmer
117.0	Greg Maddux*
101.2	Christy Mathewson
100.1	Don Sutton

Most Walks

No.	Pitcher
51	Steve Carlton
51	Tom Glavine*
50	Jim Palmer
50	John Smoltz*
48	Dave Stewart
40	David Cone
40	Orel Hershiser
38	Don Gullett
35	Catfish Hunter
34	Whitey Ford
34	Dave McNally

Most Saves

No.	Pitcher
15	Dennis Eckersley
9	Rollie Fingers
8	Goose Gossage
8	Tug McGraw
8	Randy Myers*
7	John Wetteland
7	Mark Wohlers*
6	Jose Mesa*
6	Jeff Reardon

Best Teams by Decade

New York Yankees manager Casey Stengel with rookie outfielder Mickey Mantle before the start of the 1951 World Series against the New York Giants. The Yanks won 10 American League pennants and 7 World Series under Stengel from 1949 to 1960.

Winningest Teams of the 1980s

In 1981, a 50-day players' strike (June 12-July 31) forced both the American and National leagues to split the regular season in two and create an additional postseason playoff round to determine divisional winners for the League Championship Series. The Cincinnati Reds of the NL West had the year's best overall record (66-42), but they did not win either half and therefore missed the playoffs.

	Team	Regular Season		Postseason
		Record	Pct.	Record
1	New York Yankees	854-708	.547	8-9
2	Detroit Tigers	839-727	.536	8-5
3	Kansas City Royals	826-734	.530	13-16
4	St. Louis Cardinals	825-734	.529	21-16
5	Los Angeles Dodgers	825-741	.527	21-17
6	Boston Red Sox	821-742	.525	7-11
7	New York Mets	816-743	.523	11-9
8	Toronto Blue Jays	817-746	.523	4-8
9	Houston Astros	819-750	.522	6-10
10	Montreal Expos	811-752	.519	5-5

World Series champions: Philadelphia Phillies (1980); L.A. Dodgers (1981); St. Louis (1982); Baltimore Orioles (1983); Detroit (1984); Kansas City (1985); N.Y. Mets (1986); Minnesota Twins (1987); L.A. Dodgers (1988); Oakland Athletics (1989).

Winningest Teams of the 1990s

In 1994, a 232-day players' strike began on August 12 and resulted in the cancellation of the league playoffs and World Series. In 1995 an extra playoff round, originally planned for 1994, was introduced by both leagues. The new Division Series included three division champions and a wild card team.

	Team	Regular Season		Postseason
		Record	Pct.	Record
1	Atlanta Braves	716-514	.582	40-32
2	Chicago White Sox	661-567	.538	2-4
3	Montreal Expos	643-586	.523	0-0
4	New York Yankees	639-590	.520	15-10
5	Cleveland Indians	637-590	.519	20-17
	Baltimore Orioles	637-590	.519	9-10
7	Los Angeles Dodgers	637-593	.518	0-6
8	Cincinnati Reds	636-594	.517	11-6
9	Toronto Blue Jays	629-602	.511	17-12
10	Boston Red Sox	628-603	.510	0-7
	Pittsburgh Pirates	627-603	.510	8-12

World Series champions: Cincinnati (1990); Minnesota (1991); Toronto (1992), Toronto (1993); Atlanta (1995); N.Y. Yankees (1996); Florida Marlins (1997). Note: The 1994 World Series was canceled due to a players' strike.

Winningest Teams of the 1970s

	Team	Regular Season		Postseason
		Record	Pct.	Record
1	Cincinnati Reds	953-657	.592	23-15
2	Baltimore Orioles	944-656	.590	22-16
3	Pittsburgh Pirates	916-695	.569	17-19
4	Los Angeles Dodgers	910-701	.565	14-15
5	Boston Red Sox	895-714	.556	6-4
6	New York Yankees	892-715	.555	17-13
7	Kansas City Royals	851-760	.528	5-9
8	Oakland Athletics	838-772	.520	21-18
9	Minnesota Twins	812-794	.505	0-3
10	Philadelphia Phillies	812-801	.503	2-9

World Series champions: Baltimore (1970); Pittsburgh (1971); Oakland (1972); Oakland (1973); Oakland (1974); Cincinnati (1975); Cincinnati (1976); N.Y. Yankees (1977); N.Y. Yankees (1978); Pittsburgh (1979).

Winningest Teams of the 1960s

The Major Leagues expanded from 16 to 24 teams in the 1960s and split the American and National Leagues each into two halves. Divisional champions met in the League Championship Series to determine World Series finalists starting in 1969.

	Team	Regular Season		Postseason
		Record	Pct.	Record
1	Baltimore Orioles	911-698	.566	8-4
2	San Francisco Giants	902-704	.562	3-4
3	New York Yankees	887-720	.552	14-16
4	St. Louis Cardinals	884-718	.552	11-10
5	Detroit Tigers	882-729	.547	4-3
6	Los Angeles Dodgers	878-729	.546	8-7
7	Cincinnati Reds	860-742	.537	1-4
8	Washington Senators–Minnesota Twins	862-747	.536	3-4
9	Milwaukee–Atlanta Braves	851-753	.531	0-3
10	Chicago White Sox	852-760	.529	0-0

World Series champions: Pittsburgh Pirates (1960); N.Y. Yankees (1961); N.Y. Yankees (1962); L.A. Dodgers (1963); St. Louis (1964); L.A. Dodgers (1965); Baltimore (1966); St. Louis (1967); Detroit (1968); N.Y. Mets (1969).
Note: The Washington Senators moved to Minneapolis-St. Paul and became the Minnesota Twins after the 1960 season, and the Milwaukee Braves moved to Atlanta after the 1965 season.

Winningest Teams of the 1950s

	Team	Regular Season		World Series
		Record	Pct.	
1	New York Yankees	955-582	.621	30-21
2	Brooklyn–Los Angeles Dodgers	913-630	.592	16-17
3	Cleveland Indians	904-634	.588	0-4
4	Boston–Milwaukee Braves	854-687	.554	7-7
5	Chicago White Sox	847-693	.550	2-4
6	New York–San Francisco Giants	822-721	.533	6-4
7	Boston Red Sox	814-725	.529	0-0
8	St. Louis Cardinals	776-763	.504	0-0
9	Philadelphia Phillies	767-773	.498	0-4
10	Cincinnati Reds	741-798	.481	0-0

World Series champions: N.Y. Yankees (1950-53); N.Y. Giants (1954); Brooklyn (1955); N.Y. Yankees (1956); Milwaukee (1957); N.Y. Yankees (1958); L.A. Dodgers (1959).
Note: The Boston Braves moved to Milwaukee after the 1952 season, and the Brooklyn Dodgers to Los Angeles and New York Giants to San Francisco after the 1957 season.

Winningest Teams of the 1940s

	Team	Regular Season		World Series
		Record	Pct.	
1	St. Louis Cardinals	960-580	.623	13-10
2	New York Yankees	929-609	.604	17-10
3	Brooklyn Dodgers	894-646	.581	5-12
4	Boston Red Sox	854-683	.556	3-4
5	Detroit Tigers	834-705	.542	7-7

World Series champions: Cincinnati Reds (1940); N.Y. Yankees (1941); St. Louis Cardinals (1942); N.Y. Yankees (1943); St. Louis Cardinals (1944); Detroit (1945); St. Louis Cardinals (1946); N.Y. Yankees (1947); Cleveland Indians (1948); N.Y. Yankees (1949).

Winningest Teams of the 1930s

	Team	Regular Season		World Series
		Record	Pct.	
1	New York Yankees	970-554	.636	20-3
2	Chicago Cubs	889-646	.579	2-12
3	New York Giants	868-657	.569	7-9
4	St. Louis Cardinals	869-665	.566	10-10
5	Cleveland Indians	824-708	.538	0-0

World Series champions: Philadelphia A's (1930); St. Louis Cardinals (1931); N.Y. Yankees (1932); N.Y. Giants (1933); St. Louis Cardinals (1934); Detroit Tigers (1935); N.Y. Yankees (1936-39).

Winningest Teams of the 1920s

	Team	Regular Season		World Series
		Record	Pct.	
1	New York Yankees	933-602	.608	18-15-1
2	New York Giants	890-639	.582	14-11-1
3	Pittsburgh Pirates	877-656	.572	4-7
4	St. Louis Cardinals	822-712	.536	4-7
5	Chicago Cubs	807-728	.526	1-4

World Series champions: Cleveland Indians (1920); N.Y. Giants (1921); N.Y. Giants (1922); N.Y. Yankees (1923); Washington Senators (1924); Pittsburgh (1925); St. Louis Cardinals (1926); N.Y. Yankees (1927); N.Y. Yankees (1928); Philadelphia A's (1929).

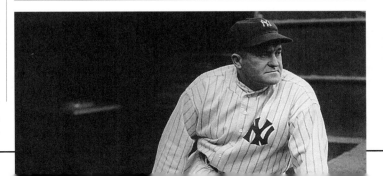

Manager Joe McCarthy guided the Yankees to five World Series championships in the 1930s and two more in 1941 and 1943.

All-Time Regular-Season Career Leaders—Batting

Asterisks (*) indicate players active in 1997.

Rogers Hornsby of the St. Louis Cardinals taking batting practice in 1926.

Highest Batting Average
Based on at least 1,500 hits; bats right (R) or left (L).

Avg.	Player	Bats	Years	AB	H
.366	Ty Cobb	L	24	11,434	4,189
.358	Rogers Hornsby	R	23	8,173	2,930
.356	Joe Jackson	L	13	4,981	1,772
.346	Ed Delahanty	R	16	7,505	2,597
.345	Tris Speaker	L	22	10,195	3,514
.344	Ted Williams	L	19	7,706	2,654
.344	Billy Hamilton	L	14	6,268	2,158
.342	Dan Brouthers	L	19	6,711	2,296
.342	Babe Ruth	L	22	8,399	2,873
.342	Harry Heilmann	R	17	7,787	2,660
.341	Pete Browning	R	13	4,820	1,646
.341	Willie Keeler	L	19	8,591	2,932
.341	Bill Terry	L	14	6,428	2,193
.340	Three players tied.				

Most Games

No.	Player
3,562	Pete Rose
3,308	Carl Yastrzemski
3,298	Hank Aaron
3,035	Ty Cobb
3,026	Stan Musial
3,026	Eddie Murray*
2,992	Willie Mays
2,973	Dave Winfield
2,951	Rusty Staub
2,896	Brooks Robinson
2,856	Robin Yount
2,834	Al Kaline
2,826	Eddie Collins
2,820	Reggie Jackson
2,808	Frank Robinson

Longest Consecutive-Game Streaks

No.	Player
2,478	Cal Ripken*
2,130	Lou Gehrig
1,307	Everett Scott
1,207	Steve Garvey
1,117	Billy Williams
1,103	Joe Sewell
895	Stan Musial
829	Eddie Yost
822	Gus Suhr
798	Nellie Fox
745	Pete Rose
740	Dale Murphy
730	Richie Ashburn

Note: Ripken's streak is ongoing; it began on May 30, 1982.

Most At-Bats

No.	Player
14,053	Pete Rose
12,364	Hank Aaron
11,988	Carl Yastrzemski
11,434	Ty Cobb
11,336	Eddie Murray*
11,008	Robin Yount
11,003	Dave Winfield
10,972	Stan Musial
10,881	Willie Mays
10,654	Brooks Robinson
10,430	Honus Wagner
10,349	George Brett
10,332	Lou Brock
10,230	Luis Aparico
10,195	Tris Speaker

Most Hits

No.	Player
4,256	Pete Rose
4,189	Ty Cobb
3,771	Hank Aaron
3,630	Stan Musial
3,514	Tris Speaker
3,419	Carl Yastrzemski
3,415	Honus Wagner
3,312	Eddie Collins
3,283	Willie Mays
3,255	Eddie Murray*
3,242	Nap Lajoie
3,178	Paul Molitor*
3,154	George Brett
3,152	Paul Waner
3,142	Robin Yount

Most Home Runs

Bats—right (R), left (L), or switch hitter (S).

No.	Player	Bats	Years	AB	RBI
755	Hank Aaron	R	23	12,364	2,297
714	Babe Ruth	L	22	8,399	2,213
660	Willie Mays	R	22	10,881	1,903
586	Frank Robinson	R	21	10,006	1,812
573	Harmon Killebrew	R	22	8,147	1,584
563	Reggie Jackson	L	21	9,864	1,702
548	Mike Schmidt	R	18	8,352	1,595
536	Mickey Mantle	S	18	8,102	1,509
534	Jimmie Foxx	R	20	8,134	1,922
521	Ted Williams	L	19	7,706	1,839
521	Willie McCovey	L	22	8,197	1,555
512	Eddie Mathews	L	17	8,537	1,453
512	Ernie Banks	R	19	9,421	1,636
511	Mel Ott	R	22	9,456	1,860
504	Eddie Murray*	S	21	11,336	1,917

Most Runs Batted In

No.	Player
2,297	Hank Aaron
2,213	Babe Ruth
1,995	Lou Gehrig
1,951	Stan Musial
1,937	Ty Cobb
1,922	Jimmie Foxx
1,917	Eddie Murray*
1,903	Willie Mays
1,879	Cap Anson
1,860	Mel Ott
1,844	Carl Yastrzemski
1,839	Ted Williams
1,833	Dave Winfield
1,827	Al Simmons
1,812	Frank Robinson
1,732	Honus Wagner

Highest Slugging Average

Based on at least 2,000 total bases.

Avg.	Player
.690	Babe Ruth
.634	Ted Williams
.632	Lou Gehrig
.609	Jimmie Foxx
.605	Hank Greenberg
.600	Frank Thomas*
.579	Joe DiMaggio
.577	Rogers Hornsby
.566	Albert Belle*
.562	Johnny Mize
.562	Ken Griffey Jr.*
.559	Stan Musial
.557	Willie Mays
.557	Juan Gonzalez*
.557	Mickey Mantle

Note: Slugging average is total bases divided by at-bats.

Most Runs Scored

No.	Player
2,246	Ty Cobb
2,174	Hank Aaron
2,174	Babe Ruth
2,165	Pete Rose
2,062	Willie Mays
1,949	Stan Musial
1,913	Rickey Henderson*
1,888	Lou Gehrig
1,882	Tris Speaker
1,859	Met Ott
1,829	Frank Robinson
1,821	Eddie Collins
1,816	Carl Yastrzemski
1,807	Paul Molitor*
1,798	Ted Williams

Most Stolen Bases

No.	Player
1,231	Rickey Henderson*
938	Lou Brock
912	Billy Hamilton
892	Ty Cobb
795	Tim Raines*
752	Vince Coleman*
744	Eddie Collins
739	Arlie Latham
738	Max Carey
722	Honus Wagner
689	Joe Morgan
668	Willie Wilson
657	Tom Brown
649	Bert Campaneris
616	George Davis

Most Walks

No.	Player
2,056	Babe Ruth
2,019	Ted Williams
1,865	Joe Morgan
1,845	Carl Yastrzemski
1,772	Rickey Henderson*
1,733	Mickey Mantle
1,708	Mel Ott
1,614	Eddie Yost
1,605	Darrell Evans
1,599	Stan Musial
1,566	Pete Rose
1,559	Harmon Killebrew
1,508	Lou Gehrig
1,507	Mike Schmidt
1,499	Eddie Collins

Times Struck Out

No.	Player
2,597	Reggie Jackson
1,936	Willie Stargell
1,883	Mike Schmidt
1,867	Tony Perez
1,816	Dave Kingman
1,757	Bobby Bonds
1,748	Dale Murphy
1,730	Lou Brock
1,710	Mickey Mantle
1,699	Harmon Killebrew
1,697	Dwight Evans
1,686	Dave Winfield
1,580	Chili Davis*
1,570	Lee May
1,556	Dick Allen

All-Time Regular-Season Career Leaders—Pitching

Asterisk (*) indicates players active in 1997.

All-time major-league strikeout leader and 324-game winner Nolan Ryan pitching for the Houston Astros in 1983.

Most Wins

Throws right (R) or left (L).

No.	Pitcher	Throws	Years	Losses	Pct.
511	Cy Young	R	22	316	.618
417	Walter Johnson	R	21	279	.599
373	Christy Mathewson	R	17	188	.665
373	Pete Alexander	R	20	208	.642
363	Warren Spahn	L	21	245	.597
361	Kid Nichols	R	15	208	.634
360	Pud Galvin	R	14	308	.540
342	Tim Keefe	R	14	225	.603
329	Steve Carlton	L	24	244	.574
328	John Clarkson	R	12	178	.648
326	Eddie Plank	L	17	194	.627
324	Don Sutton	R	23	256	.559
324	Nolan Ryan	R	27	292	.526
318	Phil Niekro	R	24	274	.537
314	Gaylord Perry	R	22	265	.542

Other 300-game winners: Gaylord Perry (314); Tom Seaver (311), Hoss Radbourn (309), Mickey Welch (307), and Lefty Grove and Early Wynn (300).

Winning Percentage

Based on at least 100 victories.

Pct.	Pitcher
.717	Spud Chandler
.690	Whitey Ford
.690	Dave Foutz
.686	Don Gullett
.682	Bob Caruthers
.682	Mike Mussina*
.680	Lefty Grove
.668	Smokey Joe Wood
.667	Vic Raschi
.665	Larry Corcoran
.665	Christy Mathewson
.660	Sam Leever
.657	Sal Maglie
.655	Sandy Koufax

Most Games

No.	Pitcher
1,070	Hoyt Wilhelm
1,050	Kent Tekulve
1,022	Lee Smith*
1,021	Dennis Eckersley*
1,002	Goose Gossage
987	Lindy McDaniel
956	Jesse Orosco*
944	Rollie Fingers
931	Gene Garber
906	Cy Young
899	Sparky Lyle
898	Jim Kaat
880	Jeff Reardon
874	Don McMahon
864	Phil Niekro

Most Games Started

No.	Pitcher
815	Cy Young
773	Nolan Ryan
756	Don Sutton
716	Phil Niekro
709	Steve Carlton
700	Tommy John
690	Gaylord Perry
685	Bert Blyleven
682	Pud Galvin
666	Walter Johnson
665	Warren Spahn
647	Tom Seaver
625	Jim Kaat
616	Frank Tanana

Most Innings Pitched

No.	Pitcher
7,356.2	Cy Young
5,941.1	Pud Galvin
5,914.2	Walter Johnson
5,404.1	Phil Niekro
5,386.0	Nolan Ryan
5,350.1	Gaylord Perry
5,282.1	Don Sutton
5,243.2	Warren Spahn
5,217.1	Steve Carlton
5,190.0	Pete Alexander
5,056.1	Kid Nichols
5,047.2	Tim Keefe
4,970.0	Bert Blyleven
4,802.0	Mickey Welch

Most Strikeouts

Listed with years played, innings pitched (IP), and average strikeouts per 9-inning game; throws right (R) or left (L).

No.	Pitcher	Throws	Years	IP	Per Game
5,714	Nolan Ryan	R	27	5,386.0	9.55
4,136	Steve Carlton	L	24	5,217.1	7.13
3,701	Bert Blyleven	R	22	4,970.0	6.70
3,640	Tom Seaver	R	20	4,782.2	6.85
3,574	Don Sutton	R	23	5,282.1	6.09
3,534	Gaylord Perry	R	22	5,350.1	5.94
3,509	Walter Johnson	R	21	5,914.2	5.33
3,342	Phil Niekro	R	24	5,404.1	5.57
3,192	Fergie Jenkins	R	19	4,500.2	6.38
3,117	Bob Gibson	R	17	3,884.1	7.22
2,882	Roger Clemens*	R	14	3,040.0	8.53
2,855	Jim Bunning	R	17	3,760.1	6.83
2,832	Mickey Lolich	L	16	3,638.1	7.01
2,803	Cy Young	R	22	7,356.2	3.42
2,773	Frank Tanana	L	21	4,188.1	5.96
2,583	Warren Spahn	L	21	5,243.2	4.43

Most Walks

No.	Pitcher
2,795	Nolan Ryan
1,833	Steve Carlton
1,809	Phil Niekro
1,775	Early Wynn
1,764	Bob Feller
1,732	Bobo Newsom
1,704	Amos Rusie
1,665	Charlie Hough
1,566	Gus Weyhing
1,541	Red Ruffing
1,442	Bump Hadley
1,434	Warren Spahn
1,431	Earl Whitehill
1,408	Tony Mullane
1,396	Sad Sam Jones
1,390	Jack Morris
1,390	Tom Seaver
1,379	Gaylord Perry

Most Home Runs Allowed

No.	Pitcher
505	Robin Roberts
484	Fergie Jenkins
482	Phil Niekro
472	Don Sutton
448	Frank Tanana
434	Warren Spahn
430	Bert Blyleven
414	Steve Carlton
399	Gaylord Perry
395	Jim Kaat
389	Jack Morris
383	Charlie Hough
380	Tom Seaver
374	Catfish Hunter
372	Jim Bunning
364	Dennis Martinez*
347	Mickey Lolich
346	Luis Tiant

Most Saves

No.	Pitcher
478	Lee Smith*
389	Dennis Eckersley*
367	Jeff Reardon
359	John Franco*
341	Rollie Fingers
319	Randy Myers*
311	Tom Henke
310	Goose Gossage
300	Bruce Sutter
278	Doug Jones*
256	Jeff Montgomery*
256	Todd Worrell*
252	Dave Righetti
244	Dan Quisenberry
238	Sparky Lyle

Most Losses

No.	Pitcher
316	Cy Young
308	Pud Galvin
292	Nolan Ryan
279	Walter Johnson
274	Phil Niekro
265	Gaylord Perry
256	Don Sutton
254	Jack Powell
251	Eppa Rixey
250	Bert Blyleven
245	Robin Roberts
245	Warren Spahn
244	Steve Carlton
244	Early Wynn
237	Jim Kaat

Most Shutouts

No.	Pitcher
110	Walter Johnson
90	Pete Alexander
79	Christy Mathewson
76	Cy Young
69	Eddie Plank
63	Warren Spahn
61	Nolan Ryan
61	Tom Seaver
60	Bert Blyleven
58	Don Sutton
57	Pud Galvin
57	Ed Walsh
56	Bob Gibson
55	Three Finger Brown
55	Steve Carlton

Lowest ERA

Earned runs allowed per game; based on at least 1,500 innings pitched. The list is divided into before and after 1961, the year the major leagues began to expand.

ERA	Pitcher
	1900-60
1.82	Ed Walsh
1.89	Addie Joss
2.06	Three Finger Brown
2.13	Christy Mathewson
	Since 1961
2.52	Hoyt Wilhelm
2.75	Whitey Ford
2.76	Sandy Koufax
2.81	Greg Maddux*
2.86	Andy Messersmith
2.86	Jim Palmer
2.86	Tom Seaver

Current Regular-Season Career Leaders—Batting

Players active during the 1997 season.

Rickey Henderson hoists stolen base No. 939 on May 1, 1991, after passing Lou Brock as baseball's all-time base-stealing leader.

Highest Batting Average

Based on at least 2,000 at-bats; listed with number of years played, at-bats (AB), and hits; bats—right (R), left (L), or switch hitter (S).

Avg.	Player	Bats	Years	AB	Hits
.340	Tony Gwynn	L	16	8,187	2,780
.334	Mike Piazza	R	6	2,558	854
.331	Wade Boggs	L	16	8,453	2,800
.330	Frank Thomas	R	8	3,821	1,261
.317	Edgar Martinez	R	11	3,818	1,210
.316	Kenny Lofton	L	7	3,314	1,047
.310	Mark Grace	L	10	5,458	1,691
.308	Paul Molitor	R	20	10,333	3,178
.305	Hal Morris	L	10	3,255	994
.304	Jeff Bagwell	R	7	3,657	1,112
.304	Chuck Knoblauch	R	7	3,939	1,197
.304	Roberto Alomar	S	10	5,460	1,659
.302	Ken Griffey Jr.	L	9	4,593	1,389
.302	Will Clark	L	12	5,941	1,795
.301	Julio Franco	R	15	7,243	2,177

Most Games

No.	Player
3,026	Eddie Murray
2,557	Paul Molitor
2,543	Cal Ripken
2,463	Harold Baines
2,460	Rickey Henderson
2,261	Gary Gaetti
2,255	Chili Davis
2,227	Wade Boggs
2,213	Brett Butler
2,191	Tim Raines
2,164	Ryne Sandberg
2,095	Tony Gwynn
2,063	Joe Carter
1,990	Tony Phillips

Most Hits

No.	Player
3,255	Eddie Murray
3,178	Paul Molitor
2,800	Wade Boggs
2,780	Tony Gwynn
2,715	Cal Ripken
2,561	Harold Baines
2,550	Rickey Henderson
2,439	Tim Raines
2,386	Ryne Sandberg
2,375	Brett Butler
2,222	Chili Davis
2,177	Julio Franco
2,118	Willie McGee
2,101	Gary Gaetti

Most Extra Base Hits

No.	Player
1,099	Eddie Murray
920	Cal Ripken
915	Paul Molitor
840	Joe Carter
826	Harold Baines
789	Barry Bonds
769	Gary Gaetti
761	Ryne Sandberg
749	Chili Davis
737	Rickey Henderson
706	Wade Boggs
683	Bobby Bonilla
671	Tim Raines
662	Rafael Palmeiro

Most Total Bases

No.	Player
5,397	Eddie Murray
4,662	Paul Molitor
4,428	Cal Ripken
4,113	Harold Baines
3,850	Rickey Henderson
3,787	Ryne Sandberg
3,780	Wade Boggs
3,731	Joe Carter
3,729	Tony Gwynn
3,656	Chili Davis
3,571	Gary Gaetti
3,539	Tim Raines
3,343	Barry Bonds
3,082	Bobby Bonilla

Most Home Runs

Listed with number of years played, at-bats (AB), and runs batted in (RBI); bats—right (R), left (L), or switch hitter (S).

No.	Player	Bats	Years	AB	RBI
504	Eddie Murray	S	21	11,336	1,917
387	Mark McGwire	R	12	4,622	983
378	Joe Carter	R	15	8,034	1,382
374	Barry Bonds	L	12	6,069	1,094
370	Cal Ripken	R	17	9,832	1,453
357	Jose Canseco	R	13	5,459	1,107
339	Harold Baines	L	18	8,818	1,423
339	Fred McGriff	L	12	5,693	1,007
332	Gary Gaetti	R	17	8,227	1,224
328	Chili Davis	S	17	8,094	1,285
308	Darryl Strawberry	L	15	5,074	937
302	Cecil Fielder	R	12	4,741	940
294	Ken Griffey Jr.	L	9	4,593	872
288	Andres Galarraga	R	13	6,074	1,051
282	Ryne Sandberg	R	16	8,385	1,061
279	Matt Williams	R	11	4,735	837
272	Albert Belle	R	9	4,075	867
271	Rafael Palmeiro	L	12	6,097	958

Most Runs Batted In

No.	Player
1,917	Eddie Murray
1,453	Cal Ripken
1,423	Harold Baines
1,382	Joe Carter
1,285	Chili Davis
1,238	Paul Molitor
1,224	Gary Gaetti
1,107	Jose Canseco
1,094	Barry Bonds
1,061	Bobby Bonilla
1,061	Ryne Sandberg
1,051	Andres Galarraga
1,036	Ruben Sierra
1,007	Fred McGriff
1,004	Will Clark
983	Mark McGwire
981	Julio Franco
973	Tony Gwynn
965	Danny Tartabull

Highest Slugging Average

Based on at least 2,000 at-bats.

Avg.	Player
.600	Frank Thomas
.576	Mike Piazza
.566	Albert Belle
.562	Ken Griffey Jr.
.557	Juan Gonzalez
.556	Mark McGwire
.551	Barry Bonds
.542	Larry Walker
.541	Jim Thome
.536	Jeff Bagwell
.532	Mo Vaughn
.527	Tim Salmon
.525	Kevin Mitchell
.525	Vinny Castilla
.521	Fred McGriff
.516	Jose Canseco
.513	Two players tied.

Note: Slugging average is total bases divided by at-bats.

Most Runs Scored

No.	Player
1,913	Rickey Henderson
1,807	Paul Molitor
1,627	Eddie Murray
1,475	Tim Raines
1,445	Cal Ripken
1,422	Wade Boggs
1,357	Brett Butler
1,318	Ryne Sandberg
1,244	Barry Bonds
1,237	Tony Gwynn
1,190	Tony Phillips
1,170	Chili Davis
1,168	Harold Baines
1,119	Joe Carter

Most Stolen Bases

No.	Player
1,231	Rickey Henderson
795	Tim Raines
752	Vince Coleman
558	Brett Butler
557	Otis Nixon
495	Paul Molitor
417	Barry Bonds
383	Juan Samuel
356	Delino DeShields
354	Kenny Lofton
345	Marquis Grissom
344	Ryne Sandberg
338	Willie McGee
335	Eric Davis

Most Walks

No.	Player
1,772	Rickey Henderson
1,333	Eddie Murray
1,328	Wade Boggs
1,227	Barry Bonds
1,209	Tim Raines
1,201	Tony Phillips
1,129	Brett Butler
1,107	Chili Davis
1,049	Paul Molitor
1,016	Cal Ripken
949	Mickey Tettleton
932	Harold Baines
890	Mark McGwire
880	Fred McGriff

Most Times Struck Out

No.	Player
1,580	Chili Davis
1,516	Eddie Murray
1,486	Gary Gaetti
1,471	Jose Canseco
1,446	Andres Galarraga
1,429	Juan Samuel
1,362	Danny Tartabull
1,355	Tony Phillips
1,326	Joe Carter
1,307	Mickey Tettleton
1,287	Harold Baines
1,276	Rickey Henderson
1,267	Pete Incaviglia
1,260	Ryne Sandberg

Current Regular-Season Career Leaders—Pitching

Players active during the 1997 season.

Roger Clemens won 192 games in 13 seasons with the Boston Red Sox before becoming a free agent and joining the Toronto Blue Jays in 1997.

Most Wins

Throws—right (R) or left (L).

Avg.	Pitcher	Throws	Years	Losses	Pct.
241	Dennis Martinez	R	22	187	.563
213	Roger Clemens	R	14	118	.644
193	Dennis Eckersley	R	23	170	.532
184	Greg Maddux	R	12	108	.630
180	Jimmy Key	L	14	114	.612
179	Orel Hershiser	R	15	123	.593
177	Dwight Gooden	R	13	97	.646
174	Mark Langston	L	14	150	.537
173	Fernando Valenzuela	L	17	153	.531
163	Danny Darwin	R	20	172	.487
153	Tom Glavine	L	11	99	.607
149	Doug Drabek	R	12	123	.548
148	David Cone	R	12	86	.632
142	Kevin Gross	R	15	158	.473
142	Chuck Finley	L	12	120	.542

Best Winning Percentage

Pct.	Pitcher
.682	Mike Mussina
.680	Andy Pettitte
.661	Kirk Rueter
.646	Dwight Gooden
.646	Randy Johnson
.644	Roger Clemens
.636	Darren Oliver
.632	David Cone
.630	Greg Maddux
.625	Pedro J. Martinez
.612	Jimmy Key
.611	Ramon Martinez
.607	Pat Hentgen
.607	Tom Glavine
.604	Jack McDowell

Most Games

No.	Pitcher
1,022	Lee Smith
1,021	Dennis Eckersley
956	Jesse Orosco
801	Rick Honeycutt
771	John Franco
760	Paul Assenmacher
694	Mike Jackson
683	Danny Darwin
680	Dan Plesac
666	Randy Myers
653	Doug Jones
639	Dennis Martinez
617	Todd Worell
595	Jeff Montgomery
583	Eric Plunk

Most Games Started

No.	Pitcher
557	Dennis Martinez
424	Fernando Valenzuela
416	Roger Clemens
407	Mark Langston
394	Orel Hershiser
378	Jimmy Key
368	Kevin Gross
366	Doug Drabek
365	Greg Maddux
364	Tom Candiotti
361	Dennis Eckersley
359	Mike Morgan
351	Dwight Gooden
346	Danny Darwin
338	Bobby Witt

Most Innings Pitched

No.	Pitcher
3,909.0	Dennis Martinez
3,246.0	Dennis Eckersley
3,040.0	Roger Clemens
2,930.0	Fernando Valenzuela
2,868.2	Danny Darwin
2,819.2	Mark Langston
2,724.2	Orel Hershiser
2,598.1	Greg Maddux
2,512.1	Jimmy Key
2,487.2	Kevin Gross
2,452.2	Tom Candiotti
2,446.2	Dwight Gooden
2,426.1	Doug Drabek
2,337.1	Mike Morgan
2,253.2	Bret Saberhagen

Most Strikeouts

Listed with the number of years played, innings pitched (IP),
and average strikeouts per 9-inning game; throws—right (R) or left (L).

No.	Pitcher	Throws	Years	IP	Per Game
2,882	Roger Clemens	R	14	3,040.0	8.53
2,379	Dennis Eckersley	R	23	3,246.0	6.59
2,365	Mark Langston	L	14	2,819.2	7.55
2,087	Dennis Martinez	R	22	3,909.0	4.81
2,074	Fernando Valenzuela	L	17	2,930.0	6.37
2,067	Dwight Gooden	R	13	2,446.2	7.60
2,034	David Cone	R	12	2,189.0	8.36
2,000	Randy Johnson	R	10	1,734.0	10.38
1,861	Danny Darwin	R	20	2,868.2	5.84
1,820	Greg Maddux	R	12	2,598.1	6.30
1,786	Orel Hershiser	R	15	2,724.2	5.90
1,769	John Smoltz	R	10	2,060.1	7.73
1,743	Sid Fernandez	L	15	1,866.2	8.40
1,739	Chuck Finley	L	12	2,238.1	6.99
1,737	Bobby Witt	R	12	2,109.1	7.41
1,727	Kevin Gross	R	15	2,487.2	6.25

Most Shutouts

No.	Pitcher
41	Roger Clemens
31	Fernando Valenzuela
29	Dennis Martinez
25	Orel Hershiser
24	Dwight Gooden
23	Greg Maddux
21	David Cone
20	Doug Drabek
20	Dennis Eckersley
20	Ramon Martinez
18	Tim Belcher
18	Mark Langston
17	Randy Johnson
16	Bret Saberhagen
15	Tom Glavine
15	Danny Jackson
14	Kevin Gross
14	Mark Gubicza

Lowest ERA

Earned runs allowed per game; based on at least 500 innings pitched.

ERA	Pitcher
2.57	John Franco
2.81	Greg Maddux
2.81	John Wetteland
2.91	Jeff Montgomery
2.96	Jesse Orosco
2.97	Roger Clemens
3.00	Pedro J. Martinez
3.03	Ismael Valdes
3.03	Lee Smith
3.06	Jeff Brantley
3.08	Randy Myers
3.09	Todd Worrell
3.10	Doug Jones
3.13	David Cone
3.25	Orel Hershiser
3.29	Jeff Fassero
3.30	Kevin Appier

Most Saves

No.	Pitcher
478	Lee Smith
389	Dennis Eckersley
359	John Franco
319	Randy Myers
278	Doug Jones
256	Jeff Montgomery
256	Todd Worrell
237	Rick Aguilera
211	John Wetteland
199	Rod Beck
173	Gregg Olson
165	Roberto Hernandez
149	Dan Plesac
133	Jesse Orosco
130	Jeff Brantley

Most Losses

No.	Pitcher
187	Dennis Martinez
172	Danny Darwin
170	Dennis Eckersley
167	Mike Morgan
158	Kevin Gross
153	Fernando Valenzuela
150	Mark Langston
143	Rick Honeycutt
142	Tom Candiotti
136	Mark Gubicza
131	Danny Jackson
131	Bobby Witt
123	Doug Drabek
123	Orel Hershiser
120	Chuck Finley

Most Walks

No.	Pitcher
1,219	Mark Langston
1,195	Bobby Witt
1,151	Fernando Valenzuela
1,146	Dennis Martinez
986	Kevin Gross
924	Roger Clemens
915	Chuck Finley
857	Randy Johnson
836	David Cone
831	Orel Hershiser
825	Danny Darwin
816	Danny Jackson
792	Dwight Gooden
790	Tom Candiotti
786	Mark Gubicza

Most Home Runs Allowed

No.	Pitcher
364	Dennis Martinez
341	Dennis Eckersley
298	Danny Darwin
291	Mark Langston
249	Jimmy Key
230	Kevin Gross
226	Doug Drabek
226	Fernando Valenzuela
213	Greg Swindell
211	Chuck Finley
206	Tom Candiotti
205	Mike Morgan
203	Roger Clemens
194	Orel Hershiser
192	Tim Belcher

All-Time Single-Season Leaders—Batting

Each category is split into two time periods: one covering from 1901 to 1960, when the American and National Leagues were each made up of 8 teams and the other from 1961 to the present, during which time the major leagues added 12 teams to the original 16. Expansion clubs in Arizona and Tampa Bay will swell the roster to 30 teams in 1998.

Most Hits

No.	Player/Team	Year
	1901–60	
257	George Sisler, Browns	1920
254	Lefty O'Doul, Phillies	1929
254	Bill Terry, Giants	1930
253	Al Simmons, A's	1925
250	Rogers Hornsby, Cardinals	1922
250	Chuck Klein, Phillies	1930
248	Ty Cobb, Tigers	1911
	Since 1961	
240	Wade Boggs, Red Sox	1985
239	Rod Carew, Twins	1977
238	Don Mattingly, Yankees	1986
234	Kirby Puckett, Twins	1988
231	Matty Alou, Pirates	1969

Longest Hitting Streaks

Games	Player/Team	Year
	1901–60	
56	Joe DiMaggio, Yankees	1941
41	George Sisler, Browns	1922
40	Ty Cobb, Tigers	1911
37	Tommy Holmes, Braves	1945
35	Ty Cobb, Tigers	1917
34	Three players tied.	
	Since 1961	
44	Pete Rose, Reds	1978
39	Paul Molitor, Brewers	1987
34	Benito Santiago, Padres	1987
31	Willie Davis, Dodgers	1969
31	Rico Carty, Braves	1970
31	Ken Landreaux, Twins	1980

Most Runs Scored

No.	Player/Team	Year
	1901–60	
177	Babe Ruth, Yankees	1921
167	Lou Gehrig, Yankees	1936
163	Lou Gehrig, Yankees	1931
163	Babe Ruth, Yankees	1928
158	Chuck Klein, Phillies	1930
158	Babe Ruth, Yankees	1920
158	Babe Ruth, Yankees	1927
	Since 1961	
146	Rickey Henderson, Yankees	1985
146	Craig Biggio, Astros	1997
143	Lenny Dykstra, Phillies	1993
143	Larry Walker, Rockies	1997
142	Ellis Burks, Rockies	1996

Joe DiMaggio hitting a home run. His consecutive-game hitting streak of 56 has been unapproached since 1941, the year he set the record.

Highest Batting Average

Based on batters averaging at least 3.1 at-bats for every game played by their teams.

Avg.	Player/Team	Year	AB	H
	1901-60			
.426	Nap Lajoie, A's	1901	544	232
.424	Rogers Hornsby, Cardinals	1924	536	227
.420	George Sisler, Browns	1922	586	246
.420	Ty Cobb, Tigers	1911	591	248
.409	Ty Cobb, Tigers	1912	553	226
	Since 1961			
.394	Tony Gwynn, Padres	1994	419	165
.390	George Brett, Royals	1980	449	175
.388	Rod Carew, Twins	1977	616	239
.372	Tony Gwynn, Padres	1997	592	220
.370	Andres Galarraga, Rockies	1993	470	174
.370	Tony Gwynn, Padres	1987	589	218

Note: The last player to hit .400 was Ted Williams of the Boston Red Sox, who hit .406 in 1941.

Most Doubles

No.	Player/Team	Year
	1901-60	
67	Earl Webb, Red Sox	1921
64	George Burns, Indians	1926
64	Joe Medwick, Cardinals	1936
63	Hank Greenberg, Tigers	1934
62	Paul Waner, Pirates	1932
60	Charlie Gehringer, Tigers	1936
59	Two players tied.	
	Since 1961	
54	Hal McRae, Royals	1977
54	John Olerud, Blue Jays	1993
54	Alex Rodriguez, Mariners	1996
54	Mark Grudzielanek, Expos	1997
53	Don Mattingly, Yankees	1986
52	Albert Belle, Indians	1995
52	Edgar Martinez, Mariners	1995
51	Four players tied.	

Most Triples

No.	Player/Team	Year
	1901-60	
36	Chief Wilson, Pirates	1912
26	Sam Crawford, Tigers	1914
26	Kiki Cuyler, Pirates	1925
26	Joe Jackson, Indians	1912
25	Sam Crawford, Tigers	1903
25	Larry Doyle, Giants	1911
25	Tom Long, Cardinals	1915
	Since 1961	
21	Willie Wilson, Royals	1985
21	Lance Johnson, Mets	1996
20	George Brett, Royals	1979
19	Garry Templeton, Cardinals	1979
19	Juan Samuel, Phillies	1984
19	Ryne Sandberg, Cubs	1984
18	Garry Templeton, Cardinals	1977
18	Willie McGee, Cardinals	1985

Most Home Runs

No.	Player/Team	Year
	1901-60	
60	Babe Ruth, Yankees	1927
59	Babe Ruth, Yankees	1921
58	Jimmie Foxx, A's	1932
58	Hank Greenberg, Tigers	1938
56	Hack Wilson, Cubs	1930
54	Babe Ruth, Yankees	1920
54	Babe Ruth, Yankees	1928
54	Ralph Kiner, Pirates	1949
	Since 1961	
61	Roger Maris, Yankees	1961
58	Mark McGwire, A's/Cardinals	1997
56	Ken Griffey Jr., Mariners	1997
54	Mickey Mantle, Yankees	1961
52	George Foster, Reds	1977
52	Willie Mays, Giants	1965
52	Mark McGwire, A's	1996

Most Total Bases

No.	Player/Team	Year
	1901-60	
457	Babe Ruth, Yankees	1921
450	Rogers Hornsby, Cardinals	1922
447	Lou Gehrig, Yankees	1927
445	Chuck Klein, Phillies	1930
438	Jimmie Foxx, A's	1932
429	Stan Musial, Cardinals	1948
	Since 1961	
409	Larry Walker, Rockies	1997
406	Jim Rice, Red Sox	1978
393	Ken Griffey Jr., Mariners	1997
392	Ellis Burks, Rockies	1996
388	George Foster, Reds	1977
388	Don Mattingly, Yankees	1986
382	Willie Mays, Giants	1962
382	Jim Rice, Red Sox	1977

Most Stolen Bases

No.	Player/Team	Year
	1901-60	
96	Ty Cobb, Tigers	1915
88	Clyde Milan, Senators	1912
83	Ty Cobb, Tigers	1911
81	Eddie Collins, A's	1910
81	Bob Bescher, Reds	1911
	Since 1961	
130	Rickey Henderson, A's	1982
118	Lou Brock, Cardinals	1974
110	Vince Coleman, Cardinals	1985
109	Vince Coleman, Cardinals	1987
108	Rickey Henderson, A's	1983
107	Vince Coleman, Cardinals	1986
104	Maury Wills, Dodgers	1962
100	Rickey Henderson, A's	1980
97	Ron LeFlore, Expos	1980

Most Runs Batted In

No.	Player/Team	Year
	1901-60	
190	Hack Wilson, Cubs	1930
184	Lou Gehrig, Yankees	1931
183	Hank Greenberg, Tigers	1937
175	Lou Gehrig, Yankees	1927
175	Jimmie Foxx, Red Sox	1938
174	Lou Gehrig, Yankees	1930
	Since 1961	
153	Tommy Davis, Dodgers	1962
150	Andres Galarraga, Rockies	1996
149	George Foster, Reds	1977
148	Johnny Bench, Reds	1970
148	Albert Belle, Indians	1996
147	Ken Griffey Jr., Mariners	1997
145	Don Mattingly, Yankees	1985
144	Juan Gonzalez, Rangers	1996

All-Time Single-Season Leaders—Pitching

Each category is split into two time periods: one covering from 1901 to 1960, when the American and National Leagues were each made up of 8 teams and the other from 1961 to the present, during which time the major leagues added 12 teams to the original 16. Expansion clubs in Arizona and Tampa Bay will swell the roster to 30 teams in 1998.

Christy Mathewson of the New York Giants in 1912, one of the 13 seasons in which he won 20 games or more.

Most Wins

No.	Pitcher/Team	Year	Losses	Pct.
	1901-60			
41	Jack Chesbro, Yankees	1904	12	.774
40	Ed Walsh, White Sox	1908	15	.727
37	Christy Mathewson, Giants	1908	11	.771
36	Walter Johnson, Senators	1913	7	.837
35	Joe McGinnity, Giants	1904	8	.814
34	Smokey Joe Wood, Red Sox	1912	5	.872
	Since 1961			
31	Denny McLain, Tigers	1968	6	.838
27	Sandy Koufax, Dodgers	1966	9	.750
27	Steve Carlton, Phillies	1972	10	.730
27	Bob Welch, A's	1990	6	.818
26	Sandy Koufax, Dodgers	1965	8	.765
26	Juan Marichal, Giants	1968	9	.743
25	Twelve players tied.			

Most Games

No.	Pitcher/Team	Year
	1901-60	
74	Jim Konstanty, Phillies	1950
71	Hoyt Wilhelm, Giants	1952
70	Ace Adams, Giants	1943
70	Mike Fornieles, Red Sox	1960
69	Ellis Kinder, Red Sox	1953
69	Don Elston, Cubs	1958
	Since 1961	
106	Mike Marshall, Dodgers	1974
94	Kent Tekulve, Pirates	1979
92	Mike Marshall, Expos	1973
91	Kent Tekulve, Pirates	1978
90	Wayne Granger, Reds	1969
90	Mike Marshall, Twins	1979
90	Kent Tekulve, Phillies	1987

Most Games Started

No.	Pitcher/Team	Year
	1901-60	
51	Jack Chesbro, Yankees	1904
49	Ed Walsh, White Sox	1908
48	Joe McGinnity, Giants	1903
46	Four players tied	
	Since 1961	
49	Wilber Wood, White Sox	1972
48	Wilber Wood, White Sox	1973
45	Mickey Lolich, Tigers	1971
44	Phil Niekro, Braves	1979
43	Wilber Wood, White Sox	1975
43	Phil Niekro, Braves	1977
42	Ten players tied.	

Most Innings Pitched

No.	Pitcher/Team	Year
	1901-60	
464	Ed Walsh, White Sox	1908
455	Jack Chesbro, Yankees	1904
434	Joe McGinnity, Giants	1903
422	Ed Walsh, White Sox	1907
	Since 1961	
377	Wilber Wood, White Sox	1972
376	Mickey Lolich, Tigers	1971
359	Wilber Wood, White Sox	1973
346	Steve Carlton, Phillies	1972
344	Gaylord Perry, Indians	1973
343	Gaylord Perry, Indians	1972
342	Phil Niekro, Braves	1979
336	Denny McLain, Tigers	1968
336	Sandy Koufax, Dodgers	1965

Consecutive Scoreless Innings

No.	Pitcher/Team	Year
	1901-60	
55.2	Walter Johnson, Senators	1913
53.0	Jack Coombs, A's	1910
50.0	Ed Reulbach, Cubs	1908-09
45.1	Carl Hubbell, Giants	1933
45.0	Cy Young, Red Sox	1904
45.0	Doc White, White Sox	1904
45.0	Sal Maglie, Giants	1950
43.2	Rube Waddell, A's	1905
	Since 1961	
59.0	Orel Hershiser, Dodgers	1988
58.0	Don Drysdale, Dodgers	1968
47.0	Bob Gibson, Cardinals	1968
41.0	Luis Tiant, Indians	1968
40.0	Gaylord Perry, Giants	1967
40.0	Luis Tiant, Red Sox	1972

Most Strikeouts

No.	Pitcher/Team	Year
	1901-60	
349	Rube Waddell, A's	1904
348	Bob Feller, Indians	1946
313	Walter Johnson, Senators	1910
303	Walter Johnson, Senators	1912
	Since 1961	
383	Nolan Ryan, Angels	1973
382	Sandy Koufax, Dodgers	1965
367	Nolan Ryan, Angels	1974
341	Nolan Ryan, Angels	1977
329	Nolan Ryan, Angels	1972
327	Nolan Ryan, Angels	1976
325	Sam McDowell, Indians	1965
319	Curt Schilling, Phillies	1997
317	Sandy Koufax, Dodgers	1966
313	J.R. Richard, Astros	1979
310	Steve Carlton, Phillies	1972

Most Shutouts

No.	Pitcher/Team	Year
	1901-60	
16	Pete Alexander, Phillies	1916
13	Jack Coombs, A's	1910
12	Pete Alexander, Phillies	1915
11	Walter Johnson, Senators	1913
11	Christy Mathewson, Giants	1908
11	Ed Walsh, White Sox	1908
10	Eight pitchers tied.	
	Since 1961	
13	Bob Gibson, Cardinals	1968
11	Sandy Koufax, Dodgers	1963
11	Dean Chance, Angels	1964
10	Juan Marichal, Giants	1965
10	Jim Palmer, Orioles	1975
10	John Tudor, Cardinals	1985
9	Six pitchers tied.	

Most Saves

No.	Pitcher/Team	Year
	1901-60	
27	Joe Page, Yankees	1949
27	Ellis Kinder, Red Sox	1953
26	Lindy McDaniel, Cardinals	1960
24	Jim Hughes, Dodgers	1954
24	Roy Face, Pirates	1960
	Since 1961	
57	Bobby Thigpen, White Sox	1990
53	Randy Myers, Cubs	1993
51	Dennis Eckersley, A's	1992
48	Rod Beck, Giants	1993
48	Dennis Eckersley, A's	1990
47	Lee Smith, Cardinals	1991
46	Dave Righetti, Yankees	1986
46	Bryan Harvey, Angels	1991
46	Lee Smith, Cards-Yankees	1993
46	Jose Mesa, Indians	1995

Lowest ERA

Earned runs allowed per game; pitchers' total innings must equal or exceed total games played by their teams.

ERA	Pitcher/Team	Year
	1901-60	
0.96	Dutch Leonard, Red Sox	1914
1.04	Three Finger Brown, Cubs	1906
1.14	Christy Mathewson, Giants	1909
1.14	Walter Johnson, Senators	1913
	Since 1961	
1.12	Bob Gibson, Cardinals	1968
1.53	Dwight Gooden, Mets	1985
1.56	Greg Maddux, Braves	1994
1.60	Luis Tiant, Indians	1968
1.63	Greg Maddux, Braves	1995
1.65	Dean Chance, Angels	1964
1.69	Nolan Ryan, Angels	1981
1.73	Sandy Koufax, Dodgers	1966
1.74	Sandy Koufax, Dodgers	1964
1.74	Ron Guidry, Yankees	1978

Most Losses

No.	Pitcher/Team	Year
	1901-60	
29	Vic Willis, Braves	1905
27	George Bell, Dodgers	1910
27	Paul Derringer, Cards-Reds	1933
27	Dummy Taylor, Giants	1901
26	Four pitchers tied.	
	Since 1961	
24	Roger Craig, Mets	1962
24	Jack Fisher, Mets	1965
22	Roger Craig, Mets	1963
22	Dick Ellsworth, Cubs	1966
22	Denny McLain, Senators	1971
22	Bill Bonham, Cubs	1974
22	Randy Jones, Padres	1974
22	Steve Rogers, Expos	1974
21	Four pitchers tied.	

Managers

Philadelphia A's manager Connie Mack (right), with his son and third-base coach Earle in 1946. The elder Mack was the A's pilot from 1901 to 1950.

Best Winning Percentages

Regular season only, through 1997; based on at least 750 major league victories.

Pct.	Manager	Years	Wins	Losses	Last Year
.615	Joe McCarthy	24	2,125	1,333	1950
.597	Billy Southworth	13	1,044	704	1951
.593	Frank Chance	11	946	648	1923
.587	John McGraw	33	2,763	1,948	1932
.584	Al Lopez	17	1,410	1,004	1969
.583	Earl Weaver	17	1,480	1,060	1986
.576	Fred Clarke	19	1,602	1,181	1977
.575	Davey Johnson*	12	985	723	active
.559	Steve O'Neill	14	1,040	821	1954
.558	Walter Alston	23	2,040	1,613	1976
.555	Bill Terry	10	823	661	1941
.555	Miller Huggins	17	1,413	1,134	1929
.553	Billy Martin	16	1,253	1,013	1988
.547	Charlie Grimm	19	1,287	1,067	1960

*Active in 1997.

Most Wins

Regular season only; through 1997.

Wins	Manager	Years
3,731	Connie Mack	53
2,763	John McGraw	33
2,194	Sparky Anderson	26
2,157	Bucky Harris	29
2,125	Joe McCarthy	24
2,040	Walter Alston	23
2,008	Leo Durocher	24
1,905	Casey Stengel	25
1,902	Gene Mauch	26
1,896	Bill McKechnie	25
1,619	Ralph Houk	20
1,602	Fred Clarke	19
1,599	Tommy Lasorda	21
1,571	Dick Williams	21
1,491	Clark Griffith	20

Most Postseason Wins

Includes 1997 World Series and league playoff games.

Record	Manager	World Series Titles
43-36	Bobby Cox*	1
37-26	Casey Stengel	7
34-21	Sparky Anderson	3
30-13	Joe McCarthy	7
31-30	Tommy Lasorda	2
26-20	Earl Weaver	1
26-20	Tony La Russa	1
26-25	Whitey Herzog	1
26-28	John McGraw	3
24-19	Connie Mack	5
23-21	Walter Alston	4
23-23	Davey Johnson*	1
21-23	Dick Williams	2
20-17	Mike Hargrove*	0

*Active in 1997 postseason.

Most Wins by Active Managers

Regular season only; as of October 20, 1997.

Wins	Manager/Team	Years
1,481	Tony La Russa, St. Louis	19
1,312	Bobby Cox, Atlanta	16
1,082	Joe Torre, N.Y. Yankees	16
985	Davey Johnson, Baltimore	12
943	Jim Leyland, Florida	12
864	Lou Piniella, Seattle	11
853	Tom Kelly, Minnesota	12
681	Bobby Valentine, N.Y. Mets	10
535	Mike Hargrove, Cleveland	7
535	Art Howe, Oakland	7
532	Johnny Oates, Texas	7
512	Jack McKeon, Cincinnati	9
470	Felipe Alou, Montreal	6
437	Phil Garner, Milwaukee	6
383	Dusty Baker, San Francisco	5

Home Fields

Biggest Major League Ballparks

Seats	Home Field	Home Team
63,000	3Com Park	San Francisco Giants
62,586	Veterans Stadium	Philadelphia Phillies
58,879	Kingdome	Seattle Mariners
57,545	Yankee Stadium	New York Yankees
57,078	Busch Stadium	St. Louis Cardinals
56,000	Dodger Stadium	Los Angeles Dodgers
55,601	Shea Stadium	New York Mets
54,313	Astrodome	Houston Astros
53,192	County Stadium	Milwaukee Brewers
52,952	Cinergy Field	Cincinnati Reds
50,516	SkyDome	Toronto Blue Jays
50,200	Coors Field	Colorado Rockies
49,831	Turner Field	Atlanta Braves
49,292	The Ballpark at Arlington	Texas Rangers
48,262	Camden Yards	Baltimore Orioles

Recently renamed: Cinergy Field (originally Riverfront Stadium, 1970-96); 3Com Park (originally Candlestick Park, 1960-94); Turner Field (originally Centennial Olympic Stadium in 1996).

Smallest Major League Ballparks

Seats	Home Field	Home Team
33,925	Fenway Park	Boston Red Sox
38,765	Wrigley Field	Chicago Cubs
40,585	Pro Player Stadium	Florida Marlins
40,625	Kauffman Stadium	Kansas City Royals
42,400	Jacobs Field	Cleveland Indians
43,662	Oakland Coliseum	Oakland Athletics
44,321	Comiskey Park	Chicago White Sox
44,457	Metrodome	Minnesota Twins
45,000	Edison International Field	Anaheim Angels
46,500	Olympic Stadium	Montreal Expos
46,510	Qualcomm Stadium	San Diego Padres
46,945	Tiger Stadium	Detroit Tigers
47,500	Bank One Ballpark	Arizona Diamondbacks
48,000	Tropicana Field	Tampa Bay Devil Rays
48,044	Three Rivers Stadium	Pittsburgh Pirates

Recently renamed: Edison International Field (originaly Anaheim Stadium, 1966-97); Kauffman Stadium (originally Royals Stadium, 1973-93); Pro Player Stadium (originally Joe Robbie Stadium, 1987-96); Qualcomm Stadium (most recently Jack Murphy/San Diego Stadium, 1982-97); Tropicana Field (most recently ThunderDome, 1993-96).

Oldest Major League Ballparks

Opened	Home Field	Home Team
1912	Fenway Park	Boston Red Sox
1912	Tiger Stadium	Detroit Tigers
1914	Wrigley Field	Chicago Cubs
1923	Yankee Stadium	New York Yankees
1953	County Stadium	Milwaukee Brewers
1960	3Com Park	San Francisco Giants
1962	Dodger Stadium	Los Angeles Dodgers
1964	Shea Stadium	New York Mets
1965	Astrodome	Houston Astros

Note: Yankee Stadium was gutted and rebuilt from 1974 to 1976, and the Yankees played at Shea Stadium during construction.

Newest Major League Ballparks

Opened	Home Field	Home Team
1998	Bank One Ballpark	Arizona Diamondbacks
1996	Turner Field	Atlanta Braves
1995	Coors Field	Colorado Rockies
1994	Ballpark at Arlington	Texas Rangers
1994	Jacobs Field	Cleveland Indians

Wrigley Field, home of the Chicago Cubs, bathed in the artificial light of its first night game on August 8, 1988. The contest against the Phillies was rained out in the 4th inning.

Awards

Most Popular Retired Numbers

Through the 1997 regular season; players listed in alphabetical order.

Jersey No.	Players Honored
42	Jackie Robinson—retired by the Los Angeles Dodgers in 1972 and by all teams in 1997 to commemorate the 50th anniversary of Robinson breaking major league baseball's color line.
1	Richie Ashburn (Phillies), Bobby Doerr (Red Sox), Fred Hutchinson (Reds), Billy Martin (Yankees), Billy Meyer (Pirates), Pee Wee Reese (Dodgers), and Ozzie Smith (Cardinals).
4	Luke Appling (White Sox), Joe Cronin (Red Sox), Lou Gehrig (Yankees), Ralph Kiner (Pirates), Mel Ott (Giants), Duke Snider (Dodgers), and Earl Weaver (Orioles).
3	Earl Averill (Indians), Harold Baines (White Sox), Harmon Killebrew (Twins), Dale Murphy (Braves), Babe Ruth (Yankees), and Bill Terry (Giants).
5	Johnny Bench (Reds), Lou Boudreau (Indians), George Brett (Royals), Joe DiMaggio (Yankees), Hank Greenberg (Tigers), and Brooks Robinson (Orioles).
9	Roger Maris (Yankees), Bill Mazeroski (Pirates), Minnie Minoso (White Sox), Enos Slaughter (Cardinals), and Ted Williams (Red Sox).
14	Ernie Banks (Cubs), Ken Boyer (Cardinals), Larry Doby (Indians), Gil Hodges (Mets), and Kent Hrbek (Twins).
20	Lou Brock (Cardinals), Frank Robinson (Orioles), Mike Schmidt (Phillies), Pie Traynor (Pirates), and Frank White (Royals).
34	Rollie Fingers (A's and Brewers), Kirby Puckett (Twins), and Nolan Ryan (Astros and Rangers).

Winners of Three Most Valuable Player Awards

Not including the 1997 regular season.

Player/Position	MVP Years
American League	
Yogi Berra, C	1955, 1954, 1951
Joe DiMaggio, OF	1947, 1941, 1939
Jimmie Foxx, 1B	1938, 1933, 1932
Mickey Mantle, OF	1962, 1957, 1956
National League	
Barry Bonds, OF	1993, 1992, 1990
Roy Campanella, C	1955, 1953, 1951
Stan Musial, OF-1B	1948, 1946, 1943
Mike Schmidt, 3B	1986, 1981, 1980

Note: Baseball has had three official MVP awards since 1911—the Chalmers Award (1911-14), presented by the Chalmers Motor Company; the League Awards (1922-29) presented by the American and National leagues; and the Baseball Writers' Award (since 1931), presented by the Baseball Writers' Association of America.

Winners of Three or More Cy Young Awards

Not including the 1997 regular season.

No.	Pitcher	Award Years
4	Steve Carlton	1982, 1980, 1977, 1972
4	Roger Clemens	1997, 1991, 1987, 1986
4	Greg Maddux	1992-95
3	Sandy Koufax*	1966, 1965, 1963
3	Jim Palmer	1976, 1975, 1973
3	Tom Seaver	1975, 1973, 1969

* The only repeat winner between 1956 and 1964, when one Cy Young Award was given out each year. Two awards, one to each league, have been presented annually since 1967.

Note: Cy Young won a major-league record 511 games in 22 seasons from 1890 to 1911 (see page 18). Voting is by selected members of the Baseball Writers' Association of America.

The Dodgers' Jackie Robinson in 1950, in a rundown between third and home in a game against the Chicago Cubs.

Perfect Games Since 1900
Retiring all 27 batters faced in a 9-inning game.

Date	Pitcher/Team	Opponent	Score
American League			
5/5/04	Cy Young, Boston	Philadelphia	3-0
10/2/08	Eddie Joss, Cleveland	Chicago	1-0
6/2317	Ernie Shore, Boston*	Washington	4-0
4/30/22	Charlie Robertson, Chicago	Detroit	2-0
5/8/68	Catfish Hunter, Oakland	Minnesota	4-0
5/15/81	Len Barker, Cleveland	Toronto	3-0
9/30/84	Mike Witt, California	Texas	1-0
7/28/94	Kenny Rogers, Texas	California	4-0
National League			
6/21/64	Jim Bunning, Philadelphia	New York Mets	6-0
9/9/65	Sandy Koufax, Los Angeles	Chicago	1-0
9/16/88	Tom Browning, Cincinnati	Los Angeles	1-0
7/28/91	Dennis Martinez. Montreal	Los Angeles	2-0
World Series			
10/8/56	Don Larsen, New York Yankees	Brooklyn	2-0

*Shore relieved Red Sox starter Babe Ruth in the first inning after Ruth was thrown out of the game by umpire Brick Owens for arguing over a lead-off walk to the Senators' Ray Morgan. Without warming up, Shore came in and retired 26 straight batters. (Morgan was erased trying to steal second.)

Note: Two 9-inning perfect games have been broken up in extra innings. In 1959 Pittsburgh's Harvey Haddix threw 12 perfect innings before losing to Milwaukee, 1-0, in the 13th; and in 1995 Pedro J. Martinez of Montreal lost his bid in the 10th inning before being lifted for a relief pitcher (the Expos won, 1-0).

Youngest Managers
Through 1997 season.

Age	Manager	First Team	First Year
23	Roger Peckinpaugh	New York Yankees	1914
24	Lou Boudreau	Cleveland Indians	1942
26	Joe Cronin	Washington Senators	1933
27	Bucky Harris	Washington Senators	1924
29	Rogers Hornsby	St. Louis Cardinals	1925

Most Valuable Player-Managers
Only two player-managers have won a pennant and the Most Valuable Player award in the same season: Detroit Tigers catcher Mickey Cochrane in 1934 and Cleveland Indians shortstop Lou Boudreau in 1948. Coincidentally, each was 31 years old the year he won.

Sandy Koufax pitched three no-hitters for the Dodgers before hurling a perfect game against the Cubs in 1965.

Triple Crown Winners
Fourteen players have led either the American or National League in batting average, home runs, and runs batted in the same season since 1901.

Year	Player/Team	Avg.	HR	RBI
American League				
1901	Nap Lajoie, A's	.422	14	125
1909	Ty Cobb, Tigers	.377	9	115
1933	Jimmie Foxx, A's	.356	48	163
1934	Lou Gehrig, Yankees	.363	49	165
1942	Ted Williams, Red Sox	.356	36	137
1947	Ted Williams, Red Sox	.343	32	114
1956	Mickey Mantle, Yankees	.353	52	130
1966	Frank Robinson, Orioles	.316	49	122
1967	Carl Yastrzemski, Red Sox	.326	44	121
National League				
1912	Heinie Zimmerman, Cubs	.372	14	103
1922	Rogers Hornsby, Cardinals	.401	42	152
1925	Rogers Hornsby, Cardinals	.403	39	143
1933	Chuck Klein, Phillies	.368	28	120
1937	Joe Medwick, Cardinals	.374	31	154

Oldest Managers
Through 1997 season.

Age	Manager	Last Team	Last Year
88	Connie Mack	Philadelphia A's	1950
75	Casey Stengel	New York Mets	1965
68	Wilbert Robinson	Brooklyn Dodgers	1931
68	Leo Durocher	Houston Astros	1973

Most Regular-Season Wins

From 1900 to 1960 and since the beginning
of the expansion era in 1961.

Record	Team	Year
1900-1960		
116-36	Chicago Cubs	1906
111-43	Cleveland Indians	1954
110-42	Pittsburgh Pirates	1909
110-44	New York Yankees	1927
107-45	Chicago Cubs	1907
107-45	Philadelphia A's	1931
107-47	New York Yankees	1932
Since 1961		
109-53	New York Yankees	1961
109-53	Baltimore Orioles	1969
108-54	Baltimore Orioles	1970
108-54	Cincinnati Reds	1975
108-54	New York Mets	1986

Most Regular-Season Losses

From 1900 to 1960 and since the beginning
of the expansion era in 1961.

Record	Team	Year
1900-1960		
36-117	Philadelphia A's	1916
38-115	Boston Braves	1935
38-113	Washington Senators	1904
42-112	Pittsburgh Pirates	1952
43-111	Boston Red Sox	1932
43-111	St. Louis Browns	1939
43-111	Philadelphia Phillies	1941
Since 1961		
40-120	New York Mets	1962
50-112	New York Mets	1965
51-111	New York Mets	1963
52-110	Montreal Expos*	1969
52-110	San Diego Padres*	1969

*Expansion teams

Longest Winning Streaks

Regular-season games only.

Games	Team	Year
1900-1960		
21	Chicago Cubs	1935
19	New York Yankees	1947
18	New York Giants	1904
18	New York Yankees	1953
Since 1961		
16	Kansas City Royals	1977
15	Minnesota Twins	1991
14	San Francisco Giants	1965
14	Baltimore Orioles	1973
14	Oakland A's	1988
14	Texas Rangers	1991
14	Kansas City Royals	1994

Longest Losing Streaks

Regular-season games only.

Games	Team	Year
1900-1960		
20	Boston Red Sox	1906
20	Philadelphia A's	1916
20	Philadelphia A's	1943
19	Two teams tied.	
Since 1961		
23	Philadelphia Phillies	1961
21	Baltimore Orioles*	1988
20	Montreal Expos	1969
19	Detroit Tigers	1975
17	New York Mets	1962
17	Atlanta Braves	1977

*Streak began on Opening Day.

Strikes & Lockouts

There have been eight work stoppages—five player strikes and three owner lockouts—
since the Players Association hired labor leader Marvin Miller as executive director in 1966.
Donald Fehr has led the union since Miller's retirement in 1983.

Year	Work Stoppage	Length	Dates	Issue
1972	Strike	13 days	April 1-13	Pensions
1973	Lockout	17 days	February 8-25	Salary arbitration
1976	Lockout	17 days	March 1-17	Free agency
1980	Strike	8 days	April 1-8	Free-agent compensation
1981	Strike	50 days	June 12-July 31	Free-agent compensation
1985	Strike	2 days	August 6-7	Salary arbitration
1990	Lockout	32 days	February 15-March 18	Salary arbitration and salary cap
1994-95	Strike	234 days	August 12-April 2	Salary cap and revenue sharing

Shortened seasons: •1972 (Opening Day pushed back to April 15, schedule reduced from 162 games to 156);
•1981 (season split in two—April 9 to June 11 and August 10 to October 5—with each part including
approximately 52 games per team); •1994 (season stopped after roughly 115 games per team; on September 14,
owners canceled playoffs and World Series guaranteeing first uncompleted season ever); •1995 (Opening Day
pushed back to April 25, schedule reduced to 144 games).

Clevleand's Jacobs Field on
August 12, 1994, the first
full day of the longest work
stoppage in professional
sports history.

FOOTBALL

Quarterback Brett Favre of the Green Bay Packers

COLLEGE FOOTBALL

PRO FOOTBALL

COLLEGE FOOTBALL

National Champions

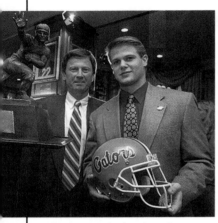

Florida quarterback and 1996 Heisman Trophy winner Danny Wuerffel (right) with head coach Steve Spurrier, who won the Gators' first Heisman Trophy in 1966.

One National Title

In alphabetical order; through 1996 Division I-A Season.

School	Year
Auburn	1957*
Brigham Young	1984
Clemson	1981
Colorado	1990*
Florida	1996
Florida State	1997
Georgia	1980
Iowa	1958*
Louisiana State	1958*
Maryland	1953
Mississippi	1960*
Syracuse	1959
Tennessee	1951
Texas A&M	1939
Texas Christian	1938
UCLA	1954*
Washington	1991*

* Championship was shared with another school.

Most National Championships

NCAA Division I.

Titles	Team	Years
9	Notre Dame	1988, 1977, 1973*, 1966*, 1964*, 1949, 1947, 1946, 1943
7	Alabama	1992, 1979, 1978*, 1973*, 1965*, 1964*, 1961*
6	Ohio State	1970*, 1968, 1961*, 1957*, 1954*, 1942
6	Oklahoma	1985, 1975, 1974*, 1956, 1955, 1950
5	Southern Cal	1978*, 1974*, 1972, 1967, 1962
4	Miami-FL	1991*, 1989, 1987, 1983
4	Minnesota	1960*, 1941, 1940, 1936
4	Nebraska	1995, 1994, 1971, 1970*
3	Michigan State	1966*, 1965*, 1952*
3	Texas	1970*, 1969, 1963
2	Army	1945, 1944
2	Georgia Tech	1990*, 1952*
2	Penn State	1986, 1982
2	Pittsburgh	1976, 1937

* Championship was shared with another school.
Source: Media polls taken by the AP (since 1936), UP (1950-57), INS; (1952-57), UPI (1958-92), FWAA (since 1954), NFF (since 1959) and USA/CNN (since 1991).

The Heisman Trophy–National Championship Double

Heisman Trophy winners whose teams were National Champions in the same season.

Year	Player/Position
1996	Danny Wuerffel, QB
1993	Charlie Ward, QB
1976	Tony Dorsett, RB
1964*	John Huarte, QB
1949	Leon Hart, End
1947	Johnny Lujack, QB
1945	Doc Blanchard, FB
1943	Angelo Bertelli, QB
1941	Bruce Smith, QB
1938	Davey O'Brian, QB

* In 1964 the National Football Foundation (NFF) selected Notre Dame as No. 1, but the Associated Press (AP) media poll ranked the team No. 3.

Head Coaches with Most National Championships

No.*	Coach	School	No.*	Coach	School
6	Bear Bryant	Alabama	3	Bud Wilkinson	Oklahoma
5	Woody Hayes	Ohio State	2	Red Blaik	Army
4	Frank Leahy	Notre Dame	2	Duffy Daugherty	Michigan St.
4	John McKay	Southern Cal	2	Bob Devaney	Nebraska
3	Bernie Bierman	Minnesota	2	Dennis Erickson	Miami-FL
3	Ara Parseghian	Notre Dame	2	Tom Osborne	Nebraska
3	Darrell Royal	Texas	2	Joe Paterno	Penn State
3	Barry Switzer	Oklahoma			

* Includes years in which there were shared national championships.
Source: Media and coaches polls taken by the AP, UP, INS, UPI, FWAA, NFF, and USA/CNN.

The Great College Dynasties

Nebraska, 1988–96
Record: 95-15-1 (.860) over 9 years
National titles: 2 (1994, 1995)
Stars: Zach Wiegert, Tommie Frazier
Coach: Tom Osborne

Florida State, 1987–96
Record: 87-14-1 (.858) over 10 years
National titles: 1 (1993)
Stars: Deion Sanders, Charlie Ward
Coach: Bobby Bowden

Miami-FL, 1983–92
Record: 107-13-0 (.892) over 10 years
National titles: 4 (1983, 1987, 1989, 1991)
Stars: Bernie Kosar, Steve Walsh
Coaches: Howard Schnellenberger, Jimmy Johnson, Dennis Erickson

Oklahoma, 1971–80
Record: 102-14-2 (.873) over 10 years
National titles: 2 (1974, 1975)
Stars: Lee Roy Selmon, Billy Sims
Coach: Barry Switzer

Alabama, 1971–80
Record: 107-13-0 (.892) over 10 years
National titles: 3 (1973, 1978, 1979)
Stars: John Hannah, Steadman Shealy
Coach: Bear Bryant

Southern Cal, 1967–79
Record: 122-23-7 (.826) over 13 years
National titles: 4 (1967, 1972, 1974, 1978)
Stars: O. J. Simpson, Charles White
Coaches: John McKay, John Robinson

Alabama, 1959–67
Record: 83-10-6 (.869) over 9 years
National titles: 3 (1961, 1964, 1965)
Stars: Joe Namath, Lee Roy Jordan
Coach: Bear Bryant

Oklahoma, 1948–58
Record: 107-8-2 (.923) over 11 years
National titles: 3 (1950, 1955, 1956)
Stars: Jim Weatherall, Billy Vessels
Coach: Bud Wilkinson

Notre Dame, 1946–53
Record: 63-8-6 (.857) over 8 years
National titles: 3 (1946, 1947, 1949)
Stars: Johnny Lujack, John Lattner
Coach: Frank Leahy

Army, 1943–50
Record: 64-5-5 (.899) over 8 years.
National titles: 2 (1944, 1945)
Stars: Doc Blanchard, Glenn Davis
Coach: Red Blaik

Minnesota, 1933–41
Record: 58-9-5 (.840) over 9 years
National titles: 5 (1934, 1935, 1936, 1940, 1941)
Stars: Ed Widseth, Bruce Smith
Coach: Bernie Bierman

Notre Dame, 1919–30
Record: 101-11-3 (.891) over 12 years
National titles: 3 (1919, 1924, 1929)
Stars: George Gipp, The Four Horsemen (Don Miller, Elmer Layden, Jim Crowley, Harry Stuhldreher)
Coach: Knute Rockne

Source: College Football Research Association

Bear Bryant built two dynasties at Alabama and won six national titles.

Abbreviations Key
AP, Associated Press
UP, United Press
INS, International News Service
UPI, United Press International
FWAA, Football Writers Association of America
NFF, National Football Foundation
USA/CNN, *USA Today*/Cable News Network

The "Four Horsemen" of Notre Dame led the Irish to a 27-2-1 record from 1922 to 1924. From left: halfback Don Miller, fullback Elmer Layden, halfback Jim Crowley, and quarterback Harry Stuhldreher.

Bowl Games

Most Appearances

No.	School	Record
48	Alabama	28-17-3
38	Southern Cal	25-13-0
37	Tennessee	21-16-0
37	Texas	17-18-2
35	Nebraska	17-18-0
33	Penn State	21-10-2
32	Georgia	15-14-3
32	Oklahoma	20-11-1
30	Louisiana State	13-16-1
29	Ohio State	13-16-0
28	Arkansas	9-16-3
28	Michigan	13-15-0
25	Georgia Tech	17-8-0
25	Mississippi	14-11-0
25	Auburn	13-10-2
25	Florida State	15-8-2

Highest-Scoring Major Bowl Games

Pts.	Final Score	Bowl
96	Texas Tech 55 Air Force 41	1995 Copper
91	Brigham Young 46 S. Methodist 45	1980 Holiday
89	Penn State 50 Brigham Young 39	1989 Holiday
86	Nebraska 62 Florida 24	1996 Fiesta
84	Arizona State 49 Missouri 35	1972 Fiesta
83	Arizona State 45 Florida State 38	1971 Fiesta
81	Kansas 51 UCLA 30	1995 Aloha
80	Colorado 47 Alabama 33	1969 Liberty
80	Washington 46 Iowa 34	1991 Rose
80	Navy 42 California 38	1996 Aloha

Most Wins

Wins	School	Games
28	Alabama	48
25	Southern Cal	38
21	Penn State	33
21	Tennessee	37
20	Oklahoma	32
17	Georgia Tech	25
17	Texas	37
17	Nebraska	35
15	Florida State	25
15	Georgia	32
14	Mississippi	25
13	Notre Dame	21
13	Auburn	25
13	Michigan	28
13	Louisiana State	30
13	Ohio State	29

Widest Victory Margins in Major Bowl Games

Pts.	Final Score	Bowl
55	Alabama 61 Syracuse 6	1953 Orange
51	Texas A&M 65 Brigham Young 14	1990 Holiday
48	Oklahoma State 62 Wyoming 14	1988 Holiday
44	Fresno State 51 Bowling Green 7	1985 California
43	Miami-FL 46 Texas 3	1991 Cotton
42	Texas 42 Maryland 0	1978 Sun
41	Syracuse 41 Clemson 0	1996 Gator
41	Southern Cal 55 Texas Tech 14	1995 Cotton
40	Houston 47 Tulane 7	1973 Bluebonnet
39	Nebraska 45 Georgia 6	1969 Sun

Lowest-Scoring Major Bowl Games

Pts.	Final Score	Bowl
0	California 0 Wash. & Jefferson 0	1922 Rose
0	Arizona State 0 Catholic 0	1940 Sun
0	Arkansas 0 Louisiana State 0	1947 Cotton
0	Air Force 0 Texas Christian 0	1959 Cotton
2	Fordham 2 Missouri 0	1942 Sugar
3	Tennessee 3 Texas A&M 0	1957 Gator
5	Texas Christian 3 Louisiana State 2	1936 Sugar
6	Auburn 6 Michigan St. 0	1938 Orange
6	Santa Clara 6 Louisiana State 0	1938 Sugar
6	Tulsa 6 Texas Tech 0	1942 Sun
6	Alabama 3 Texas 3	1960 Bluebonnet
6	Oregon State 6 Villanova 0	1962 Liberty

Southern Cal's twenty Rose Bowl victories include the epic 42-37 defeat of Wisconsin in 1963.

Most Rose Bowls

No.	School	Record
28	Southern Cal	20-8-0
16	Michigan	7-9-0
13	Washington	6-6-1
13	Ohio State	6-7-0
11	Stanford	5-5-1
11	UCLA	5-6-0

Most Sugar Bowls

No.	School	Record
12	Alabama	8-4-0
10	Louisiana State	3-7-0
8	Mississippi	5-3-0
7	Tennessee	4-3-0
6	Florida	2-4-0
6	Georgia	2-4-0

Most Orange Bowls

No.	School	Record
16	Oklahoma	11-5-0
16	Nebraska	7-9-0
8	Miami-FL	5-3-0
7	Alabama	4-3-0
5	Florida State	3-2-0
5	Georgia Tech	3-2-0
5	Colorado	2-3-0
5	Louisiana State	2-3-0
5	Notre Dame	2-3-0

Most Cotton Bowls

No.	School	Record
19	Texas	9-9-1
9	Texas A&M	4-5-0
8	Arkansas	2-5-1
7	Notre Dame	5-2-0
6	Texas Christian	2-3-1
6	Alabama	2-4-0

The Rose Bowl, the oldest college bowl game, began in 1902 and plays annually to crowds of more than 100,000 spectators.

Battles of the Unbeaten

Bowl games in which both teams had undefeated and untied records during the regular season.

Date	Bowl	Winner vs. Loser	Score
1/2/96	Fiesta	Nebraska vs. Florida	62-24
1/1/93	Sugar	Alabama vs. Miami-FL	34-13
1/2/89	Fiesta	Notre Dame vs. West Virginia	34-21
1/1/88	Orange	Miami-FL vs. Oklahoma	20-14
1/2/87	Fiesta	Penn St. vs. Miami-FL	14-10
12/31/73	Sugar	Notre Dame vs. Alabama	24-23
1/1/72	Orange	Nebraska vs. Alabama	38-6
1/2/56	Orange	Oklahoma vs. Maryland	20-6
1/1/52	Sugar	Maryland vs. Tennessee	28-13
1/1/41	Sugar	Boston College vs. Tennessee	19-13
1/2/39	Orange	Tennessee vs. Oklahoma	17-0
1/1/31	Rose	Alabama vs. Washington	24-0
1/1/27	Rose	Stanford vs. Alabama	7-7*
1/2/22	Rose	Washington & Jefferson vs. California	0-0*
1/1/21	Rose	California vs. Ohio State	28-0

* Tie score.

Best Teams by Decade

Winningest Teams of the 1990s

Through the 1996 season.

	Team	Overall Record	Pct.	Nat'l. Titles	Bowl Record
1	Florida State	75-10-1	.878	1	6-1-1
2	Nebraska	74-11-1	.866	2	3-4-0
3	Florida	73-14-1	.835	1	3-3-0
4	Miami-FL	69-14-0	.831	1	3-3-0
5	Colorado	67-14-4	.812	1	5-2-0
6	Alabama	70-16-1	.810	1	5-1-0
7	Penn State	69-17-0	.802	0	5-2-0
8	Tennessee	66-17-2	.788	0	5-2-0
	Texas A&M	66-17-2	.788	0	2-3-0
10	Notre Dame	63-19-2	.762	0	3-3-0
	Ohio State	64-19-3	.762	0	2-5-0

National champions: 1990—Colorado (AP) and Georgia Tech (UPI); 1991—Miami–FL (AP) and Washington (USA/CNN); 1992—Alabama; 1993—Florida State; 1994—Nebraska; 1995—Nebraska; 1996—Florida.
Sources: National titles according to AP, FWAA, NFF, and the UPI coaches' poll, plus the USA Today/CNN coaches' poll since 1991.

Florida State head coach Bobby Bowden.

Winningest Teams of the 1980s

	Team	Overall Record	Pct.	Nat'l. Titles	Bowl Record
1	Nebraska	103-20-0	.837	0	4-6-0
2	Miami-FL	98-20-0	.831	3	5-3-0
3	Brigham Young	102-26-0	.797	1	5-5-0
4	Oklahoma	91-25-2	.780	1	4-4-0
5	Clemson	86-25-4	.765	1	5-1-0
6	Penn State	89-27-2	.763	2	6-2-0
7	Georgia	88-27-4	.756	1	4-4-2
8	Florida State	87-28-3	.750	0	7-1-1
9	Michigan	89-29-2	.750	0	5-5-0
10	Auburn	86-31-1	.733	0	5-2-1

National champions: 1980—Georgia; 1981—Clemson; 1982—Penn State; 1983—Miami-FL; 1984—Brigham Young; 1985—Oklahoma; 1986—Penn State; 1987—Miami-FL; 1988—Notre Dame; 1989—Miami-FL.
Sources: National titles according to AP, FWAA, NFF, and the UPI coaches' poll.

Winningest Teams of the 1970s

	Team	Overall Record	Pct.	Nat'l. Titles	Bowl Record
1	Oklahoma	102-13-3	.877	2	6-1-1
2	Alabama	103-16-1	.863	3	5-4-1
3	Michigan	96-16-3	.848	0	0-6-0
4	Nebraska	98-20-4	.820	2	7-3-0
5	Penn State	96-22-0	.814	0	5-4-0
6	Ohio State	91-20-3	.811	1	2-7-0
7	Notre Dame	91-22-0	.805	2	6-1-0
8	Southern Cal	93-21-5	.803	3	7-1-0
9	Texas	88-26-1	.770	1	3-6-0
10	Arizona State	90-28-0	.763	0	6-1-0

National champions: 1970—Nebraska (AP, FWAA), Texas (UPI, NFF-tie) and Ohio State (NFF-tie); 1971—Nebraska; 1972—Southern Cal; 1973—Notre Dame (AP, FWAA, NFF) and Alabama (UPI); 1974—Oklahoma (AP) and Southern Cal (UPI, FWAA, NFF); 1975—Oklahoma; 1976—Pittsburgh; 1977—Notre Dame; 1978—Alabama (AP, FWAA, NFF) and Southern Cal (UPI); 1979—Alabama.
Sources: National titles according to AP, FWAA, NFF, and the UPI coaches' poll.

Winningest Teams of the 1960s

	Team	Overall Record	Pct.	Nat'l. Titles	Bowl Record
1	Alabama	90-16-4	.836	3	5-4-1
2	Texas	86-19-3	.810	2	6-1-1
3	Arkansas	82-24-1	.771	1	2-5-0
4	Ohio State	68-21-2	.758	1	1-0-0
5	Dartmouth	68-22-0	.756	0	0-0-0
6	Missouri	76-23-6	.752	0	4-1-0
7	Bowling Green	71-23-2	.750	0	0-1-0
8	Southern Cal	76-25-4	.743	2	3-2-0
9	Mississippi	77-25-6	.741	1	5-5-0
10	Penn State	77-27-1	.738	0	4-1-1

National champions: 1960—Minnesota (AP, UPI, NFF) and Mississippi (FWAA); 1961—Alabama (AP, UPI, NFF) and Ohio State (FWAA); 1962—Southern Cal; 1963—Texas; 1964—Alabama (AP, UPI), Arkansas (FWAA), and Notre Dame (NFF); 1965—Alabama (AP, FWAA-tie) and Michigan State (UPI, NFF, FWAA-tie); 1966—Notre Dame (AP, UPI, FWAA, NFF-tie) and Michigan State (NFF-tie); 1967—Southern Cal; 1968—Ohio State; 1969—Texas.
Source: National titles according to AP, FWAA, NFF, and the UPI coaches' poll.

Coach Bud Wilkinson's Oklahoma Sooners dominated the 1950s with three national championships and a 47-game winning streak that is still an NCAA Division I record.

Winningest Teams of the 1950s

	Team	Overall Record	Pct.	Nat'l. Titles	Bowl Record
1	Oklahoma	93-10-2	.895	3	4-1-0
2	Mississippi	80-21-5	.778	0	4-2-0
3	Michigan State	70-21-1	.766	1	2-0-0
4	Princeton	67-22-1	.750	0	0-0-0
5	Georgia Tech	79-26-6	.739	1	6-1-0
6	UCLA	68-26-3	.716	1	0-2-0
7	Ohio State	63-24-5	.712	2	2-0-0
8	Tennessee	71-31-4	.692	1	2-3-0
9	Penn State	62-28-4	.681	0	1-0-0
10	Maryland	67-31-3	.678	1	1-2-0

National champions: 1950—Oklahoma; 1951—Tennessee; 1952—Michigan State (AP, UP) and Georgia Tech (INS); 1953—Maryland; 1954—Ohio State (AP, INS) and UCLA (UP, FWAA); 1955—Oklahoma; 1956—Oklahoma; 1957—Auburn (AP) and Ohio State (UP, FWAA, INS); 1958—Louisiana State (AP, UPI) and Iowa (FWAA); 1959—Syracuse.
Sources: National titles according to AP, INS (1952–57), FWAA (starting in 1954), NFF (starting in 1959), the coaches' poll by UP (1950–57) and by UPI (starting in 1958).

Winningest Teams of the 1940s

	Team	Overall Record	Pct.	Nat'l. Titles	Bowl Record
1	Notre Dame	82-9-6	.876	4	0-0-0
2	Michigan	74-15-3	.821	1	1-0-0
3	Texas	78-21-3	.779	0	4-0-1
4	Army	68-17-7	.777	2	0-0-0
5	Tennessee	67-19-5	.764	0	1-3-0
6	Penn State	62-20-5	.741	0	0-0-1
7	Georgia	78-27-4	.734	0	4-1-1
8	Alabama	66-23-4	.731	0	3-2-0
9	Pennsylvania	57-21-4	.720	0	0-0-0
10	Oklahoma	69-27-4	.710	0	3-0-0

National champions: 1940—Minnesota; 1941—Minnesota; 1942—Ohio State; 1943—Notre Dame; 1944—Army; 1945—Army; 1946—Notre Dame; 1947—Notre Dame; 1948—Michigan; 1949—Notre Dame.
Source: National titles according to AP media poll.

Abbreviations Key

AP, Associated Press; UP, United Press; INS, International News Service; UPI, United Press International; FWAA, Football Writers Association of America; NFF, National Football Foundation; USA/CNN, *USA Today*/Cable News Network.

Winningest Teams

Through the 1996 season.

All-Time Winning Records
Ranked by percentage.

	Team	Years	Total Games	Won	Lost	Tied	Pct.	Bowl Record
1	Notre Dame	108	1,010	746	222	42	.759	13-8-0
2	Michigan	117	1,054	764	254	36	.742	13-15-0
3	Alabama	102	1,009	713	253	43	.728	28-17-3
4	Oklahoma	102	985	673	259	53	.710	20-11-1
5	Texas	104	1,030	713	284	33	.708	17-18-2
6	Ohio State	107	1,015	690	272	53	.706	13-16-0
7	Nebraska	107	1,041	709	292	40	.700	17-18-0
8	Southern Cal	104	972	653	265	54	.700	25-13-0
9	Penn State	110	1,043	706	296	41	.697	21-10-2
10	Tennessee	100	1,001	666	283	52	.691	21-16-0
11	Florida State	50	544	347	180	17	.653	16-8-2
12	Central Michigan	96	805	498	271	36	.641	0-2-0
13	Washington	106	944	578	317	49	.638	12-10-1
14	Army	107	999	607	341	51	.633	2-2-0
15	Miami-OH	108	929	565	320	44	.632	5-2-0
16	Louisiana State	103	979	594	338	47	.631	13-16-1
17	Arizona State	84	757	464	269	24	.629	9-6-1
18	Georgia	103	1,009	606	349	54	.627	15-14-3
19	Auburn	104	974	583	344	47	.623	13-10-2
20	Colorado	107	977	588	353	36	.620	9-12-0
21	Miami-FL	70	725	438	268	19	.617	11-11-0
22	Florida	90	901	525	336	40	.605	11-13-0
23	Bowling Green	78	716	407	257	52	.605	2-3-0
24	Michigan State	100	927	538	345	44	.604	5-8-0
25	Texas A&M	102	992	574	370	48	.603	11-10-0

Note: NCAA teams classified as Division I-A for at least 10 years. Records include all bowl games.

Extra Point
The Associated Press weekly nationwide Top 25 poll of Division I-A college football teams began in 1936 and has been voted on since then by sportswriters and broadcasters. In the six decades of the poll, the two top-ranked teams have met on 31 occasions—20 times during the regular season and 11 in bowl games. Since the first No.1 vs. No. 2 meeting in 1943, the top-ranked team has won 18 times, lost 11, and there have 2 ties, both involving Notre Dame (1946 and 1966).

All-Time Victories
Division I-A.

	School	Wins
1	Michigan	764
2	Notre Dame	746
3	Alabama	713
	Texas	713
5	Nebraska	709
6	Penn State	706
7	Ohio State	690
8	Oklahoma	673
9	Tennessee	666
10	Southern Cal	653
11	Syracuse	608
12	Army	607
13	Georgia	606
14	Louisiana State	594
15	Colorado	588
16	Washington	585
17	Auburn	583
18	West Virginia	577
19	Pittsburgh	576
20	Texas A&M	574

All-Time Victories
Division I-AA.

	School	Wins
1	Yale	783
2	Princeton	724
3	Pennsylvania	715
4	Harvard	711
5	Fordham	677
6	Dartmouth	612
7	Lafayette	578
8	Cornell	564
9	Delaware	533
10	Holy Cross	529

Note: The NCAA divided Division I in Division I-A and Division I-AA for football only in January 1978.

No. 1 vs. No. 2

Most Appearances in No. 1 vs. No. 2 Games

Through the 1996 season.

No.	School	Record
9	Notre Dame	5-2-2
6	Oklahoma	1-5-0
5	Nebraska	3-2-0
5	Miami-FL	3-2-0
4	Army	3-0-1
4	Florida State	2-2-0
4	Southern Cal	2-2-0
3	Texas	3-0-0
3	Alabama	2-1-0
3	Penn State	2-1-0
3	Michigan	0-3-0
3	Navy	0-3-0

Ron Vanderkelen of the Number 2 team, Wisconsin, during their Rose Bowl loss to the Number 1 team, Southern Cal, in the 1963 Rose Bowl.

King of the Hill

Showdowns between the two top-ranked college football teams from the first year of the Associated Press media poll in 1936 through the 1996 season. Each team is listed with its record going into the contest. Sites are listed as either the place or the bowl game.

Date	Rank/Winner	Rank/Loser	Score	Site
11/30/96	2, Florida State (10-0)	1, Florida (10-0)	24-21	Tallahassee
1/2/96	1, Nebraska (11-0)	2, Florida (12-0)	62-24	Fiesta Bowl
1/1/94	1, Florida State (11-1)	2, Nebraska (11-0)	18-16	Orange Bowl
11/13/93	2, Notre Dame (9-0)	1, Florida State. (9-0)	31-24	South Bend
1/1/93	2, Alabama (12-0)	1, Miami-FL (11-0)	34-13	Sugar Bowl
11/16/91	2, Miami-FL (8-0)	1, Florida State (10-0)	17-16	Tallahassee
9/16/89	1, Notre Dame (1-0)	2, Michigan (0-0)	24-19	Ann Arbor
11/26/88	1, Notre Dame (10-0)	2, Southern Cal (10-0)	27-10	Los Angeles
1/1/88	2, Miami-FL (11-0)	1, Oklahoma (11-0)	20-14	Orange Bowl
11/21/87	2, Oklahoma (10-0)	1, Nebraska (10-0)	17-7	Lincoln
1/2/87	2, Penn State (11-0)	1, Miami-FL (11-0)	14-10	Fiesta Bowl
9/27/86	2, Miami-FL (3-0)	1, Oklahoma (2-0)	28-16	Miami
10/19/85	1, Iowa (5-0)	2, Michigan (5-0)	12-10	Iowa City
1/1/83	2, Penn State (10-1)	1, Georgia (11-0)	27-23	Sugar Bowl
9/26/81	1, Southern Cal (2-0)	2, Oklahoma (1-0)	28-24	Los Angeles
1/1/79	2, Alabama (10-1)	1, Penn State (11-0)	14-7	Sugar Bowl
1/1/72	1, Nebraska (12-0)	2, Alabama (11-0)	38-6	Orange Bowl
11/25/71	1, Nebraska (10-0)	2, Oklahoma (9-0)	35-31	Norman
12/6/69	1, Texas (9-0)	2, Arkansas (9-0)	15-14	Fayetteville
1/1/69	1, Ohio State (9-0)	2, Southern Cal (9-0-1)	27-16	Rose Bowl
9/28/68	1, Purdue (1-0)	2, Notre Dame (1-0)	37-22	South Bend
11/19/66	1, Notre Dame (8-0)	2, Michigan State (9-0)	10-10	East Lansing
1/1/64	1, Texas (10-0)	2, Navy (9-1)	28-6	Cotton Bowl
10/12/63	2, Texas (3-0)	1, Oklahoma (2-0)	28-7	Dallas
1/1/63	1, Southern Cal (10-0)	2, Wisconsin (8-1)	42-37	Rose Bowl
11/9/46	1, Army (7-0)	2, Notre Dame (5-0)	0-0	New York
12/1/45	1, Army (8-0)	2, Navy (7-0-1)	32-13	Philadelphia
11/10/45	1, Army (6-0)	2, Notre Dame (5-0-1)	48-0	New York
12/2/44	1, Army (8-0)	2, Navy (6-2)	23-7	Baltimore
11/20/43	1, Notre Dame (8-0)	2, Iowa Pre-Flight (8-0)	14-13	South Bend
10/9/43	1, Notre Dame (2-0)	2, Michigan (3-0)	35-12	Ann Arbor

Rivalries

Most-Played Division I-A Series
Number of games played through the 1996 season.

No.	Rivals	Leader/Record
106	Minnesota–Wisconsin	Minnesota, 57-41-8
105	Kansas–Missouri	Missouri, 49-47-9
103	Baylor–Texas Christian*	Baylor, 49-47-7
103	Kansas–Nebraska	Nebraska, 79-21-3
103	Texas–Texas A&M	Texas, 66-32-5
101	Cincinnati–Miami–OH	Miami–OH, 54-40-7
101	North Carolina–Virginia	N. Carolina, 54-43-4
100	Auburn–Georgia	Auburn, 47-45-8
100	Oregon–Oregon State	Oregon, 50-40-10
99	Indiana–Purdue	Purdue, 59-34-6
99	California–Stanford	Stanford, 49-39-11
97	Army–Navy	Army, 47-43-7
94	Clemson–South Carolina	Clemson, 55-35-4
94	Kansas–Kansas State	Kansas, 61-28-5
94	Kansas–Oklahoma	Oklahoma, 62-26-6
94	Utah–Utah State	Utah, 62-28-4
93	Louisiana State–Tulane	LSU, 64-22-7
93	Michigan–Ohio State	Michigan, 53-34-6
93	Mississippi–Mississippi State	Mississippi, 53-34-6
93	North Carolina–Wake Forest	N. Carolina, 62-29-2
92	Penn State–Pittsburgh#	Penn State, 47-41-4
92	Kentucky–Tennessee	Tennessee, 60-23-9
91	Georgia–Georgia Tech	Georgia, 51-35-5
91	Iowa State–Nebraska	Nebraska, 75-14-2
91	Oklahoma–Oklahoma State	Oklahoma, 72-12-7
91	Oklahoma–Texas	Texas, 52-34-5
90	Auburn–Georgia Tech#	Auburn, 47-39-4
90	Illinois–Northwestern	Illinois, 47-38-5
90	Missouri–Nebraska	Nebraska, 55-32-3
90	Tennessee–Vanderbilt	Tennessee, 59-26-5

* Did not play during 1996 season.
# Penn State and Pittsburgh last played in 1992; Auburn and Georgia Tech in 1989.

The Army-Navy Game of 1932 was won by the Cadets, 20-0.

Best-Known Division I-A Trophy Games
In alphabetical order.

Trophy	Rivals	First Year
Axe	California–Stanford	1933
Beer Barrel	Kentucky–Tennessee	1925
Commander-in-Chief	Air Force–Army–Navy	1972
Floyd of Rosendale	Iowa–Minnesota	1935
Golden Egg	Mississippi–Mississippi State	1927
Little Brown Jug	Michigan–Minnesota	1909
Old Oaken Bucket	Indiana–Purdue	1925
Paul Bunyan Axe	Minnesota–Wisconsin	1948
Tomahawk	Illinois–Northwestern	1945
Victory Bell	Southern Cal–UCLA	1942

Most-Played Division I-AA Series
Number of games played through 1996 season.

No.	Rivals	Leader/Record
132	Lafayette–Lehigh	Lafayette, 71-56-5
119	Yale–Princeton	Yale, 64-45-10
113	Yale–Harvard	Yale, 61-44-8
106	William & Mary–Richmond	Wm. & Mary, 54-47-5
103	Pennsylvania–Cornell	Penn, 58-40-5
101	Yale–Brown	Yale, 72-24-5
100	Harvard–Dartmouth	Harvard, 52-43-5
98	W. Illinois–Illinois State	Western IL, 40-35-3
96	Montana–Montana State	Montana, 59-32-5
96	Harvard–Brown	Harvard, 68-26-2

Streaks

Division I-A and Division I-AA, through 1996.

Longest Winning Streaks
Number of games, including bowl games.

No.	School	Seasons	Ended by	Score
47	Oklahoma	1953–57	Notre Dame	7-0
39	Washington	1908–14	Oregon State	0-0
37	Yale	1890–93	Princeton	6-0
37	Yale	1887–89	Princeton	10-0
35	Toledo	1969–71	Tampa	21-0
34	Pennsylvania	1894–96	Lafayette	6-4
31	Oklahoma	1948–50	Kentucky	13-7
31	Pittsburgh	1914–18	Cleveland Naval Reserve	10-9
31	Pennsylvania	1896–98	Harvard	10-0
30	Texas	1968–70	Notre Dame	24-11
29	Miami–FL	1990–93	Alabama	34-13
29	Michigan	1901–03	Minnesota	6-6
28	Alabama	1991–93	Tennessee	17-17
28	Alabama	1978–80	Mississippi State	24-11
28	Oklahoma	1973–75	Kansas	23-3
28	Michigan State	1950–53	Purdue	6-0

Longest Losing Streaks
Number of games.

No.	School	Seasons
68	Prairie View A&M	1989–96*
44	Columbia	1983–88
34	Northwestern	1979–82
28	Kansas State	1944–48
28	Virginia	1958–61
27	Eastern Michigan	1980–82
27	New Mexico State	1988–90
26	Colorado State	1960–63
21	New Mexico	1967–69
21	Kent	1981–83

* Before the 1997 season, Prairie View's last victory was a 21–12 decision against Mississippi Valley State on Oct. 28, 1989.
Note: Prairie View and Columbia are the only Division I-AA schools listed

Last 10 Undefeated and Untied Division I-A Teams
Bowls included, through 1996 season.

Year	School	Won	Bowl
1995	Nebraska	12	Fiesta
1994	Nebraska	13	Orange
1994	Penn State	11	Rose
1993	Auburn	11	no bowl*
1992	Alabama	13	Sugar
1991	Miami-FL	12	Orange
1991	Washington	12	Rose
1988	Notre Dame	12	Fiesta
1987	Miami-FL	12	Orange
1986	Penn State	12	Fiesta

* On probation and ineligible for bowl game participation.

Longest Winning Streaks at Home
Number of games.

No.	School	Years
58	Miami–FL	1985–94
57	Alabama	1963–82
56	Harvard	1890–95
50	Michigan	1901–07
42	Texas	1968–76
40	Notre Dame	1907–18
38	Notre Dame	1919–27
37	Yale	1900–1903
37	Yale	1904–08
33	Harvard	1900–1903

Most Consecutive Winning Seasons

No.	School	Years
42	Notre Dame	1889–1932
38	Alabama	1911–50
35	Nebraska	1962–96*
29	Oklahoma	1966–94
28	Virginia	1888–1915
27	Michigan	1892–1918
26	Penn State	1939–64

* Ongoing streak.

Longest Unbeaten Streaks
Number of games, including bowl games.

No.	School	Record	Seasons
63	Washington	59-0-4	1907–17
56	Michigan	55-0-1	1901–05
50	California	46-0-4	1920–25
48	Yale	47-0-1	1885–89
48	Oklahoma	47-0-1	1953–57
47	Yale	42-0-5	1879–85
44	Yale	42-0-2	1894–96
42	Yale	39-0-3	1904–08

All-Time Career Leaders

NCAA Division I-A only, through 1996.

Most Yards Rushing

Yards	Player/School/Years
6,082	Tony Dorsett, Pittsburgh, 1973–76
5,598	Charles White, Southern Cal, 1976–79
5,259	Herschel Walker, Georgia, 1980–82
5,177	Archie Griffin, Ohio State, 1972–75
5,012	Darren Lewis, Texas A&M, 1987–90
4,965	Anthony Thompson, Indiana, 1986–89
4,958	George Rogers, South Carolina, 1977–80
4,948	Trevor Cobb, Rice, 1989–92
4,895	Paul Palmer, Temple, 1983–86
4,813	Steve Bartalo, Colorado State, 1983–86

Most Yards Rushing Per Game

Yards	Player/School/Years
174.6	Ed Marinaro, Cornell, 1969–71
164.4	O. J. Simpson, Southern Cal, 1967–68
159.4	Herschel Walker, Georgia, 1980–82
150.6	LeShon Johnson, N. Illinois, 1992–93
148.0	Marshall Faulk, San Diego State, 1991–93
147.9	George Jones, San Diego State, 1995–96
141.4	Tony Dorsett, Pittsburgh, 1973–76
141.4	Troy Davis, Iowa State, 1994–96
136.6	Mike Rozier, Nebraska, 1981–83
136.2	Howard Stevens, Louisville, 1971–72

Most Yards Passing

Yards	Player/School/Years
15,031	Ty Detmer, Brigham Young, 1988–91
11,425	Todd Santos, San Diego State, 1984–87
11,153	Eric Zeier, Georgia, 1991–94
10,913	Alex Van Pelt, Pittsburgh, 1989–92
10,875	Danny Wuerffel, Florida, 1993–96
10,623	Kevin Sweeney, Fresno State, 1982–86
10,579	Doug Flutie, Boston College, 1981–84
10,531	Steve Stenstrom, Stanford, 1991–94
10,280	Brian McClure, Bowling Green, 1982–85
10,258	Troy Kopp, Pacific, 1989–92

Boston College quarterback Doug Flutie.

Best Passing-Efficiency Ratings

At least 400 completions, with the percentage of completed passes (Cmp. Pct.) and the total number of interceptions (Int.), touchdown passes, and yards.

Rating	Player/School/Years	Cmp. Pct.	Int.	TD	Yards
163.6	Danny Wuerffel/Florida, 1993–96	.605	42	114	10,875
162.7	Ty Detmer/Brigham Young, 1988–91	.626	65	121	15,031
162.0	Steve Sarkisian/Brigham Young, 1995–96	.669	26	53	7,464
157.1	Billy Blanton/San Diego St., 1993–96	.639	25	67	8,165
156.9	Jim McMahon/Brigham Young, 1977–78, 1980–81	.616	34	84	9,536
152.9	Vinny Testaverde/Miami-FL, 1982, 1984–86	.613	25	48	6,058
152.7	Josh Wallwork/Wyoming, 1995–96	.616	28	54	6,453
151.2	Trent Dilfer/Fresno St., 1991–93	.596	21	51	6,944
149.8	Steve Young/Brigham Young, 1981–83	.652	33	56	7,733
149.7	Troy Aikman/Oklahoma, 1984–85; UCLA, 1987–88	.630	18	40	5,436

Most Receptions

No.	Player/School/Years
266	Aaron Turner Pacific, 1989–92
264	Chad Mackey Louisiana Tech, 1993–96
263	Terance Mathis New Mexico, 1985–87, 1989
262	Mark Templeton Long Beach State, 1983–86
261	Howard Twilley Tulsa, 1963–65
259	Marcus Harris Wyoming, 1993–96
245	David Williams Illinois, 1983–85
236	Marc Zeno Tulane, 1984–87
235	Jason Wolf S. Methodist, 1989–92

Most Points Scored by Nonkickers

Pts.	Player/School/Years
394	Anthony Thompson Indiana, 1986–89
376	Marshall Faulk San Diego St., 1991–93
356	Tony Dorsett Pittsburgh, 1973–76
354	Glenn Davis Army, 1943–46
337	Art Luppino Arizona, 1953–56
336	Steve Owens Oklahoma, 1967–69
327	Wilford White* Arizona State, 1947–50
324	Barry Sanders Oklahoma State, 1986–88
320	Allen Pinkett Notre Dame, 1982–85

* Includes 4 field goals.

Most Points Scored by Kickers

Pts.	Player/School/Years
423	Roman Anderson Houston, 1988–91
397	Carlos Huerta Miami-FL, 1988–91
395	Jason Elam Hawaii, 1988–92
393	Derek Schmidt Florida State, 1984–87
368	Luis Zendejas Arizona State, 1981–84
358	Jeff Jaeger Washington, 1983–86
353	John Lee UCLA, 1982–85
353	Max Zendejas Arizona, 1982–85
353	Kevin Butler Georgia, 1981–84

Most Field Goals

No.	Player/School/Years
80	Jeff Jaeger Washington, 1983–86
79	John Lee UCLA, 1982–85
79	Jason Elam Hawaii, 1988–92
78	Philip Doyle Alabama, 1987–90
78	Luis Zendejas Arizona State, 1981–84
77	Kevin Butler Georgia, 1981–84
77	Max Zendejas Arizona, 1982–85
73	Carlos Huerta Miami–FL, 1988–91
73	Derek Schmidt Florida State, 1984–8

Most Touchdowns Rushing

No.	Player/School/Years
64	Anthony Thompson Indiana, 1986–89
57	Marshall Faulk San Diego State, 1991–93
56	Steve Owens Oklahoma, 1967–69
55	Tony Dorsett Pittsburgh, 1973–76
51	Pete Johnson Ohio State, 1973–76
50	Ed Marinaro Cornell, 1969–71
50	Mike Rozier Nebraska, 1982–83
50	Billy Sims Oklahoma, 1975, 1977–79
49	Three players tied.

Most Touchdowns Passing

No.	Player/School/Years
121	Ty Detmer Brigham Young, 1988–91
114	Danny Wuerffel Florida, 1993–96
91	David Klingler Houston, 1988–91
87	Troy Kopp Pacific, 1989–92
84	Jim McMahon Brigham Young, 1977–78, 1980–81
81	Joe Adams Tennessee State, 1977–80
77	John Elway Stanford, 1979–82
75	Andre Ware Houston, 1987–89
74	Dan Marino Pittsburgh, 1979–82

Single-Season Leaders

NCAA Division I-A only, through 1996.

Most Yards Rushing

Yards	Player/School/Season
2,628	Barry Sanders/Oklahoma St., 1988
2,342	Marcus Allen/Southern Cal, 1981
2,185	Troy Davis/Iowa State, 1996
2,148	Mike Rozier/Nebraska, 1983
2,084	Byron Hanspard/Texas Tech, 1996
2,055	Rashaan Salaam/Colorado, 1994
2,010	Troy Davis/Iowa State, 1995
1,976	LeShon Johnson/N. Illinois, 1993
1,948	Tony Dorsett/Pittsburgh, 1976
1,908	Lorenzo White/Michigan St. 1985
1,905	Wasean Tait, Toledo, 1995
1,891	Herschel Walker, Georgia, 1981
1,890	Brian Pruitt, Central Michigan, 1994
1,881	Ed Marinaro, Cornell, 1971
1,877	Ernest Anderson, Oklahoma State, 1982

Best Passing Efficiency Ratings

At least 15 attempts per game, with the percentage of completed passes (Cmp. Pct.) and the total number of interceptions (Int.), touchdown passes, and yards.

Rating	Player/School/Season	Cmp. Pct.	Int.	TD	Yards
178.4	Danny Wuerffel/Florida, 1995	.646	10	35	3,266
176.9	Jim McMahon/Brigham Young, 1980	.638	18	47	4,571
175.6	Ty Detmer/Brigham Young, 1989	.643	15	32	4,560
173.6	Steve Sarkisian/Brigham Young, 1996	.688	12	33	4,027
173.1	Trent Dilfer/Fresno State, 1993	.652	4	28	3,276
172.9	Kerry Collins/Penn State, 1994	.667	7	21	2,679
172.6	Jerry Rhome/Tulsa, 1964	.687	4	32	2,870
170.6	Danny Wuerffel/Florida, 1996	.575	13	39	3,625
170.4	Bobby Hoying/Ohio State, 1995	.634	11	28	3,023
169.6	Billy Blanton/San Diego State, 1996	.656	5	29	3,221

Tony Dorsett of Pittsburgh, 1976 Heisman Trophy winner, led the Panthers to the national title.

Most Yards Rushing Per Game

Yds.	Player/School/Season
238.9	Barry Sanders/Oklahoma St., 1988
212.9	Marcus Allen/Southern Cal, 1981
209.0	Ed Marinaro/Cornell, 1971
198.6	Troy Davis/Iowa State, 1996
189.5	Byron Hanspard/Texas Tech, 1996
186.8	Rashaan Salaam/Colorado, 1994
182.7	Troy Davis/Iowa State, 1995
180.3	Charles White/Southern Cal, 1979
179.6	LeShon Johnson/N. Illinois, 1993
179.0	Mike Rozier/Nebraska, 1983

Most Yards Passing

Yards	Player/School/Season
5,188	Ty Detmer/BYU, 1990
5,140	David Klingler/Houston, 1990
4,699	Andre Ware/Houston, 1989
4,571	Jim McMahon/BYU, 1980
4,560	Ty Detmer/BYU, 1989
4,322	Scott Mitchell/Utah, 1988
4,273	Robbie Bosco/BYU, 1985
4,265	Chris Vargas/Nevada, 1993
4,090	Josh Wallwork/Wyoming, 1996
4,031	Ty Detmer/BYU, 1991

Most Receptions

No.	Player/School/Season
142	Manny Hazard/Houston, 1989
134	Howard Twilley/Tulsa, 1965
129	Alex Van Dyke/Nevada, 1995
114	Damond Wilkins/Nevada, 1996
109	Marcus Harris/Wyoming, 1996
108	Jason Phillips/Houston, 1988
106	Fred Gilbert/Houston, 1991
105	Chris Penn/Tulsa, 1993
103	Sherman Smith/Houston, 1992
102	James Dixon/Houston, 1988

Most Points Scored
Nonkickers.

Pts.	Player/School	Season	TD	FG	XPt.
234	Barry Sanders, Oklahoma State	1988	39	0	0
174	Lydell Mitchell, Penn State	1971	29	0	0
174	Mike Rozier, Nebraska	1983	29	0	0
166	Art Luppino, Arizona	1954	24	0	22
157	Bobby Reynolds, Nebraska	1950	22	0	25
154	Anthony Thompson, Indiana	1989	25	0	4
152	Fred Wendt, Texas–El Paso	1948	20	0	32
150	Pete Johnson, Ohio State	1975	25	0	0
148	Ed Marinaro, Cornell	1971	24	0	4
145	Bob Gaiters, New Mexico State	1960	23	0	7

Most Touchdowns Passing

No.	Player/School, Season
54	David Klingler/Houston, 1990
47	Jim McMahon/Brigham Young, 1980
46	Andre Ware/Houston, 1989
41	Ty Detmer/Brigham Young, 1990
39	Dennis Shaw/San Diego State, 1969
39	Danny Wuerffel/Florida, 1996
38	Doug Williams/Grambling, 1977
37	Troy Kopp/Pacific, 1991
35	Danny Wuerffel/Florida, 1995
35	Ty Detmer/Brigham Young, 1991

Most Touchdowns Rushing

No.	Player/School/Season
37	Barry Sanders/Oklahoma St., 1988
29	Mike Rozier/Nebraska, 1983
24	Rashaan Salaam/Colorado, 1994
24	Ed Marinaro/Cornell, 1971
24	Anthony Thompson/Indiana, 1988
24	Anthony Thompson/Indiana, 1989
23	Steve Owens/Oklahoma, 1969
23	Pete Johnson/Ohio State, 1975
23	Ki-Jana Carter/PennState, 1994

Most Touchdowns Receiving

No.	Player/School/Season
22	Manny Hazard/Houston, 1989
19	Desmond Howard/Michigan, 1991
18	Reidel Anthony/Florida, 1996
18	Tom Reynolds/San Diego St., 1971
18	Dennis Smith/Utah, 1989
18	Aaron Turner/Pacific, 1991
17	Mario Bailey/Washington, 1991
17	Chris Doering/Florida, 1995
17	Terry Glenn/Ohio State, 1995
17	Clarkston Hines/Duke, 1989
17	Bryan Reeves/Nevade, 1993
17	J. J. Stokes/UCLA, 1993

Most Combined Yards
Rushing, receiving, and kick returns.

Yards	Player/SchoolSeason
3,250	Barry Sanders/Oklahoma State, 1988
2,995	Ryan Benjamin/Pacific, 1991
2,690	Mike Pringle/Cal State-Fullerton, 1989
2,633	Paul Palmer/Temple, 1986
2,597	Ryan Benjamin/Pacific, 1992
2,559	Marcus Allen/Southern Cal, 1981

In 1988 Oklahoma State running back Barry Sanders set single-season records for touchdowns, rushing, and combined yards that still stand.

Extra Point
Ohio State running back Archie Griffin, who won back-to-back Heisman Trophies as Player of the Year in 1974 and 1975, holds the NCAA Division I record of 31 consecutive games gaining 100 yards or more.

Most Field Goals

No.	Player/School, Season
29	John Lee/UCLA, 1984
28	Paul Woodside/West Virginia, 1982
28	Luis Zendajas/Arizona State, 1983
27	Fuad Reveiz/Tennessee, 1982
25	John Diettrich/Ball State, 1985
25	Chris Jacke/Texas–El Paso, 1988
25	Chuck Nelson/Washington, 1982
24	Seven kickers tied.

Single-Game Leaders

NCAA Division I-A only, through 1996; in each case player's team is the first listed.

Most Yards Rushing

Yds.	Player/Game/Year
396	Tony Sands, Kansas vs. Missouri, 1991
386	Marshall Faulk, San Diego State vs. Pacific, 1991
378	Troy Davis, Iowa State vs. Missouri, 1996
377	Anthony Thompson, Indiana vs. Wisconsin, 1989
357	Two players tied.

Most Receptions

No.	Player/Game/Year
23	Randy Gatewood, UNLV vs. Idaho, 1994
22	Jay Miller, Brigham Young vs. New Mexico, 1973
20	Rick Eber, Tulsa vs. Idaho State, 1967
19	Howard Twilley, Tulsa vs. Colorado State, 1965
19	Ron Fair, Arizona Stat. vs. Washington State, 1989
19	Manny Hazard, Houston vs. Texas Christian, 1989
19	Manny Hazard, Houston vs. Texas, 1989

Most Passing Yards

Yds.	Player/Game/Year
716	David Klingler, Houston vs. Arizona State, 1990
690	Matt Vogler, Texas Christian vs. Houston, 1990
631	Scott Mitchel,l Utah vs. Air Force, 1988
622	Jeremy Leach, New Mexico vs. Utah, 1989
621	Dave Wilson, Illinois vs. Ohio State, 1980

Most Combined Yards

Rushing, recieving, and kick returns.

Yds.	Player/Game/Year
435	Brian Pruitt, Central Michigan vs. Toledo, 1994
429	Moe Williams, Kentucky vs. South Carolina, 1995
422	Marshall Faulk, San Diego State vs. Pacific, 1991
419	Randy Gatewood, UNLV vs. Idaho, 1994
417	Greg Allen, Florida State vs. Western Carolina, 1981
417	Paul Palmer, Temple vs. East Carolina, 1986

Most Total Yards

Passing and rushing combined.

Yds.	Player/Game/Year
732	David Klingler, Houston vs. Arizona State, 1990
696	Matt Vogler, Texas Christian vs. Houston, 1990
625	David Klingler, Houston vs. Texas Christian, 1990
625	Scott Mitchell, Utah vs. Air Force, 1988
612	Jimmy Klingler, Houston vs. Rice, 1992

Most Yards Receiving

Yds.	Player/Game/Year
363	Randy Gatewood, UNLV vs. Idaho, 1994
349	Chuck Hughes, Texas–El Paso vs. North Texas, 1965
322	Rick Eber, Tulsa vs. Idaho State., 1967
318	Harry Wood, Tulsa vs. Idaho State, 1967
316	Jeff Evans, New Mexico State vs. Southern Illinois, 1978

Longest Field Goals with Kicking Tee

Yds.	Player/Game/Year
67	Russell Erxleben, Texas vs. Rice, 1977
67	Steve Little, Arkansas vs. Texas, 1977
67	Joe Williams, Wichita St. vs. Southern Illinois, 1978
65	Tony Franklin, Texas A&M vs. Baylor, 1976

Longest Field Goals Without Kicking Tee

Yds.	Player/Game/Year
62	Jason Hanson, Washington St. vs. UNLV, 1991
61	Dan Eichloff, Kansas vs. Ball St., 1992
61	Kyle Bryant, Texas A&M vs. Southern Miss, 1994

Note: The NCAA banned the use of kicking tees after 1988 and narrowed the goal posts to 18 feet, 6 inches, in 1991.

Most Points Scored

Pts.	Player/Game/Year
48	Howard Griffith/Illinois vs. Southern Illinois, 1990
44	Marshall Faulk/San Diego State vs. Pacific, 1991
43	Jim Brown/Syracuse vs. Colgate, 1956
42	Fred Wendt/Texas–El Paso vs. New Mexico State, 1948
42	Arnold Boykin/Mississippi vs. Mississippi State, 1951
38	Dick Bass, Pacific vs. San Diego State, 1958
37	Jimmy Nutter, Wichita State. vs. Northern State, 1949
36	Twelve players tied.

Head Coaches

NCAA Division I-A only, through 1996.

Best Winning Percentages

Based on a minimum of 13 years as Division I-A coach. Bowl games are included.

Pct.	Coach	Yrs.	Record	Last Year
.881	Knute Rockne	13	105-12-5	1930
.864	Frank Leahy	13	107-13-9	1953
.837	Barry Switzer	16	157-29-4	1988
.832	Percy Houghton	13	96-17-6	1924
.829	Bob Neyland	21	173-31-12	1952
.828	Hurry Up Yost	29	196-36-12	1926
.828	Tom Osborne*	24	242-49-3	active
.826	Bud Wilkinson	17	145-29-4	1963
.812	Jock Sutherland	20	144-28-14	1938
.806	Bob Devaney	16	136-30-7	1972
.795	Frank Thomas	19	141-33-9	1946
.794	Joe Paterno*	31	289-74-3	active
.786	Henry Williams	23	141-34-12	1921
.781	Gil Dobie	33	180-45-15	1938
.780	Bear Bryant	38	323-85-17	1982

* Active in 1997.

Knute Rockne in his playing days was captain of the unbeaten 1913 Notre Dame team.

Most Wins

Based on at least 10 years as Division I-A head coach.

Wins	Coach	Yrs.
323	Bear Bryant	38
319	Pop Warner	44
314	Amos Alonzo Stagg	57
289	Joe Paterno*	31
270	Bobby Bowden*	31
242	Tom Osborne*	24
238	Woody Hayes	33
234	Bo Schembechler	27
228	LaVell Edwards*	25
222	Hayden Fry*	35

* Active in 1997.
Note: Eddie Robinson at Division I-AA Grambling is the all-time Division I leader in coaching victories with a record of 405-157-15 in 54 seasons, (through 1996).

Most Wins by Active Coaches

Based on at least 5 years as Division I-A head coach

Wins	Coach/School	Yrs.
289	Joe Paterno, Penn State	31
270	Bobby Bowden, Florida State	31
242	Tom Osborne, Nebraska	24
228	LaVell Edwards, BYU	25
222	Hayden Fry, Iowa	35
176	Don Nehlen, W. Virgnia	26
160	George Welsh, Virginia	24
157	John Cooper, Ohio State	20
139	Jackie Sherrill, Miss. State	19
128	Dick Tomey, Arizona	20
127	Ken Hatfield, Rice	18
121	Larry Smith, Missouri	20
118	Danny Ford, Arkansas	16

Most Bowl Appearances

No.	Coach	Record
29	Bear Bryant	15-12-2
27	Joe Paterno*	18-8-1
24	Tom Osborne*	11-13-0
20	Bobby Bowden*	15-4-1
20	Lou Holtz	10-8-2
20	Vince Dooley	8-10-2
20	LaVell Edwards*	7-12-1
18	John Vaught	10-8-0
17	Bo Schembechler	5-12-0
16	Darrell Royal	8-7-1
16	Johnny Majors	9-7-0
16	Hayden Fry*	7-8-1
15	Don James	10-5-0

* Active in 1997.

Home Fields

Largest Division I-A Stadiums

Seats	Stadium	School	Conference
102,501	Michigan	Michigan	Big 10
102,485	Neyland	Tennessee	SEC
100,089	Rose Bowl*	UCLA	Pac-10
93,967	Beaver	Penn State	Big 10
92,000	L.A. Coliseum*	Southern Cal	Pac-10
89,841	Ohio	Ohio State	Big 10
86,117	Sanford	Georgia	SEC
85,500	Stanford	Stanford	Pac-10
85,214	Jordan-Hare	Auburn	SEC
83,091	Legion Field*	Alabama#	SEC
83,000	Florida Field	Florida	SEC
81,474	Memorial	Clemson	ACC
80,250	Williams-Brice	South Carolina	SEC
80,225	Notre Dame	Notre Dame	Indep
79,940	Tiger	Louisiana State.	SEC
77,500	Doak Campbell	Florida State	ACC
76,129	Camp Randall	Wisconsin	Big 10
76,000	Spartan	Michigan State.	Big 10
75,662	Memorial	California	Pac-10
75,512	Memorial	Texas	Big 12

* Stadium is not on campus.
# Independent Alabama-Birmingham also uses Legion Field.

Newest Division I Stadiums
With more than 30,000 seats.

Built	Stadium	School	Seats
1994	Rutgers	Rutgers	42,500
1991	Marshall	Marshall*	30,000
1983	Fred Yager	Miami-OH	30,000
1982	Metrodome	Minnesota	63,669
1980	Bulldog	Fresno State	41,031
1980	Carrier Dome	Syracuse	50,000
1980	Mountaineer	West Virginia	63,500

*Division I-AA school.

Notre Dame Stadium held 60,000 when Paul Hornung (above) played in the mid-1950s; it expanded its capacity to 80,000 in 1997.

Largest Division I-AA Stadiums
Listed with home teams, conference and seating capacity.

Seats	Stadium	School	Conference
62,512	Miss. Veterans*	Jackson St.	SWAC
60,546	Franklin Field	Pennsylvania	Ivy
60,000	Yale Bowl	Yale	Ivy
37,967	Harvard	Harvard	Ivy
30,000	Marshall	Marshall	Southern
27,000	Schoelkopf Field	Cornell	Ivy
25,500	Bragg Memorial	Florida A&M	MEAC
25,000	Jack Spinks	Alcorn State	SWAC

* Stadium is not on campus.

Oldest Division I Stadiums
With more than 30,000 seats.

Built	Stadium	School	Seats
1895	Franklin Field	Pennsylvania*	60,546
1903	Harvard	Harvard*	37,967
1913	Dodd/Grant Field	Georgia Tech	46,000
1914	Yale Bowl	Yale*	60,000
1915	Scott Field	Mississippi State	40,656
1915	Schoellkopf Field	Cornell*	27,000
1916	Nippert	Cincinnati	35,000
1917	Camp Randall	Wisconsin	76,129

*All four Ivy League schools are in Division I-AA

After the 1996 season, Division I-AA Princeton tore down Palmer Stadium, which had been built in 1914 with 45,725 seats. A new 30.000-seat stadium will open in 1998.

Miscellaneous

Schools With Most Heisman Trophy Winners

Winners are listed with the positions they played and the year in which they won.

No. School/Winners

Notre Dame

7   Angelo Bertelli, QB (1943); Johnny Lujack, QB (1947); Leon Hart, End (1949); Johnny Lattner, HB (1953); Paul Hornung, QB (1956); John Huarte, QB (1964); and Tim Brown, WR (1987).

Ohio State

6   Les Horvath, QB-HB (1944); Vic Janowicz, HB (1950); Howard Cassady, HB (1955); Archie Griffin, RB (1974, 1975); and Eddie George, RB (1995).

Southern Cal

4   Mike Garrett, HB (1965); O. J. Simpson, HB (1968); Charles White, RB (1979); and Marcus Allen, RB (1981).

Army

3   Doc Blanchard, FB (1945); Glenn Davis, HB (1946); and Pete Dawkins, HB (1958).

Oklahoma

3   Billy Vessels, HB (1952); Steve Owens, HB (1969); and Billy Sims, RB (1978).

Television's All-Time Top-Rated College Football Bowl Games

Bowl opponents listed with national ranking going into the game and with TV audience share out of 100 percent viewership in U.S.

Rating	Bowl	Winner	Loser	Score	Share
41.1	1956 Rose	No. 2, Michigan State	No. 4, UCLA	17-14	67%
37.5	1957 Rose	No. 3, Iowa	No. 10, Oregon State	35-19	63
34.6	1964 Rose	No. 3, Illinois	Washington	17-7	58
33.5	1969 Rose	No. 1, Ohio State	No. 2, Southern Cal	27-16	56
33.3	1971 Cotton	No. 6, Notre Dame	No. 1, Texas	24-11	63
33.3	1959 Rose	No. 2, Iowa	No. 16, California	38-12	57
32.8	1963 Rose	No. 1, Southern Cal	No. 2, Wisconsin	42-37	57
32.5	1961 Rose	No. 6, Washington	No. 1, Minnesota	17-7	58
31.3	1975 Rose	No. 5, Southern Cal	No. 3, Ohio St.	18-17	51
30.6	1976 Rose	No. 11, UCLA	No. 1, Ohio State	23-10	52

Best ratings for other major bowls: • 1975 Orange Bowl, in which Notre Dame (no. 9) defeated Alabama (no. 2), 13-11—28.8 rating, 43 share; • 1973 Sugar Bowl, in which Notre Dame (no. 3) defeated Alabama (no. 1), 24-23—25.3 rating, 44 share; • 1987 Fiesta Bowl, in which Penn State (no. 2) defeated Miami-FL (no. 1), 14-10—25.1 rating, 38 share.

Associated Press Athletes of the Year

From 1939 to 1955 eight Heisman Trophy winners were named Male Athlete of the Year by the Associated Press. In order they were: Nile Kinnick, Iowa (1939); Tom Harmon, Michigan (1940); Frank Sinkwich, Georgia (1942); Glenn Davis, Army (1946); Johnny Lujack, Notre Dame (1947); Leon Hart, Notre Dame (1949); Dick Kazmaier, Princeton (1951); and Hopalong Cassady, Ohio State (1955).

Army's backfield tandem of Doc Blanchard (right) and Glenn Davis won back-to-back Heisman Trophies in 1945 and 1946.

Last 5 Running Backs To Win the Heisman Trophy

Year	Player/School
1995	Eddie George, Ohio State
1994	Rashaan Salaam, Colorado
1988	Barry Sanders, Oklahoma St.
1985	Bo Jackson, Auburn
1983	Mike Rozier, Nebraska

The 12 Juniors Who Won the Heisman Trophy

Year	Player/Position/School
1994	Rashaan Salaam,* RB, Colorado
1991	Desmond Howard,* WR, Mich.
1990	Ty Detmer, QB, Brigham Young
1989	Andre Ware,* QB, Houston
1988	Barry Sanders,* RB, Okla. State
1982	Herschel Walker,* RB, Georgia
1978	Billy Sims, RB, Oklahoma
1974	Archie Griffin, RB, Ohio State
1963	Roger Staubach, QB, Navy
1950	Vic Janowicz, HB, Ohio State
1948	Doak Walker, HB, SMU
1945	Doc Blanchard, FB, Army

* Turned pro after their junior year.

PRO FOOTBALL

Super Bowl Champions

All-Time Appearances

No.	Team	Record
8	Dallas Cowboys	5-3
5	San Francisco 49ers	5-0
5	Pittsburgh Steelers	4-1
5	Washington Redskins	3-2
5	Miami Dolphins	2-3
4	Oakland–L.A. Raiders	3-1
4	Buffalo Bills	0-4
4	Denver Broncos	0-4
4	Minnesota Vikings	0-4
3	Green Bay Packers	3-0
2	New York Giants	2-0
2	Baltimore Colts	1-1
2	Kansas City Chiefs	1-1
2	Cincinnati Bengals	0-2
2	New England Patriots	0-2
1	Chicago Bears	1-0
1	New York Jets	1-0
1	Los Angeles Rams	0-1
1	Philadelphia Eagles	0-1
1	San Diego Chargers	0-1

Note: Since their last Super Bowl appearances, the Baltimore Colts have moved to Indianapolis (1984) and the L.A. Rams to St. Louis (1995). After the 1995 season, the Cleveland Browns franchise moved to Baltimore and was renamed the Ravens; the NFL has frozen all records of the Browns until an expansion team takes their place in Cleveland.

Super Bowl No-Shows

Eleven teams have never played in the Super Bowl: Arizona Cardinals, Atlanta Falcons, Baltimore Ravens, Carolina Panthers, Cleveland Browns, Detroit Lions, Jacksonville Jaguars, New Orleans Saints, Seattle Seahawks, Tampa Bay Buccaneers, and Tennessee Oilers.

All-Time Winners
Only 12 teams have won the Super Bowl in 31 seasons.

Titles	Team	Super Bowl Numbers*	Championship Seasons
5	Dallas Cowboys	6, 12, 27, 28, 30	1971, 1977, 1992, 1993, 1995
5	San Francisco 49ers	16, 19, 23, 24, 29	1981, 1984, 1988, 1989, 1994
4	Pittsburgh Steelers	9, 10, 13, 14	1974, 1975, 1978, 1979
3	Green Bay Packers	1, 2, 31	1966, 1967, 1996
3	Oakland–L.A. Raiders	11, 15, 18	1976, 1980, 1983
3	Washington Redskins	17, 22, 26	1982, 1987, 1991
2	Miami Dolphins	7, 8	1972, 1973
2	New York Giants	21, 25	1986, 1990
1	Baltimore Colts#	5	1970
1	Chicago Bears	20	1985
1	Kansas City Chiefs	4	1969
1	New York Jets	3	1968

* The Roman numerals used by the NFL to designate Super Bowls have been converted to Arabic numerals to save space.
# The Baltimore Colts moved to Indianapolis after the 1983 season.

Greatest Underdogs
According to consensus Super Bowl point spreads.

Pts.	Super Bowl	Year	Underdog	Final Score
19	III	1969	New York Jets	Jets 16, Baltimore Colts 7
18	XXIX	1995	San Diego Chargers	San Francisco 49ers 49, Chargers 26
14	I	1967	Kansas City Chiefs	Green Bay Packers 35, Chiefs 10
14	XXXI	1997	New England Patriots	Green Bay Packers 35, Patriots 21
13½	II	1968	Oakland Raiders	Green Bay Packers 33, Raiders 14
13½	XXX	1996	Pittsburgh Steelers	Dallas Cowboys 27, Steelers 17
12½	XXIV	1990	Denver Broncos	San Francisco 49ers 55, Broncos 10
12	IV	1970	Kansas City Chiefs	Chiefs 23, Minnesota Vikings 7
10½	XIV	1980	Los Angeles Rams*	Pittsburgh Steelers 31, Rams 19
10½	XXVIII	1994	Buffalo Bills	Dallas Cowboys 30, Bills 13

* The Los Angeles Rams moved to St. Louis after the 1994 season.
Note: The New York Jets (1969) and Kansas City Chiefs (1970) were the only underdogs to upset their heavily favored opponents. Of the others, only the 1996 Pittsburgh Steelers were able to beat the point spread.

Closest Games

Margin	Winner	Loser	Score	Year
1 pt.	N.Y. Giants	Buffalo	20-19	1987
3 pts.	Baltimore	Dallas	16-13	1971
4 pts	Pittsburgh	Dallas	21-17	1976
4 pts.	Pittsburgh	Dallas	35-31	1979
4 pts.	San Francisco	Cincinnati	20-16	1989
5 pts.	San Francisco	Cincinnati	26-21	1982
7 pts.	Miami	Washington	14-7	1973
9 pts.	N.Y. Jets	Baltimore	16-7	1969
10 pts.	Pittsburgh	Minnesota	16-6	1975
10 pts.	Washington	Miami	27-17	1983
10 pts.	Dallas	Pittsburgh	27-17	1996

Note: Through January 1997 the average margin of victory after 31 Super Bowls has been 17 points. No Super Bowl game has ever been decided in overtime.

Biggest Blowouts

Margin	Winner	Loser	Score	Year
45 pts.	San Francisco	Denver	55-10	1990
36 pts.	Chicago	New England	46-10	1986
35 pts.	Dallas	Buffalo	52-17	1993
32 pts.	Washington	Denver	42-10	1988
29 pts.	L.A. Raiders	Washington	38-9	1984
25 pts.	Green Bay	Kansas City	35-10	1967
23 pts.	San Francisco	San Diego	49-26	1995
22 pts.	San Francisco	Miami	38-16	1985
21 pts.	Dallas	Miami	24-3	1972
19 pts.	Green Bay	Oakland	33-14	1968
19 pts.	N.Y. Giants	Denver	39-20	1987

Note: Prior to the first Super Bowl in January 1967, the widest margin of victory in an NFL championship game was 73 points, scored by the Chicago Bears against the Washington Redskins on December 8, 1940; final score, 73-0.

The First Super Bowl

On January 15, 1967, seven months after the rival American and National football leagues agreed to merge, the first AFL-NFL World Championship Game was played. Two years later, the contest was officially dubbed the Super Bowl. In 1971 the Super Bowl Trophy was named in honor of Vince Lombardi, who coached the Green Bay Packers to victory in the first two Super Bowls; Lombardi died in 1970.

Most Starts by a Quarterback

No.	Player/Team	W–L
4	Terry Bradshaw, Pittsburgh	4-0
4	Joe Montana, San Francisco	4-0
4	Roger Staubach, Dallas	2-2
4	Jim Kelly, Buffalo	0-4
3	Troy Aikman, Dallas	3-0
3	Bob Griese, Miami	2-1
3	John Elway, Denver	0-3
3	Fran Tarkenton, Minnesota	0-3
2	Jim Plunkett,* Raiders	2-0
2	Bart Starr, Green Bay	2-0
2	Len Dawson, Kansas City	1-1
2	Joe Theismann, Washington	1-1
2	Craig Morton,# Dallas/Denver	0-2

* Plunket is the only QB to have started for the same team representing two cities—the Oakland Raiders (1981) and the L.A. Raiders (1984).

Morton is the only QB to have started for two different Super Bowl teams—the Dallas Cowboys (1971) and the Denver Broncos (1978).

Note: Earl Morrall started the 1969 Super Bowl for the Baltimore Colts and was relieved by teammate Johnny Unitas; two years later, the roles were reversed and Morrall relieved Unitas.

Most Appearances by a Head Coach

No.	Coach/Team	Record
6	Don Shula, Baltimore/Miami	2-4
5	Tom Landry, Dallas	2-3
4	Chuck Noll, Pittsburgh	4-0
4	Joe Gibbs, Washington	3-1
4	Bud Grant, Minnesota	0-4
4	Marv Levy, Buffalo	0-4
3	Bill Walsh, San Francisco	3-0
3	Bill Parcells, N.Y. Giants/ New England	2-1
3	Dan Reeves, Denver	0-3
2	Tom Flores, Oakland– L.A. Raiders	2-0
2	Jimmy Johnson, Dallas	2-0
2	Vince Lombardi, Green Bay	2-0
2	George Seifert, San Francisco	2-0
2	Hank Stram, Kansas City	1-1

Quarterback Joe Montana threw five touchdown passes in San Francisco's 55-10 rout of the Denver Broncos in 1990.

Super Bowl Career Leaders

San Francisco's Jerry Rice caught 10 passes for 149 yards and 3 touchdowns against San Diego in 1995.

Most Yards Rushing

Listed with carries, average yards per carry, and touchdowns

Yards	Player/Team	Car.	Avg.	TD
354	Franco Harris, Pittsburgh	101	3.5	4
297	Larry Csonka, Miami	57	5.2	2
289	Emmitt Smith, Dallas	70	4.1	5
230	John Riggins, Washington	64	3.6	2
204	Timmy Smith, Washington	22	9.3	2
204	Thurman Thomas, Buffalo	52	3.9	4
201	Roger Craig, San Francisco	52	3.9	2
191	Marcus Allen, L.A. Raiders	20	9.5	2
162	Tony Dorsett, Dallas	31	5.2	1
153	Mark van Eeghen, Oakland	37	4.1	0

Games: Harris and Thomas (4); Craig, Csonka, and E. Smith (3); Dorsett, Riggins and van Eeghen (2); Allen and T. Smith (1)

Most Yards Receiving

Listed with receptions, average yards per catch, and touchdowns.

Yards	Player/Team	Rec.	Avg.	TD
512	Jerry Rice, San Francisco	28	18.3	7
364	Lynn Swann, Pittsburgh	16	22.8	3
323	Andre Reed, Buffalo	27	12.0	0
268	John Stallworth, Pittsburgh	11	24.4	3
256	Michael Irvin, Dallas	16	16.0	2
234	Ricky Sanders, Washington	10	23.4	2
212	Roger Craig, San Francisco	20	10.6	3
181	Cliff Branch, Oakland/ L.A. Raiders	14	12.9	3
179	Art Monk, Washington	9	19.9	0
173	Max McGee, Green Bay	8	21.6	2

Games: Reed, Stallworth and Swann (4); Branch, Craig, Irvin, Monk, and Rice (3); McGee and Sanders (2).

Most Receptions

Listed with yards gained, average yards per catch, and touchdowns.

No.	Player/Team	Yds.	Avg.	TD
28	Jerry Rice, San Francisco	512	18.3	7
27	Andre Reed, Buffalo	323	12.0	0
20	Roger Craig, San Francisco	212	10.6	3
20	Thurman Thomas, Buffalo	144	7.2	0
17	Jay Novacek, Dallas	148	8.7	2
16	Lynn Swann, Pittsburgh	364	22.8	3
16	Michael Irvin, Dallas	256	16.0	2
15	Chuck Foreman, Minnesota	139	9.3	0
14	Cliff Branch, Oakland	181	12.9	3
12	Don Beebe, Buffalo/Green Bay	171	14.3	2
12	Preston Pearson, Baltimore/Pittsburgh/Dallas	105	8.8	0
12	Kenneth Davis, Buffalo	72	6.0	0

Games: Pearson (5); Beebe, Davis, Reed, Swann and Thomas (4); Branch, Craig, Foreman, Irvin, Novacek, and Rice (3).

Most Frequent Super Bowl Sites

While the New Orleans Saints have yet to play in the Super Bowl, their hometown has served as host for the Big Game a record 8 times. The first 3 games were played outdoors at Tulane Stadium and the last 5 at the Louisiana Superdome. Seven Super Bowls have been played in Miami—5 at the Orange Bowl and 2 at Pro Player Stadium (formerly Joe Robbie Stadium).

Most Yards Passing

Listed with attempts, completions, and completion percentage.

Yards	Player/Team	Att.	Cmp.	Pct.
1,142	Joe Montana, San Francisco	122	83	68.0
932	Terry Bradshaw, Pittsburgh	84	49	58.3
829	Jim Kelly, Buffalo	145	81	55.9
734	Roger Staubach, Dallas	98	61	62.2
689	Troy Aikman, Dallas	80	56	70.0
669	John Elway, Denver	101	46	45.5
489	Fran Tarkenton, Minnesota	89	46	51.7
452	Bart Starr, Green Bay	47	29	61.7
433	Jim Plunkett, Oakland–L.A. Raiders	46	29	63.0
386	Joe Theismann, Washington	58	31	53.4

Games: Bradshaw, Kelly, Montana, and Staubach (4); Aikman, Elway, and Tarkenton (3); Plunkett, Starr, and Theismann (2).

Most Points Scored

Including touchdowns, field goals, and points after touchdowns.

Pts.	Player/Team	TD	FG	PAT
42	Jerry Rice, San Francisco	7	0	0
30	Emmitt Smith, Dallas	5	0	0
24	Roger Craig, San Francisco	4	0	0
24	Franco Harris, Pittsburgh	4	0	0
24	Thurman Thomas, Buffalo	4	0	0
22	Ray Wersching, San Francisco	0	5	7
20	Don Chandler, Green Bay	0	4	8
18	Cliff Branch, Oakland	3	0	0
18	John Stallworth, Pittsburgh	3	0	0
18	Lynn Swann, Pittsburgh	3	0	0
18	Ricky Watters, San Francisco	3	0	0

Games: Harris, Stallworth, Swann, and Thomas (4); Branch, Craig, Rice, and E. Smith (3); Chandler and Wersching (2); Watters (1).

All-time Super Bowl rushing leader Franco Harris (32) of Pittsburgh on his way to a 158-yard performance against Minnesota in 1975.

Best Passing Efficiency Ratings

Based on at least 25 attempts.

Rating	Player/Team	Games	Cmp./Pct.	Int.	TD
150.9	Phil Simms, N.Y. Giants	1	88.0	0	3
134.1	Steve Young, San Francisco	2	66.7	0	6
128.1	Doug Williams, Washington	1	62.1	1	4
127.8	Joe Montana, San Francisco	4	68.0	0	11
122.8	Jim Plunkett, Oakland–L.A. Raiders	2	63.0	0	4
112.8	Terry Bradshaw, Pittsburgh	4	58.3	4	9
111.9	Troy Aikman, Dallas	3	70.0	1	5
107.9	Brett Favre, Green Bay	1	51.2	0	2
95.4	Roger Staubach, Dallas	4	62.2	4	8
95.2	Ken Anderson, Cincinnati	1	73.5	2	2

Note: Passers are rated against a fixed performance standard adopted by the NFL in 1973. The ratings are based on percentage of touchdown passes, completions, interceptions, and the average yards gained per passing attempt.

Most Player Appearances

Eight players have played in five games each.

Player	Teams/Games
Marv Fleming	Green Bay (2) Miami (3)
Larry Cole	Dallas (5)
Cliff Harris	Dallas (5)
Charles Haley	San Francisco (2) Dallas (3)
D.D. Lewis	Dallas (5)
Preston Pearson	Baltimore (1) Pittsburgh (1) Dallas (3)
Charlie Waters	Dallas (5)
Rayfield Wright	Dallas (5)

Super Bowl Game Leaders

Most Yards Rushing

Yds.	Player/Game/Year
204	Timmy Smith, Washington vs. Denver (1988)
191	Marcus Allen, L.A. Raiders vs. Washington (1984)
166	John Riggins, Washington vs. Miami (1983)
158	Franco Harris, Pittsburgh vs. Minnesota (1975)
145	Larry Csonka, Miami vs. Minnesota (1974)

Most Yards Passing

Yds.	Player/Game/Year
357	Joe Montana, San Francisco vs. Cincinnati (1989)
340	Doug Williams, Washington vs. Denver (1988)
331	Joe Montana, San Francisco vs. Miami (1985)
325	Steve Young, San Francisco vs. San Diego (1995)
318	Terry Bradshaw, Pittsburgh vs. Dallas (1979)

Most Touchdown Passes

No.	Player/Game/Year
6	Steve Young, San Francisco vs. San Diego (1995)
5	Joe Montana, San Francisco vs. Denver (1990)
4	Terry Bradshaw, Pittsburgh vs. Dallas (1979)
4	Doug Williams, Washington vs. Denver (1988)
4	Troy Aikman, Dallas vs. Buffalo (1993)

Most Pass Completions
Listed with pass attempts.

No.	Player/Game/Year
31	Jim Kelly, Buffalo vs. Dallas (1994)
29	Dan Marino, Miami vs. San Francisco (1985)
28	Jim Kelly, Buffalo vs. Washington (1992)
28	Neil O'Donnell, Pittsburgh vs. Dallas (1996)
25	Ken Anderson, Cincinnati vs. San Francisco (1982)

Most Receptions

No.	Player/Game/Year
11	Dan Ross, Cincinnati vs. San Francisco (1982)
11	Jerry Rice, San Francisco vs. Cincinnati (1989)
10	Tony Nathan, Miami vs. San Francisco (1985)
10	Jerry Rice, San Francisco vs. San Diego (1995)
10	Andre Hastings, Pittsburgh vs. Dallas (1996)

Most Yards Receiving

Yds.	Player/Game/Year
215	Jerry Rice, San Francisco vs. Cincinnati (1989)
193	Ricky Sanders, Washington vs. Denver (1988)
161	Lynn Swann, Pittsburgh vs. Dallas (1976)
152	Andre Reed, Buffalo vs. Dallas (1993)
149	Jerry Rice, San Francisco vs. San Diego (1995)

Most Combined Yards
Rushing, receiving, and kick returns.

Yds.	Player/Game/Year
244	Desmond Howard, Green Bay vs. New England (1997)
242	Andre Coleman, San Diego vs. San Francisco (1995)
235	Ricky Sanders, Washington vs. Denver (1988)
220	Jerry Rice, San Francisco vs. Cincinnati (1989)
213	Timmy Smith, Washington vs. Denver (1988)

Note: Both Howard and Coleman gained all their yardage on kick returns.

Most Points Scored
by Individual Players

Pts.	Player/Game/Year
18	Roger Craig, San Francisco vs. Miami (1985)
18	Jerry Rice, San Francisco vs. Denver (1990)
18	Jerry Rice, San Francisco vs. San Diego (1995)
18	Ricky Watters, San Francisco vs. San Diego (1995)
15	Don Chandler, Green Bay vs. Oakland (1968)

Most Combined Points Scored
by Two Teams

Pts.	Final Score/Site/Year
75	San Francisco 49, San Diego 26, at Miami (1995)
69	Dallas 52, Buffalo 17, at Pasadena (1993)
66	Pittsburgh 35, Dallas 31, at Miami (1979)
65	San Francisco 55, Denver 10, at New Orleans (1990)
61	Washington 37, Buffalo 24, at Minneapolis (1992)

Single-Play Leaders

Longest Runs from Scrimmage

Yds.	Player/Game/Year
74	Marcus Allen, L.A. Raiders vs. Washington (1984)
58	Timmy Smith, Washington vs. Denver (1988)
58	Tom Matte, Baltimore vs. New York Jets (1969)
49	Larry Csonka, Miami vs. Washington (1973)
43	John Riggins, Washington vs. Miami (1983)

Note: Allen, T. Smith, and Riggins scored touchdowns on their returns.

Longest Kickoff Returns

Yds.	Player/Game/Year
99	Desmond Howard, Green Bay vs. New England (1997)
98	Fulton Walker, Miami vs. Washington (1983)
98	Andre Coleman, San Diego vs. San Francisco (1995)
93	Stanford Jennings, Cincinnati vs. San Francisco (1989)
67	Rick Upchurch, Denver vs. Dallas (1978)

Note: All returns, except Upchurch's, went for touchdowns.

Extra Point

In thirty-one Super Bowls, the winning quarterback has been named Most Valuable Player sixteen times. Joe Montana of the 49ers won it three times, and Terry Bradshaw of the Steelers and Bart Starr of the Packers were each honored twice. The other quarterbacks are Troy Aikman (Cowboys), Len Dawson (Chiefs), Joe Namath (Jets), Jim Plunkett (Raiders), Mark Rypien (Redskins), Phil Simms (Giants), Roger Staubach (Cowboys), Doug Williams (Redskins), and Steve Young (49ers).

Longest Pass Plays

Yds.	Players/Game/Year
81	Brett Favre to Antonio Freeman Washington vs. New Eng. (1997)
80	Jim Plunkett to Kenny King Oakland vs. Philadelphia (1981)
80	Doug Williams to Ricky Sanders Washington vs. Denver (1988)
76	David Woodley to Jimmy Cefalo Miami vs. Washington (1983)
75	Johnny Unitas to John Mackey Baltimore vs. Dallas (1971)

Note: All plays went for touchdowns.

Longest Punt Returns

Yds.	Player/Game/Year
45	John Taylor, San Francisco vs. Cincinnati (1989)
34	Darrell Green, Washington vs. L.A. Raiders (1984)
34	Desmond Howard, Green Bay vs. New England (1997)
32	Desmond Howard, Green Bay vs. New England (1997)
31	Willie Wood, Green Bay vs. Oakland (1968)

Note: No returns went for touchdowns.

Longest Fumble Returns

Yds.	Player/Game/Year
64	Leon Lett, Dallas vs. Buffalo (1993)
49	Mike Bass, Washington vs. Miami (1973)
46	James Washington, Dallas vs. Buffalo (1994)
37	Mike Hegman, Dallas vs. Pittsburgh (1979)
19	Randy Hughes, Dallas vs. Denver (1978)

Note: Bass, Washington, and Hegman scored touchdowns on their returns.

Longest Interception Returns

Yds.	Player/Game/Year
75	Willie Brown, Oakland vs. Minnesota (1977)
60	Herb Adderley, Green Bay vs. Oakland (1968)
55	Jake Scott, Miami vs. Washington (1973)
50	Willie Wood, Green Bay vs. Kansas City (1967)
47	Jim Morrissey, Chicago vs. New England (1986)

Note: Brown and Adderley scored touchdowns on their returns.

Longest Field Goals

Yds.	Player/Game/Year
54	Steve Christie, Buffalo vs. Dallas (1994)
48	Jan Stenerud, Kansas City vs. Minnesota (1970)
48	Rich Karlis, Denver vs. New York Giants (1987)
47	Jim Turner, Denver vs. Dallas (1978)
46	Chris Bahr, Oakland vs. Philadelphia (1981)
46	Norm Johnson, Pittsburgh vs. Dallas (1996)

Green Bay's Desmond Howard.

NFL Playoff Leaders

All postseason games through the 1997 Super Bowl.

Dallas quarterback Troy Aikman.

Best Winning Percentages

Since 1933; including Super Bowls and all NFL and AFL playoff games. Listed with years teams have qualified for postseason play (Playoff Berths).

Pct.	Team	Record	Playoff Berths
.714	Green Bay Packers	20-8	17
.667	Jacksonville Jaguars	2-1	1
.629	San Francisco 49ers	22-13	18
.627	Dallas Cowboys	32-19	24
.600	Washington Redskins*	21-14	19
.588	Pittsburgh Steelers	20-14	18
.583	Oakland Raiders#	21-15	18
.548	Miami Dolphins	17-14	16
.519	Buffalo Bills	14-13	15
.500	Chicago Bears	14-14	21
.500	Indianapolis Colts†	10-10	13
.500	Carolina Panthers	1-1	1

* Includes 1 game while the franchise was in Boston.
\# Includes 12 games while in Los Angeles.
† Includes 15 games while in Baltimore.

Most Appearances in NFL-NFC Championship Games

Since 1933; listed with title game records.

No.	Team	Record
16	Dallas Cowboys	8-8
16	New York Giants	5-11
13	Chicago Bears	7-6
12	Green Bay Packers	9-3
12	Washington Redskins*	7-5
12	St. Louis Rams#	3-9
11	San Francisco 49ers	5-6
11	Cleveland Browns†	4-7
6	Minnesota Vikings	4-2
6	Detroit Lions	4-2

* Includes 1 game while franchise was in Boston.
\# Includes 1 game while in Cleveland and 11 in Los Angeles.
† Browns moved to AFC after 1969 season.

Most Appearances in AFL-AFC Championship Games

Since 1960; listed with title game records.

No.	Team	Record
12	Oakland Raiders*	4-8
9	Pittsburgh Steelers	5-4
8	Buffalo Bills	6-2
8	San Diego Chargers#	2-6
7	Miami Dolphins	5-2
6	Houston Oilers	2-4
5	Denver Broncos	4-1
4	Kansas City Chiefs†	3-1
3	Indianapolis Colts‡	1-2
3	Cleveland Browns	0-3
3	New England Patriots	2-1

* Includes 2 games while franchise was in Los Angeles.
\# Includes 1 game while in Los Angeles.
† Includes 1 game while in Dallas as the Texans.
‡ Includes 2 games while in Baltimore.

Best-Rated Quarterbacks

Based on at least 150 attempts.

Rating	Player	Cmp. Pct.	TD
104.8	Bart Starr	61.0	15
96.0	Troy Aikman*	66.5	22
95.6	Joe Montana	62.7	45
94.7	Brett Favre*	61.2	18
93.5	Ken Anderson	66.3	9
91.4	Joe Theismann	60.7	11
89.7	Steve Young*	62.0	15
84.9	Warren Moon	64.3	17

* Played in the 1996 playoffs.
Games: Montana (23); Young (18); Aikman (14); Stabler (13); Favre, Kosar, Moon, Starr and Theismann (10); Anderson (6).
Note: Passers are rated against a fixed performance standard adopted by the NFL in 1973. The ratings are based on percentage of touchdown passes, completions, interceptions, and the average yards gained per passing attempt.

Most Yards Rushing

Yds.	Player/Team
1,556	Franco Harris, Pittsburgh
1,413	Emmitt Smith,* Dallas
1,399	Thurman Thomas,* Buffalo
1,383	Tony Dorsett, Dallas
1,310	Marcus Allen, Oakland–L.A. Raiders/Kansas City

* Played in the 1996 playoffs.

Most Pass Completions

No.	Player/Team
460	Joe Montana, San Fran./K.C.
322	Jim Kelly,* Buffalo
291	Dan Marino, Miami
259	Warren Moon, Houston
276	Troy Aikman,* Dallas

* Played in the 1996 playoffs.

Most Receptions

Rec.	Player/Team
120	Jerry Rice,* San Francisco
80	Andre Reed,* Buffalo
83	Michael Irvin,* Dallas
75	Thurman Thomas,* Buffalo
73	Cliff Branch, Oakland–L.A. Raiders
70	Fred Biletnikoff, Oakland

* Played in the 1996 playoffs.

Most Yards Passing

Yds.	Player/Team
5,772	Joe Montana, San Fran./K.C.
3,863	Jim Kelly,* Buffalo
3,833	Terry Bradshaw, Pittsburgh
3,600	Dan Marino, Miami
3,587	John Elway,* Denver

* Played in the 1996 playoffs.

Most Touchdown Passes

No.	Player/Team
45	Joe Montana, San Francisco/K.C.
30	Terry Bradshaw, Pittsburgh
29	Dan Marino, Miami
24	Roger Staubach, Dallas
22	Troy Aikman,* Dallas

* Played in the 1996 playoffs.

Most Yards Receiving

Yds.	Player/Team
1,742	Jerry Rice,* San Francisco
1,289	Cliff Branch, Oakland/L.A. Raiders
1,283	Michael Irvin,* Dallas
1,169	Andre Reed,* Buffalo
1,167	Fred Biletnikoff, Oakland
1,121	Paul Warfield, Cleveland/Miami

* Played in the 1996 playoffs.

Most Points Scored

At least 100 points.

ts.	Player/Team
120	Emmitt Smith,* Dallas
120	Thurman Thomas,* Buffalo
115	George Blanda, Chicago Bears/Houston/Oakland
108	Jerry Rice,* San Francisco
103	Matt Bahr, Pittsburgh-Cleveland/New York. Giants/New England
102	Franco Harris, Pittsburgh

* Played in the 1996 playoffs.

Most Playoff Games as Head Coach

No.	Coach/Team
36	Tom Landry, Dallas
36	Don Shula, Baltimore/Miami
24	Chuck Noll, Pittsburgh
22	Bud Grant, Minnesota
21	Joe Gibbs, Washington
19	Marv Levy,* Buffalo
18	Chuck Knox, L.A. Rams/Buffalo/Seattle
16	John Madden, Oakland
15	Dan Reeves, Denver/N.Y. Giants
15	Bill Parcells,* N.Y. Giants/New England
15	Marty Schottenheimer, Cleveland/Kansas City

* Coached in the 1996 playoffs.

Bart Starr (15) led Green Bay to five NFL titles and two Super Bowl victories between 1961 and 1968.

Best Teams by Decade

Winningest Teams of the 1990s
Through the 1996 season

	Team	Regular Season	Pct.	Playoffs
1	San Francisco 49ers	84-28-0	.750	7-5
2	Dallas Cowboys	77-35-0	.688	12-3
3	Buffalo Bills	76-36-0	.679	10-6
4	Kansas City Chiefs	73-39-0	.652	3-6
5	Pittsburgh Steelers	69-43-0	.616	4-5
6	Miami Dolphins	67-45-0	.598	3-4
7	Philadelphia Eagles	66-46-0	.589	2-4
8	Oakland–L.A.Raiders	62-50-0	.554	2-3
	Denver Broncos	62-50-0	.554	1-3
10	Green Bay Packers	61-51-0	.545	7-3
	Minnesota Vikings	61-51-0	.545	0-4

Super Bowl championship seasons: 1990—New York Giants; 1991—Washington; 1992—Dallas; 1993—Dallas; 1994—San Francisco; 1995—Dallas; 1996—Green Bay.

Winningest Teams of the 1970s

	Team	Regular Season	Pct.	Playoffs
1	Dallas Cowboys	105-39-0	.729	14-7
2	Miami Dolphins	104-39-1	.726	8-4
3	Oakland Raiders	100-38-6	.715	8-6
4	Minnesota Vikings	99-43-2	.694	7-8
5	Los Angeles Rams	98-42-4	.694	6-7
6	Pittsburgh Steelers	99-44-1	.691	14-4
7	Washington Redskins	91-52-1	.635	2-4
8	Denver Broncos	75-64-5	.538	2-3
9	Cincinnati Bengals	74-70-0	.514	0-3
10	Baltimore Colts	73-70-1	.510	4-4

Super Bowl championship seasons: 1970—Baltimore; 1971—Dallas; 1972—Miami; 1973—Miami; 1974—Pittsburgh; 1975—Pittsburgh; 1976—Oakland; 1977—Dallas; 1978—Pittsburgh; 1979—Pittsburgh.

Winningest Teams of the 1980s

	Team	Regular Season	Pct.	Playoffs
1	San Francisco 49ers	104-47-1	.688	13-4
2	Washington Redskins	97-55-0	.638	11-3
3	Miami Dolphins	94-57-1	.622	6-5
4	Denver Broncos	93-58-1	.615	6-5
5	Chicago Bears	92-60-0	.605	5-4
6	Oakland–L.A Raiders	89-63-0	.586	8-3
7	Los Angeles Rams	86-66-0	.566	4-7
8	Cleveland Browns	83-68-1	.549	3-7
9	New York Giants	81-70-1	.536	6-4
10	Cincinnati Bengals	81-71-0	.533	4-3

Super Bowl championship seasons: 1980—Oakland; 1981—San Francisco; 1982—Washington; 1983—Los Angeles Raiders; 1984—San Francisco; 1985—Chicago; 1986—New York Giants; 1987—Washington; 1988—San Francisco; 1989—San Francisco.

Head coach Paul Brown won three NFL titles with the Cleveland Browns in the 1950s then continued his winning ways with the Cincinnati Bengals in the 1970s.

Winningest Teams of the 1960s

The NFL and AFL merged after the 1969 season.

	Team	Regular Season	Pct.	Playoffs
1	Green Bay Packers	96-37-5	.714	9-1
2	Cleveland Browns	92-41-5	.685	3-3
3	Baltimore Colts	92-42-4	.681	2-3
4	Kansas City Chiefs*	87-48-5	.639	5-1
5	San Diego Chargers*	86-48-6	.636	1-4
6	Oakland Raiders*	77-58-5	.568	3-3
7	New York Giants	69-63-6	.522	0-3
8	Detroit Lions	66-61-11	.518	0-0
9	St. Louis Cardinals	67-63-8	.515	0-0
10	Houston Oilers*	70-66-4	.514	2-3
	New York Jets*	69-65-6	.514	2-1

* AFL teams.
Super Bowl championship seasons: 1966—Green Bay; 1967—Green Bay; 1968—New York Jets; 1969—Kansas City. The first 2 Super Bowls were officially known as "The AFL-NFL World Championship Game."
NFL titles: 1960—Philadelphia; 1961—Green Bay; 1962—Green Bay; 1963—Chicago; 1964—Cleveland; 1965—Green Bay; 1966—Green Bay; 1967—Green Bay; 1968—Baltimore; 1969—Minnesota.
AFL titles: 1960—Houston; 1961—Houston; 1962—Dallas Texans; 1963—San Diego; 1964—Buffalo; 1965—Buffalo; 1966—Kansas City; 1967—Oakland; 1968—New York Jets; 1969—Kansas City.
Note: The Chicago Cardinals moved to St. Louis after the 1959 season; the Los Angeles Chargers moved to San Diego after the 1960 season; the Dallas Texans moved to Kansas City and became the Chiefs after the 1962 season; and the New York Titans were renamed the Jets following the 1962 season.

Winningest Teams of the 1950s

	Team	Regular Season	Pct.	NFL Titles
1	Cleveland Browns	88-33-2	.742	3
2	New York Giants	76-41-3	.646	1
3	Chicago Bears	70-48-1	.592	0
4	Detroit Lions	68-48-4	.583	3
5	Los Angeles Rams	68-49-3	.579	1
6	San Francisco 49ers	63-54-3	.538	0
7	Baltimore Colts	41-42-1	.494	2
8	Pittsburgh Steelers	54-63-3	.463	0
9	Philadelphia Eagles	51-64-5	.446	0
10	Washington Redskins	47-70-3	.404	0

Note: The Cleveland Rams moved to Los Angeles after the 1945 season. In 1949 the Cleveland Browns and San Francisco entered the NFL after the demise of the All-America Football Conference. The Baltimore Colts joined the NFL in 1950 but folded after one season, and a new Baltimore Colts franchise joined the NFL in 1953.

Chicago Bears owner George Halas (right), seen here with Red Grange in 1935, served intermittently as his own head coach for forty years between 1920 and 1967.

Winningest Teams of the 1940s

	Team	Regular Season	Pct.	NFL Titles
1	Chicago Bears	81-26-3	.750	4
2	Washington Redskins	65-41-4	.609	1
3	Green Bay Packers	62-44-4	.582	1
4	Philadelphia Eagles	58-47-5	.550	2
5	New York Giants	55-47-8	.536	0

Other NFL titles: Chicago Cardinals and Cleveland Rams.
Note: From 1946 to 1949 the Cleveland Browns went 47-4-3 (.898) in the All-American Football Conference and won all four league championships.

Winningest Teams of the 1930s

	Team	Regular Season	Pct.	NFL Titles
1	Chicago Bears	85-28-11	.730	2
2	Green Bay Packers	86-35-4	.704	4
3	New York Giants	80-39-8	.661	2
4	Detroit Lions	73-39-9	.640	1
5	Washington Redskins	46-36-8	.556	1

Note: The Detroit Lions originated as the Portsmouth, OH, Spartans (1930–33), and Washington as the Boston Braves (1932) and Boston Redskins (1933–36).

All-Time Career Leaders

NFL regular season career leaders through the 1996 season; players with asterisks (*) were active in 1996.

Running back Walter Payton, who played his entire 13-year career with the Chicago Bears, retired in 1987 as the NFL's all-time rushing leader.

Best-Rated Passers

Based on at least 1,500 attempts.

Rating	Player	Yrs.	Cmp. Pct.	TD	Yds.
96.2	Steve Young*	12	64.5	174	25,479
92.3	Joe Montana	15	63.2	273	40,551
88.6	Brett Favre*	6	61.9	147	18,724
88.3	Dan Marino*	14	59.9	369	51,636
84.4	Jim Kelly*	11	60.1	237	35,467
83.4	Roger Staubach	11	57.0	153	22,700
83.0	Troy Aikman*	8	62.9	110	22,733
82.7	Neil Lomax	8	57.6	136	22,771
82.6	Sonny Jurgensen	18	57.1	255	32,224
82.6	Len Dawson	19	57.1	239	28,711
82.1	Jeff Hostetler*	11	58.2	89	15,531
81.9	Ken Anderson	16	59.3	197	32,838
81.8	Bernie Kosar*	12	59.3	124	23,301
81.7	Danny White	13	59.7	155	21,959

Note: Passers are rated against a fixed performance standard adopted by the NFL in 1973. The ratings are based on percentage of touchdown passes, completions, and interceptions, and the average yards gained per passing attempt.

Most Points Scored

Listed with years played, touchdowns, field goals, and points after touchdowns.

Pts.	Player	Yrs.	TD	FG	PAT
2,002	George Blanda	26	9	335	943
1,711	Nick Lowery*	18	0	383	562
1,699	Jan Stenerud	19	0	373	580
1,556	Gary Anderson*	15	0	356	488
1,537	Morten Andersen*	15	0	355	472
1,473	Eddie Murray	16	0	325	498
1,470	Pat Leahy	18	0	304	558
1,452	Norm Johnson*	15	0	300	552
1,439	Jim Turner	16	1	304	521
1,422	Matt Bahr	17	0	300	522
1,382	Mark Moseley	16	0	300	482

Most Touchdowns

Listed with the years played; touchdowns rushing, receiving, and on kick returns; and total points scored.

TD	Player	Yrs.	Rush	Rec.	Ret.	Pts.
165	Jerry Rice*	12	10	154	1	994#
134	Marcus Allen*	15	112	21	1	806#
126	Jim Brown	9	106	20	0	756
125	Walter Payton	13	110	15	0	750
116	John Riggins	14	104	12	0	696
115	Emmitt Smith*	7	108	7	0	690
113	Lenny Moore	12	63	48	2	678
105	Don Hutson	11	3	99	3	630
101	Steve Largent	14	1	100	0	606
100	Franco Harris	13	91	9	0	600

Totals include 2-point conversions: two for Rice and one for Allen.

Most Yards Passing

Yds.	Player	Yrs.
51,636	Dan Marino*	14
47,003	Fran Tarkenton	18
45,034	John Elway*	14
43,787	Warren Moon*	13
43,040	Dan Fouts	15
40,551	Joe Montana	15
40,239	Johnny Unitas	18
37,946	Dave Krieg*	17
36,442	Boomer Esiason*	13
35,467	Jim Kelly*	11
34,665	Jim Hart	19
34,380	Jim Everett*	11
33,872	Steve DeBerg	16
33,503	John Hadl	16
33,462	Phil Simms	14

Most Touchdown Passes

TD	Player	Yrs.
369	Dan Marino*	14
342	Fran Tarkenton	18
290	Johnny Unitas	18
273	Joe Montana	15
261	Dave Krieg*	17
255	Sonny Jurgensen	18
254	Warren Moon*	13
254	Dan Fouts	15
251	John Elway*	14
244	John Hadl	16
239	Len Dawson	19
237	Jim Kelly*	11
236	George Blanda	26
234	Boomer Esiason*	13
214	John Brodie	17

Most Yards Rushing

Yds.	Player	Yrs.
16,726	Walter Payton	13
13,259	Eric Dickerson	11
12,739	Tony Dorsett	12
12,312	Jim Brown	9
12,120	Franco Harris	13
11,738	Marcus Allen*	15
11,725	Barry Sanders*	8
11,352	John Riggins	14
11,236	O.J. Simpson	11
10,762	Thurman Thomas*	9
10,273	Ottis Anderson	14
10,160	Emmitt Smith*	7
9,407	Earl Campbell	8
8,597	Jim Taylor	10
8,378	Joe Perry	14

Most Times Intercepted

No.	Player	Yrs.
277	George Blanda	26
268	John Hadl	16
266	Fran Tarkenton	18
253	Norm Snead	15
253	Johnny Unitas	18
247	Jim Hart	19
243	Bobby Layne	15
242	Dan Fouts	15
224	John Brodie	17

Most Yards Receiving

Yds.	Player	Yrs.
16,377	Jerry Rice*	12
14,004	James Lofton	16
13,177	Henry Ellard*	14
13,089	Steve Largent	14
12,721	Art Monk	16
12,146	Charlie Joiner	18
11,834	Don Maynard	15
10,884	Andre Reed*	12
10,856	Gary Clark	11
10,716	Stanley Morgan	14
10,372	Harold Jackson	16
10,266	Lance Alworth	11
10,111	Irving Fryar*	13
9,831	Drew Hill	15
9,500	Michael Irvin	9

Most Receptions

No.	Player	Yrs.
1,050	Jerry Rice*	12
940	Art Monk	16
819	Steve Largent	14
775	Henry Ellard*	14
766	Andre Reed*	12
764	James Lofton	16
750	Charlie Joiner	18
699	Gary Clark	11
667	Cris Carter*	10
662	Ozzie Newsome	13
650	Irving Fryar*	13
649	Charley Taylor	13
634	Drew Hill	15
633	Don Maynard	15
631	Raymond Berry	13

Most Sacks

The NFL began compiling statistics for this category in 1982.

Sacks	Player	Yrs.
165½	Reggie White*	12
140	Bruce Smith*	12
133	Richard Dent*	14
132½	Lawrence Taylor	12

Note: The unofficial career leader in sacks is Deacon Jones with 172. Jones, who invented the term "sack," retired in 1974 after a 14-year career as a defensive end.

Extra Point
Quarterback and placekicker George Blanda is the only NFL player whose career touched four decades of the century. He began as a 22-year-old rookie with the Chicago Bears in 1949, then led the Houston Oilers to consecutive titles in 1960 and 1961, and finished his career as placekicker at age 48 with the Oakland Raiders. He set three all-time records: most seasons played (26), most games (340), and most points (2,002).

Current Career Leaders

NFL career leaders who were active during 1996 regular season.

Best-Rated Quarterbacks

Based on at least 1,500 attempts; listed with the years played, the completion percentage, and the touchdown passes and passing yards.

Rating	Player	Yrs.	Cmp. Pct.	TD	Yds.
96.2	Steve Young	12	64.5	174	25,479
88.6	Brett Favre	6	61.9	147	18,724
88.3	Dan Marino	14	59.9	369	51,636
84.4	Jim Kelly	11	60.1	237	35,467
83.0	Troy Aikman	8	62.9	110	22,733
82.1	Jeff Hostetler	11	58.2	89	15,531
81.8	Bernie Kosar	12	59.3	124	23,301
81.5	Dave Krieg	17	58.5	261	37,946

Note: Passers are rated against a fixed performance standard adopted by the NFL in 1973. The ratings are based on percentage of touchdown passes, completions, interceptions, and average yards gained per passing attempt.

Most Points Scored

Listed with years played, touchdowns, field goals, and points after touchdowns

Pts.	Player	Yrs.	TD	FG	PAT
1,711	Nick Lowery	18	0	383	562
1,556	Gary Anderson	15	0	356	488
1,537	Morten Andersen	15	0	355	472
1,452	Norm Johnson	15	0	300	552
1,175	Kevin Butler	12	0	257	404
1,111	Al Del Greco	13	0	236	403
994	Jerry Rice	12	165	0	4*
913	Chip Lohmiller	9	0	204	301
859	Pete Stoyanovich	8	0	193	280
822	Jeff Jaeger	9	0	185	267

* Includes two 2-point conversions.

Most Yards Passing

Yards	Player	Yrs.
51,636	Dan Marino	14
45,034	John Elway	14
43,787	Warren Moon	13
37,946	Dave Krieg	17
36,442	Boomer Esiason	13
35,467	Jim Kelly	11
34,380	Jim Everett	11
26,252	Vinny Testaverde	10
25,479	Steve Young	12
23,301	Bernie Kosar	12

Most Passing Yards Per Game

Based on at least 1,500 attempts.

Avg.	Player	Yrs.
259.5	Dan Marino	14
244.0	Drew Bledsoe	4
243.3	Warren Moon	13
231.2	Brett Favre	6
223.2	Jim Everett	11

Most Touchdown Passes

TD	Player	Yrs.
369	Dan Marino	14
261	Dave Krieg	17
254	Warren Moon	13
251	John Elway	14
237	Jim Kelly	11
234	Boomer Esiason	13
202	Jim Everett	11
174	Steve Young	12
157	Vinny Testaverde	10
147	Brett Favre	6

Most Times Intercepted

Int.	Player	Yrs.
209	Dan Marino	14
208	Warren Moon	13
205	John Elway	14
199	Dave Krieg	17
182	Boomer Esiason	13

Most Sacks

The NFL began compiling statistics for this category in 1982.

Sacks	Player	Yrs.
165½	Reggie White	12
140	Bruce Smith	12
133	Richard Dent	14
122½	Kevin Greene	12
115½	Chris Doleman	12
113	Sean Jones	13
112½	Leslie O'Neal	10
105½	Pat Swilling	11

Most Times Sacked

Sacks	Player	Yrs.
492	Dave Krieg	17
464	John Elway	14
401	Warren Moon	13
323	Jim Kelly	11
311	Boomer Esiason	13

Most Touchdowns

Listed with the years played; touchdowns rushing, receiving, and on kick returns; and total points scored.

TD	Player	Yrs.	Rush	Rec.	Ret.	Pts.
165	Jerry Rice	12	10	154	1	994*
134	Marcus Allen	15	112	21	1	806*
115	Emmitt Smith	7	108	7	0	690
91	Barry Sanders	8	84	7	0	546
82	Thurman Thomas	9	62	20	0	492
82	Herschel Walker	11	61	19	2	492
77	Cris Carter	10	0	76	1	466*
76	Andre Reed	12	1	75	0	456
73	Irving Fryar	13	1	69	3	442*
72	Earnest Byner	13	56	15	1	432

* Includes 2-point conversions: two each for Rice, Carter, and Fryar; one for Allen.

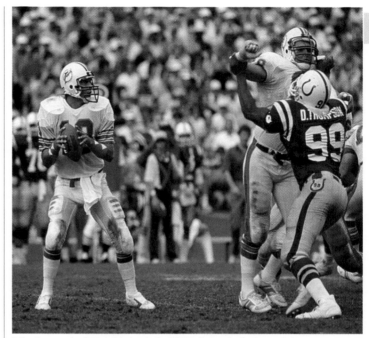

Miami quarterback Dan Marino is the NFL's all-time leader in touchdown passes and yards passing.

Most Yards Rushing

Yards	Player	Yrs.
11,738	Marcus Allen	15
11,725	Barry Sanders	8
10,762	Thurman Thomas	9
10,160	Emmitt Smith	7
8,205	Herschel Walker	11
7,948	Earnest Byner	13
6,816	Rodney Hampton	7
5,859	Chris Warren	7
5,524	Ricky Watters	5
5,457	Terry Allen	5
4,522	Jerome Bettis	4
4,250	Harold Green	7
4,202	Craig Heyward	9

Most Interceptions Caught

Int.	Player	Yrs.
48	Eugene Robinson	12
43	Darrell Green	14
40	Albert Lewis	14
38	Rod Woodson	10
38	Kevin Ross	13

Most Yards Per Carry

Based on at least 750 rushing attempts.

Avg.	Player	Yrs.
4.9	Barry Sanders	8
4.4	Emmitt Smith	7
4.3	Chris Warren	15
4.2	Craig Heyward	9
4.2	Herschel Walker	11
4.2	Thurman Thomas	9

Most Yards Receiving

Yds.	Player	Yrs.
16,377	Jerry Rice	12
13,177	Henry Ellard	14
10,884	Andre Reed	12
10,111	Irving Fryar	13
9,500	Michael Irvin	9
8,503	Anthony Miller	9
8,367	Cris Carter	10
8,026	Mark Carrier	10
8,018	Webster Slaughter	11
8,001	Bill Brooks	11

Most Receptions

Rec.	Player	Yrs.
1,050	Jerry Rice	12
775	Henry Ellard	14
766	Andre Reed	12
667	Cris Carter	10
650	Irving Fryar	13
591	Michael Irvin	9
583	Bill Brooks	11
576	Marcus Allen	15
569	Andre Rison	8
564	Keith Byars	11
563	Ronnie Harmon	11
549	Anthony Miller	9
536	Brian Blades	9

Most Yards Per Catch

Based on at least 200 catches.

Avg.	Player	Yrs.
20.1	Flipper Anderson	9
17.0	Henry Ellard	14
16.5	Willie Davis	6
16.3	Willie Green	6
16.3	Michael Jackson	6

Single-Season Leaders

The NFL regular season schedule has grown from 12 games (1947–60) to 14 games (1961–77) to 16 games (since 1978).
The AFL regular season schedule was always 14 games (1960–69).

Best Quarterback Efficiency Ratings
Based on at least 175 attempts.

Rating	Player/Team	Year	Cmp. Pct.	TD	Int.	Yds.
112.8	Steve Young, San Francisco	1994	70.2	35	10	3,969
112.4	Joe Montana, San Francisco	1989	70.2	26	8	3,521
110.4	Milt Plum, Cleveland	1960	60.4	21	5	2,297
109.9	Sammy Baugh, Washington	1945	70.3	11	4	1,669
108.9	Dan Marino, Miami	1984	64.2	48	17	5,084
107.5	Sid Luckman, Chicago Bears	1943	54.5	28	12	2,194
107.0	Steve Young, San Francisco	1992	66.7	25	7	3,465
105.0	Bart Starr, Green Bay	1966	62.2	14	3	2,257
104.8	Roger Staubach, Dallas	1971	59.7	15	4	1,882
104.8	Y.A. Tittle, New York Giants	1963	60.2	36	14	3,145
104.3	Bart Starr, Green Bay	1968	63.7	15	8	1,617
103.4	Ken Stabler, Oakland	1976	66.7	27	17	2,737

Note: Passers are rated against a fixed performance standard adopted by the NFL in 1973. The ratings are based on percentage of touchdown passes, completions, interceptions, and average yards gained per passing attempt.

Most Combined Yards
Rushing, receiving, and kick returns.

Yds.	Player/Team/Year
2,535	Lionel James, San Diego, 1985
2,477	Brian Mitchell, Washington, 1994
2,462	Terry Metcalf, St. Louis, 1975
2,444	Mack Herron, New England, 1974
2,440	Gale Sayers, Chicago, 1966
2,428	Timmy Brown, Philadelphia, 1963
2,348	Brian Mitchell, Washington, 1995
2,317	Tim Brown, L.A. Raiders, 1988
2,308	Marcus Allen, L.A. Raiders, 1985
2,306	Timmy Brown, Philadelphia, 1962
2,272	Gale Sayers, Chicago, 1965
2,259	Eric Dickerson, L.A. Rams, 1984
2,243	O.J. Simpson, Buffalo, 1975
2,216	Walter Payton, Chicago, 1977

Most Yards Passing

Yds.	Player/Team/Year
5,084	Dan Marino, Miami, 1984
4,802	Dan Fouts, San Diego, 1981
4,746	Dan Marino, Miami, 1986
4,715	Dan Fouts, San Diego, 1980
4,690	Warren Moon, Houston, 1991
4,689	Warren Moon, Houston, 1990
4,614	Neil Lomax, St. Louis, 1984
4,555	Drew Bledsoe, New England, 1994
4,458	Lynn Dickey, Green Bay, 1983
4,453	Dan Marino, Miami, 1994
4,434	Dan Marino, Miami, 1988
4,413	Brett Favre, Green Bay, 1995
4,367	Mark Brunell, Jacksonville, 1996
4,348	Bill Kenney, Kansas City, 1983
4,338	Scott Mitchell, Detroit, 1995

Most Yards Rushing

Yds.	Player/Team/Year
2,105	Eric Dickerson, L.A. Rams, 1984
2,003	O.J. Simpson, Buffalo, 1973
1,934	Earl Campbell, Houston, 1980
1,883	Barry Sanders, Detroit, 1994
1,863	Jim Brown, Cleveland, 1963
1,852	Walter Payton, Chicago, 1977
1,821	Eric Dickerson, L.A. Rams, 1986
1,817	O.J. Simpson, Buffalo, 1975
1,808	Eric Dickerson, L.A. Rams, 1983
1,773	Emmitt Smith, Dallas, 1995
1,759	Marcus Allen, L.A Raiders, 1985
1,719	Gerald Riggs, Atlanta, 1985
1,713	Emmitt Smith, Dallas, 1992
1,697	Earl Campbell, Houston, 1979
1,690	Barry Foster, Pittsburgh, 1992

Most Receptions

Rec.	Player/Team/Year
123	Herman Moore, Detroit, 1995
122	Cris Carter, Minnesota, 1994
122	Cris Carter, Minnesota, 1995
122	Jerry Rice, San Francisco, 1995
119	Isaac Bruce, St. Louis, 1995
112	Jerry Rice, San Francisco, 1994
112	Sterling Sharpe, Green Bay, 1993
111	Michael Irvin, Dallas, 1995
111	Terance Mathis, Atlanta, 1994
108	Sterling Sharpe, Green Bay, 1992
108	Brett Perriman, Detroit, 1995
108	Jerry Rice, San Francisco, 1996
106	Art Monk, Washington, 1984
106	Herman Moore, Detroit, 1996
104	Eric Metcalf, Atlanta, 1995

Most Points Scored

Pts.	Player/Team/Year
176	Paul Hornung, Green Bay, 1960
161	Mark Moseley, Washington, 1961
155	Gino Cappelletti, Boston, 1964
150	Emmitt Smith, Dallas, 1995
149	Chip Lohmiller, Washington, 1991
147	Gino Cappelletti, Boston, 1961
146	Paul Hornung, Green Bay, 1961
145	Jim Turner, N.Y. Jets, 1968
145	John Kasay, Carolina, 1996
144	John Riggins, Washington, 1983
144	Kevin Butler, Chicago, 1985
141	Norm Johnson, Dallas, 1995
140	Tony Franklin, New Eng., 1986
139	Gary Anderson, Pittsburgh, 1985
139	Nick Lowery, Kansas City, 1990

Most Touchdowns Passing

TD	Player/Team/Year
48	Dan Marino, Miami, 1984
44	Dan Marino, Miami, 1986
39	Brett Favre, Green Bay, 1996
38	Brett Favre, Green Bay, 1995
36	George Blanda, Houston, 1961
36	Y.A. Tittle, N.Y. Giants, 1963
35	Steve Young, San Francisco, 1994
34	Daryle Lamonica, Oakland, 1969
33	Y.A. Tittle, N.Y. Giants, 1962
33	Dan Fouts, San Diego, 1981
33	Warren Moon, Houston, 1990
33	Jim Kelly, Buffalo, 1991
33	Brett Favre, Green Bay, 1994
33	Warren Moon, Minnesota, 1995
33	Vinny Testaverde, Baltimore, 1996

Extra Point
It comes as no surprise that Jerry Rice set the single-season record of 22 touchdown receptions in 1987.

Most Touchdowns

TD	Player/Team/Year
25	Emmitt Smith, Dallas, 1995
24	John Riggins, Washington, 1983
23	O.J. Simpson, Buffalo, 1975
23	Jerry Rice, San Francisco, 1987
22	Gale Sayers, Chicago, 1965
22	Chuck Foreman, Minnesota, 1975
22	Emmitt Smith, Dallas, 1994
21	Jim Brown, Cleveland, 1965
21	Joe Morris, N.Y. Giants, 1985
21	Terry Allen, Washington, 1996
20	Lenny Moore, Baltimore, 1964
20	Leroy Kelly, Cleveland, 1968
19	Five players tied.

Most Field Goals

FG	Player/Team/Year
37	John Kasay, Carolina, 1996
36	Cary Blanchard, Indianapolis, 1996
35	Ali Haji-Sheikh, N.Y. Giants, 1983
35	Jeff Jaeger, L.A. Rams, 1993
34	Jim Turner, N.Y. Jets, 1968
34	Nick Lowery, Kansas City, 1990
34	Jason Hanson, Detroit, 1993
34	John Carney, San Diego, 1994
34	Fuad Reveiz, Minnesota, 1994
34	Norm Johnson, Dallas, 1995

Most Interceptions Caught

Int.	Player/Team/Year
14	Night Train Lane, L.A. Rams, 1952
13	Dan Standifer, Washington, 1948
13	Spec Sanders, N.Y. Yanks, 1950
13	Lester Hayes, Oakland, 1980
12	Nine players tied.

Most Yards Receiving

Yds.	Player/Team/Year
1,848	Jerry Rice, San Francisco, 1995
1,781	Isaac Bruce, St. Louis, 1995
1,746	Charley Hennigan, Houston, 1961
1,686	Herman Moore, Detroit, 1995
1,603	Michael Irvin, Dallas, 1995
1,602	Lance Alworth, San Diego, 1965
1,570	Jerry Rice, San Francisco, 1986
1,555	Roy Green, St. Louis, 1984
1,546	Charley Hennigan, Houston, 1964
1,523	Michael Irvin, Dallas, 1991
1,503	Jerry Rice, San Francisco, 1993
1,502	Jerry Rice, San Francisco, 1990
1,499	Jerry Rice, San Francisco, 1994
1,497	Robert Brooks, Green Bay, 1995
1,495	Elroy Hirsch, L.A. Rams, 1951

Most Sacks

No.	Player/Team/Year
22	Mark Gastineau, N.Y. Jets, 1984
21	Reggie White, Philadelphia, 1987
21	Chris Doleman, Minnesota, 1989
20½	Lawrence Taylor, N.Y. Giants, 1986
20	Derrick Thomas, Kansas City, 1990

Jim Brown of Cleveland led the NFL in rushing eight of his nine seasons in the league.

Single-Game Leaders

Most Yards Rushing

Yds.	Player/Game/Date
275	Walter Payton, Chicago vs. Minnesota (11/20/77)
273	O.J. Simpson, Buffalo vs. Detroit (11/25/76)
250	O.J. Simpson, Buffalo vs. New England (9/16/73)
247	Willie Ellison, L.A. Rams vs. New Orleans (12/5/71)
243	Cookie Gilchrist, Buffalo vs. N.Y. Jets (12/8/63)

Most Receptions

Rec.	Player/Game/Date
18	Tom Fears, Los Angeles vs. Green Bay (12/3/50)
17	Clark Gaines, N.Y. Jets vs. San Francisco (9/21/80)
16	Sonny Randle, St. Louis vs. N.Y. Giants (11/4/62)
16	Jerry Rice, San Francisco vs. L.A. Rams (11/20/94)
16	Keenan McCardell, Jacksonville vs. St. Louis (10/20/96)

Most Yards Receiving

Yds.	Player/Game/Date
336	Flipper Anderson, L.A. Rams vs. New Orleans,* (11/26/89)
309	Stephone Paige, Kansas City vs. San Diego (12/22/85)
303	Jim Benton, Cleveland vs. Detroit (11/22/45)
302	Cloyce Box, Detroit vs. Baltimore (12/3/50)
289	Jerry Rice, San Francisco vs. Minnesota (12/18/95)
286	John Taylor, San Francisco vs. L.A. Rams (12/11/89)

*Overtime.

Most Yards Passing

Yds.	Player/Game/Date
554	Norm Van Brocklin, L.A. Rams vs. N.Y. Yanks (9/28/51)
527	Warren Moon, Houston vs. Kansas City (12/16/90)
522	Boomer Esiason, Arizona vs. Washington (11/10/96)
521	Dan Marino, Miami vs. N.Y. Jets (10/23/88)
513	Phil Simms, N.Y. Giants vs. Cincinnati (10/13/85)

Most Combined Yards

Rushing, receiving, and kick returns.

Yds.	Player/Game/Date
404	Glyn Milburn, Denver vs. Seattle (12/10/95)
373	Billy Cannon, Houston vs. N.Y. Titans (12/10/61)
347	Tyrone Hughes, New Orleans vs. L.A. Rams (10/23/94)
345	Lionel James, San Diego vs. L.A. Raiders* (11/10/85)
341	Timmy Brown, Philadelphia vs. St. Louis (12/16/62)

* Overtime.

Highest-Scoring Games

Pts.	Final Score	Date
113	Washington 72 N.Y. Giants 41	11/27/66
101	Oakland 52 Houston 49	12/22/63
99	Seattle 51* Kansas City 48	11/27/83
98	Chicago Cards 63 N.Y. Giants 35	10/17/48
97	L.A. Rams 70 Baltimore 27	10/22/50

* Overtime.
Note: The highest-scoring playoff game was a 58-37 Philadelphia victory over Detroit in the 1995 NFC wild card game.

Most Touchdown Passes

TD	Player/Game/Date
7	Sid Luckman, Chicago Bears vs. N.Y. Giants (11/14/43)
7	Adrian Burk, Philadelphia vs. Washington (10/17/54)
7	George Blanda, Houston vs. N.Y. Titans (11/19/61)
7	Y.A. Tittle, N.Y. Giants vs. Washington (10/28/62)
7	Joe Kapp, Minnesota vs. Baltimore (9/28/69)

Most Points Scored

Pts.	Player/Game/Date
40	Ernie Nevers,* Chicago Cards vs. Chicago Bears (11/28/29)
36	Dub Jones, Cleveland vs. Chicago Bears (11/25/51)
36	Gale Sayers, Chicago vs. San Francisco (12/12/65)
33	Paul Hornung, Green Bay vs. Baltimore (10/8/61)
30	Seven players tied.

* On Thanksgiving 1929, Nevers scored 6 touchdowns and 4 points after; final score—Cards 40, Bears 6.

Longest Field Goals

Yds.	Player/Game/Date
63	Tom Dempsey, New Orleans vs. Detroit (11/8/70)
60	Steve Cox, Cleveland vs. Cincinnati (10/21/84)
60	Morten Andersen, New Orleans vs. Chicago (10/27/91)
59	Four players tied.

Note: Dempsey was born with no right hand and a toeless right foot. He kicked with the right foot in a specially designed shoe.

Head Coaches

NFL records through 1996.

Most Wins

Through the 1996 season, including playoffs.

Wins	Coach	Years
347	Don Shula	33
324	George Halas	40
270	Tom Landry	29
229	Curly Lambeau	33
209	Chuck Noll	23
193	Chuck Knox	22
170	Paul Brown	21
168	Bud Grant	18
153	Steve Owen	23
149	Dan Reeves*	16
148	Marv Levy*	16
140	Joe Gibbs	12
136	Hank Stram	17
134	Weeb Ewbank	20
130	Marty Schottenheimer*	13

* Active in 1997.

Best Winning Percentages

Based on at least 90 NFL victories, including playoffs.

Pct.	Coach	Years	W	L	T	Last Year
.755	George Seifert	8	108	35	0	1996
.740	Vince Lombardi	10	105	35	6	1969
.731	John Madden	10	112	39	7	1978
.683	Joe Gibbs	12	140	65	0	1992
.681	George Allen	12	118	54	5	1977
.671	George Halas	40	324	151	31	1967
.665	Don Shula	33	347	173	6	1995
.623	Curly Lambeau	33	229	134	22	1953
.622	Mike Ditka*	11	112	68	0	active
.617	Bill Walsh	10	102	63	1	1988
.610	Marty Schottenheimer*	13	130	83	1	active
.609	Paul Brown#	21	170	108	6	1975
.607	Bud Grant	18	168	108	5	1985
.601	Tom Landry	29	270	178	6	1988

* Active in 1997.
\# The NFL does not recognize records from the defunct All-American Football Conference (1946-49), erasing Paul Brown's record of 52-4-3.

Most Wins by Active Coaches

Through the 1996 season, including playoffs.

Wins	Coach/Team	Years
149	Dan Reeves, Atlanta	16
148	Marv Levy, Buffalo	16
130	Marty Schottenheimer, Kansas City	13
119	Bill Parcells, New York Jets	12
112	Mike Ditka, New Orleans	11
77	Ted Marchibroda, Baltimore	10
66	Jimmy Johnson, Miami	6
58	Mike Holmgren, Green Bay	5
57	Bill Cowher, Pittsburgh	5
57	Dick Vermeil, St. Louis	7
50	Bobby Ross, Detroit	5
47	Dennis Green, Minnesota	5
39	Barry Switzer, Dallas	3

Youngest Head Coaches

Listed with first season as NFL coach.

Age	Coach	First Team
31	Harland Svare	L.A. Rams (1962)
32	Dave Shula	Cincinnati (1992)
33	John Madden	Oakland (1969)
33	Don Shula	Baltimore (1963)
34	Al Davis	Oakland (1963)

Oldest Head Coaches

Listed with last season as NFL coach.

Age	Coach	Last Team
72	George Halas	Chicago (1967)
69	Marv Levy	Buffalo (active)
67	Paul Brown	Cincinnati (1975)
66	Weeb Ewbank	N.Y. Jets (1973)

Green Bay coach Vince Lombardi raises the game ball after the Packers beat Kansas City in the first Super Bowl.

Home Fields

Biggest NFL Stadiums

Seats	Home Field	Home Team
80,365	Pontiac Silverdome	Detroit Lions
80,116	Jack Kent Cooke Stadium	Washington Redskins
80,024	Rich Stadium	Buffalo Bills
79,101	Arrowhead Stadium	Kansas City Chiefs
77,716	Giants Stadium	New York Giants & New York Jets
76,123	Mile High Stadium	Denver Broncos
74,916	Pro Player Park	Miami Dolphins
74,321	Houlihan's Stadium	Tampa Bay Buccaneers
73,273	Sun Devil Stadium	Arizona Cardinals
73,000	Municipal Stadium	Jacksonville Jaguars
72,520	Ericsson Stadium	Carolina Panthers
71,228	Georgia Dome	Atlanta Falcons
70,207	3Com Park	San Francisco 49ers
66,944	Soldier Field	Chicago Bears
66,400	Kingdome	Seattle Seahawks

Recently renamed: Pro Player Park (formerly Joe Robbie Stadium, 1987–96); Houlihan's Stadium (Tampa Stadium, 1976–96); and 3Com Park (Candlestick Park, 1960–94)

Smallest NFL Stadiums

Seats	Home Field	Home Team
59,600	Three Rivers Stadium	Pittsburgh Steelers
60,272	RCA Dome	Indianapolis Colts
60,292	Foxboro Stadium	New England Patriots
60,389	Cinergy Field	Cincinnati Bengals
60,789	Qualcomm Stadium	San Diego Chargers
60,790	Lambeau Field	Green Bay Packers
62,380	Liberty Bowl*	Tennessee Oilers
62,500	Oakland Coliseum	Oakland Raiders
64,035	Metrodome	Minnesota Vikings
64,522	Memorial Stadium	Baltimore Ravens
64,899	Veterans Stadium	Philadelphia Eagles
64,992	Louisiana Superdome	New Orleans Saints
65,812	Texas Stadium	Dallas Cowboys
66,000	Trans World Dome	St. Louis Rams

* The temporary home in Memphis of the former Houston Oilers, who plan to move into a new stadium in Nashville by 1999.
Recently renamed: RCA Dome (formerly Hoosier Dome, 1984–94); Cinergy Field (Riverfront Stadium, 1970–96); and Qualcomm Stadium (San Diego/Jack Murphy Stadium, 1967–97).

Oldest NFL Stadiums

Opened	Home Field	Home Team
1924	Soldier Field	Chicago Bears
1948	Mile High Stadium	Denver Broncos
1954	Memorial Stadium	Baltimore Ravens
1957	Lambeau Field	Green Bay Packers
1958	Sun Devil Stadium	Arizona Cardinals

Newest NFL Stadiums

Opened	Home Field	Home Team
1997	Jack Kent Cooke Stadium	Washington Redskins
1996	Ericsson Stadium	Carolina Panthers
1995	Municipal Stadium	Jacksonville Jaguars
1995	Trans World Dome	St. Louis Rams
1992	Georgia Dome	Atlanta Falcons

Chicago's Soldier Field, the NFL's oldest stadium at age 73.

Awards

Most Popular Retired Numbers

Through the 1996 NFL season.

Jersey No.	Players Honored
14	Dan Fouts (San Diego), Otto Graham (Cleveland), Steve Grogan (New England), Don Hutson (Green Bay), and Y.A. Tittle (N.Y. Giants).
7	Dutch Clark (Detroit), George Halas (Chicago), Mel Hein (N.Y. Giants), and Bob Waterfield (St. Louis Rams).
12	John Brodie (San Francisco), Bob Griese (Miami), Joe Namath, (N.Y. Jets), and Seattle Mariners fans as the "12th Man."
40	Tom Brookshier (Philadelphia), Mike Haynes (New England), Joe Morrison (N.Y. Giants), and Gale Sayers (Chicago).
3	Bronko Nagurski (Chicago), Tony Canadeo (Green Bay), and Jan Stenerud (Kansas City).
34	Earl Campbell (Houston), Walter Payton (Chicago), and Joe Perry (San Francisco).
56	Bill Hewitt (Chicago), Joe Schmidt (Detroit), and Lawrence Taylor (N.Y. Giants).
63	Willie Lanier (Kansas City), Mike Munchak (Houston), and Lee Roy Selmon (Tampa Bay).
70	Art Donovan (Indianapolis), Charlie Krueger (San Francisco), and Al Wistert (Philadelphia).
77	Red Grange (Chicago), Stan Mauldin (Arizona), and Jim Parker (Indianapolis).
88	J. V. Cain (Arizona), Alan Page (Minnesota), and Charlie Sanders (Detroit).

Most Frequent Most Valuable Players

Based on the Carr Trophy presented by the NFL (1938-46, wire service awards presented by United Press International (1953-69) and Associated Press (since 1957), and the Pro Football Writers Assn. (since 1978); through the 1996 season.

No.	Player/Team/Years
4	Jim Brown, Cleveland, 1965 (AP, UPI), 1963 (UPI), 1958 (UPI), 1957 (AP)
3	Y.A. Tittle, San Francisco–N.Y. Giants 1963 (AP), 1962 (UPI), 1957 (UPI)
3	Johnny Unitas, Baltimore, 1967 (AP-UPI), 1964 (AP, UPI), 1959 (UPI)
2	Earl Campbell, Houston, 1979 (AP, FW), 1978 (FW)
2	Brett Favre, Green Bay, 1996 (AP, FW), 1995 (AP, FW)
2	Otto Graham, Cleveland, 1955 (UPI), 1953 (UPI)
2	Don Hutson, Green Bay, 1941–42 (Carr)
2	Joe Montana, San Francisco, 1990 (AP), 1989 (AP, FW)
2	Steve Young, San Francisco, 1994 (AP, FW), 1992 (AP, FW)

Note: All are quarterbacks, except Brown (fullback), Campbell (running back), and Hutson (end).

Heisman Trophy Winners
Now in Pro Football Hall of Fame

Listed with year player won Heisman.

Year	Player/Team/Position
1977	Earl Campbell, Texas, RB
1976	Tony Dorsett, Pittsburgh, RB
1968	O.J. Simpson, Southern Cal, HB
1963	Roger Staubach, Navy, QB
1956	Paul Hornung, Notre Dame, QB
1948	Doak Walker, SMU, HB

Year inducted into Hall of Fame: Simpson and Staubach (1985); Hornung and Walker (1986); Campbell (1991) and Dorsett (1994).
Note: The Heisman Trophy has been presented to the college football Player of the Year since 1935.

The New York Giants retired quarterback Y.A. Tittle's number in 1965.

NFL Rookies of the Year
Now in Pro Football Hall of Fame

Listed with players NFL rookie year.

Year	Player/Team/Position
1978	Earl Campbell, Houston, RB
1977	Tony Dorsett, Dallas, RB
1976	Mike Haynes, New Eng., DB
1974	Jack Lambert, Pittsburgh, LB
1972	Franco Harris, Pittsburgh, RB
1965	Joe Namath, N.Y. Jets, QB
	Gale Sayers, Chicago, HB
1964	Charley Taylor, Washington
1961	Mike Ditka, Chicago, TE
1957	Jim Brown, Cleveland, FB
1956	Lenny Moore, Baltimore, HB

Year inducted into Hall of Fame: Brown (1971), Campbell (1991), Ditka (1988), Dorsett (1994), Harris (1990), Haynes (1997), Lambert (1990) Moore (1975), Namath (1985), Sayers (1977) and Taylor (1984).
Note: United Press International has been selecting NFL Rookies of the Year since 1955 and AP since 1974.

Miscellaneous

Winningest Teams Since NFL-AFL Merger in 1970

Based on at least 100 games played; through 1996 playoffs.

Pct.	Team	W	L	T	Division Titles
.645	Miami Dolphins	282	155	2	11
.643	Dallas Cowboys	292	162	0	14
.621	Oakland–L.A. Raiders	269	163	6	9
.614	San Francisco 49ers	270	169	3	15
.602	Pittsburgh Steelers	265	175	1	13
.600	Washington Redskins	261	174	1	5
.571	Minnesota Vikings	248	186	2	12
.565	Denver Broncos	239	183	6	8
.537	L.A.–St. Louis Rams	230	198	4	8
.515	Chicago Bears	218	205	1	6

Losingest Teams Since NFL-AFL Merger in 1970

Based on at least 100 games played; through 1996 playoffs.

Pct.	Team	W	L	T	Division Titles
.309	Tampa Bay Buccaneers	101	226	1	2
.399	New York Jets	165	249	2	0
.402	Atlanta Falcons	165	246	4	1
.405	New Orleans Saints	165	243	4	1
.421	St.Louis-Arizona Cards	170	235	6	2
.430	Baltimore–Indianapolis Colts	180	239	2	5
.445	Houston Oilers	188	235	2	2
.450	Detroit Lions	185	227	4	3
.452	New England Patriots	190	230	0	3
.456	Seattle Seahawks	151	180	0	1

Note: Tampa Bay and Seattle were expansion teams in 1976.

Best Single-Season Team Records

Since 1933, including playoffs.

W-L	Team	Season
17-0	Miami Dolphins	1972
18-1	San Francisco 49ers	1984
18-1	Chicago Bears	1985
16-1	Oakland Raiders	1976
14-1	Green Bay Packers	1962
13-1	Chicago Bears	1934
12-1	Washington Redskins	1982*
12-1	Chicago Bears	1941
12-1	Philadelphia Eagles	1949
11-1	Washington Redskins	1942
11-1	Chicago Bears	1942

* A 57-day players' strike reduced the regular season from 16 games to 9.
Note: All teams listed above won NFL or Super Bowl championships except the 1934 and 1942 Chicago Bears, who went undefeated and untied through the regular season but lost the NFL title game.

Worst Single-Season Team Records

Since 1933.

W-L	Team	Season
0-14	Tampa Bay Bucs	1976
0-11	Detroit Lions	1942
0-10	Chicago Cards	1943
0-10	Brooklyn Tigers	1944
0-10	Card-Pitt*	1944
0-8	Cincinnati Reds	1934
0-11-1	Dallas Cowboys	1960
0-8-1	Baltimore Colts	1982#
1-15	New Orleans Saints	1980
1-15	Dallas Cowboys	1989
1-15	New England Patriots	1990
1-15	Indianapolis Colts	1991
1-15	New York Jets	1996

* In 1944, the Chicago Cardinals and Pittsburgh merged for one season as "Card-Pitt."
# A 57-day players' strike reduced the regular season schedule from 16 games to 9.

Most Victories on "Monday Night Football"

Through 1996; series debuted on ABC-TV in 1970.

Wins	Team	Record
33	Oakland–L.A. Raiders	33-14-1
32	Miami Dolphins	32-22-0
29	Dallas Cowboys	29-21-0
27	San Francisco 49ers	27-17-0
25	Pittsburgh Steelers	25-15-0
22	Washington Redskins	22-21-0
17	L.A.–St. Louis Rams	17-20-0
16	Minnesota Vikings	16-16-0
15	Buffalo Bills	15-18-0
15	Chicago Bears	15-27-0
14	Kansas City Chiefs	14-10-0
14	Philadelphia Eagles	14-12-0
14	San Diego Chargers	14-12-0
14	Denver Broncos	14-19-1
14	New York Giants	14-21-1

Most appearances: Miami (54), Dallas (50), Oakland (48), San Francisco (44), and Washington (43).
Fewest appearances: Carolina and Jacksonville (0), Tampa Bay (3), Arizona (15), and Seattle (16).

BASKETBALL

Michael Jordan drives for the basket in the 1997 NBA Finals.

COLLEGE BASKETBALL

PRO BASKETBALL

COLLEGE BASKETBALL
NCAA National Champions

Most NCAA Titles
Schools with more than one NCAA title since the Division I tournament began in 1939.

No.	School	Championship Years
11	UCLA	1995, 1975, 1967-73, 1965, 1964
6	Kentucky	1996, 1978, 1958, 1951, 1949, 1948
5	Indiana	1987, 1981, 1976, 9153, 1940
3	North Carolina	1993, 1982, 1957
2	Cincinnati	1962, 1961
2	Duke	1992, 1991
2	Kansas	1988, 1952
2	Louisville	1986, 1980
2	N. Carolina State	1983, 1974
2	Oklahoma State	1946, 1945
2	San Francisco	1956, 1955

Larry Bird of Indiana State with Magic Johnson (background) and Jay Vincent of Michigan State closing in during the 1979 NCAA championship game.

Schools with One NCAA Title

School/Year	School/Year
Arizona (1997)	Mich. St. (1979)
Arkansas (1994)	Ohio St. (1960)
California (1959)	Oregon (1939)
City College of New York (1950)	Stanford (1942)
Georgetown (1984)	Texas Western* (1966)
Holy Cross (1947)	UNLV (1990)
La Salle (1954)	Utah (1944)
Loyola–IL (1963)	Villanova (1985)
Marquette (1977)	Wisconsin (1941)
Michigan (1989)	Wyoming (1943)

*Texas Western is now Texas–El Paso.

Most NCAA Tournament Appearances
Through 1997 Division I tournament.

No.	School	Tourn. Record	Titles
39	Kentucky	77-35	6
33	UCLA	77-26	11
31	North Carolina	72-31	3
27	Louisville	48-29	2
26	Indiana	50-21	5
26	Kansas	56-26	2
24	Notre Dame	25-28	0
24	Villanova	37-24	1
23	St. John's	23-25	0
23	Syracuse	35-24	0
22	Arkansas	37-22	1
22	Kansas State	27-26	0

Most NCAA Final Four Appearances

No.	School	1	2	3	4
15	UCLA	11	1	2	1
13	N. Carolina	3	4	4	2
12	Kentucky	6	3	3	0
11	Duke	2	5	4	0
10	Kansas	2	4	2	2
8	Ohio State	1	3	4	0
7	Indiana	5	0	2	0
7	Louisville	2	0	3	2
6	Arkansas	1	1	4	0
6	Cincinnati	2	1	3	0
6	Michigan	1	4	1	0
5	Houston	0	2	2	1

Note: Consolation games for third place were held from 1946 to 1981, after which losers in semifinals have shared third place.

Most Consecutive Tournament Appearances

No.	School	Years
23	North Carolina	1975-97*
14	Georgetown	1979-92
13	UCLA	1967-79
13	Arizona	1986-97*
12	Indiana	1986-97*
11	Duke	1984-94
10	Marquette	1971-80
10	Syracuse	1983-92
10	Louisiana State	1984-93

*Indicates ongoing streak.

Most Frequent Most Valuable Players

No.	Player/School	Years
3	Lew Alcindor,* UCLA	1967-69
2	Alex Groza, Kentucky	1948-49
2	Bob Kurland, Okla. State	1945-46
2	Jerry Lucas, Ohio State	1960-61
2	Bill Walton, UCLA	1972-73

*Alcindor changed his name to Kareem Abdul-Jabbar after turning professional.

MVPs Whose Teams Did Not Win the Title

Year	Player/School/Place
1983	Akeem Olajuwon,* Houston, 2nd
1971	Howard Porter,# Villanova, 2nd
1966	Jerry Chambers, Utah, 4th
1965	Bill Bradley, Princeton, 3rd
1963	Art Heyman, Duke, 3rd
1961	Jerry Lucas, Ohio State, 2nd
1959	Jerry West, West Virginia, 2nd
1958	Elgin Baylor, Seattle, 2nd
1957	Wilt Chamberlain, Kansas, 2nd
1956	Hal Lear, Temple, 3rd
1953	B. H. Born, Kansas, 2nd

*Olajuwon later changed the spelling of his first name to Hakeem.
Declared ineligible by the NCAA and his award was vacated.

All-Time NCAA All-Tournament Teams

All-Time Team

Player/School	Years
Lew Alcindor, UCLA	1967-69
Larry Bird, Indiana State	1979
Wilt Chamberlain, Kansas	1957
Magic Johnson, Michigan State	1979
Michael Jordan, N. Carolina	1982

1980–87 Team

Player/School	Years
Steve Alford, Indiana	1987
Johnny Dawkins, Duke	1986
Patrick Ewing, Georgetown	1982-84
Darrell Griffith, Louisville	1980
Michael Jordan, N. Carolina	1982
Rodney McCray, Louisville	1980
Akeem Olajuwon, Houston	1983-84
Ed Pinckney, Villanova	1985
Isiah Thomas, Indiana	1981
James Worthy, N. Carolina	1982

All-1970s Team

Player/School	Years
Kent Benson, Indiana	1976
Larry Bird, Indiana State	1979
Jack Givens, Kentucky	1978
Magic Johnson, Michigan State	1979
Marques Johnson, UCLA	1975-76
Scott May, Indiana	1976
David Thompson, N.C. State	1974
Bill Walton, UCLA	1972-74
Sidney Wicks, UCLA	1969-71
Keith Wilkes, UCLA	1972-74

Selection Committee, 1988
The 50th anniversary teams were picked by coaches Denny Crum, Joe Hall, Jud Heathcote, Hank Iba, Pete Newell, Dean Smith, John Thompson and John Wooden; and administrators Wayne Duke, Dave Gavitt, and Vic Bubas.

All-1960s Team

Player/School	Years
Lew Alcindor, UCLA	1967-69
Bill Bradley, Princeton	1965
Gail Goodrich, UCLA	1964-65
John Havlicek, Ohio State	1961-62
Elvin Hayes, Houston	1967
Walt Hazzard, UCLA	1964
Jerry Lucas, Ohio State	1960-61
Jeff Mullins, Duke	1964
Cazzie Russell, Michigan	1965
Charlie Scott, North Carolina	1968-69

All-1950s Team

Player/School	Years
Elgin Baylor, Seattle	1958
Wilt Chamberlain, Kansas	1957
Tom Gola, La Salle	1954
K.C. Jones, San Francisco	1955
Clyde Lovellette, Kansas	1952
Oscar Robertson, Cincinnati	1959-60
Guy Rodgers, Temple	1958
Lennie Rosenbluth, N. Carolina	1957
Bill Russell, San Francisco	1955-56
Jerry West, West Virginia	1959

All-1940s Team (1939–49)

Player/School	Years
Ralph Beard, Kentucky	1948-49
Howie Dallmer, Stanford	1942
Dwight Eddleman, Illinois	1949
Arnie Ferrin, Utah	1944
Alex Groza, Kentucky	1948-49
George Kaftan, Holy Cross	1947
Bob Kurland, Oklahoma State	1945-46
Jim Pollard, Stanford	1942
Kenny Sailors, Wyoming	1943
Gerry Tucker, Oklahoma	1947

Final Four Single-Game Leaders

Division I; year column also indicates whether Final Four game was a semifinal (S), final (F), or third place game (3rd).
Consolation games for third place were played from 1946 to 1981.

Most Points

Pts.	Player/School	Opponent	Year
58	Bill Bradley, Princeton	Wichita State	1965–3rd
48	Hal Lear, Temple	SMU	1956–3rd
44	Bill Walton, UCLA	Memphis State.	1973–F
42	Bob Houbregs, Washington	Louisiana State	1953–3rd
42	Jack Egan, St. Joseph's–PA	Utah	1961–3rd
42	Gail Goodrich, UCLA	Michigan	1965–F
41	Jack Givens, Kentucky	Duke	1978–F
39	Oscar Robertson, Cincinnati	Louisville	1959–3rd
39	Al Wood, North Carolina	Virginia	1981–S
38	Jerry West, West Virginia	Louisville	1959–S
38	Jerry Chambers, Utah	Texas Western	1966–S
38	Freddie Banks, UNLV	Indiana	1987–S

Most Rebounds

No.	Player/School	Opponent	Year
27	Bill Russell, San Francisco	Iowa	1956–F
24	Elvin Hayes, Houston	UCLA	1967–S
23	Bill Russell, San Francisco	SMU	1956–S
22	Elgin Baylor, Seattle	Kansas State	1958–S
22	Tom Sanders, NYU	Ohio State	1960–S
22	Larry Kenon, Memphis State	Providence	1973–S
22	Akeem Olajuwon, Houston	Louisville	1983–S

Most Assists

No.	Player/School	Opponent	Year
18	Mark Wade, UNLV	Indiana	1987–S
12	Rumeal Robinson, Michigan	Illinois	1989–S
12	Edgar Padilla, UMass	Kentucky	1996–S
11	Michael Jackson, Georgetown	St. John's	1985–S
11	Milt Wagner, Louisville	Louisiana State	1986–S
11	Rumeal Robinson, Michigan	Seton Hall*	1989–F

*Overtime game.

Most Field Goals

No.	Player/School	Opponent	Year
22	Bill Bradley, Princeton	Wichita State	1965–3rd
21	Bill Walton, UCLA	Memphis State	1973–F
18	Jack Givens, Kentucky	Duke	1978–F
17	Three players tied.		

Most 3-Point Field Goals

No.	Player/School	Opponent	Year
10	Freddie Banks, UNLV	Indiana	1987–S
7	Steve Alford, Indiana	Syracuse	1987–F
7	Dave Seiger, Oklahoma	Kansas	1988–F
7	Dennis Scott, Georgia Tech	UNLV	1990–S
7	Tony Delk, Kentucky	Syracuse	1996–F

Most Free Throws

No.	Player/School	Opponent	Year
18	Gail Goodrich, UCLA	Michigan	1965–F
15	Oscar Robertson, Cincinnati	Louisville	1959–3rd
15	Bill Buntin, Michigan	Kansas State	1964–3rd

Closest Championship Games

Points	Final Score	Year
1	Indiana 69, Kansas 68	1953
1	North Carolina 54, Kansas 53 (3OT)	1957
1	California 71, West Virginia 70	1959
1	North Carolina 63, Georgetown 62	1982
1	Indiana 74, Syracuse 73	1987
1	Michigan 80, Seton Hall 79 (OT)	1989

Extra Point

The most one-sided victory in an NCAA Division I title game occurred in 1990 when the University of Nevada at Las Vegas beat Duke by thirty points. The Blue Devils returned to the Final Four the next two years and won back-to-back championships.

Single-Tournament Leaders

Most Points

Pts.	Player/School	Year
184	Glen Rice, Michigan	1989
177	Bill Bradley, Princeton	1965
167	Elvin Hayes, Houston	1968
163	Danny Manning, Kansas	1988
160	Hal Lear, Temple	1956
160	Jerry West, West Virginia	1959
158	Austin Carr, Notre Dame	1970
158	Joe Barry Carroll, Purdue	1980
153	Johnny Dawkins, Duke	1986
153	Dennis Scott, Ga. Tech	1990

Games: Rice, Manning, Carroll, and Dawkins (6); Bradley, Hayes, Lear, West, and Scott (5); Carr (3).

Highest Scoring Average
At least 3 games played.

Avg.	Player/School	Year
52.7	Austin Carr, Notre Dame	1970
41.7	Austin Carr, Notre Dame	1971
35.8	Jerry Chambers, Utah	1966
35.8	Bo Kimble, Loyola-CA	1990
35.4	Bill Bradley, Princeton	1965
35.3	Clyde Lovellette, Kansas	1959
35.0	Gail Goodrich, UCLA	1965
35.0	Jerry West, W. Virginia	1960
34.8	Bob Houbregs, Wash.	1953
33.4	Elvin Hayes, Houston	1968

Games: Bradley, Lovellette, and Hayes (5); Chambers, Kimble, Goodrich, and Houbregs (4); Carr, 1970 and 1971, and West (3).

Most Field Goals

No.	Player/School	Year
75	Glen Rice, Michigan	1989
70	Elvin Hayes, Houston	1968
69	Danny Manning, Kansas	1988
68	Austin Carr, Notre Dame	1970
66	Johnny Dawkins, Duke	1986
65	Bill Bradley, Princeton	1965

Games: Rice, Manning, and Dawkins (6); Hayes and Bradley (5); Carr (3).

Most 3-Point Field Goals

No.	Player/School	Year
27	Glen Rice, Michigan	1989
26	Freddie Banks, UNLV	1987
24	Dennis Scott, Georgia Tech	1990
23	Jeff Fryer, Loyola–CA	1990
22	Donald Williams, N. Carolina	1993

Games: Rice and Williams (6); Banks and Scott (5); Fryer (4).

Most Rebounds

No.	Player/School	Year
97	Elvin Hayes, Houston	1968
93	Artis Gilmore, Jacksonville	1970
91	Elgin Baylor, Seattle	1958
90	Sam Lacey, New Mexico State	1970
89	Clarence Glover, W. Kentucky	1971

Games: Five each.

Most Assists

No.	Player/School	Year
61	Mark Wade, UNLV	1987
56	Rumeal Robinson, Michigan	1989
49	Sherman Douglas, Syracuse	1987
47	Bobby Hurley, Duke	1992
46	Lazarus Sims, Syracuse	1996

Games: Six each, except Wade (5).

Most Blocked Shots

No.	Player/School	Year
23	David Robinson, Navy	1986
21	Marcus Camby, UMass	1996
20	Tim Perry, Temple	1988
19	Alonzo Mourning, G'town	1989
18	Cherokee Parks, Duke	1994
18	Marcus Camby, UMass	1995

Games: Parks (6); Camby, 1996 (5); Robinson, Perry, Mourning, and Camby, 1995 (4).

Bill Bradley (42) of Princeton scored 58 points against Wichita State in 1965.

Most Points in One Game
Not including Final Four games.

Points	Player/School/Opponent
61	Austin Carr, Notre Dame vs. Ohio Univ. (1st Round, 1970)
56	Oscar Robertson, Cincinnati vs. Arkansas (Regional 3rd Place game, 1958)
52	Austin Carr, Notre Dame vs. Kentucky (2nd Round, 1970)
52	Austin Carr, Notre Dame vs. Texas Christian (1st Round, 1971)

Tournament Career Leaders

Listed with number of years each player appeared in NCAA Division I tournament; asterisks (*) indicate players active in 1997 tournament.

Most Points

Pts.	Player/School	Yrs.	Gm.	Avg.
407	Christian Laettner, Duke	4	23	17.7
358	Elvin Hayes, Houston	3	13	27.5
328	Danny Manning, Kansas	4	16	20.5
324	Oscar Robertson, Cincinnati	3	10	32.4
308	Glen Rice, Michigan	4	13	23.7
304	Lew Alcindor, UCLA	3	12	25.3
303	Bill Bradley, Princeton	3	9	33.7
303	Corliss Williamson, Arkansas	3	15	20.2
289	Austin Carr, Notre Dame	3	7	41.3
280	Juwan Howard, Michigan	3	16	17.5
279	Calbert Cheaney, Indiana	4	13	21.5
275	Jerry West, West Virginia	3	9	30.6
269	Danny Ferry, Duke	4	19	14.2
269	Grant Hill, Duke	4	20	13.5
266	Jerry Lucas, Ohio State	3	12	22.2
260	Reggie Williams, Georgetown	4	17	15.3
256	Patrick Ewing, Georgetown	4	18	14.2
254	Bill Walton, UCLA	3	12	21.2
250	Jalen Rose, Michigan	3	16	15.6
247	Tony Delk, Kentucky	4	17	14.5

Last year played: Alcindor (1969), Bradley (1965), Carr (1971), Cheaney (1993), Delk (1996), Ewing (1985), Ferry (1989), Hayes (1968), Hill (1994), Howard (1994), Laettner (1992), Lucas (1962), Manning (1988), Rice (1989), Robertson (1960), Rose (1994), Walton (1974), West (1960), Williams (1987), and Williamson (1995).

Highest Scoring Average
Based on at least 6 games played.

Avg.	Player/School	Yrs.	Gm.	Pts.
41.3	Austin Carr, Notre Dame	3	7	289
33.7	Bill Bradley, Princeton	3	9	303
32.4	Oscar Robertson, Cincinnati	3	10	324
30.6	Jerry West, West Virginia	3	9	275
30.5	Bob Pettit, Louisiana State	2	6	183
29.3	Dan Issel, Kentucky	3	6	176
29.3	Jim McDaniels, Western Kentucky	2	6	176
29.2	Dwight Lamar, SW Louisiana	2	6	175
29.1	Bo Kimble, Loyola, Calif.	3	7	204
28.6	David Robinson, Navy	3	7	200
27.6	Len Chappell, Wake Forest	2	8	221
27.5	Elvin Hayes, Houston	3	13	358
27.4	Bob Houbregs, Washington	2	7	192
27.0	Don Schlundt, Indiana	2	6	162
25.7	Kenny Anderson, Ga. Tech	2	7	180
25.4	Adrian Dantley, Notre Dame	3	8	203
25.3	Lew Alcindor, UCLA	3	12	304
25.2	Barry Kramer, NYU	2	6	151
25.2	Bob Lanier, St. Bonaventure	2	6	151
25.1	Cazzie Russell, Michigan	3	9	226

Last year played: Alcindor (1969), Anderson (1991), Bradley (1965), Carr (1971), Chappell (1962), Dantley (1976), Hayes (1968), Houbregs (1953), Issel (1970), Kimble (1990), Kramer (1963), Lamar (1973), Lanier (1970), McDaniels (1971), Pettit (1954), Robertson (1960), Robinson (1987), Russell (1966), Schlundt (1954), and West (1960).

Most Games

No.	Player/School	Years
23	Christian Laettner, Duke	1989-92
22	Brian Davis, Duke	1989-92
22	Greg Koubek, Duke	1988-91
20	Grant Hill, Duke	1991-94
20	Thomas Hill, Duke	1990-93
20	Bobby Hurley, Duke	1990-93
20	Antonio Lang, Duke	1991-94

Best Field Goal Percentage
Based on at least 70 made.

Pct.	Player/School
.686	Bill Walton, UCLA
.684	Stephen Thompson, Syracuse
.680	Brad Daugherty, North Carolina
.651	Akeem Olajuwon, Houston
.649	Eric Montross, North Carolina

Best 3-Point Field Goal Percentage
Based on at least 20 made.

Pct.	Player/School
.650	William Scott, Kansas State
.625	Sam Cassell, Florida State
.618	Steve Alford, Indiana
.565	Glen Rice, Michigan
.553	Rex Walters, Kansas

Most Rebounds

No.	Player/School	Yrs.	Gm.	Avg.
222	Elvin Hayes, Houston	3	13	17.1
201	Lew Alcindor, UCLA	3	12	16.8
197	Jerry Lucas, Ohio State	3	12	16.4
176	Bill Walton, UCLA	3	12	14.7
169	Christian Laettner, Duke	4	23	7.3
165	Tim Duncan,* Wake Forest	4	11	15.0
160	Paul Hogue, Cincinnati	3	12	13.3
157	Sam Lacey, New Mexico State	3	11	14.3
155	Derrick Coleman, Syracuse	4	14	11.1
153	Akeem Olajuwon, Houston	3	15	10.2
144	Patrick Ewing, Georgetown	4	18	8.0
138	Marques Johnson, UCLA	4	16	8.6
138	George Lynch, North Carolina	4	17	8.1
137	Len Chappell, Wake Forest	2	8	17.1
135	Ed Pinckney, Villanova	4	14	9.6
134	Grant Hill, Duke	4	20	6.7
131	Oscar Robertson, Cincinnati	3	10	13.1
131	Curtis Rowe, UCLA	3	12	10.9
131	Danny Ferry, Duke	4	19	6.9
129	Sam Perkins, North Carolina	4	15	8.6

Last year played: Alcindor (1969), Chappell (1962), Coleman (1990), Duncan (1997), Ewing (1985), Ferry (1989), Hayes (1968), Hill (1994), Hogue (1962), Johnson (1977), Lacey (1970), Laettner (1992), Lucas (1962), Lynch (1993), Olajuwon (1984), Perkins (1984), Pinckney (1985), Robertson (1960), Rowe (1971), and Walton (1974).

This Christian Laettner buzzer-beater against Kentucky in 1992 sent Duke to its fifth straight Final Four.

Best Free-Throw Percentage
Based on at least 30 made.

Pct.	Player/School
.977	Keith Van Horn,* Utah
.957	LaBradford Smith, Louisville
.949	Phil Ford, North Carolina
.943	Lawrence Moten, Syracuse
.927	Rodney Monroe, N.C. State

Most Assists

No.	Player/School
145	Bobby Hurley, Duke
106	Sherman Douglas, Syracuse
100	Greg Anthony, UNLV
93	Mark Wade, UNLV
93	Rumeal Robinson, Michigan
93	Jacque Vaughn, Kansas
93	Anthony Epps,* Kentucky

Most Steals

No.	Player/School
39	Grant Hill, Duke
34	Anthony Epps,* Kentucky
32	Mookie Blaylock, Oklahoma
32	Christian Laettner, Duke
31	Lee Mayberry, Arkansas
31	Bobby Hurley, Duke
31	Clint McDaniel, Arkansas

Best Teams By Decade

Winningest Teams of the 1990s

Through 1997 NCAA Division I Tournament.

	School	Overall Record	Pct.	NCAA Titles	NCAA Tourn.
1	Kansas	228-46	.832	0	20-8
2	Kentucky	219-50	.814	1	22-5
3	Arizona	204-55	.788	1	15-7
4	Arkansas	213-63	.772	1	23-6
5	North Carolina	212-64	.768	1	24-7
6	UCLA	194-61	.761	1	15-7
7	Massachusetts	202-67	.751	0	11-6
8	Connecticut	193-67	.742	0	13-6
9	Princeton	161-56	.742	0	1-5
10	Utah	192-67	.741	0	9-5
11	Duke	202-72	.737	2	24-5
12	Cincinnati	192-71	.730	0	12-6

NCAA champions: UNLV (1990); Duke (1991); Duke (1992); North Carolina (1993); Arkansas (1994); UCLA (1995); Kentucky (1996); Arizona (1997).

Bill Russell (6) led the University of San Francisco to a 57-1 record and two NCAA titles in 1955 and 1956, but the Dons were only 115-85 the rest of the decade.

Winningest Teams of the 1980s

	School	Overall Record	Pct.	NCAA Titles	NCAA Tourn.
1	North Carolina	281-63	.817	1	25-9
2	UNLV	271-65	.807	0	13-7
3	Georgetown	269-69	.796	1	23-8
4	DePaul	235-67	.778	0	7-9
5	Temple	225-78	.743	0	7-5
6	Syracuse	243-87	.736	0	14-8
7	Texas-El Paso	227-82	.735	0	3-6
8	Oklahoma	245-90	.731	0	14-7
9	Kentucky	233-86	.730	0	13-9
10	St. John's	228-85	.728	0	8-8
11	Indiana	228-86	.726	2	18-7
12	Oregon State	212-80	.726	0	2-7

NCAA champions: Louisville (1980); Indiana (1981); North Carolina (1982); North Carolina State (1983); Georgetown (1984); Villanova (1985); Louisville (1986); Indiana (1987); Kansas (1988); Michigan (1989).

Winningest Teams of the 1970s

	School	Overall Record	Pct.	NCAA Titles	NCAA Tourn.
1	UCLA	273-27	.910	5	32-5
2	Marquette	251-41	.860	1	17-9
3	Pennsylvania	223-56	.799	0	10-10
4	North Carolina	239-65	.786	0	11-7
5	Kentucky	223-69	.764	1	14-7
6	Louisville	224-70	.762	0	8-8
7	Syracuse	213-69	.755	0	7-8
8	Long Beach State	209-71	.746	0	7-6
9	Indiana	208-75	.735	1	11-3
10	Florida State	201-74	.731	0	4-2
11	UNLV	203-78	.722	0	5-1
12	North Carolina State	208-80	.722	1	7-3

NCAA champions: UCLA (1970); UCLA (1971); UCLA (1972); UCLA (1973); North Carolina State (1974); UCLA (1975); Indiana (1976); Marquette (1977); Kentucky (1978); Michigan State (1979).

Winningest Teams of the 1960s

	School	Overall Record	Pct.	NCAA Titles	NCAA Tourn.
1	UCLA	234-52	.818	5	22-4
2	Cincinnati	214-63	.773	2	14-4
3	Providence	204-64	.761	0	2-3
4	Duke	213-67	.761	0	11-4
5	Kentucky	197-69	.741	0	7-7
6	Ohio State	188-69	.732	1	13-3
7	St. Joseph's–PA	201-74	.731	0	8-10
8	Dayton	207-77	.729	0	7-5
9	Bradley	197-74	.727	0	0-0
10	Princeton	188-71	.726	0	8-9
11	Vanderbilt	182-69	.725	0	1-1
12	North Carolina	184-72	.719	0	7-5

NCAA champions: Ohio State (1960); Cincinnati (1961); Cincinnati (1962); Loyola of Chicago (1963); UCLA (1964); UCLA (1965); Texas Western (1966); UCLA (1967); UCLA (1968); UCLA (1969).

National Invitation Tournament (NIT)champions: Bradley (1960); Providence (1961); Dayton (1962); Providence (1963); Bradley (1964); St. John's (1965); Brigham Young (1966); Southern Illinois (1967); Dayton (1968); Temple (1969). The NIT began in 1938, a year before the first NCAA tournament, and is held at Madison Square Garden in New York.

Winningest Teams of the 1950s

	School	Overall Record	Pct.	NCAA Titles	NCAA Tourn.
1	Kentucky	224-33	.872	2	13-5
2	N.Carolina State	240-65	.787	0	6-6
3	Seattle	233-69	.772	0	8-7
4	La Salle	209-65	.763	1	9-1
5	Dayton	228-71	.763	0	1-1
6	Holy Cross	199-65	.754	0	2-4
7	Kansas State	179-63	.740	0	7-5
8	Connecticut	187-67	.736	0	1-7
9	West Virginia	205-74	.735	0	4-5
10	Louisville	202-77	.724	0	3-3
11	Illinois	165-64	.721	0	6-2
12	Western Kentucky	205-82	.714	0	0-0

NCAA champions: City College of New York (1950); Kentucky (1951); Kansas (1952); Indiana (1953); La Salle (1954); San Francisco (1955); San Francisco (1956); North Carolina (1957); Kentucky (1958); California (1959).

National Invitation Tournament champions: City College of New York (1950); Brigham Young (1951); La Salle (1952); Seton Hall (1953); Holy Cross (1954); Duquesne (1955); Louisville (1956); Bradley (1957); Xavier-OH (1958); St. John's (1959).

Winningest Teams of the 1940s

	School	Overall Record	Pct.	NCAA Titles	NCAA Tourn.
1	Kentucky	239-42	.851	2	8-2
2	Oklahoma State	237-55	.812	2	8-1
3	Rhode Island	178-44	.802	0	0-0
4	Eastern Kentucky	145-40	.784	0	0-0
5	Western Kentucky	222-66	.771	0	0-1
6	Tennessee	152-46	.768	0	0-0
7	Bowling Green	204-66	.756	0	0-0
8	Notre Dame	162-55	.747	0	0-0
9	Toledo	176-65	.730	0	0-0
10	St. John's	162-60	.730	0	0-0
11	West Virginia	157-59	.727	0	0-0
12	Illinois	150-57	.725	0	2-3

NCAA champions: Indiana (1940); Wisconsin (1941); Stanford (1942); Wyoming (1943); Utah (1944); Oklahoma State (1945); Oklahoma State (1946); Holy Cross (1947); Kentucky (1948); Kentucky (1949).

National Invitation Tournament champions: Colorado (1940); LIU-Brooklyn (1941); West Virginia (1942); St. John's (1943); St. John's (1944); DePaul (1945); Kentucky (1946); Utah (1947); Saint Louis (1948); San Francisco (1949).

Note: Oklahoma State was known as Oklahoma A&M until 1957.

Lew Alcindor (later Kareem Abdul Jabbar) and UCLA coach John Wooden in 1969, Alcindor's senior year. By then Wooden had won five NCAA championships at UCLA and would go on to win five more in the 1970s.

Winningest Teams

Most Division I Wins

	School	Wins
1	Kentucky	1,685
2	North Carolina	1,675
3	Kansas	1,630
4	St. John's	1,532
5	Duke	1,516
6	Temple	1,475
7	Syracuse	1,451
8	Oregon State	1,441
9	Pennsylvania	1,437
10	Notre Dame	1,414
11	Indiana	1,410
12	UCLA	1,398
13	Washington	1,365
14	Princeton	1,359
15	Western Kentucky	1,356
16	Purdue	1,355
17	Utah	1,346
18	West Virginia	1,325
	Louisville	1,325
20	Bradley	1,323
21	Illinois	1,321
22	Fordham	1,313
23	North Carolina State	1,309
24	Washington State	1,300
25	Cincinnati	1,283

Most Wins in One Season

Including postseason tournaments.

Record	School	Year
37-2	UNLV	1987
37-3	Duke	1986
36-3	Kentucky	1948
35-2	Massachusetts	1996
35-3	Georgetown	1985
35-3	Arizona	1988

All-Time Won-Lost Records

Ranked by percentage; based on at least 30 years in Division I. Won-lost records include all NCAA and NIT tournament games.

	School	Years	Games	Won	Lost	Pct.	NCAA Tourn.
1	Kentucky	94	2,211	1,685	525	.762	77-35
2	North Carolina	87	2,270	1,675	595	.738	72-31
3	UNLV	39	1,105	811	294	.734	30-11
4	UCLA	78	2,002	1,398	604	.698	77-26
5	Kansas	99	2,340	1,630	710	.697	56-26
6	St. John's	90	2,228	1,532	696	.688	23-25
7	Syracuse	96	2,134	1,451	683	.680	35-24
8	Western Kentucky	78	2,006	1,356	650	.676	15-17
9	Duke	92	2,265	1,516	749	.669	57-19
10	Arkansas	74	1,930	1,268	662	.657	37-22
11	Louisville	83	2,021	1,325	696	.656	48-29
12	DePaul	74	1,793	1,174	619	.655	20-23
13	Indiana	97	2,165	1,410	755	.651	50-21
14	Notre Dame	92	2,177	1,414	762	.650	25-28
15	Utah	89	2,074	1,346	728	.649	25-22
16	Temple	101	2,279	1,475	804	.647	24-21
17	Weber State	35	991	640	351	.646	5-12
18	Purdue	99	2,105	1,355	750	.644	19-16
19	Illinois	92	2,057	1,321	736	.642	22-19
20	Villanova	77	1,961	1,256	705	.640	37-24

Note: Tie games from early in the century included Kentucky and Notre Dame (1 each).

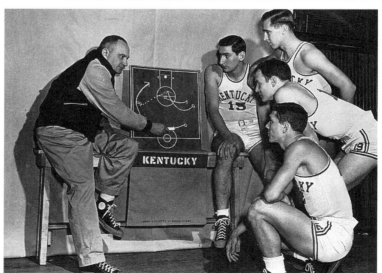

In 41 years at Kentucky, coach Adolph Rupp's teams won 876 games and 4 national championships.

Streaks

Longest Winning Streaks—Full Season

Including postseason tournament games.

Wins	School	Years	Ended by	Score
88	UCLA	1971-74	Notre Dame	71-70
60	San Francisco	1955-57	Illinois	62-33
47	UCLA	1966-68	Houston	71-69
45	UNLV	1990-91	Duke	79-77
44	Texas	1913-17	Rice	24-18
43	Seton Hall	1939-41	LIU-Brooklyn	49-26
43	LIU-Brooklyn	1935-37	Stanford	45-31
41	UCLA	1968-69	Southern Cal	46-44
39	Marquette	1970-71	Ohio State	60-59
37	Cincinnati	1962-63	Wichita State	65-64
37	North Carolina	1957-58	West Virginia	75-64
36	N.C. State	1974-75	Wake Forest	83-78
35	Arkansas	1927-29	Texas	26-25

Longest Winning Streaks—Regular Season

Not including postseason tournament games.

Wins	School	Years	Ended by	Score
76	UCLA	1971-74	Notre Dame	71-70
57	Indiana	1975-77	Toledo	59-57
56	Marquette	1970-72	Detroit	70-49
54	Kentucky	1952-55	Georgia Tech	59-58
51	San Francisco	1955-57	Illinois	62-33
48	Pennsylvania	1970-72	Temple	57-52
47	Ohio State	1960-62	Wisconsin	86-67
44	Texas	1913-17	Rice	24-18
43	UCLA	1966-68	Houston	71-69
43	LIU-Brooklyn	1935-37	Stanford	45-31

Undefeated for an Entire Season

Tournament games included.

Season	School	W–L	NCAA final
1938-39	LIU-Brooklyn	24-0	won NIT title*
1939-40	Seton Hall	19-0	no postseason
1943-44	Army	15-0	no postseason
1953-54	Kentucky	25-0	refused bid to NCAAs#
1955-56	San Francisco	29-0	beat Iowa, 83-71
1956-57	North Carolina	32-0	beat Kansas, 54-53 (3OT)
1963-64	UCLA	30-0	beat Duke, 98-83
1966-67	UCLA	30-0	beat Dayton, 79-64
1971-72	UCLA	30-0	beat Florida St., 81-76
1972-73	UCLA	30-0	beat Memphis St., 87-66
1972-73	N.C. State	27-0	Ineligible for NCAAs†
1975-76	Indiana	32-0	beat Michigan, 86-68

* Once a more important tournament than the NCAAs, the National Invitation Tournament (NIT) has been held since 1938 with the championship game played every year at Madison Square Garden.
\# Kentucky declined the tournament bid after the NCAA declared fifth-year seniors Cliff Hagan, Frank Ramsey, and Lou Tsioropoulos ineligible for the postseason.
† North Carolina State was declared ineligible for the NCAA tournament for using improper methods in recruiting freshman star forward David Thompson.

Longest Home-Court Winning Streaks

Wins	School	Years	Ended by	Score
129	Kentucky	1943-55	Georgia Tech	59-58
99	St. Bonaventure	1948-61	Detroit	77-70
98	UCLA	1970-76	Oregon	65-45
86	Cincinnati	1957-64	Kansas	51-47
81	Arizona	1945-51	Kansas State	76-57
81	Marquette	1967-73	Notre Dame	71-69
80	Lamar	1978-84	La. Tech	68-65
75	Long Beach St.	1968-74	San Francisco	94-84
72	UNLV	1974-78	New Mexico	102-98
71	Arizona	1987-92	UCLA	89-87

Indiana coach Bobby Knight flanked by Quinn Buckner (left) and Scott May after winning the 1976 NCAA championship. The 1976 Indiana Hoosiers were the last NCAA Division I team to be undefeated for an entire season.

All-Time Career Leaders

NCAA Division I career leaders through the 1996–97 season; statistics include regular season and postseason tournament games; asterisks (*) indicate players active in 1996–97.

Most Points

Pts.	Player/School	Gm.	Last Year
3,667	Pete Maravich, Louisiana State	83	1970
3,249	Freeman Williams, Portland State	106	1978
3,217	Lionel Simmons, La Salle	131	1990
3,165	Alphonso Ford, Miss. Valley State	109	1993
3,066	Harry Kelly, Texas Southern	110	1983
3,008	Hersey Hawkins, Bradley	125	1988
2,973	Oscar Robertson, Cincinnati	88	1960
2,951	Danny Manning, Kansas	147	1988
2,914	Alfredrick Hughes, Loyola-IL	120	1985
2,884	Elvin Hayes, Houston	93	1968
2,850	Larry Bird, Indiana State	94	1979
2,832	Otis Birdsong, Houston	116	1977
2,804	Kevin Bradshaw, U.S. International	111	1991
2,801	Allan Houston, Tennessee	128	1993
2,723	Hank Gathers, Loyola-CA	117	1990

Years played: 4 each, except Maravich, Robertson, Hayes, and Bird (3 each).
Note: Bradshaw played freshman year at Bethune-Cookman and Gathers at Southern Cal.

Highest Scoring Average

Based on at least 45 games or 1,400 points; Division I games only.

Avg.	Player/School	Gm.	Last Year
44.2	Pete Maravich, Louisiana State	83	1970
34.6	Austin Carr, Notre Dame	74	1971
33.8	Oscar Robertson, Cincinnati	88	1960
33.1	Calvin Murphy, Niagara	77	1970
32.7	Dwight Lamar, S.W. Louisiana	57	1973
32.5	Frank Selvy, Furman	78	1954
32.3	Rick Mount, Purdue	72	1970
32.1	Darrell Floyd, Furman	71	1956
32.0	Nick Werkman, Seton Hall	71	1964
31.5	Willie Humes, Idaho State	48	1971
31.4	Bird Averitt, Pepperdine	49	1973
31.3	Elgin Baylor, Seattle	80	1958
31.0	Elvin Hayes, Houston	93	1968
30.7	Freeman Williams, Portland State	106	1978
30.3	Larry Bird, Indiana State	94	1979

Years played: 3 each, except Williams (4) and Lamar, Humes, and Averitt (2 each).

Highest Rebound Average

Based on at least 800 rebounds.

Avg.	Player/School	Gm.	Last Year
22.7	Artis Gilmore, Jacksonville	54	1971
21.8	Charlie Slack, Marshall	88	1956
21.6	Paul Silas, Creighton	81	1964
21.5	Leroy Wright, Pacific	67	1960
21.5	Art Quimby, Connecticut	80	1955
21.1	Walter Dukes, Seton Hall	59	1953
20.3	Bill Russell, San Francisco	79	1956
20.2	Kermit Washington, American	73	1973
20.2	Julius Erving, Massachusetts	52	1971
19.5	Joe Holup, George Washington	104	1956

Years played: 3 each, except Slack, Quimby, Holup, and Gola (4 each); and Gilmore, Dukes, and Erving (2 each).

Most Combined Points and Rebounds

Total	Player/School	Pts.	Reb.	Gm.
4,663	Tom Gola, La Salle	2,462	2,201	118
4,646	Lionel Simmons, La Salle	3,217	1,429	131
4,486	Elvin Hayes, Houston	2,884	1,602	93
4,389	Dickie Hemric, Wake Forest	2,587	1,802	104
4,311	Oscar Robertson, Cincinnati	2,973	1,338	88
4,256	Joe Holup, G. Washington	2,226	2,030	104
4,151	Harry Kelly, Tex. Southern	3,066	1,085	110
4,138	Danny Manning, Kansas	2,951	1,187	147
4,097	Larry Bird, Indiana State	2,850	1,247	94
4,059	Elgin Baylor, Seattle	2,500	1,559	80
4,000	Michael Brooks, La Salle	2,628	1,372	114

Years played: 4 each, except Hayes, Robertson, Bird, and Baylor (3 each).
Note: Baylor played freshman year at College of Idaho and Gathers at Southern Cal.

Most Games Played

Including postseason tournaments.

No.	Player/School
148	Christian Laettner, Duke
147	Danny Manning, Kansas
145	Stacey Augman, UNLV
143	Derrick Coleman, Syracuse
143	Patrick Ewing, Georgetown
143	Danny Ferry, Duke
141	Brian Davis, Duke
141	Anthony Epps, Kentucky
139	Ralph Beard, Kentucky
139	Lee Mayberry, Arkansas
138	Greg Anthony, Portland/UNLV
138	Sherman Douglas, Syracuse
138	Doug West, Villanova
138	Reggie Williams, Georgetown

Last year played: Anthony (1991), Augman (1991), Beard (1949), Coleman (1990), Davis (1992), Douglas (1989), Epps (1997), Ewing (1985), Ferry (1989), Laettner (1992), Manning (1988), Mayberry (1992), West (1989), and Williams (1987).

Best Free-Throw Percentage

Based on at least 300 made.

No.	Player/School
.909	Greg Starrick, Kentucky/S. Ill.
.901	Jack Moore, Nebraska
.900	Steve Henson, Kansas State
.898	Steve Alford, Indiana
.898	Bob Lloyd, Rutgers
.895	Jim Barton, Dartmouth
.892	Tommy Boyer, Arkansas
.888	Rob Robbins, New Mexico
.885	Sean Miller, Pittsburgh
.885	Ron Perry, Holy Cross
.885	Joe Dykstra, Western Illinois

Last year played: Alford (1987), Barton (1989), Boyer (1963), Dykstra (1983), Henson (1990), Joseph (1990), Lloyd (1967), Macy (1980), Miller (1992), Moore (1982), Perry (1980), Robbins (1991), and Starrick (1972).

Most Assists

No.	Player/School
1,076	Bobby Hurley, Duke
1,038	Chris Corchiani, N.C. State
983	Keith Jennings, E. Tenn. State
960	Sherman Douglas, Syracuse
956	Tony Miller, Marquette
950	Greg Anthony, Portland/UNLV
939	Gary Payton, Oregon State
902	Orlando Smart, San Francisco
894	Andre LaFleur, Northeastern
884	Jim Les, Bradley
883	Frank Smith, Old Dominion
877	Taurence Chisholm, Delaware

Last year played: Anthony (1991), Chisholm (1988), Corchiani (1991), Douglas (1989), Hurley (1993), Jennings (1991), LaFleur (1987), Les (1986), Miller (1995), Payton (1990), Smart (1994), and Smith (1988).

Most Steals

No.	Player/School
376	Eric Murdock, Providence
344	Gerald Walker, San Francisco
344	Johnny Rhodes, Maryland
341	Michael Anderson, Drexel
341	Kenny Robertson, Cleveland State
334	Keith Jennings, E. Tenn. State
329	Greg Anthony, Portland/UNLV
328	Chris Corchiani, N.C. State
321	Gary Payton, Oregon State
321	Chris Garner,* Memphis
314	Mark Woods, Wright State
314	Pointer Williams, McNesse State
310	Scott Burrell, Connecticut
310	Clarence Ceasar, Louisiana State

Last year played: Anderson (1988), Anthony (1991), Burrell (1993), Ceasar (1995), Corchiani (1991), Garner (1997), Jennings (1991), Murdock (1991), Payton (1990), Rhodes (1996), Robertson (1990), Walker (1996), Williams (1996), and Woods (1993).

Duke guard and all-time NCAA assist leader Bobby Hurley looking for a receiver.

Most Blocked Shots

No.	Player/School
492	Adonal Foyle,* Colgate
481	Tim Duncan,* Wake Forest
453	Alonzo Mourning, Georgetown
437	Lorenzo Coleman,* Tenn. Tech
425	Theo Ratliff, Wyoming
419	Rodney Blake, St. Joseph's–PA
412	Shaquille O'Neal, Louisiana State
409	Kevin Roberson, Vermont
399	Jim McIlvaine, Marquette
392	Tim Perry, Temple
375	Jason Lawson,* Villanova
374	Pervis Ellison, Louisville

Last year played: Blake (1988), Coleman (1997), Duncan (1997), Ellison (1989), Foyle (1997), Lawson (1997), McIlvaine (1994), Mourning (1992), O'Neal (1992), Perry (1988), Ratliff (1995), and Roberson (1992).

Single-Season Leaders

NCAA Division I career leaders through the 1996–97 season; statistics include regular season and postseason tournament games; asterisks (*) incidate players active in 1996–97.

Most Points

Points	Player/School	Year	Avg.
1,381	Pete Maravich, Louisiana State	1970	44.5
1,214	Elvin Hayes, Houston	1968	36.8
1,209	Frank Selvy, Furman	1954	41.7
1,148	Pete Maravich, Louisiana State	1969	44.2
1,138	Pete Maravich, Louisiana State	1968	43.8
1,131	Bo Kimble, Loyola–CA	1990	35.3
1,125	Hersey Hawkins, Bradley	1988	36.3
1,106	Austin Carr, Notre Dame	1970	38.1
1,101	Austin Carr, Notre Dame	1971	38.0
1,090	Otis Birdsong, Houston	1977	30.3
1,054	Dwight Lamar, S.W. Louisiana	1972	36.3
1,054	Kevin Bradshaw, U.S. International	1991	37.6
1,030	Glenn Robinson, Purdue	1994	30.3
1,015	Hank Gathers, Loyola–CA	1989	32.7
1,011	Oscar Robertson, Cincinnati	1960	33.7

Although Pete Maravich (23) of Louisiana State led the nation in scoring averages for three straight years (1968–70), he never played in the NCAA tournament.

Highest Scoring Average

Avg.	Player/School	Year	Points
44.5	Pete Maravich, Louisiana State	1970	1,381
44.2	Pete Maravich, Louisiana State	1969	1,148
43.8	Pete Maravich, Louisiana State	1968	1,138
41.7	Frank Selvy, Furman	1954	1,209
40.1	Johnny Neumann, Mississippi	1971	923
38.8	Freeman Williams, Portland State	1977	1,010
38.8	Billy McGill, Utah	1962	1,009
38.2	Calvin Murphy, Niagara	1968	916
38.1	Austin Carr, Notre Dame	1970	1,106
38.0	Austin Carr, Notre Dame	1971	1,101
37.6	Kevin Bradshaw, U.S. International	1991	1,054
37.4	Rick Barry, Miami–FL	1965	973
36.8	Elvin Hayes, Houston	1968	1,214
36.8	Marshall Rogers, Pan American	1976	919
36.7	Howie Komives, Bowling Green	1964	844

Highest Rebound Average
Based on at least 800 rebounds

Avg.	Player/School	Year	Rebounds
25.6	Charlie Slack, Marshall	1955	538
25.1	Leroy Wright, Pacific	1959	652
24.4	Art Quimby, Connecticut	1955	611
23.6	Charlie Slack, Marshall	1956	520
23.5	Ed Conlin, Fordham	1953	612
23.2	Joe Holup, George Washington	1956	604
23.2	Artis Gilmore, Jacksonville	1971	603
23.2	Art Quimby, Connecticut	1954	588
22.5	Paul Silas, Creighton	1962	563
22.4	Leroy Wright, Pacific	1960	360
22.2	Walter Dukes, Seton Hall	1953	734
22.2	Charlie Tyra, Louisville	1956	645
22.2	Charlie Slack, Marshall	1954	466
22.2	Artis Gilmore, Jacksonville	1970	621
21.8	Four players tied.		

Most Assists

No.	Player/School	Year
406	Mark Wade, UNLV	1987
399	Avery Johnson, Southern U.	1988
373	Anthony Manuel, Bradley	1988
333	Avery Johnson, Southern U.	1987
328	Mark Jackson, St. John's	1986
326	Sherman Douglas, Syracuse	1989
310	Greg Anthony, UNLV	1991
310	Sam Crawford, New Mexico State	1993
309	Reid Gettys, Houston	1984
305	Carl Golston, Loyola–CA	1985
303	Craig Neal, Georgia Tech	1988
301	Keith Jennings, E. Tennessee State	1991

Best Free-Throw Percentage

Based on at least 2.5 made per game.

Pct.	Player/School	Year
.959	Craig Collins, Penn State	1985
.950	Rod Foster, UCLA	1982
.944	Carlos Gibson, Marshall	1978
.944	Danny Basile, Marist	1994
.942	Jim Barton, Dartmouth	1986
.939	Jack Moore, Nebraska	1982
.935	Rob Robbins, New Mexico	1990
.935	Dandrea Evans, Troy State	1994
.933	Tommy Boyer, Arkansas	1962
.931	Damon Goodwin, Dayton	1986
.929	Brian Magid, George Washington	1980
.929	Mike Joseph, Bucknell	1990

Most Steals

No.	Player/School	Year
150	Mookie Blaylock, Oklahoma	1988
142	Aldwin Ware, Fla. A&M	1988
139	Darron Brittman, Chicago St.	1986
138	Nadav Henefeld, UConn	1990
131	Mookie Blaylock, Oklahoma	1989
130	Ronn McMahon, East. Wash.	1990
124	Marty Johnson, Towson St.	1988
124	Allen Iverson, Georgetown	1996
120	Jim Paguaga, St. Francis–NY	1986
120	Shawn Griggs, SW Louisiana	1994

Best 3-Point Field Goal Percentage

Based on at least 1.5 made per game.

Pct.	Player/School	Year
.634	Glenn Tropf, Holy Cross	1988
.632	Sean Wightman, W. Mich.	1992
.592	Keith Jennings, E. Tenn. State	1991
.585	Dave Calloway, Monmouth	1989
.573	Steve Kerr, Arizona	1988
.571	Reginald Jones, Prairie View A&M	1987
.563	Joe Tribelhorn, Colorado State.	1989
.560	Mike Joseph, Bucknell	1988
.558	Brian Jackson, Evansville	1995
.557	Christian Laettner, Duke	1992
.548	Reginald Jones, Prairie View A&M	1988
.547	Eric Rhodes, Stephen F. Austin	1987

Most Blocked Shots

No.	Player/School	Year
207	David Robinson, Navy	1986
180	Adonal Foyle, Colgate	1997
178	Keith Kloss, Central Connecticut State	1996
177	Shawn Bradley, BYU	1991
169	Alonzo Mourning, Georgetown	1989
165	Adonal Foyle, Colgate	1996
160	Alonzo Mourning, Georgetown	1992
157	Shaquille O'Neal, LSU	1992
156	Roy Rogers, Alabama	1996
151	Dikembe Mutombo, Georgetown	1991
147	Adonal Foyle, Colgate	1995
144	Theo Ratliff, Wyoming	1995
144	David Robinson, Navy	1987

Best Field Goal Percentage

Based on at least 5 made per game.

Pct.	Player/School	Year
.746	Steve Johnson, Oregon State	1981
.722	Dwayne Davis, Florida	1989
.713	Keith Walker, Utica	1985
.710	Steve Johnson, Oregon State.	1980
.704	Oliver Miller, Arkansas	1991
.703	Alan Williams, Princeton	1987
.702	Mark McNamara, Calif.	1982
.700	Warren Kidd, Middle Tennessee State	1991
.700	Pete Freeman, Akron	1991
.699	Joe Senser, West Chester	1977
.698	Lee Campbell, S.W. Missouri State.	1990
.698	Stephen Scheffler, Purdue	1990

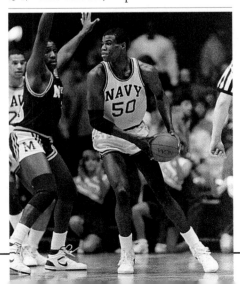

David Robinson of Navy set the all-time single season record for blocked shots in 1986.

Single-Game Leaders

NCAA Division I career leaders through the 1996–97 season. Statistics include regular season and postseason tournament games; asterisks (*) indicate players active in 1996–97.

Highest Scoring Games

Between Division I teams.

Pts.	Final Score/Date
331	Loyola-CA 181, U.S. International 150 (1/31/89)
326	Loyola-CA 186, U.S. International 140 (1/5/91)
306	Loyola-CA 162, U.S. International 144 (1/7/89)
289	Loyola-CA 152, U.S. International 137 (12/7/89)
289	Louisiana State 148, Loyola-CA 141, OT (2/3/90)

Most Points

Against a Division I opponent.

Pts.	Player/Game/Date
72	Kevin Bradshaw, U.S. International vs. Loyola–CA (1/5/91)
69	Pete Maravich, Louisiana State vs. Alabama (2/7/70)
68	Calvin Murphy, Niagara vs. Syracuse (12/7/68)
66	Jay Handlan, Washington & Lee vs. Furman (2/17/51)
66	Pete Maravich, Louisiana State vs. Tulane (2/10/69)
66	Anthony Roberts, Oral Roberts vs. N. Carolina A&T (2/19/77)
65	Anthony Roberts, Oral Roberts vs. Oregon (3/9/77)
65	Scott Haffner, Evansville vs. Dayton (2/18/89)
64	Pete Maravich, Louisiana State vs. Kentucky (2/21/70)
63	Johnny Neumann, Mississippi vs. LSU (1/30/71)
63	Hersey Hawkins, Bradley vs. Detroit (2/22/88)
62	Three players tied.

Most Rebounds

No.	Player/Game/Date
51	Bill Chambers, Wm. & Mary vs. Virginia (2/14/53)
43	Charlie Slack, Marshall vs. Morris Harvey (1/12/54)
42	Tom Heinsohn, Holy Cross vs. Boston College (3/1/55)
40	Art Quimby, Connecticut vs. Boston Univ. (1/11/55)
39	Maurice Stokes, St. Francis–NY vs. John Carroll (1/28/55)
39	Dave DeBusschere, Detroit vs. Central Michigan (1/30/60)
39	Keith Swagerty, Pacific vs. UC–Santa Barbara (3/5/65)
38	Five players tied.

Most Assists

No.	Player/Game/Date
22	Tony Fairley, Charleston Southern vs. Armstrong Atlantic (2/9/87)
22	Avery Johnson, Southern U. vs. Texas Southern (1/25/88)
22	Sherman Douglas, Syracuse vs. Providence (1/28/89)
21	Mark Wade, UNLV vs. Navy (12/29/86)
21	Kelvin Scarborough, New Mexico vs. Hawaii (2/13/87)
21	Anthony Manuel, Bradley vs. UC–Irvine (12/19/87)
21	Avery Johnson, Southern U. vs. Alabama State (1/16/88)

Most 3-Point Field Goals

No.	Player/Game/Date
14	Dave Jamerson, Ohio University vs. Charleston-SC (12/21/89)
14	Askia Jones, Kansas State vs. Fresno State (3/24/94)
12	Five players tied.

Most Steals

No.	Player/Game/Date
13	Mookie Blaylock, Oklahoma vs. Centenary (12/12/87)
13	Mookie Blaylock, Oklahoma vs. Loyola-CA (12/17/88)
12	Kenny Robertson, Cleveland St. vs. Wagner (12/3/88)
12	Terry Evans, Oklahoma vs. Florida A&M (1/27/93)

Most Blocked Shots

No.	Player/Game/Date
14	David Robinson, Navy vs. NC-Wilmington (1/4/86)
14	Shawn Bradley, Brigham Young vs. Eastern Kentucky (12/7/90)
14	Roy Rogers, Alabama vs. Georgia (2/10/96)
13	Kevin Roberson, Vermont vs. New Hampshire (1/9/92)
13	Jim McIlvaine, Marquette vs. N.E. Illinois (12/9/92)
13	Keith Gloss, Central Conn. State vs. St. Francis-PA (12/21/94)

Extra Point

Pete Maravich of Louisiana State ranks as the most prolific scorer in the history of college basketball. In each of three seasons, ending in 1970, Maravich, a 6-foot 5-inch guard, led the nation in scoring and achieved a scoring average of 44.2 points per game that set an all-time career record.

Head Coaches

NCAA Division I only, through 1996–97 season.

Best Winning Percentages

Based on at least 10 seasons in Division I; includes postseason tournaments.

Pct.	Head Coach	Yrs.	W	L	Last Year
.826	Clair Bee	21	412	87	1951
.822	Adolph Rupp	41	876	190	1972
.821	Jerry Tarkanian*	26	667	145	active
.804	John Wooden	29	664	162	1975
.776	Dean Smith*	36	879	254	active
.770	Harry Fisher	13	147	44	1925
.768	Frank Keaney	27	387	117	1948
.767	George Keogan	24	385	117	1943
.765	Jack Ramsey	11	231	71	1966
.761	Vic Bubas	10	213	67	1969
.748	Chick Davies	21	314	106	1948
.747	Ray Mears	21	399	135	1977
.745	Jim Boeheim*	21	502	172	active
.739	Rick Pitino*	15	352	124	1997
.739	Al McGuire	20	405	143	1977

* Active during 1996–97 season.

Fresno State's Jerry Tarkanian has the best winning percentage of all active Division I coaches.

Most Wins

Based on at least 10 seasons in Division I; includes postseason tournaments.

Wins	Head Coach	Yrs.
879	Dean Smith*	36
876	Adolph Rupp	41
767	Henry Iba	41
759	Ed Diddle	42
746	Phog Allen	48
724	Ray Meyer	42
700	Bob Knight*	32
694	Norm Stewart*	36
691	Don Haskins*	36
683	Lefty Driesell*	35
667	Jerry Tarkanian*	26
664	John Wooden	29

* Active during 1996–97 season.

Most Wins by Active Coaches

Through 1996-97 season. Based on 5 years as Division I-A coach; includes tournaments.

Wins	Head Coach/School/Yrs.
879	Dean Smith, North Carolina (36)
772	Jim Phelan, Mount St. Mary's (43)
700	Bob Knight, Indiana (32)
694	Norm Stewart, Missouri (36)
691	Don Haskins, Texas–El Paso (36)
683	Lefty Driesell, Georgia St. (35)
667	Jerry Tarkanian, Fresno St. (26)
613	Denny Crum, Louisville (26)
587	Eddie Sutton, Oklahoma St. (27)
573	John Thompson, Georgetown (25)
560	John Chaney, Temple (25)
558	Eldon Miller, Northern Iowa (35)
532	Lute Olson, Arizona (24)

Most Appearances in NCAA Tournament

No.	Head Coach/Titles	Record
27	Dean Smith (2)*	65-27
21	Denny Crum (2)*	42-21
21	Bob Knight (3)*	40-18
20	Adolph Rupp (4)	30-18
20	John Thompson (1)*	34-19
18	Lou Carnesecca	17-20
18	Lou Henson	19-19
18	Lute Olson (1)*	28-18
18	Eddie Sutton	27-18
17	Jim Boeheim	27-17
16	John Wooden (10)	47-10
16	Jerry Tarkanian (1)	37-16

* Team participated in 1997 NCAA tournament.

Home Courts

Matthews Arena at Northeastern University opened in 1912 as Boston Arena and is the oldest multipurpose athletic facility in the world.

Largest Division I Arenas

Principal home courts; listed with home teams.

Seats	Home Court	School
33,000	Carrier Dome	Syracuse
24,535	Thompson-Boling Arena	Tennessee
23,000	Rupp Arena*	Kentucky
22,700	Marriott Center	Brigham Young
21,572	Dean Smith Center	North Carolina
21,500	MCI Center*	Georgetown
20,142	The Pyramid*	Memphis
20,029	Continental Airlines Arena*	Seton Hall
20,000	Kiel Center*	Saint Louis
19,524	Madison Square Garden*	St. John's
19,200	Marine Midland Arena*	Canisius
19,200	Bud Walton Arena	Arkansas
18,865	Freedom Hall*	Louisville
18,592	Bradley Center*	Marquette
18,500	Thomas & Mack Center	UNLV
18,018	University Arena (The Pit)	New Mexico
17,357	Assembly Hall	Indiana
17,500	Rosemont Horizon*	DePaul
16,450	Assembly Hall	Illinois
16,300	Allen Fieldhouse	Kansas

*Arena is off campus.

Oldest Division I Arenas

Opened	Home Court	School	Seats
1910	Matthews Arena	Northeastern	6,000
1926	Rose Hill Gym	Fordham	3,470
1926	Lavietes Pavilion	Harvard	2,195
1927	McArthur Court	Oregon	10,063
1927	The Palestra	Penn	8,700
1927	Edmundson Pavilion	Washington	7,900
1928	Hinkle Fieldhouse	Butler	11,043
1928	Williams Arena	Minnesota	14,300
1930	Wisconsin Field House	Wisconsin	11,500
1932	Lee Ampitheater*	Yale	3,100
1933	Harmon Gym	California	6,578
1933	Fogelman Arena	Tulane	3,600

*Known as Payne Whitney Gymnasium until 1996-97 season.

Newest Division I Arenas

Opened	Home Court	School	Seats
1997	MCI Center	Georgetown	21,500
1997	Special Events Center	Murray State	8,200
1997	Aztec Bowl Arena	San Diego State	12,414
1996	Bryce Jordan Center	Penn State	15,300
1996	Dale Halton Arena	N.C.-Charlotte	9,105
1996	Loyola Events Center	Loyola–IL	5,200
1996	Marine Midland Arena	Canisius	19,200
1995	Whittemore Center	New Hampshire	7,200

Miscellaneous

Most Popular Division I Team Nicknames

No.	Nickname/School
12	**Bulldogs** Butler, The Citadel, Drake, Fresno State, Georgia, Gonzaga (AKA the Zags), Louisiana Tech, Mississippi State, NC-Asheville, Stanford, South Carolina State, and Yale
12	**Tigers** Auburn, Clemson, Grambling State, Jackson State, LSU, Memphis, Missouri, Pacific, Princeton, Tennessee State, Texas Southern, Towson State
9	**Eagles** American, Boston College, Coppin State, Eastern Michigan, Eastern Washington, Georgia Southern, Morehead State, North Texas, Winthrop
9	**Wildcats** Arizona, Bethune-Cookman, Davidson, Kansas State, Kentucky, New Hampshire, Northwestern, Villanova, Weber State
7	**Bears** Baylor, Brown, California (Golden Bears), Maine (Black Bears), Mercer, Morgan State, and Southwest Missouri State
7	**Panthers** Eastern Illinois, Florida International (Golden Panthers), Georgia State, Northern Iowa, Pittsburgh, Prairie View A&M, and Wisconsin-Milwaukee

No.	Nickname/School
7	**Red . . .** Red Raiders, Colgate Redbirds, Illinois State Red Foxes, Marist Red Hawks, Miami–OH Red Flash, St. Francis–PA Red Storm, St. John's Red Raiders , Texas Tech
6	**Fighting . . .** Fighting Camels, Campbell Fighting Blue Hens, Delaware Fighting Illini, Illinois Fighting Tigers, LSU Fighting Irish, Notre Dame Fighting Gamecocks, South Carolina
5	**Blue . . .** Blue Devils, Central Connecticut State Bluejays, Creighton Blue Demons, DePaul Blue Devils, Duke Blue Raiders, Middle Tennessee State
5	**Broncos** Boise State, Rider (Broncs), Santa Clara, Texas–Pan American (Broncs), Western Michigan
5	**Cougars** Brigham Young, Chicago State, College of Charleston, Houston, Washington State.
5	**Golden Eagles** Marquette, Northeastern Illinois, Oral Roberts, Southern Miss, Tennessee Tech

The 1997 NCAA Division I championship game between Arizona and Kentucky was the first time two schools with the same nickname met in the final.

Sneaker Wars

Exclusive shoe and apparel contracts with major Division I basketball programs are big business. The following shoes have made it to the Men's Final Four over the last 10 years.

Year	Shoe/Final Four
1997	Nike (Arizona,* Minnesota, North Carolina) Converse (Kentucky)
1996	Nike (Massachusetts, Miss. St., Syracuse) Converse (Kentucky*)
1995	Nike (North Carolina, Okla. St.) Converse (Arkansas) Reebok (UCLA*)
1994	Nike (Arizona, Duke) Converse (Arkansas*) Reebok (Florida)
1993	Converse (Kansas, Kentucky, North Carolina*) Nike (Michigan)
1992	Adidas (Duke*, Indiana) Nike (Cincinnati, Michigan)
1991	Converse (Kansas, N. Carolina) Adidas (Duke*) Nike (UNLV)
1990	Nike (Georgia Tech, UNLV*) Adidas (Duke) Converse (Arkansas)
1989	Nike (Michigan,* Seton Hall) Adidas (Duke) Converse (Illinois)
1988	Nike (Arizona, Kansas*) Adidas (Duke) Converse (Oklahoma)

*Eventual National Champion.

Triumphant Exits
Three Division I head coaches ended their college careers by winning the NCAA championship game: John Wooden of UCLA was first, in 1975, followed by Al McGuire of Marquette in 1977, and Larry Brown of Kansas in 1988.

NCAA Women's National Champions

Rebecca Lobo (50) led unbeaten Connecticut to its first NCAA basketball title in 1995.

Most NCAA Final Four Appearances

No.	School	1	2	3*
10	Tennessee	5	2	3
8	Louisiana Tech	2	3	3
6	Stanford	2	0	4
4	Georgia	0	2	2
3	Southern Cal	2	1	0
3	Old Dominion	1	1	1
3	Connecticut	1	0	2
3	Auburn	0	3	0
3	Virginia	0	1	2
3	W. Kentucky	0	1	2
2	Texas	1	0	1
2	Long Beach State	0	0	2
2	Maryland	0	0	2

*Both losing teams in semifinals share third place.

Most NCAA Titles

Schools with more than one NCAA title since the Division I tournament began in 1982.

No.	School	Championship Years
5	Tennessee	1997, 1996, 1991, 1989, 1987
2	Louisiana Tech	1988, 1982
2	Stanford	1992, 1990
2	Southern Cal	1984, 1983
1	Connecticut	1995
1	North Carolina	1994
1	Old Dominion	1985
1	Texas	1986
1	Texas Tech	1993

AIAW Champions

The tournament of the Association of Intercollegiate Athletics for Women decided the women's national championship from 1972 to 1981. The AIAW's last tournament was in 1982.

No.	School	Championship Years
3	Delta State—MS	1972-74
3	Immaculata—PA	1975-77
2	Old Dominion	1980, 1979
1	Louisiana Tech	1981
1	Rutgers	1982
1	UCLA	1978

Most Frequent Most Valuable Player

In NCAA Division I Tournament.

No.	Player/School	Years
2	Cheryl Miller, Southern Cal	1984, 1983

Extra Point
Since 1982 there have been only two undefeated women's national Division I champions: Texas (34-0) in 1986 and Connecticut (35-0) in 1995.

Most NCAA Tournament Appearances

No.	School	Tourn. Record	Titles
16	Tennessee	55-11	5
16	Louisiana Tech	46-17	2
14	Mississippi	15-14	0
14	Penn State	14-14	0
14	Georgia	28-14	0
14	Virginia	26-14	0
14	Texas	22-13	1
14	Old Dominion	23-13	1
13	Southern Cal	27-11	2
13	Auburn	25-13	0
12	Montana	6-12	0
12	N.C. State	10-12	0
12	Stephen F. Austin	9-12	0
12	W. Kentucky	15-12	0

Most NCAA Tournament Appearances by a Head Coach

No.	Head Coach/School	Record
16	Pat Summitt, Tennessee	55-11
15	Leon Barmore, La. Tech	46-17
14	Andy Landers, Georgia	28-14
14	Debbie Ryan, Virginia	26-14
14	Jody Conradt, Texas	22-13
14	Van Chancellor, Ole Miss	15-14
14	Rene Portland, Penn State	14-14
13	Joe Ciampi, Auburn	25-13
12	Tara Van Derveer, Ohio State, Stanford	30-10
12	Jim Foster, St. Joseph's—PA, Vanderbilt	17-12
12	Paul Sandeford, W. Kentucky	15-12
12	Kay Yow, N.C. State	10-12
12	Robin Selvig, Montana	6-12

NCAA titles: Summitt (5); VanDerveer (2); Barmore and Conradt (1).

Winningest Women's Teams

All-Time Won-Lost Records

Division I teams with at least 350 wins, including all postseason tournament games through 1996–97 season.

Pct.	School	Record
.840	Louisiana Tech	645-123
.807	Montana	457-109
.805	Texas	618-150
.802	Tennessee	693-171
.753	Stephen F. Austin	594-195
.752	Mount St. Mary's	463-153
.738	Old Dominion	593-210
.731	Virginia	509-187
.728	Mississippi	517-193
.727	Auburn	525-197
.722	Long Beach State	604-232
.716	Penn State	523-207
.715	Maine	408-163
.712	St. Peter's	503-203
.710	Utah	466-190
.707	North Carolina State	481-199
.705	Tennessee Tech	584-244
.705	Rutgers	469-196
.697	Ohio State	543-236
.696	St. Joseph's–PA	450-197

All-Time Division I Victories

	School	Wins
1	Tennessee	693
2	Louisiana Tech	645
3	Texas	618
4	James Madison	616
5	Long Beach State	604
6	Stephen F. Austin	594
7	Old Dominion	593
8	Tennessee Tech	584
9	Ohio State	543
10	Western Kentucky	527
11	Auburn	525
12	Penn State	523
13	Kansas State	522
14	Southern Illinois	521
15	Mississippi	517
16	Virginia	509
17	St. Peter's	503
18	Texas Tech	482
19	North Carolina State	481
	Georgia	481
	Memphis	481

Longest Winning Streaks

Including postseason tournament games.

Wins	School	Season(s)
54	Louisiana Tech	1980-82
40	Texas	1985-87
35	Connecticut	1994-96
33	Connecticut	1996-97
33	Old Dominion	1996-97
32	North Carolina	1993-95
30	Miami–FL	1991-92
29	Vermont	1991-92
29	Auburn	1988-89
28	Vermont	1992-93
28	Southern Cal	1982-84
26	Montana	1987-88
26	Central Michigan	1983-84
25	Stanford	1996-97
25	Colorado	1994-95
25	Mississippi	1991-92
24	Texas Tech	1992-94
23	Four teams tied.	

Best Head-Coach Winning Percentages

Based on at least 10 seasons in Division I; includes postseason tournament. All coaches were active in 1996–97.

Pct.	Head Coach/School	Yrs.	W	L
.865	Leon Barmore, Louisiana Tech	15	428	67
.814	Pat Summitt, Tennessee	23	625	143
.807	Robin Selvig, Montana	19	457	109
.792	Tara VanDerveer, Stanford	18	437	115
.781	Jody Conradt, Texas	28	697	195
.774	Geno Auriemma, Connecticut	12	294	86
.773	Andy Landers, Georgia	18	442	130
.771	Joe Ciampi, Auburn	20	471	140
.767	Gary Blair, Arkansas	12	287	87

Coach Pat Summitt celebrating a gold medal at the 1984 Olympics. She has also won five NCAA championships at Tennessee.

Women's Tournament Career Leaders

Includes the number of appearances (Years) in NCAA Division I tournament.

Most Points—Career

Pts.	Player/School	Yrs.	Games	Avg.
388	Bridgette Gordon, Tennessee	4	18	21.6
333	Cheryl Miller, Southern Cal	4	16	20.8
312	Janice Lawrence, Louisiana Tech	3	14	22.3
291	Penny Toler, Long Beach State	4	13	22.4
274	Dawn Staley, Virginia	4	15	18.3
263	Cindy Brown, Long Beach State	4	12	21.9
263	Venus Lacy, Louisiana Tech	3	14	18.8
261	Clarissa Davis, Texas	3	12	21.8
254	Janet Harris, Georgia	4	13	19.5

Last year played: Brown (1987), Davis (1989), Gordon (1989), Harris (1985), Lacy (1990), Lawrence (1984), Miller (1986), Staley (1992), Toler (1989).
Note: Penny Toler played for San Diego State in the 1985 tournament.

Most Points—One Game

Included with the year of the game is the round it was played in the tournament: first round (1st); second round (2nd); regional semifinal (RS); regional championship (RF); national final (F).

Pts.	Player/School	Opponent	Year
50	Lorri Bauman, Drake	Maryland	1982–RF
47	Sheryl Swoopes, Texas Tech	Ohio St.	1993–F
43	Barbara Kennedy, Clemson	Penn St.	1982–1st
40	LaTaunya Pollard, L. Beach St.	Howard	1982–1st
40	Cindy Brown, Long Beach St.	Ohio St.	1987–RF
39	Sheri Sam, Vanderbilt	Harvard	1996–1st
39	Kerry Bascom, Connecticut	Toledo	1991–2nd
39	Portia Hill, Stephen F. Austin	Arkansas	1990–RS
39	Delmonica DeHorney, Arkansas	Stanford	1990–RF
38	Connie Swift, Tenn. St.	Oregon St.	1995–1st

Most Rebounds—Career

No.	Player/School	Yrs.	Games	Avg.
170	Cheryl Miller, Southern Cal	4	16	10.6
162	Sheila Frost, Tennessee	4	18	9.0
161	Val Whiting, Stanford	4	16	10.1
148	Venus Lacy, Louisiana Tech	3	14	10.6
142	Bridgette Gordon, Tennessee	4	18	7.9
136	Kirsten Cummings, L.Beach St.	4	13	10.5
130	Nora Lewis, Louisiana Tech	3	14	9.3
127	Pam McGee, Southern Cal	3	13	9.8
125	Charlotte Smith, N.Carolina	4	12	10.4
125	Daedra Charles, Tennessee	3	13	9.6
125	Paula McGee, Southern Cal	3	13	9.6

Last year played: Charles (1991), Cummings (1985), Frost (1989), Gordon (1989), Lacy (1990), Lewis (1989), Miller (1986), Pam McGee (1984), Paula McGee (1984), Smith (1995), and Whiting (1993).

Most Rebounds—One Game

Included with the year of the game is the round it was played in the tournament: first round (1st); second round (2nd); regional semifinal (RS); and national final (F).

No.	Player/School	Opponent	Year
23	Cheryl Taylor, Tenn. Tech	Georgia	1985–1st
23	Charlotte Smith, Virginia	La. Tech	1994–F
22	Daedra Charles, Tennessee	SW Mo. St.	1991–2nd
21	Cherie Nelson, Southern Cal	Western Ky.	1987–2nd
20	Alison Long, Oregon	Missouri	1982–1st
20	Shelda Arceneaux, San Diego St.	Long Beach	1984–RS
20	Tracy Claxton, Old Dom.	Georgia	1985–F
20	Brigette Combs, Western Ky.	West Va.	1989–1st
20	Tandreia Green, Western Ky.	West Va.	1989–1st
19	Seven players tied.		

Best Scoring Average—One Tournament

Avg.	Player/School	Year	Games	Pts.	Avg.	Player/School	Year	Games	Pts.
36.7	Lorri Bauman, Drake	1982	3	110	27.5	Delmonica DeHorney, Arkansas	1990	4	110
35.4	Sheryl Swoopes, Texas Tech	1993	5	177	26.8	Bridgette Gordon, Tennessee	1989	5	134
28.3	Sheri Sam, Vanderbilt	1996	4	113	24.8	Penny Toler, Long Beach State	1988	4	99

Women's All-Time Career Leaders

NCAA Division I career leaders through the 1996–97 season, including regular season and postseason tournament games.

Most Points—NCAA Era
After 1981–82 season.

Pts.	Player/School	Gm.	Last Year
3,122	Patricia Hoskins, Miss. Valley State	110	1989
3,115	Lorri Bauman, Drake	120	1984
3,018	Cheryl Miller, Southern Cal	128	1986
2,944	Valorie Whiteside, Appalachian State	116	1988
2,906	Joyce Walker, Louisiana State	117	1984
2,860	Sandra Hodge, New Orleans	107	1984
2,796	Andrea Congreaves, Mercer	108	1993
2,746	Karen Pelphrey, Marshall	114	1986
2,696	Cindy Brown, Long Beach State	128	1987
2,655	Carolyn Thompson, Texas Tech	121	1984

Years played: 4 years each.

Most Points—Pre-NCAA Era
Before 1981–82 season.

Pts.	Player/School	Gm.	Last Year
3,649	Lynette Woodward, Kansas	139	1981
3,204	Cindy Brogdon, Mercer/Tennessee	128	1979
3,199	Carol Blazejowski, Montclair State.	101	1978
3,198	Denise Curry, UCLA	130	1981
3,137	Susie Snider Eppers, Baylor	123	1977
3,018	Susan Taylor, Valdosta State	128	1980
3,001	LaTaunya Pollard, Long Beach State	128	1983
2,986	Queen Brumfield, SE Louisiana	133	1979
2,981	Lusia Harris, Delta State	115	1977
2,979	Pam Kelly, Louisiana Tech	153	1982

Years played: 4 years each, except Eppers (3).

Best Rebound Average
Based on at least 800 rebounds, NCAA Era.

Avg.	Player/School
16.1	Wanda Ford, Drake
15.1	Patricia Hoskins, Miss. Valley St.
13.9	Tarcha Hollis, Grambling
13.4	Katie Beck, East Tennessee St.
13.0	Marilyn Stephens, Temple
12.8	Natalie Williams, UCLA
12.8	Cheryl Taylor Tennessee Tech
12.7	DeShawne Blocker, E. Tenn. St.
12.7	Olivia Bradley, West Virginia
12.6	Judy Mosley, Hawaii

Most Assists
NCAA Era.

No.	Player/School
1,307	Suzie McConnell, Penn State
1,165	Andrea Nagy, Florida Int'l
1,088	Tine Freil, Pacific
987	Shanya Evans, Providence
892	Nancy Kennelly, Northwestern
869	Neacole Hall, Alabama State
858	Teresa Weatherspoon, La. Tech
851	Stephany Raines, Mercer
833	Gaynor O'Donnell, E. Carolina
826	Tina Nicholson, Penn State

Cheryl Miller was tournament MVP in 1983 and 1984, and Southern Cal won the NCAA title both years.

Most Points—Single Game
NCAA Era.

No.	Player/School	No.	Player/School
60	Cindy Brown, Long Beach State vs. San Jose State (2/16/87)	55	Patricia Hoskins, Miss. Valley St vs. Southern U. (2/13/89)
58	Lorri Bauman, Drake vs. SW Missouri State (1/6/84)	55	Patricia Hoskins, Miss. Valley St vs. Alabama State (2/25/89)
58	Kim Perrot, SW Louisiana vs. SE Louisiana (2/5/90)	54	Three players tied.

PRO BASKETBALL
NBA Champions

All-Time Appearances in NBA Finals
Through 1996–97 season.

No.	Team	Record
24	Los Angeles Lakers	11-13
19	Boston Celtics	16-3
8	Philadelphia 76ers	3-5
7	New York Knicks	2-5
6	Golden State Warriors	3-3
5	Chicago Bulls	5-0
5	Detroit Pistons	2-3
4	Houston Rockets	2-2
4	Atlanta Hawks	1-3
4	Washington Wizards	1-3
3	Portland Trail Blazers	1-2
3	Seattle SuperSonics	1-2
2	Milwaukee Bucks	1-1
2	Phoenix Suns	0-2
1	Baltimore Bullets	1-0
1	Sacramento Kings	1-0
1	Chicago Stags (folded 1950)	0-1
1	Orlando Magic	0-1
1	Utah Jazz	0-1
1	Washington Capitols	0-1

Note: The Baltimore Bullets folded in 1955 and the Washington Capitols in 1951.

Most Titles Won
Only 15 franchises have won the NBA Finals since 1947.

No.	Team	Championship Years	Playoff Berths	Record
16	Boston Celtics	1986, 1984, 1981, 1976, 1974, 1969, 1968, 1959-66, 1957	41	272-189
11	Los Angeles Lakers	1988, 1987, 1985, 1982, 1980, 1972, 1952-54, 1950, 1949	45	305-211
5	Chicago Bulls	1997, 1996, 1991-93	23	132-100
3	Golden State Warriors	1975, 1956, 1947	27	99-115
3	Philadelphia 76ers	1983, 1967, 1955	37	175-153
2	Detroit Pistons	1990, 1989	30	113-111
2	Houston Rockets	1995, 1994	19	97-93
2	New York Knicks	1973, 1970	33	152-147
1	Baltimore Bullets	1948	3	9-7
1	Milwaukee Bucks	1971	19	85-84
1	Portland Trail Blazers	1977	20	70-78
1	Sacramento Kings	1951	21	46-72
1	Atlanta Hawks	1958	34	113-143
1	Seattle SuperSonics	1979	18	93-93
1	Washington Wizards	1978	21	69-97

Franchise Moves & Name Changes: •Lakers—Minneapolis (5 titles), Los Angeles (6 titles); •Warriors—Philadelphia (2 titles), San Francisco (0 titles), Oakland (1 title); •76ers—as Syracuse Nationals (1 title), as Philadelphia 76ers (2 titles); •Pistons—Ft. Wayne, Ind. (0 titles), Detroit (2 titles); •Rockets—San Diego (0 titles), Houston (2 titles); •Kings—as Rochester Royals (1 title), as Cincinnati Royals, Kansas City-Omaha Kings, Kansas City Kings, and Sacramento Kings (0 titles); •Hawks—Tri-Cities and Milwaukee (0 titles), St. Louis (1 title), Atlanta (0 titles); •Wizards—as Chicago Packers and Zephyrs (0 titles), as Baltimore and Capital Bullets (0 titles), as Washington Bullets (1 title). Bullets changed name to Wizards after 1996–97 season.

Extra Point
The Basketball Association of America (BAA) merged with its rival, the National Basketball League, following the 1948–49 season to form the National Basketball Association. The champions and league records of the 1946–47 and 1947–48 BAA seasons are considered official by the NBA.

From left, Michael Jordan, Bill Cartwright, and Scottie Pippen with three of the Chicago Bulls' five NBA trophies. The Bulls won three straight NBA titles (1991–93) and added two more in 1996 and 1997.

Four-Game Sweeps in the NBA Finals
Listed with margins of victory in each game.

Year	Winner/Loser	Margins
1959	Boston Celtics over Minneapolis	3, 20, 13, 5
1971	Milwaukee Bucks over Baltimore	10, 19, 8,12
1975	Golden St. Warriors over Washington	6, 1, 8, 1
1983	Philadelphia 76ers over L.A. Lakers	6, 10, 17, 7
1989	Detroit Pistons over L.A. Lakers	12, 3, 4, 8
1995	Houston Rockets over Orlando	2, 11, 3, 12

Most Championships—Players

No.	Player/Team	No.	Player/Team
11	Bill Russell, Celtics	7	Jim Loscutoff, Celtics
10	Sam Jones, Celtics	7	Frank Ramsey, Celtics
8	John Havlicek, Celtics	6	Kareem Abdul-Jabbar, Bucks and Lakers
8	Tom Heinsohn, Celtics		
8	K.C. Jones, Celtics	6	Bob Cousy, Celtics
8	Tom Sanders, Celtics		

Most Championships—Coaches

No.	Coach/Team	No.	Coach/Team
9	Red Auerbach, Celtics	2	Tom Heinsohn, Celtics
5	Phil Jackson, Bulls	2	Red Holzman, Knicks
5	John Kundla, Lakers	2	K.C. Jones, Celtics
4	Pat Riley, Lakers	2	Bill Russell, Celtics
2	Chuck Daly, Pistons	2	Rudy Tomjanovich, Rockets
2	Alex Hannum, Hawks and 76ers		

Note: Alex Hannum is the only head coach in league history to win NBA championships with two different franchises—the St. Louis Hawks (1958) and the Philadelphia 76ers (1967).

Most Points

Series	Pts.	Player/Team/Opponent	Year
4-Gm	131	Hakeem Olajuwon, Houston vs. Orlando	1995
5-Gm	169	Jerry West, L.A. Lakers vs. Boston	1965
6-Gm	245	Michael Jordan, Chicago vs. Phoenix	1993
7-Gm	284	Elgin Baylor, L.A. Lakers vs. Boston	1962

Most Assists

Series	No.	Player/Team/Opponent	Year
4-Gm	51	Bob Cousy, Boston vs. Minneapolis	1959
5-Gm	62	Magic Johnson, L.A. Lakers vs. Chicago	1991
6-Gm	84	Magic Johnson, L.A. Lakers vs. Boston	1985
7-Gm	95	Magic Johnson, L.A. Lakers vs. Boston	1984

Most Rebounds

Series	No.	Player/Team/Opponent	Year
4-Gm	118	Bill Russell, Boston vs. Minneapolis	1959
5-Gm	144	Bill Russell, Boston vs. St. Louis	1961
6-Gm	171	Wilt Chamberlain, Phila. vs. San Fran.	1967
7-Gm	189	Bill Russell, Boston vs. L.A. Lakers	1962

Most Steals
Compiled by the NBA since 1974.

Series	No.	Player/Team/Opponent	Year
4-Gm	14	Rick Barry, Golden St. vs. Washington	1975
5-Gm	14	Michael Jordan, Chi. vs. L.A. Lakers	1991
6-Gm	16	Julius Erving, Philadelphia vs. Portland	1977
	16	Magic Johnson, L.A. Lakers vs. Phila.	1980
	16	Larry Bird, Boston vs. Houston	1986
7-Gm	20	Isiah Thomas, Detroit vs. L.A. Lakers	1988

Most 3-Point Field Goals

Series	No.	Player/Team/Opponent	Year
4-Gm	11	Penny Hardaway, Orlando vs. Houston	1995
	11	Robert Horry, Houston vs. Orlando	1995
5-Gm	11	Isiah Thomas, Detroit vs. Portland	1990
6-Gm	17	Dan Marjerle, Phoenix vs. Chicago	1993
7-Gm	17	Derek Harper, New York vs. Houston	1994

Most Points in a Single Game

No.	Player/Team/Opponent	Finals	Year
61	Elgin Baylor, L.A. Lakers vs.Boston	Gm. 5	1962
55	Rick Barry, San Francisco vs. Philadelphia	Gm. 3	1967
55	Michael Jordan, Chicago vs. Phoenix	Gm. 4	1993

Playoff Career Leaders

Listed with number of appearances in playoffs (Years); asterisks (*) indicate players and teams that played in 1997 postseason.

Most Points

Points	Player	Yrs.	Gm.	Avg.
5,762	Kareem Abdul-Jabbar	18	237	24.3
5,307	Michael Jordan*	12	158	33.6
4,457	Jerry West	13	153	29.1
3,897	Larry Bird	12	164	23.8
3,776	John Havlicek	13	172	22.0
3,701	Magic Johnson	13	190	19.5
3,623	Elgin Baylor	12	134	27.0
3,607	Wilt Chamberlain	13	160	22.5
3,572	Hakeem Olajuwon*	12	131	27.3
3,182	Kevin McHale	13	169	18.8
3,165	Karl Malone*	12	117	27.1
3,116	Dennis Johnson	13	180	17.3
3,088	Julius Erving	11	141	21.9
3,022	James Worthy	9	143	21.1
2,909	Sam Jones	12	154	18.9

Highest Scoring Average

Based on at least 25 games or 700 points.

Avg.	Player	Yrs.	Gm.	Points
33.6	Michael Jordan*	12	158	5,307
29.1	Jerry West	13	153	4,457
27.3	Hakeem Olajuwon*	12	131	3,572
27.1	Karl Malone*	12	117	3,165
27.0	Elgin Baylor	12	134	3,623
27.0	George Gervin	9	59	1,592
25.8	Dominique Wilkins	9	55	1,421
25.5	Bob Pettit	9	88	2,240
25.6	Shaquille O'Neal*	4	45	1,153
24.8	Rick Barry	7	74	1,833
24.7	Reggie Miller	7	49	1,211
24.5	Bernard King	5	28	687
24.4	Alex English	10	68	1,661
24.3	Kareem Abdul-Jabbar	18	237	5,762
24.2	Paul Arizin	8	49	1,186

Best Field Goal Percentage

Based on at least 150 made.

Pct.	Player
.627	James Donaldson
.612	Bob Davies
.580	Otis Thorpe*
.574	Mark West
.574	Kurt Rambis
.568	Artis Gilmore
.567	Shaquille O'Neal*
.561	Kevin McHale
.559	Bernard King
.550	Horace Grant#
.546	Darryl Dawkins
.545	Cedric Maxwell

Active but did not play in the 1997 playoffs.

Best 3-Point Field Goal Percentage

Based on at least 45 made.

Pct.	Player
.500	Bobby Hansen
.454	B.J. Armstrong
.448	Kenny Smith
.436	Reggie Miller
.434	Jeff Hornacek*
.417	Trent Tucker
.409	Mario Elie*
.404	Chuck Person
.397	Danny Ainge
.396	Byron Scott
.395	Steve Smith*
.390	Penny Hardaway

Best Free Throw Percentage

Pct.	Player
.944	Mark Price
.932	Calvin Murphy
.916	Hersey Hawkins*
.911	Bill Sharman
.907	Kiki Vanderweghe
.897	Jeff Hornacek*
.890	Larry Bird
.889	Vince Boryla
.880	Bobby Wanzer
.875	Rick Barry
.869	Rolando Blackman
.866	Ricky Pierce*

Most Assists

No.	Player
2,346	Magic Johnson
1,366	John Stockton*
1,062	Larry Bird
1,006	Dennis Johnson
987	Isiah Thomas
970	Jerry West
948	Michael Jordan*
937	Bob Cousy
922	Maurice Cheeks
893	Kevin Johnson*
868	Clyde Drexler*
825	John Havlicek

Most Rebounds

No.	Player
4,104	Bill Russell
3,913	Wilt Chamberlain
2,481	K. Abdul-Jabbar
1,777	Wes Unseld
1,765	Robert Parish*
1,724	Elgin Baylor
1,683	Larry Bird
1,527	Paul Silas
1,519	Hakeem Olajuwon*
1,506	Charles Barkley*
1,465	Magic Johnson
1,428	Dennis Rodman*
1,339	Karl Malone*
1,305	Bill Bridges

Most Games

No.	Player
237	Kareem Abdul-Jabbar
193	Danny Ainge
190	Magic Johnson
184	Robert Parish*
183	Byron Scott*
180	Dennis Johnson
172	John Havlicek
169	Kevin McHale
168	Michael Cooper
165	Bill Russell
164	Larry Bird
163	Paul Silas
160	Wilt Chamberlain
158	Michael Jordan*

Kareem Abdul-Jabbar, 1988. He set all-time NBA records for points scored in the playoffs and regular season before he retired in 1989.

Most Steals

No.	Player
358	Magic Johnson
344	Michael Jordan*
299	Scottie Pippen*
296	Larry Bird
295	Maurice Cheeks
270	Clyde Drexler*
247	Dennis Johnson
247	John Stockton*
235	Julius Irving
234	Isiah Thomas
228	Hakeem Olajuwon*
226	Byron Scott*

Most Blocked Shots

No.	Player
476	Kareem Abdul-Jabbar
449	Hakeem Olajuwon*
309	Robert Parish*
281	Kevin McHale
266	Patrick Ewing*
239	Julius Erving
223	Caldwell Jones
222	Elvin Hayes
210	Mark Eaton
165	Darryl Dawkins
165	David Robinson
153	John Salley

Most Personal Fouls

No.	Player
797	Kareem Abdul-Jabbar
617	Robert Parish*
575	Dennis Johnson
571	Kevin McHale
546	Bill Russell
542	Dennis Rodman*
533	Danny Ainge
527	John Havlicek
524	Magic Johnson
523	Scottie Pippen*
508	Tom Sanders
474	Michael Cooper

Most Years—Players

Yrs.	Player
18	Kareem Abdul-Jabbar
16	Robert Parish*
15	Tree Rollins
15	Dolph Schayes
14	Clyde Drexler*
14	Paul Silas

Most Years—Teams

Yrs.	Team
45	Los Angeles Lakers*
41	Boston Celtics
37	Philadelphia 76ers
34	Atlanta Hawks*
32	New York Knicks*
30	Detroit Pistons*
27	Golden State Warriors
21	Sacramento Kings
21	Washington Wizards*

Note: Includes all cities each franchise has represented.

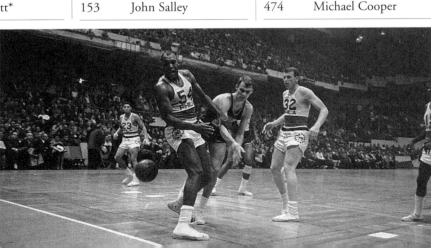

During a game in 1965, Warriors' Rick Berry (right) knocks the ball out of 76ers Lucious Jackson's hands.

Playoff Single-Season Leaders

Jerry West of the Los Angeles Lakers (left), the only player to average more than 40 points a game in a single season of the NBA playoffs.

Best Records

Pct.	Team	Record	Rounds	Year
.923	Philadelphia 76ers	12-1	3	1983
.882	Detroit Pistons	15-2	4	1989
.882	Chicago Bulls	15-2	4	1991
.857	Milwaukee Bucks	12-2	3	1971
.857	Los Angeles Lakers	12-2	3	1982
.833	Minneapolis Lakers	10-2	4	1950
.833	Boston Celtics	15-3	4	1986
.833	Los Angeles Lakers	15-3	4	1987
.833	Chicago Bulls	15-3	4	1996

Best Field Goal Percentage
Based on at least 40 field goals made; listed with attempts.

Pct.	Player/Team	Year	Gm.	FG/Att.
.654	James Donaldson, Dallas	1988	17	68/104
.652	Kurt Rambis, L.A. Lakers	1984	21	60/92
.641	Alton Lister, Milwaukee	1986	14	66/103
.635	Otis Thorpe, Houston	1993	12	73/115
.634	Cedric Maxwell, Boston	1980	9	59/93

Highest Scoring Average
Based on at least 8 games played.

Avg.	Player/Team	Year	Gm.	Pts
40.6	Jerry West, L.A. Lakers	1965	11	447
38.6	Elgin Baylor, L.A. Lakers	1962	13	502
38.1	Elgin Baylor, L.A. Lakers	1961	12	457
36.7	Michael Jordan, Chicago	1990	16	587
36.3	Michael Jordan, Chicago	1988	10	363

Best 3-Point Field Goal Percentage
Based on at least 5 three-point field goals made; listed with attempts.

Pct.	Player/Team	Year	Gm.	FG/Att.
.857	Muggsy Bogues, Charlotte	1997	2	6/7
.750	Ricky Pierce, Milwaukee	1989	9	6/8
.714	Anthony Bowie, Orlando	1995	17	5/7
.692	Chris Mullin, Golden State	1991	8	9/13
.667	Brad Davis, Dallas	1986	10	10/15

Most Rebounds Per Game
Based on at least 8 games played.

Avg.	Player/Team	Year	Gm.	No.
29.9	Bill Russell, Boston	1961	10	299
29.1	Wilt Chamberlain, Phila.	1967	15	437
27.7	Bill Russell, Boston	1959	11	305
27.2	Bill Russell, Boston	1964	10	272
27.2	Wilt Chamberlain, San Fran.	1965	11	299

Best Free Throw Percentage
Based on at least 20 free throws made; listed with attempts.

Pct.	Player/Team	Year	Gm.	FT/Att.
1.000	Kiki Vandeweghe, Port.	1986	4	32/32
1.000	Mark Price, Cleveland	1990	5	30/30
.980	Jack Sikma, Milwaukee	1987	12	48/49
.970	Mark Price, Cleveland	1995	4	32/33

Most Assists Per Game
Based on at least 8 games played.

Avg.	Player/Team	Year	Gm.	No.
15.2	Magic Johnson, L.A. Lakers	1985	19	289
15.1	Magic Johnson, L.A. Lakers	1986	14	211
14.8	John Stockton, Utah	1988	11	163
14.6	Johnny Moore, San Antonio	1983	11	161

Playoff Single-Game Leaders

Most Assists

No.	Player/Game/Date
24	Magic Johnson, L.A. Lakers vs. Phoenix (5/15/84)
24	John Stockton, Utah vs. L.A. Lakers (5/17/88)
23	Magic Johnson, L.A. Lakers vs. Portland (5/3/85)
23	John Stockton, Utah vs. Portland (4/25/96)
22	Doc Rivers, Atlanta vs. Boston (5/16/88)

Most Rebounds

No.	Player/Game/Date
41	Wilt Chamberlain, Philadelphia vs. Boston (4/5/67)
40	Bill Russell, Boston vs. Philadelphia (3/23/58)
40	Bill Russell, Boston vs. St. Louis (3/29/60)
40	Bill Russell, Boston vs. L.A. Lakers, OT (4/18/62)
39	Three-way tie between Russell (twice) and Chamberlain (once).

Most Field Goals
Listed with attempts.

FG/Att.	Player/Game/Date
24/36	John Havlicek, Boston vs. Atlanta (4/1/73)
24/42	Wilt Chamberlain, Philadelphia vs. Syracuse (3/14/60)
24/45	Michael Jordan, Chicago vs. Cleveland (5/1/88)
23/31	Charles Barkley, Phoenix vs. Golden St. (5/4/94)

Most Free Throws
Listed with attempts

FT/Att.	Player/Game/Date
30/32	Bob Cousy, Boston vs. Syracuse, 4OT (3/21/53)
23/28	Michael Jordan, Chicago vs. New York (5/14/89)
22/27	Michael Jordan, Chicago vs. Cleveland, OT (5/5/89)
22/24	Karl Malone, Utah vs. L.A. Clippers (5/3/92)

Most 3-Point Field Goals
Listed with attempts

FG/Att.	Player/Game/Date
9/17	Rex Chapman, Phoenix vs. Seattle (4/25/97)
8/10	Dan Majerle, Phoenix vs. Seattle (6/1/93)
7	Ten players tied.

Most Steals

No.	Player/Game/Date
8	Ricky Barry, Golden State vs. Seattle (4/14/75)
8	Lionel Hollins, Portland vs. L.A. Lakers (5/8/77)
8	Maurice Cheeks, Philadelphia vs. New Jersey (4/11/79)
8	Craig Hodges, Milwaukee vs. Philadelphia (5/9/86)
8	Tim Hardaway, Golden State vs. L.A. Lakers (5/8/91)
8	Tim Hardaway, Golden State vs. Seattle (4/30/92)
8	Mookie Blaylock, Atlanta vs. Indiana (4/29/96)

Most Points

Pts.	Player/Team	Opponent	Date
63	Michael Jordan, Chicago	vs. Boston, 2OT	4/20/86
61	Elgin Baylor, L.A. Lakers	vs. Boston	4/14/62
56	Wilt Chamberlain, Phila.	vs. Syracuse	3/22/62
56	Michael Jordan,* Chicago	vs. Miami	4/29/92
56	Charles Barkley,* Phoenix	vs. Golden State	5/4/94
55	Rick Barry, San Francisco	vs. Phila.	4/18/67
55	Michael Jordan, Chicago	vs. Cleveland	5/1/88
55	Michael Jordan,* Chicago	vs. Phoenix	6/16/93
55	Michael Jordan,* Chicago	vs. Wash.	4/27/97
54	John Havlicek, Boston	vs. Atlanta	4/1/73
54	Michael Jordan,* Chicago	vs. New York	5/31/93
53	Wilt Chamberlain, Phila.	vs. Syracuse	3/14/60
53	Jerry West, L.A. Lakers	vs. Boston	4/23/69
53	Jerry West, L.A. Lakers	vs. Baltimore	4/5/65

* High scorers since 1990.

The Lakers' Elgin Baylor scored 61 points against Boston in Game 5 of the 1962 NBA Finals, setting a record that stood for almost a quarter century (24 years and 6 days).

Best Teams by Decade

Winningest NBA Teams of the 1990s

Through the 1996-97 season.

	Team	Regular Season		Playoff
		Record	Pct.	Record
1	Chicago Bulls	483-173	.736	96-35
2	Utah Jazz	443-213	.675	50-44
3	Seattle SuperSonics	425-231	.648	38-37
4	Phoenix Suns	420-236	.640	42-39
5	Portland Trail Blazers	414-242	.631	39-39
6	New York Knicks	411-245	.627	49-45
7	San Antonio Spurs	403-253	.614	27-29
8	Houston Rockets	400-256	.610	49-39
9	Los Angeles Lakers	393-263	.599	29-31
10	Atlanta Hawks	366-290	.558	15-27

NBA champions: Detroit Pistons (1990); Chicago (1991); Chicago (1992); Chicago (1993); Houston (1994); Houston (1995); Chicago (1996); Chicago (1997).

Winningest NBA Teams of the 1980s

	Team	Regular Season		Playoff
		Record	Pct.	Record
1	Boston Celtics	592-228	.722	91-59
2	Los Angeles Lakers	591-229	.721	111-48
3	Philadelphia 76ers	535-285	.652	63-43
4	Milwaukee Bucks	522-298	.637	42-51
5	Atlanta Hawks	449-371	.548	20-30
6	Portland Trail Blazers	442-378	.539	14-28
7	Phoenix Suns	439-381	.535	25-32
8	Denver Nuggets	430-390	.524	24-34
9	Seattle SuperSonics	424-396	.517	24-33
10	Detroit Pistons	423-397	.516	47-26

NBA champions: L.A. Lakers (1980); Boston (1981); L.A. Lakers; Philadelphia (1983); Boston (1984); L.A. Lakers (1985); Boston (1986); L.A. Lakers (1987); L.A. Lakers (1988); Detroit (1989).

Winningest NBA Teams of the 1970s

	Team	Regular Season		Playoff
		Record	Pct.	Record
1	Milwaukee Bucks	492-328	.600	42-27
2	Los Angeles Lakers	485-335	.591	46-43
3	Washington Bullets	483-337	.589	55-61
	Denver Nuggets	145-101	.589	9-13
5	San Antonio Spurs	144-102	.585	9-13
6	Boston Celtics	477-343	.582	47-33
7	New York Knicks	458-362	.559	48-37
8	Golden St. Warriors	447-373	.545	31-30
9	Chicago Bulls	438-382	.534	19-31
10	Phoenix Suns	411-409	.501	22-21

NBA champions: New York (1970); Milwaukee (1971); L.A. Lakers (1972); New York (1973); Boston (1974); Golden State (1975); Boston (1976); Portland Trail Blazers (1977); Washington (1978); Seattle SuperSonics (1979).

Note: Denver and San Antonio, along with the Indiana Pacers and the New Jersey Nets, were the four American Basketball Association teams that joined the NBA when the ABA folded, after the 1975–76.

How dominant were Bill Russell (left), Red Auerbach, and the Boston Celtics in the 1960s? They won 85 more regular season games and 28 more playoff games than any other team and captured 9 out of 10 NBA championships.

Winningest NBA Teams of the 1960s

	Team	Regular Season		Playoff
		Record	Pct.	Record
1	Boston Celtics	571-228	.715	87-48
2	Philadelphia 76ers	486-313	.608	37-38
3	Los Angeles Lakers	447-352	.559	59-54
4	Atlanta Hawks	444-355	.556	43-46
5	Cincinnati Royals	404-395	.506	15-24
6	San Fran. Warriors	403-396	.504	30-37
7	Baltimore Bullets	262-383	.406	5-12
8	New York Knicks	314-485	.392	9-11
9	Detroit Pistons	313-486	.392	10-17
10	Chicago Bulls	95-150	.388	1-7

NBA champions: Boston nine times (1960-66, 1968, and 1969) and Philadelphia once (1967).

Franchise moves (5): • Minneapolis Lakers to Los Angeles after the 1959-60 season; • Philadelphia Warriors to San Francisco after the 1961-62 season; • Chicago Zephyrs to Baltimore and renamed the Bullets after the 1962-63 season; • Syracuse Nationals to Philadelphia and renamed the 76ers after the 1962-63 season; • St. Louis Hawks to Atlanta after the 1967-68 season.

Winningest NBA Teams of the 1950s

	Team	Regular Season		Playoff
		Record	Pct.	Record
1	Syracuse Nationals	404-295	.578	41-35
2	Boston Celtics	408-298	.578	31-28
3	New York Knicks	388-314	.553	26-27
4	Minneapolis Lakers	388-316	.551	52-33
5	Rochester Royals	364-340	.517	17-19
6	Ft. Wayne Pistons	352-351	.501	21-33
7	Indianapolis Olympians	132-137	.491	4-9
8	Philadelphia Warriors	324-377	.460	11-16
9	St. Louis Hawks	302-399	.431	21-17
10	Baltimore Bullets	104-252	.292	0-2

NBA champions:Minneapolis (1950); Rochester (1951); Minneapolis (1952); Minneapolis (1953); Minneapolis (1954); Syracuse (1955); Philadelphia (1956); Boston (1957); St. Louis (1958); Boston (1959).

Franchise moves (4): •Tri-Cities Blackhawks became the Milwaukee Hawks after the 1950-51 season then moved to St. Louis after the 1954-55 season; •Ft. Wayne (Ind.) Pistons moved to Detroit after the 1956-57 season; •Rochester Royals moved to Cincinnati after the 1956-57 season.

Franchise failures (8): •Indianapolis after the 1952-53 season; • Baltimore after 14 games in the 1954-55 season; and the •Anderson Packers (37-27); •Chicago Stags (40-28); •Denver Nuggets (11-51); •St. Louis Bombers (26-42); •Sheboygan Redskins (22-40); •Waterloo Hawks (19-43) after the 1949-50 season.

George Mikan (99) was pro basketball's first big man at 6 feet 10 1/2 inches and the reason the Minneapolis Lakers won four NBA titles in the 1950s. He later became the first commissioner of the ABA.

Winningest ABA Teams (1968–76)

	Team	Regular Season		Playoff
		Record	Pct.	Record
1	Kentucky Colonels	448-296	.602	55-46
2	Indiana Pacers	427-317	.574	69-50
3	Denver Nuggets	413-331	.555	27-35
4	Utah Stars	366-310	.541	46-34
5	San Antonio Spurs	378-366	.508	17-32
6	New York Nets	374-370	.503	37-32
7	Spirits of St. Louis	334-410	.449	12-21
8	Miami Floridians	189-219	.463	11-21
9	Virginia Squires	326-417	.439	30-26
10	Pittsburgh Condors	180-228	.441	14-8

ABA champions: Pittsburgh Pipers (1968); Oakland Oaks (1969); Indiana (1970); Utah (1971); Indiana (1971); Indiana (1973); New York (1974); Kentucky (1975); New York (1976).

Franchise moves and name changes: •Denver—from Rockets to Nuggets after the 1973-74 season; •Miami—originally Minnesota Muskies became the Miami Floridians after the 1967-68 season, The Floridians after the 1969-70 season, and folded in 1972; •New York— originally New Jersey Americans became the New York Nets after the 1967-68 season; •Pittsburgh—originally Pittsburgh Pipers became the Minnesota Pipers after the 1968-69 season, the Pittsburgh Condors after the 1969-70 season, and folded in 1972; •St. Louis—originally Houston Mavericks became the Carolina Cougars after the 1968-69 season and the Spirits of St. Louis after the 1973-74 season; •San Antonio—originally Dallas Chaparrals became the Texas Chaparrals after the 1971-72 season and the San Antonio Spurs after the 1972-73 season; •Utah—originally Anaheim Amigos became the Los Angeles Stars after the 1967-68 season, moved to Salt Lake City after the 1969-70 season, and folded after 16 games in 1975-76 season; •Virginia—original Oakland Oaks became the Washington Capitols after the 1968-69 season and the Virginia Squires after the 1969-70 season.

All-Time Career Leaders

NBA regular-season career leaders through the 1996-97 season; asterisks (*) indicate players active in 1996–97.

Most Points
NBA games only.

Points	Player	Yrs.	Games	Last Year
38,387	Kareem Abdul-Jabbar	20	1,560	1989
31,419	Wilt Chamberlain	14	1,045	1973
27,409	Moses Malone	19	1,329	1995
27,313	Elvin Hayes	16	1,303	1984
26,920	Michael Jordan*	12	848	active
26,710	Oscar Robertson	14	1,040	1974
26,534	Dominique Wilkins*	14	1,047	active
26,395	John Havlicek	16	1,270	1978
25,613	Alex English	15	1,193	1991
25,592	Karl Malone*	12	980	active
25,192	Jerry West	14	932	1974
23,650	Hakeem Olajuwon*	13	978	active
23,334	Robert Parish*	21	1,568	active
23,177	Adrian Dantley	15	955	1991
23,149	Elgin Baylor	14	846	1972

Highest Scoring Average
Based on at least 400 games or 12,000 points; NBA games only.

Avg.	Player	Yrs.	Games	Last Year
31.7	Michael Jordan*	12	848	active
30.1	Wilt Chamberlain	14	1,045	1973
27.4	Elgin Baylor	14	846	1972
27.0	Jerry West	14	932	1974
26.4	Bob Pettit	11	792	1965
26.2	George Gervin	10	791	1986
26.1	Karl Malone*	12	980	active
25.7	Oscar Robertson	14	1,040	1974
25.5	David Robinson*	8	563	active
25.3	Dominique Wilkins*	14	1,047	active
24.6	Kareem Abdul-Jabbar	20	1,560	1989
24.3	Larry Bird	13	897	1992
24.3	Adrian Dantley	15	955	1991
24.2	Pete Maravich	10	658	1980
24.2	Hakeem Olajuwon*	13	978	active

Most Seasons

No.	Player
21	Robert Parish*
20	Kareem Abdul-Jabbar
19	James Edwards
19	Moses Malone
18	Tree Rollins
16	John Havlicek
16	Elvin Hayes
16	Rick Mahorn*
16	Danny Schayes*
16	Dolph Schayes
16	Paul Silas
16	Buck Williams*
16	Herb Williams*

Most Games

No.	Player
1,611	Robert Parish*
1,560	Kareem Abdul-Jabbar
1,329	Moses Malone
1,303	Elvin Hayes
1,270	John Havlicek
1,266	Buck Williams*
1,254	Paul Silas
1,193	Alex English
1,168	James Edwards
1,156	Tree Rollins
1,122	Hal Greer
1,107	Jack Sikma

Most Consecutive Games

No.	Player
906	Randy Smith
896	A.C. Green*
844	Johnny Kerr
706	Dolph Schayes
685	Bill Laimbeer
682	Harry Gallatin
657	Michael Cage*
609	Jack Twyman
609	John Stockton*
586	James Donladson
574	Terry Tyler
542	Otis Thorpe

Most Rebounds

No.	Player
23,924	Wilt Chamberlain
21,620	Bill Russell
17,440	Kareem Abdul-Jabbar
16,279	Elvin Hayes
16,212	Moses Malone
14,715	Robert Parish*
14,464	Nate Thurmond
14,241	Walt Bellamy
13,769	Wes Unseld
12,942	Jerry Lucas
12,849	Bob Pettit
12,834	Buck Williams*
12,357	Paul Silas
11,739	Hakeem Olajuwon*

Combined NBA-ABA Career Points

Including service in American Basketball Assn. (1968-76).

Points	Player	Yrs.	Avg.	Last Year
38,387	Kareem Abdul-Jabbar	20	24.6	1989
31,419	Wilt Chamberlain	14	30.1	1973
30,026	Julius Erving#	16	24.2	1987
29,580	Moses Malone#	21	20.3	1995
27,482	Dan Issel#	15	22.6	1985
27,313	Elvin Hayes	16	21.0	1984
26,920	Michael Jordan*	12	31.7	active
26,710	Oscar Robertson	14	25.7	1974
26,595	George Gervin#	14	25.1	1986
26,534	Dominique Wilkins*	14	25.3	active
26,395	John Havlicek	16	20.8	1978
25,613	Alex English	15	21.5	1991
25,592	Karl Malone*	12	26.1	active
25,279	Rick Barry#	14	24.8	1980
25,192	Jerry West	14	27.0	1974
24,941	Artis Gilmore#	17	18.8	1988

#Active in both ABA and NBA.
Years in ABA: Issel (6); Erving and Gilmore (5); Barry and Gervin (4); M. Malone (2).
Scoring championships: NBA—Jordan (9), Chamberlain (7), Gervin (4), Abdul-Jabbar (3); ABA—Erving (3), Barry and Issel (1).

Archrivals and all-time NBA rebound leaders Wilt Chamberlain (left) and Bill Russell.

Most Assists

No.	Player
12,170	John Stockton*
10,141	Magic Johnson
9,887	Oscar Robertson
9,061	Isiah Thomas
7,392	Maurice Cheeks
7,211	Lenny Wilkens
6,955	Bob Cousy
6,917	Guy Rodgers
6,825	Mark Jackson*
6,476	Nate Archibald
6,454	John Lucas
6,453	Reggie Theus

Most Field Goals

No.	Player
15,837	Kareem Abdul-Jabbar
12,681	Wilt Chamberlain
10,976	Elvin Hayes
10,659	Alex English
10,513	John Havlicek
10,081	Michael Jordan*
9,913	Dominique Wilkins*
9,614	Robert Parish*
9,510	Karl Malone*
9,508	Oscar Robertson
9,435	Moses Malone
9,400	Hakeem Olajuwon*

Most Free Throws

No.	Player
8,531	Moses Malone
7,694	Oscar Robertson
7,160	Jerry West
6,979	Dolph Schayes
6,832	Adrian Dantley
6,712	Kareem Abdul-Jabbar
6,505	Karl Malone*
6,233	Michael Jordan*
6,182	Bob Pettit
6,057	Wilt Chamberlain
5,790	Charles Barkley*
5,763	Elgin Baylor

Most Steals

Compiled since 1973–74.

No.	Player
2,531	John Stockton*
2,310	Maurice Cheeks
2,165	Michael Jordan*
2,112	Alvin Robertson
2,081	Clyde Drexler*
1,861	Isiah Thomas
1,841	Derek Harper*
1,811	Hakeem Olajuwon*
1,724	Magic Johnson
1,692	Scottie Pippen*
1,666	Fat Lever
1,638	Gus Williams

All-Time All-Stars

Center Kareem Abdul-Jabbar is one of five players who have been named to the All-NBA First Team 10 times. The other four are forwards Elgin Baylor and Bob Pettit, and guards Bob Cousy and Jerry West. Nine-time honorees include forwards Larry Bird and Karl Malone, and guards Magic Johnson, Michael Jordan and Oscar Robertson.

Current Career Leaders

Active NBA regular season career leaders through the 1996–97 season.

Most Points

Points	Player	Yrs.	Games	Avg.	First Year
26,920	Michael Jordan	12	848	31.7	1985
26,534	Dominique Wilkins	14	1,047	25.3	1983
25,592	Karl Malone	12	980	26.1	1986
23,650	Hakeem Olajuwon	13	978	24.2	1985
23,334	Robert Parish	21	1,611	14.5	1977
21,756	Charles Barkley	13	943	23.1	1985
21,539	Patrick Ewing	12	913	23.6	1986
20,908	Clyde Drexler	14	1,016	20.6	1984
18,557	Eddie Johnson	15	1,121	16.6	1982
18,355	Terry Cummings	15	1,037	17.7	1983
17,397	Dale Ellis	14	1,040	16.7	1984
16,582	Buck Williams	16	1,266	13.1	1982
16,120	Chris Mullin	12	787	20.5	1986
15,877	Otis Thorpe	13	1,034	15.4	1985
15,824	Reggie Miller	10	801	19.8	1988

Highest Scoring Average

Based on at least 225 games or 4,500 points.

Avg.	Player	Yrs.	Games	Points	First Year
31.7	Michael Jordan	12	848	26,920	1985
27.0	Shaquille O'Neal	5	346	9,355	1993
26.1	Karl Malone	12	980	25,592	1986
25.5	David Robinson	8	563	14,366	1990
25.3	Dominique Wilkins	14	1,047	26,534	1983
24.2	Hakeem Olajuwon	13	978	23,650	1985
23.6	Patrick Ewing	12	913	21,539	1986
23.1	Mitch Richmond	9	681	15,748	1989
23.1	Charles Barkley	13	943	21,756	1985
21.1	Glenn Robinson	3	242	5,104	1995
20.6	Clyde Drexler	14	1,016	20,908	1984
20.6	Glen Rice	8	636	13,073	1990
20.5	Grant Hill	3	230	4,722	1995
20.5	Chris Mullin	12	787	16,120	1986
20.0	Latrell Sprewell	5	386	7,733	1993

Most Seasons

No.	Player
21	Robert Parish
16	Rick Mahorn
16	Danny Schayes
16	Buck Williams
16	Herb Williams
15	Terry Cummings
15	Eddie Johnson
15	Ricky Pierce
14	Clyde Drexler
14	Dale Ellis
14	Derek Harper
14	Byron Scott
14	Dominique Wilkins

Most Games

No.	Player
1,611	Robert Parish
1,266	Buck Williams
1,121	Eddie Johnson
1,088	Derek Harper
1,073	Byron Scott
1,069	Herb Williams
1,047	Dominique Wilkins
1,045	Danny Schayes
1,042	Rick Mahorn
1,040	Dale Ellis
1,037	Terry Cummings
1,034	Otis Thorpe

Most Personal Fouls

No.	Player
4,443	Robert Parish
4,174	Buck Williams
3,695	Hakeem Olajuwon
3,468	Otis Thorpe
3,413	Terry Cummings
3,354	Rick Mahorn
3,301	Patrick Ewing
3,289	Danny Schayes
3,213	Karl Malone
3,167	Alton Lister
3,143	LaSalle Thompson
3,092	Clyde Drexler

Most Rebounds

No.	Player
14,715	Robert Parish
12,834	Buck Williams
11,739	Hakeem Olajuwon
11,027	Charles Barkley
10,542	Karl Malone
10,324	Dennis Rodman
9,513	Patrick Ewing
9,371	Charles Oakley
9,188	Otis Thorpe
9,151	Kevin Willis
8,257	Michael Cage
7,985	Terry Cummings

Most Assists

No.	Player
12,170	John Stockton
6,825	Mark Jackson
6,442	Kevin Johnson
6,157	Derek Harper
6,066	Terry Porter
5,957	Muggsy Bogues
5,743	Clyde Drexler
4,969	Rod Strickland
4,901	Tim Hardaway
4,838	Nate McMillan
4,566	Mark Price
4,538	Jeff Hornacek

Most Free Throws

No.	Player
6,505	Karl Malone
6,233	Michael Jordan
6,002	Dominique Wilkins
5,790	Charles Barkley
4,829	Hakeem Olajuwon
4,622	Patrick Ewing
4,421	Clyde Drexler
4,168	David Robinson
4,106	Robert Parish
4,034	Reggie Miller
3,919	Buck Williams
3,787	Detlef Schremp

Most Steals
Compiled since 1973–74.

No.	Player
2,531	John Stockton
2,165	Michael Jordan
2,081	Clyde Drexler
1,841	Derek Harper
1,811	Hakeem Olajuwon
1,692	Scottie Pippen
1,530	Nate McMillan
1,520	Charles Barkley
1,460	Mookie Blaylock
1,417	Karl Malone
1,374	Dominique Wilkins
1,344	Chris Mullin

Most Blocked Shots
Compiled since 1973–74.

No.	Player
3,363	Hakeem Olajuwon
2,516	Patrick Ewing
2,361	Robert Parish
2,012	David Robinson
1,750	Dikembe Mutombo
1,594	Herb Williams
1,576	Benoit Benjamin
1,472	Alton Lister
1,378	John Williams
1,373	Mark West
1,128	Charles Jones
1,085	Buck Williams

Most Field Goals

No.	Player
10,081	Michael Jordan
9,913	Dominique Wilkins
9,614	Robert Parish
9,510	Karl Malone
9,400	Hakeem Olajuwon
8,449	Patrick Ewing
7,883	Clyde Drexler
7,728	Charles Barkley
7,583	Terry Cummings
7,494	Eddie Johnson
6,735	Dale Ellis
6,329	Buck Williams
6,154	Otis Thorpe

Most 3-Point Field Goals

No.	Player
1,461	Dale Ellis
1,432	Reggie Miller
1,086	Glen Rice
1,038	Vernon Maxwell
981	Dennis Scott
974	Hersey Hawkins
970	Mitch Richmond
968	Derek Harper
935	Dan Majerle
924	Mark Price
913	Dell Curry
911	Terry Porter

Note: Three-point play was instituted by NBA during 1979–80 season.

Utah Jazz guard John Stockton entered the 1997–98 NBA season as the league's all-time leader in assists and steals.

Extra Point
Michael Jordan has won nine scoring championships and averaged 31.7 points a game during his twelve-year career with the Chicago Bulls. In college, however, he averaged just 17.7 points a game in three years at North Carolina.

Single-Season Leaders

Most categories are divided into two parts: one covering the period from the NBA's inaugural 1946–47 season though 1975–76, when the rival American Basketball Association folded, and the other beginning with the 1976–77 season, when 4 former ABA teams—the Denver Nuggets, Indiana Pacers, New Jersey Nets, and San Antonio Spurs—joined the NBA, increasing league membership to 22 teams.

In 1972–73, Nate Archibald (10) of the Kansas City-Omaha Kings became the only player to lead the NBA in scoring and assists in the same season.

Highest Scoring Average
Based on at least 70 games or 1,400 points.

Avg.	Player/Team	Season	Points
1946–47 to 1975–76			
50.4	Wilt Chamberlain, Philadelphia	1961-62	4,029
44.8	Wilt Chamberlain, San Francisco	1962-63	3,586
38.4	Wilt Chamberlain, Philadelphia	1960-61	3,033
38.3	Elgin Baylor, L.A. Lakers	1961-62	1,836
37.6	Wilt Chamberlain, Philadelphia	1959-60	2,707
36.9	Wilt Chamberlain, San Francisco	1963-64	2,948
35.6	Rick Barry, San Francisco	1966-67	2,775
Since 1976–77			
37.1	Michael Jordan, Chicago	1986-87	3,041
35.0	Michael Jordan, Chicago	1987-88	2,868
33.6	Michael Jordan, Chicago	1989-90	2,753
33.1	George Gervin, San Antonio	1979-80	2,585
32.9	Bernard King, New York	1984-85	1,809
32.6	Michael Jordan, Chicago	1992-93	2,541
32.5	Michael Jordan, Chicago	1988-89	2,633

Most Rebounds Per Game
Compiled by NBA since 1950–51 season.

Avg.	Player/Team	Season
1950–51 to 1975–76		
27.2	Wilt Chamberlain, Phila.	1960-61
27.0	Wilt Chamberlain, Phila.	1959-60
25.7	Wilt Chamberlain, Phila.	1961-62
24.7	Bill Russell, Boston	1963-64
24.6	Wilt Chamberlain, Phila.	1965-66
Since 1976–77		
18.7	Dennis Rodman, Det.	1991-92
18.3	Dennis Rodman, Det.	1992-93
17.6	Moses Malone, Houston	1978-79
17.3	Dennis Rodman, S.A.	1993-94

Most Assists Per Game

Avg.	Player/Team	Season
1946–47 to 1975–76		
11.5	Oscar Robertson, Cinn.	1964-65
11.4	Oscar Robertson, Cinn.	1961-62
11.4	Nate Archibald, K.C.	1972-73
11.2	Guy Rodgers, Chicago	1966-67
11.1	Oscar Robertson, Cinn.	1965-66
Since 1976–77		
14.5	John Stockton, Utah	1989-90
14.2	John Stockton, Utah	1990-91
13.9	Isiah Thomas, Detroit	1984-85
13.8	John Stockton, Utah	1987-88
13.7	John Stockton, Utah	1991-92

Most Personal Fouls

No.	Player/Team	Season
1946–47 to 1975–76		
366	Bill Bridges, St. Louis	1967-68
356	Charlie Scott, Boston	1975-76
350	Dave Cowens, Boston	1970-71
345	Bailey Howell, Balt.	1964-65
344	Zelmo Beaty, St.Louis	1966-67
344	Joe Strawder, Detroit	1966-67
344	Don Adams, San Diego	1970-71
Since 1976–77		
386	Darryl Dawkins, N.J.	1983-84
379	Darryl Dawkins, N.J.	1982-83
372	Steve Johnson, K.C.	1981-82
367	Bill Robinzine, K.C.	1978-79

Best Field Goal Percentage

Pct.	Player/Team	Season
1946–47 to 1975–76		
.727	Wilt Chamberlain, L.A.	1972-73
.683	Wilt Chamberlain, Phila.	1966-67
.649	Wilt Chamberlain, L.A.	1971-72
.595	Wilt Chamberlain, Phila.	1967-68
.583	Wilt Chamberlain, L.A.	1968-69
.559	Johnny Green, Cinn.	1969-70
Since 1976–77		
.670	Artis Gilmore, Chicago	1980-81
.652	Artis Gilmore, Chicago	1981-82
.637	James Donaldson, L.A. Clippers	1984-85
.633	Chris Gatling, Gold. St.	1994-95
.632	Steve Johnson, San Ant.	1985-86
.631	Artis Gilmore, Chicago	1983-84

Best Free Throw Percentage

Pct.	Player/Team	Season
1946–47 to 1975–76		
.932	Bill Sharman, Boston	1958-59
.921	Bill Sharman, Boston	1960-61
.905	Bill Sharman, Boston	1956-57
.904	Bob Wanzer, Rochester	1951-52
.904	Dolph Schayes, Syra.	1956-57
.904	Dolph Schayes, Syra.	1957-58
Since 1976–77		
.958	Calvin Murphy, Houston	1980-81
.956	Mahmoud Abdul-Rauf, Denver	1993-94
.948	Mark Price, Cleveland	1992-93
.947	Rick Barry, Houston	1978-79
.947	Mark Price, Cleveland	1991-92
.945	Ernie DiGregorio, Buf.	1976-77

Most Blocked Shots Per Game

Compiled by NBA since 1973–74 season.

Avg.	Player/Team	Season
5.56	Mark Eaton, Utah	1984-85
4.96	Manute Bol, Wash.	1985-86
4.85	Elmore Smith, L.A.	1973-74
4.61	Mark Eaton, Utah	1985-86
4.59	Hakeem Olajuwon, Hou.	1989-90
4.49	David Robinson, San Ant.	1991-92
4.34	Hakeem Olajuwon, Hou.	1991-92
4.31	Manute Bol, Golden St.	1988-89
4.29	Tree Rollins, Atlanta	1982-83
4.28	Mark Eaton, Utah	1983-84
4.17	Hakeem Olajuwon, Hou.	1992-93
4.12	Kareem Abdul-Jabbar, L.A. Lakers	1975-76

Best 3-Point Field Goal Percentage

Compiled by NBA since 1979–80 season.

Pct.	Player/Team	Season
.524	Steve Kerr, Chicago	1994-95
.522	Jon Sundvold, Miami	1988-89
.522	Tim Legler, Wash.	1995-96
.515	Steve Kerr, Chicago	1995-96
.514	Detlef Schrempf, Sea.	1994-95
.507	Steve Kerr, Cleveland	1989-90
.491	Craig Hodges, Mil-Pho.	1987-88
.486	Mark Price, Cleveland	1987-88
.481	Kiki Vanderweghe, Port	1986-87
.481	Craig Hodges, Chicago	1989-90

Note: The three-point shot had been the signature play of the ABA from 1967-68 through 1975-76 and was not adopted by the NBA until four years after the ABA folded.

Most Steals Per Game

Compiled by NBA since 1973–74 season.

Avg.	Player/Team	Season
3.67	Alvin Robertson, San Ant.	1985-86
3.47	Don Buse, Indiana	1976-77
3.43	Magic Johnson, L.A.	1980-81
3.23	M. R. Richardson, N. Y.	1979-80
3.21	Alvin Robertson, San Ant.	1986-87
3.21	John Stockton, Utah	1988-89
3.18	Slick Watts, Seattle	1975-76
3.16	Michael Jordan, Chi.	1987-88
3.04	Alvin Robertson, Mil.	1990-91
3.03	Alvin Robertson, San Ant.	1988-89
2.98	John Stockton, Utah	1991-92
2.96	Three players tied.	

Highest ABA Scoring Average

Based on at least 1,000 points.

Avg.	Player/Team	Season
34.6	Charlie Scott, Virginia	1971-72
34.0	Rick Barry, Oakland	1968-69
31.9	Julius Erving, Virginia	1972-73
31.5	Rick Barry, New York	1971-72
30.6	Dan Issel, Kentucky	1971-72
30.0	Spencer Haywood, Den	1969-70
29.9	Dan Issel, Kentucky	1970-71
29.8	George McGinnis, Ind.	1974-75
29.3	John Brisker, Pitts.	1970-71
29.3	Julius Erving, N.Y.	1975-76

Note: Of these players, Barry, Brisker, Haywood, McGinnis and Scott moved to the NBA before the ABA folded in 1976. Erving and Issel played their first NBA seasons in 1976–77.

Extra Point

Oscar Robertson, who was an All-Star guard for the Cincinnati Royals and Milwaukee Bucks during his thirteen-year NBA career, showed his versatility when he averaged a triple-double for the entire 1961–62 season. His final statistics that year showed per-game averages of 30.8 points, 11.4 assists and 12.5 rebounds in 79 games.

Oscar Robertson of the Cincinnati Royals in action against the Boston Celtics in 1963.

Single-Game Leaders

Most Points

Pts.	Player/Team	Opponent	Date
	1946–47 to 1975–76		
100	Wilt Chamberlain, Philadelphia	New York*	3/2/62
78	Wilt Chamberlain, Philadelphia	L.A. Lakers, 3OT	12/8/61
73	Wilt Chamberlain, Philadelphia	Chicago	1/13/62
73	Wilt Chamberlain, San Francisco	New York	11/16/62
72	Wilt Chamberlain, San Francisco	L.A. Lakers	11/3/62
71	Elgin Baylor, L.A. Lakers	New York	11/15/60
70	Wilt Chamberlain, San Francisco	Syracuse	3/10/63
68	Wilt Chamberlain, Philadelphia	Chicago	12/16/67
	Since 1976–77 Season		
73	David Thompson, Denver	Detroit	4/9/78
71	David Robinson, San Antonio	L.A. Clippers	4/24/94
69	Michael Jordan, Chicago	Cleveland, OT	3/28/90
68	Pete Maravich, New Orleans	New York	2/25/77
64	Rick Barry, Golden St.	Portland	3/26/74
64	Michael Jordan, Chicago	Orlando, OT	1/16/93
63	George Gervin, San Antonio	New Orleans	4/9/78
61	Three times (Michael Jordan twice, Karl Malone once).		

*Game was played at Hershey, PA (final score: Philadelphia 169, New York 147).

Wilt Chamberlain, 1961.

Most Field Goals
Listed with attempts.

FG/Att.	Player/Game/Date
36/63	Wilt Chamberlain, Philadelphia vs. New York (3/2/62)
31/62	Wilt Chamberlain, Philadelphia vs. L.A. Lakers, 3OT (12/8/61)
30/40	Wilt Chamberlain, Philadelphia vs. Chicago (12/16/67)
30/45	Rick Barry, Golden State vs. Portland (3/26/74)

Most Rebounds

No.	Player/Game/Date
55	Wilt Chamberlain, Philadelphia vs. Boston (11/24/60)
51	Bill Russell, Boston vs. Syracuse (2/5/60)
49	Bill Russell, Boston vs. Philadelphia (11/16/57)
49	Bill Russell, Boston vs. Detroit (3/11/65)
45	Wilt Chamberlain, Philadelphia vs. Syracuse (2/6/60)
45	Wilt Chamberlain, Philadelphia vs. L.A. Lakers (1/21/61)

Most Assists

No.	Player/Game/Date
30	Scott Skiles, Orlando vs. Denver (12/30/90)
29	Kevin Porter, New Jersey vs. Houston (2/24/78)
28	Bob Cousy, Boston vs. Minneapolis (2/27/59)
28	Guy Rodgers, San Francisco vs. St. Louis (3/14/63)
28	John Stockton, Utah vs. San Antonio (1/15/91)
27	Geoff Huston, Cleveland vs. Golden St. (1/27/82)
27	John Stockton, Utah vs. New York (12/19/89)

Most 3-Point Field Goals
Listed with attempts.

FG/Att.	Player/Game/Date
11/17	Dennis Scott, Orlando vs. Atlanta (4/18/96)
10/15	Brian Shaw, Miami vs. Milwaukee (4/8/93)
10/18	Joe Dumars, Detroit vs. Minnesota (11/8/94)
10/12	George McCloud, Dallas vs. Phoenix, OT (12/16/95)

Note: The 3-point shot was introduced to the NBA during the 1979-80 season.

Head Coaches

Best Winning Percentages
Regular season only; based on at least 250 NBA victories.

Pct.	Head Coach	Yrs.	W	L	Last Year
.736	Phil Jackson*	8	483	173	active
.705	Pat Riley*	15	859	360	active
.698	Billy Cunningham	8	454	196	1985
.674	K.C. Jones	10	522	252	1992
.662	Red Auerbach	20	938	479	1966
.639	Rudy Tomjanovich*	6	281	159	active
.620	Les Harrison	7	295	181	1955
.619	Tom Heinsohn	9	427	263	1978
.616	Jerry Sloan*	12	577	359	active
.598	Chuck Daly*	12	564	379	active
.592	George Karl*	10	442	305	active
.589	Larry Costello	10	430	300	1979
.586	Rick Adelman	8	357	252	1997
.583	John Kundla	11	423	302	1959
.581	Bill Sharman	7	333	240	1976

*Active at the start of the 1997–98 regular season.

In fifteen years, coach Pat Riley has never had a losing season.

Most Wins
Through 1996–97 season, not including playoffs.

Wins	Head Coach	Yrs.
1,070	Lenny Wilkens*	24
938	Red Auerbach	20
935	Dick Motta	25
927	Bill Fitch*	24
864	Jack Ramsay	21
859	Pat Riley*	15
851	Don Nelson	19
832	Cotton Fitzsimmons	21
784	Gene Shue	22
707	John MacLeod	18
696	Red Holzman	18
628	Doug Moe	15
624	Larry Brown*	14

* Active in 1996–97 season.

Most Wins by Active Coaches
Regular season only; through 1996–97.

Wins	Head Coach/Team	Yrs.
1,070	Lenny Wilkens, Atlanta	24
927	Bill Fitch, L.A. Clippers	24
859	Pat Riley, Miami	15
624	Larry Brown, Philadelphia	14
577	Jerry Sloan, Utah	12
564	Chuck Daly, Orlando	12
503	Mike Fratello, Cleveland	12
489	Del Harris, L.A. Lakers	12
483	Phil Jackson, Chicago	8
442	George Karl, Seattle	10
283	Bernie Bickerstaff, Wash.	8
281	Rudy Tomjanovich, Houston	6
255	Chris Ford, Milwaukee	6
237	Doug Collins, Detroit	5

Most Playoff Wins

Wins	Head Coach	NBA Titles
145	Pat Riley*	4
99	Red Auerbach	9
96	Phil Jackson*	5
81	K.C. Jones	2
74	Chuck Daly	2
68	Lenny Wilkens*	1
66	Billy Cunningham	1
60	John Kundla	5
58	Red Holzman	2
56	Dick Motta	1
55	Bill Fitch*	1
52	Jerry Sloan*	0
51	Don Nelson	0

* Active in 1997 playoffs.

Home Courts

Biggest NBA Arenas

Seats	Home Court	Home Team
24,042	Charlotte Coliseum	Charlotte Hornets
21,711	United Center	Chicago Bulls
21,570	Georgia Dome*	Atlanta Hawks
21,500	MCI Center	Washington Wizards
21,454	Palace at Auburn Hills	Detroit Pistons
21,401	Rose Garden	Portland Trail Blazers
21,000	CoreStates Center	Philadelphia 76ers
20,562	Gund Arena	Cleveland Cavaliers
20,557	Alamodome#	San Antonio Spurs
20,125	SkyDome	Toronto Raptors
20,039	Continental Airlines	New Jersey Nets
19,911	Delta Center	Utah Jazz
19,763	Madison Square Garden	New York Knicks
19,200	Oakland Coliseum	Golden St. Warriors
19,193	General Motors Place	Vancouver Grizzlies

*The Hawks will play 28 games at the Georgia Dome and 13 at Alexander Memorial Coliseum during the 1997–98 season.
#The Alamodome capacity can be expanded to 34,215 seats.
Recently renamed: Continental Airlines Arena (originally Meadowlands Arena, 1981–96).

Oldest NBA Arenas

Opened	Home Court	Home Team
1959	L.A. Sports Arena	Los Angeles Clippers
1962	Key Arena	Seattle SuperSonics
1966	Oakland Coliseum	Golden St. Warriors
1967	Great Western Forum	Los Angeles Lakers
1968	Madison Square Garden	New York Knicks
1972	The Omni	Atlanta Hawks
1974	Market Sqare Arena	Indiana Pacers
1975	McNichols Arena	Denver Nuggets
1975	The Summit	Houston Rockets
1980	Reunion Arena	Dallas Mavericks

Smallest NBA Arenas

Seats	Home Court	Home Team
15,200	Miami Arena	Miami Heat
16,021	L.A. Sports Arena	Los Angeles Clippers
16,285	The Summit	Houston Rockets
16,530	Market Square Arena	Indiana Pacers
17,072	Key Arena	Seattle SuperSonics
17,171	McNichols Arena	Denver Nuggets
17,248	Orlando Arena	Orlando Magic
17,317	ARCO Arena	Sacramento Kings
17,505	Great Western Forum	Los Angeles Lakers
18,042	Reunion Arena	Dallas Mavericks
18,624	FleetCenter	Boston Celtics
18,633	Bradley Center	Milwaukee Bucks
19,006	Target Center	Minnesota Timberwolves
19,023	America West Arena	Phoenix Suns

Recently renamed: Great Western Forum (originally The Forum, 1967–90); Key Arena at Seattle Center (originally Seattle Coliseum before being rebuilt and reopened in 1995).

Newest NBA Arenas

Opened	Home Court	Home Team
1997	MCI Center	Washington Wizards
1996	CoreStates Center	Philadelphia 76ers
1995	FleetCenter	Boston Celtics
1995	Rose Garden	Portland Trail Blazers
1995	General Motors Place	Vancouver Grizzlies

The Los Angeles Memorial Sports Arena, which opened in 1959, has been home to the NBA Clippers since the team moved from San Diego in 1984.

Awards

Most Popular Retired Numbers

Through the 1996–97 regular season.

Jersey No.	Persons Honored
15	Brad Davis (Mavericks), Hal Greer (76ers), Tom Heinsohn (Celtics), Vinnie Johnson (Pistons), Dick McGuire and Earl Monroe (both Knicks), and Larry Steele (Trail Blazers).
32	Fred Brown (Sonics), Billy Cunningham (76ers), Julius Erving (Nets), Magic Johnson (Lakers), Kevin McHale (Celtics), Bill Walton (Trail Blazers), and Brian Winters(Bucks).
1	Nate Archibald (Kings), Walter Brown (Celtics), Frank Layden (Jazz), Oscar Robertson (Bucks), and Larry Weinberg (Trail Blazers).
6	Walter Davis (Suns), Julius Erving (76ers) and Bill Russell (Celtics), and fans of the Hornets and the Kings honored as the "6th man."
23	Lou Hudson (Hawks), Michael Jordan (Bulls), Calvin Murphy (Rockets), Frank Ramsey (Celtics), and John Williamson (Nets).
33	Kareem Abdul-Jabbar (twice—Bucks and Lakers), Alvan Adams (Suns), Larry Bird (Celtics), and David Thompson (Nuggets).
44	George Gervin (Spurs), Dan Issel (Nuggets), Sam Lacey (Kings), Jerry West (Lakers), and Paul Westphal (Suns).

Earl Monroe of the New York Knicks.

Most Frequent Most Valuable Players

Through the 1996–97 season.

No.	Player/Team/Years
6	Kareem Andul-Jabbar, Milwaukee and L.A. Lakers, 1971, 1972, 1974,1976, 1977, 1980
5	Bill Russell, Boston, 1958, 1961-63, 1965
4	Wilt Chamberlain, Philadelphia, Warriors, and 76ers, 1960,1966-68
4	Michael Jordan, Chicago, 1988, 1991, 1992, 1996
3	Larry Bird, Boston, 1984-86
3	Magic Johnson, L.A. Lakers, 1987, 1989, 1990
3	Moses Malone, Houston and Philadelphia, 1979, 1982, 1983

Positions: All are centers except forward Bird and guards Johnson and Jordan.

Note: The Maurice Podoloff Trophy for regular season MVP has been presented by the NBA since 1956.

Rookies of the Year Who Became MVPs

First Year	Player	First MVP
1955	Bob Pettit	1956
1960	Wilt Chamberlain*	1960
1961	Oscar Robertson	1964
1965	Willis Reed	1970
1969	Wes Unseld*	1969
1970	Kareem Abdul-Jabbar#	1971
1971	Dave Cowens	1973
1973	Bob McAdoo	1975
1980	Larry Bird	1984
1985	Michael Jordan	1988
1990	David Robinson	1995

* Centers Chamberlain of the Philadelphia Warriors and Unseld of the Baltimore Bullets are the only players to win both the Rookie of the Year and MVP awards in the same season.

Abdul-Jabbar won Rookie of the Year as Lew Alcindor and changed his name after the 1970–71 season.

Note: Five players have won the MVP award more than once: Abdul-Jabbar (6), Bird (3), Chamberlain (4), Jordan (4), and Pettit (2).

The 50 Greatest Players in NBA History

Players are listed alphabetically.

Centers (14)

Kareen Abdul-Jabbar, Wilt Chamberlain, Dave Cowens, Patrick Ewing,* Elvin Hayes, Moses Malone, George Mikan, Hakeem Olajuwon,* Shaquille O'Neal,* Robert Parish,* Willis Reed, David Robinson,* Bill Russell, and Bill Walton.

Forwards (11)

Charles Barkley,* Rick Barry, Elgin Baylor, Larry Bird, Billy Cunningham, Dave DeBusschere, Julius Erving, Karl Malone,* Kevin McHale, Scottie Pippen,* and James Worthy.

Center/Forwards (5)

Jerry Lucas, Bob Pettit, Dolph Schayes, Nate Thurmond, and Wes Unseld.

Forward/Guards (2)

Paul Arizin and John Havlicek.

Guards (18)

Nate Archibald, Dave Bing, Bob Cousy, Clyde Drexler,* Walt Frazier, George Gervin, Hal Greer, Magic Johnson, Sam Jones, Michael Jordan,* Pete Maravich, Earl Monroe, Oscar Robertson, Bill Sharman, John Stockton,* Isiah Thomas, Jerry West, and Lenny Wilkens.

* Active in 1997.

Note: The NBA's 50th Anniversary Team was selected in 1996 by a national panel consisting of members of the media, former players and coaches, current and former general managers, and team executives.

Miscellaneous

Most Regular-Season Wins

Since 1946–47 season.

W-L	Team	Season
72-10	Chicago Bulls*	1995-96
69-13	L.A. Lakers*	1971-72
69-13	Chicago Bulls*	1996-97
68-13	Philadelphia 76ers*	1966-67
68-14	Boston Celtics	1972-73
67-15	Boston Celtics*	1985-86
67-15	Chicago Bulls*	1991-92

* Went on to win NBA title.

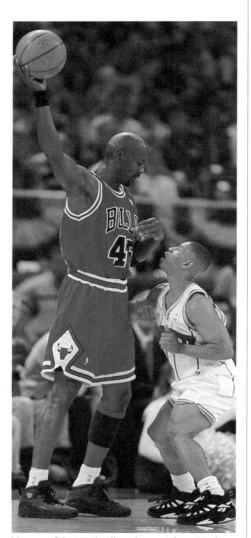

Not one of the NBA's tallest players, 6-foot, 6-inch Michael Jordan has no trouble keeping the ball away from 5-foot, 3-inch Muggsy Bogues, the NBA's shortest player.

Most Regular-Season Losses

Since 1946–47 season.

W-L	Team	Season
9-73	Philadelphia 76ers	1972-73
11-71	Dallas Mavericks	1992-93
12-70	Los Angeles Clippers	1986-87
14-68	Houston Rockets	1982-83
14-68	Vancouver Grizzlies	1996-97
15-67	Seven teams tied.	

Note: None of the teams above were NBA expansion clubs in the years noted.

Tallest Players in NBA History

Height	Player	Years
7-7	Manute Bol	1985-95
7-7	Gheorge Muresan	1993–
7-6	Shawn Bradley	1993–
7-4	Mark Eaton	1982-93
7-4	Priest Lauderdale	1996–
7-4	Rik Smits	1988–

Shortest Players in NBA History

Height	Player	Years
5-3	Muggsy Bogues	1987–
5-7	Greg Grant	1989–
5-7	Keith Jennings	1992-95
5-7	Louis Klotz	1947-48
5-7	Spud Webb	1985–

Longest Winning Streaks

Single season, regular season games only.

Gm.	Team	Dates
33	L.A. Lakers	11/5/71 to 1/7/72
20	Milwaukee	2/6 to 3/8/71
18	New York	10/24 to 11/28/69
18	Boston	2/24 to 3/26/82
18	Chicago	12/29/95 to 2/2/96

Highest-Scoring Games

Most points, regular season games only.

Pts.	Final Score/Date
370	Detroit 186, Denver 184 (3OT), Dec. 13, 1983
337	San Antonio 171, Milw. 166 (3OT), March 6, 1982
320	Golden St. 162, Denver 158, Nov. 2, 1990
318	Denver 163, San Antonio 155, Jan. 11, 1984
316	Three games tied.

Lowest-Scoring Games

Most points, regular season games only.

Pts	Final Score/Date
119	Boston 62, Milwaukee Hawks 57, Feb. 27, 1955
123	Miami 66, Philadelphia 5, Feb. 21, 1996
133	Detroit 72, New York 61, April 12, 1992
135	Ft. Wayne 69, Syracuse 66, Jan. 25, 1955
141	Cleveland 84, Orlando 57 Dec. 4, 1996

Longest Losing Streaks

Single season, regular season games only.

Gm.	Team	Dates
23	Vancouver	2/16 to 4/2/96
20	Philadelphia	1/9 to 2/11/73
20	Dallas	11/13 to 12/22/93
19	Cleveland	3/19 to 4/18/82
19	San Diego Clippers	3/11 to 4/13/82
19	L.A. Clippers	12/30/88 to 2/6/89
19	Dallas	2/6 to 3/15/93
19	Vancouver	11/7 to 12/13/96

HOCKEY

Steve Yzerman, captain of the Detroit Red Wings, hoists the team's eighth Stanley Cup, won in 1997.

Stanley Cup Champions

Most Appearances in Final

Since the National Hockey League took possession of the Stanley Cup in 1918.

No.	Team	Record
32	Montreal Canadiens	23-8*
21	Toronto Maple Leafs	13-8
20	Detroit Red Wings	8-12
17	Boston Bruins	5-12
10	New York Rangers	4-6
10	Chicago Blackhawks	3-7
7	Philadelphia Flyers	2-5
6	Edmonton Oilers	5-1
5	New York Islanders	4-1
5	Vancouver Millionaires	0-5
4	Ottawa Senators#	4-0
3	Montreal Maroons	2-1
3	St. Louis Blues	0-3
2	Pittsburgh Penguins	2-0
2	Calgary Flames	1-1
2	Victoria Cougars	1-1
2	Minnesota North Stars	0-2
2	Seattle Metropolitans	0-2
2	Vancouver Canucks	0-2

*The 1919 Stanley Cup Final between the Montreal Canadiens of the National Hockey League and the Seattle Metropolitans of the Pacific Coast Hockey Association was canceled due to an influenza epidemic with the series tied 2-2 after four games. The Canadiens also won the cup in 1916 as a member of the National Hockey Association.

#The original Ottawa Senators played in the NHL from 1917 to 1931 and from 1932 to 1934. The franchise also played one season as the St. Louis Eagles before folding in 1935. The current Ottawa Senators franchise joined the NHL as an expansion team in 1992.

Note: The Vancouver Millionaires, Victoria Cougars, and Seattle Metropolitans were the only members of the Western Canada Hockey League, Western Hockey League, or Pacific Coast Hockey League to compete against NHL teams for the Stanley Cup between 1918 and 1926.

Most Titles Won

Only 16 franchises have won the Stanley Cup since the NHL took possession of the trophy in 1918.

No.	Team	Championship Years	Playoffs Berths	Record
23	Montreal Canadiens	1993, 1986, 1976-79, 1973, 1971, 1969, 1968, 1966, 1965, 1956-60, 1953, 1946, 1944, 1931, 1930, 1924	71	377-243-8
13	Toronto Maple Leafs	1967, 1962-64, 1951, 1947-49, 1945, 1942, 1932, 1922, 1918	58	210-230-4
8	Detroit Red Wings	1997, 1955, 1954, 1952, 1950, 1943, 1937, 1936	46	206-201-1
5	Boston Bruins	1972, 1970, 1941, 1939, 1929	57	228-242-6
5	Edmonton Oilers	1990, 1988, 1987, 1985, 1984	14	125-67-0
4	New York Rangers	1994, 1940, 1933, 1928	48	183-195-8
4	New York Islanders	1980-83	17	128-90-0
4	(original) Ottawa Senators	1927, 1923, 1921, 1920	10	18-17-6
3	Chicago Blackhawks	1961, 1938, 1934	52	187-214-5
2	Montreal Maroons	1935, 1926	11	21-21-8
2	Philadelphia Flyers	1975, 1974	23	144-125-0
2	Pittsburgh Penguins	1992, 1991	17	86-74-0
1	Calgary Flames	1989	21	69-87-0
1	Colorado Avalanche	1996	11	61-58-0
1	New Jersey Devils	1995	9	52-45-0
1	Victoria Cougars	1925	3	9-5-4

Franchise moves & name changes: •Toronto—as Arenas (1 Stanley Cup title), as St. Pats (1) and as Maple Leafs (11); •Flames—in Atlanta (0 titles), in Calgary (1); •Avalanche—as Quebec Nordiques (0 titles), as Colorado Avalanche (1); •Devils—as Kansas City Scouts and Colorado Rockies (0 titles), as New Jersey Devils (1 title).

Franchise failures: •Ottawa Senators became the St. Louis Eagles after 1933-34 season and folded in 1935; •Montreal Maroons folded after the 1937-38 season; •Victoria Cougars folded along with the Western Hockey League after the 1925-26 season (the Cougars were the only member of the WHL, Western Canada Hockey League, or Pacific Coast Hockey League to win the cup final against an NHL team).

The Stanley Cup

Frederick Arthur Lord Stanley of Preston, a British sportsman, became a ice hockey enthusiast while serving as the sixth Governor-General of Canada (1888–93). Before returning to England, he donated a sterling silver bowl to be awarded annually to the amateur hockey champion of Canada. The trophy passed into professional hands in 1910 when teams in the new National Hockey Association began to compete for it. The NHA reorganized as the National Hockey League in 1917. The Stanley Cup is the oldest championship trophy competed for by professional athletes in North America.

Stanley Cup Final Leaders

Seven-Game Final

Since the best-of-seven format was adopted in 1939;
listed with the final score of Game 7.

Year	Winner/Loser	Game 7/Site
1994	N.Y. Rangers over Vancouver	3-2, at New York
1987	Edmonton over Philadelphia	3-1, at Edmonton
1971	Montreal over Chicago	3-2, at Chicago
1965	Montreal over Chicago	4-0, at Montreal
1964	Toronto over Detroit	4-0, at Toronto
1955	Detroit over Montreal	3-1, at Detroit
1954	Detroit over Montreal	2-1 (OT), at Detroit
1950	Detroit over N.Y. Rangers	4-3 (2 OT), at Detroit
1945	Toronto over Detroit	2-1, at Detroit
1942	Toronto over Detroit	3-1, at Toronto

Note: The 1942 Toronto Maple Leafs are the only team in Stanley Cup history to lose the first three games of the final and then come back to win the championship.

Most Championships—Players

No.	Player/Team	No.	Player/Team
11	Henri Richard, Montreal	8	Maurice Richard, Montreal
10	Jean Beliveau, Montreal	8	Red Kelly, Detroit and Toronto
10	Yvan Cournoyer, Montreal	7	Serge Savard, Montreal
9	Claude Provost, Montreal	7	Jean-Guy Talbot, Montreal
8	Jacques Lemaire, Montreal		

Most Points

Series	Pts.	Player/Team/Opponent	Year
4-Gm	13*	Wayne Gretzky, Edmonton vs. Boston	1988
5-Gm	11	Paul Coffey, Edmonton vs. Philadelphia	1985
	11	Wayne Gretzky, Edmonton vs. Philadelphia	1985
6-Gm	12	Mario Lemieux, Pittsburgh vs. Minnesota	1991
	12	Yvan Cournoyer, Montreal vs Chicago	1973
	12	Jacques Lemaire, Montreal vs. Chicago	1973
7-Gm	12	Gordie Howe, Detroit vs. Montreal	1955

*Edmonton's 4-game sweep of Boston included a suspended Game 4 which was tied at 3 when a power failure at Boston Garden ended the contest at 16:37 in the second period. While the game did not count, the NHL considers individual statistics to be official, and Gretzky had 2 assists.
Points breakdown: •4 Games—Gretzky (3 Goals, 10 Assists); •5 Games—Coffey (3G, 8A), Gretzky (7G, 4A; •6 Games—Lemieux (5G, 7A), Cournoyer (6G, 6A), Lemaire (3G, 9A); •7 Games—Howe (5G, 7A).

Most Goals

Series	No.	Player/Team/Opponent	Year
4-Gm	7	Mike Bossy, N.Y. Islanders vs. Vancouver	1982
5-Gm	7	Jean Beliveau, Montreal vs. Detroit	1956
	7	Wayne Gretzky, Edmonton vs. Philadelphia	1985
6-Gm	6	Yvan Cournoyer, Montreal vs. Chicago	1973
7-Gm	6	Alex Delvecchio, Detroit vs. Montreal	1955

Most Assists

Series	No.	Player/Team/Opponent	Year
4-Gm	10	Wayne Gretzky, Edmonton vs. Boston	1988
5-Gm	8	Bert Olmstead, Montreal vs. Detroit	1956
	8	Paul Coffey, Edmonton vs. Philadelphia	1985
6-Gm	9	Jacques Lemaire, Montreal vs. Chicago	1973
	9	Larry Murphy, Pittsburgh vs. Minnesota	1991
7-Gm	9	Wayne Gretzky, Edmonton vs. Philadelphia	1987

Fewest Goals Against

One goaltender, entire series.

Series	No.	Player/Team/Opponent	Year
4-Gm	2	Terry Sawchuk, Detroit vs. Montreal	1955
5-Gm	6	Frankie Brimsek, Boston vs. Toronto	1939
	6	Jacques Plante, Montreal vs. Boston	1957
6-Gm	11	Dave Kerr, N.Y. Rangers vs. Toronto	1940
7-Gm	9	Harry Lumley, Detroit vs. Toronto	1945
	9	Frank McCool, Toronto vs. Detroit	1945

Note: In 1945 Toronto and Detroit held each other to 9 goals apiece as the Maple Leafs won the 7-game Final by scores of 1-0, 2-0, 1-0, 3-5, 0-2, 0-1, and 2-1. McCool had 3 shutouts and Lumley had 2.

Most Championships—Coaches

No.	Coach/Team	No.	Coach/Team
8	Toe Blake, Montreal	4	Al Arbour, NY Islanders
7	Scotty Bowman,* Montreal, Pittsburgh, and Detroit	4	Punch Imlach, Toronto
		4	Dick Irvin, Toronto and Montreal
5	Hap Day, Toronto	4	Glen Sather, Edmonton

*Bowman is the only head coach in NHL history to win Stanley Cup championships with 3 different franchises. He also reached the Final 3 times with St. Louis.

Playoff Career Leaders

Asterisks (*) indicate players who participated in 1997 playoffs; (DNP) indicates players active in 1997
who did not participate, either because they were injured or their teams failed to qualify.

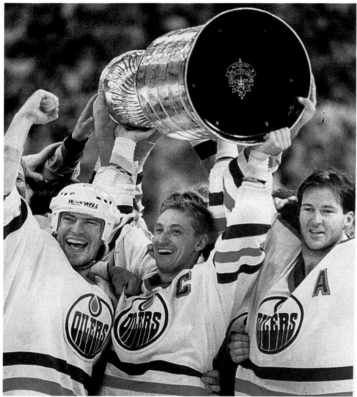

All-time scoring leaders Wayne Gretzky (center) and Mark Messier (left) won four
Stanley Cups together in Edmonton between 1984 and 1988.

Most Points

Years indicate number of appearances in Stanley Cup playoffs;
listed with goals (G) and assists (A).

Pts.	Player	Yrs.	Gm.	G	A
382	Wayne Gretzky*	16	208	122	260
295	Mark Messier*	17	236	109	186
233	Jari Kurri*	14	196	106	127
214	Glenn Anderson	15	225	93	121
195	Paul Coffey*	15	189	59	136
184	Bryan Trottier	17	221	71	113
176	Jean Beliveau	17	162	79	97
175	Denis Savard*	16	164	66	109
164	Doug Gilmour*	13	146	49	115
164	Denis Potvin	14	185	56	108
160	Mike Bossy	10	129	85	75
160	Gordie Howe	20	157	68	92
160	Bobby Smith	13	184	64	96
155	Mario Lemieux*	7	89	70	85

Most Goals

No.	Player
122	Wayne Gretzky*
109	Mark Messier*
106	Jari Kurri*
93	Glenn Anderson
85	Mike Bossy
82	Maurice Richard
79	Jean Beliveau
73	Dino Ciccarelli (DNP)
71	Bryan Trottier
70	Claude Lemieux*
70	Mario Lemieux*
69	Esa Tikkanen*
68	Gordie Howe
66	Brett Hull*
66	Denis Savard*

Most Assists

No.	Player
260	Wayne Gretzky*
186	Mark Messier*
136	Paul Coffey*
127	Jari Kurri*
121	Glenn Anderson
116	Larry Robinson
115	Doug Gilmour*
113	Bryan Trottier
112	Ray Bourque (DNP)
109	Denis Savard*
108	Denis Potvin
97	Jean Beliveau
97	Larry Murphy*
96	Bobby Smith
92	Gordie Howe

Most Penalty Minutes

No.	Player
661	Dale Hunter (DNP)
541	Chris Nilan
466	Willi Plett
455	Claude Lemieux*
455	Tiger Williams
442	Glenn Anderson
426	Tim Hunter (DNP)
412	Dave Schultz
405	Duane Sutter
383	Rick Tocchet (DNP)
382	Jim Peplinski
382	Al Secord
352	Andre DuPont
335	Terry O'Reilly
325	Ken Linseman

Most Appearances

No.	Player
20	Gordie Howe
20	Larry Robinson
19	Red Kelly
18	Henri Richard
18	Stan Mikita
17	Six players tied.

Most Appearances— Goaltenders

No.	Player
16	Jacques Plante
15	Glenn Hall
15	Andy Moog*
15	Terry Sawchuk
14	Tony Esposito

Best Goals-Against Averages

Based on at least 48 games played; goals against (GA).

Avg.	Goaltender	Games	Min.	GA
1.80	Clint Benedict	48	2,907	87
1.83	Martin Brodeur*	48	3,084	94
1.93	George Hainsworth	52	3,486	112
1.98	Turk Broda	101	6,348	211
2.17	Jacques Plante	112	6,651	241
2.37	Patrick Roy*	153	9,452	374
2.40	Ken Dryden	112	6,846	274
2.43	Bernie Parent	71	4,302	174
2.50	Ed Belfour (DNP)	68	3,942	164
2.50	Harry Lumley	76	4,778	199
2.54	Johnny Bower	74	4,350	184
2.54	Terry Sawchuk	106	6,311	267
2.56	Frankie Brimsek	68	4,365	186
2.69	Mike Richter*	76	4,514	202
2.69	Gerry Cheevers	88	5,396	242
2.69	Mike Vernon*	123	7,308	328

Most Wins

Record	Player
96-55	Patrick Roy*
88-36	Billy Smith
80-32	Ken Dryden
80-40	Grant Fuhr*
73-45	Mike Vernon*
71-37	Jacques Plante
64-52	Andy Moog*
58-42	Turk Broda
54-48	Terry Sawchuk
51-39	Tom Barrasso (DNP)
49-65	Glenn Hall
47-35	Gerry Cheevers
47-43	Ron Hextall*
45-53	Tony Esposito
41-25	Gump Worsley
41-33	Mike Richter*

Most Shutouts

No.	Player
15	Clint Benedict
15	Jacques Plante
13	Turk Broda
12	Terry Sawchuk
11	Patrick Roy*
10	Ken Dryden
9	Mike Richter*
8	Gerry Cheevers
8	George Hainsworth
8	Dave Kerr
8	John Roach
7	Harry Lumley
7	Tiny Thompson
6	Martin Brodeur*
6	Tony Esposito
6	Glenn Hall
6	Bernie Parent

Goaltender Clint Benedict played with Ottawa and the Montreal Maroons from 1917 to 1930.

Most Games

No.	Player
236	Mark Messier*
227	Larry Robinson
225	Glenn Anderson
221	Bryan Trottier
213	Kevin Lowe*
208	Wayne Gretzky*
196	Jari Kurri*
189	Paul Coffey*
185	Denis Potvin
184	Bobby Smith
182	Bob Gainey
180	Henri Richard
172	Claude Lemieux*
172	John Tonelli
169	Denis Savard

Most Games—Goaltenders

No.	Player
153	Patrick Roy*
132	Billy Smith
127	Grant Fuhr*
123	Andy Moog*
123	Mike Vernon*
115	Glenn Hall
112	Jacques Plante
112	Ken Dryden
106	Terry Sawchuk
102	Turk Broda
99	Tony Esposito
94	Tom Barrasso (DNP)
92	Ron Hextall*
88	Gerry Cheevers
84	Kelly Hrudey (DNP)

Most Losses

Record	Player
49-65	Glenn Hall
96-55	Patrick Roy*
45-53	Tony Esposito
64-52	Andy Moog*
54-48	Terry Sawchuk
29-47	Harry Lumley
36-46	Kelly Hrudey (DNP)
73-45	Mike Vernon*
47-43	Ron Hextall*
58-42	Turk Broda
80-40	Grant Fuhr*
51-39	Tom Barrasso (DNP)
71-37	Jacques Plante
88-36	Billy Smith
47-35	Gerry Cheevers

Playoff Single-Season Leaders

Right winger Reggie Leach of the Philadelphia Flyers scored 19 goals in 16 games in the 1976 playoffs.

Most Penalty Minutes

No.	Player/Team	Year	Games
141	Chris Nilan, Montreal	1986	18
139	Dave Schultz, Philadelphia	1974	17
116	Tiger Williams, Vancouver	1982	17
108	Tim Hunter, Calgary	1986	19
107	Jim Peplinski, Calgary	1986	22

Best Goaltender Winning Percentage
Based on at least 8 games played.

Pct.	Player/Team	Year	Record
1.000	Gump Worsley, Montreal	1968	11-0
1.000	Jacques Plante, Montreal	1960	8-0
1.000	Terry Sawchuk, Detroit	1952	8-0
.923	Gerry Cheevers, Boston	1970	12-1
.923	Ken Dryden, Montreal	1976	12-1

Note: Grant Fuhr of Edmonton went 16-2 (.889) in 1988, while Bill Durnan of Montreal and Turk Broda of Toronto, each went 8-1 in two separate playoff seasons—Durnan in 1944 and 1946, and Broda in 1948 and 1949.

Best Records
Based on at least 8 games.

Pct.	Team	Record	Rounds	Year
1.000	Detroit Red Wings	8-0	2	1952
1.000	Montreal Canadiens	8-0	2	1960
.923	Montreal Canadiens	12-1	3	1968
.923	Montreal Canadiens	12-1	3	1976
.889	Edmonton Oilers	16-2	4	1988
.889	Montreal Canadiens	8-1	2	1944
.889	Montreal Canadiens	8-1	2	1946
.889	Toronto Maple Leafs	8-1	2	1948
.889	Toronto Maple Leafs	8-1	2	1949
.857	Three teams tied at 12-2.			

Most Points

Pts.	Player/Team	Year	Games	G
47	Wayne Gretzky, Edmonton	1985	18	17
44	Mario Lemieux, Pittsburgh	1991	23	16
43	Wayne Gretzky, Edmonton	1988	19	12
40	Wayne Gretzky, Los Angeles	1993	24	15
38	Wayne Gretzky, Edmonton	1983	16	12
37	Paul Coffey, Edmonton	1985	18	12

Most Goals

No.	Player/Team	Year	Games	Pts.
19	Reggie Leach, Philadelphia	1976	16	24
19	Jari Kurri, Edmonton	1985	18	31
18	Joe Sakic, Colorado	1996	22	34
17	Seven players tied.			

Most Assists

No.	Player/Team	Year	Games	Pts.
31	Wayne Gretzky, Edmonton	1988	19	43
30	Wayne Gretzky, Edmonton	1985	18	47
29	Wayne Gretzky, Edmonton	1987	21	34
28	Mario Lemieux, Pittsburgh	1991	23	44
26	Wayne Gretzky, Edmonton	1983	16	38

Playoff Single-Game Leaders

Most Points

Listed with goals (G) and assists (A).

No.	Player/Team	Opponent	G	A	Date
8	Patrik Sundstrom, New Jersey	Washington	3	5	4/22/88
8	Mario Lemieux, Pittsburgh	Philadelphia	5	3	4/25/89
7	Wayne Gretzky, Edmonton	Calgary	4	3	4/17/83
7	Wayne Gretzky, Edmonton	Winnipeg	3	4	4/25/85
7	Wayne Gretzky, Edmonton	Los Angeles	1	6	4/9/87
6	Dickie Moore, Montreal	Boston	2	4	3/25/54
6	Phil Esposito, Boston	Toronto	4	2	4/2/69
6	Darryl Sittler, Toronto	Philadelphia	5	1	4/22/76
6	Guy Lafleur, Montreal	St. Louis	3	3	4/11/77
6	Mikko Leinonen, N.Y. Rangers	Philadelphia	0	6	4/8/82
6	Paul Coffey, Edmonton	Chicago	1	5	5/14/85
6	John Anderson, Hartford	Quebec	2	4	4/12/86
6	Mario Lemieux, Pittsburgh	Washington	3	3	4/23/92

The Richard brothers, Maurice (left) and Henri, played together on five Stanley Cup Championship teams for Montreal, from 1956 to 1960.

Most Goals

No.	Player/Game/Date
5	Newsy Lalonde, Montreal vs. Ottawa (3/1/19)
5	Maurice Richard, Montreal vs. Toronto (3/23/44)
5	Darryl Sittler, Toronto vs. Philadelphia (4/22/76)
5	Reggie Leach, Philadelphia vs. Boston (5/6/76)
5	Mario Lemieux, Pittsburgh vs. Philadelphia (4/25/89)

Most Assists

No.	Player/Game/Date
6	Mikko Leinonen, N.Y. Rangers vs. Philadelphia (4/8/82)
6	Wayne Gretzky, Edmonton vs. Los Angeles (4/9/87)
5	Ten players tied.

Most Goals—One Game

Two teams combined.

No.	Final Score/Round/Date
18	Los Angeles 10, Edmonton 8, 1st round (4/7/82)
17	Pittsburgh 10, Philadelphia 7, 2nd round (4/25/89)
16	Edmonton 13, Los Angeles 3, 1st round (4/9/87)
16	Los Angeles 12, Calgary 4, 1st round (4/10/90)

Most Goals—One Period

Two teams combined.

No.	Teams/Round/Date
9	NY Rangers (6), Philadelphia (3), 2nd round, 3rd period (4/24/79)
9	Los Angeles (5), Calgary (4), 1st round, 2nd period (4/10/90)
8	Five tied.

Most Penalty Minutes

No.	Player/Team/Opponent/Date
42	Dave Schultz, Philadelphia vs. Toronto (4/22/76)

Note: Schultz received one minor penalty, two majors, one 10- minute misconduct, and two game misconducts.

Most Career Overtime Goals

No.	Player	Last Year
6	Maurice Richard	1960
5	Glenn Anderson	1996
4	Bob Nystrom	1986
4	Wayne Gretzky	active
4	Dale Hunter	active
4	Joe Murphy	1996
4	Stephane Richter	active

Best Teams by Decade

Jean Drapeau, the mayor of Montreal (left), congratulates Canadiens' captain Yvan Cournoyer (center) and coach Scotty Bowman after the Montreal Canadiens won another Stanley Cup in 1976.

Winningest NHL Teams of the 1990s
Through the 1996-97 season.

	Team	Regular Season		Playoff
		Record	Pct.	Record
1	Detroit Red Wings	331-209-80	.598	51-38
2	Pittsburgh Penguins	328-234-58	.576	58-40
3	Chicago Blackhawks	310-228-82	.566	45-41
4	Boston Bruins	312-232-76	.565	39-43
5	New York Rangers	309-234-77	.560	47-41
6	New Jersey Devils	298-234-88	.552	41-34
7	Montreal Canadiens	299-236-85	.551	38-35
8	Calgary Flames	294-240-86	544	13-24
9	St. Louis Blues	293-242-85	.541	34-38
10	Washington Capitals	294-260-66	.527	29-34

Stanley Cup champions: •Edmonton Oilers (1990); •Pittsburgh (1991, 1992); •Montreal (1993); •N.Y. Rangers (1994); •New Jersey (1995); •Colorado Avalanche (1996); •Detroit (1997).
Franchise move and name change: Quebec Nordiques to Denver after the 1994-95 season, becoming the Colorado Avalanche.

Winningest NHL Teams of the 1980s

	Team	Regular Season		Playoff
		Record	Pct.	Record
1	Edmonton Oilers	446-250-104	.623	89-37
2	Philadelphia Flyers	446-254-100	.620	62-55
3	Montreal Canadiens	435-252-113	.614	67-50
4	Boston Bruins	418-281-101	.586	38-46
5	New York Islanders	414-288-98	.579	85-47
6	Calgary Flames	398-288-114	.569	55-51
7	Buffalo Sabres	389-293-118	.560	25-30
8	Washington Capitals	379-311-110	.543	24-29
9	New York Rangers	353-348-99	.503	33-43
10	St. Louis Blues	341-344-115	.498	39-48

Stanley Cup champions: •N.Y. Islanders (1980–83); •Edmonton (1984, 1985); •Montreal (1986); •Edmonton (1987, 1988); •Calgary (1989).
Franchise moves: Atlanta Flames moved to Calgary after the 1979- 80 season; Colorado Rockies to New Jersey after the 1981-82 season, becoming the Devils.
Note: Four World Hockey Assn. teams joined the NHL when the WHA folded after the 1978-79 season—the Edmonton Oilers, Hartford Whalers, Quebec Nordiques, and Winnipeg Jets.

Winningest NHL Teams of the 1970s

	Team	Regular Season		Playoff
		Record	Pct.	Record
1	Montreal Canadiens	499-155-134	.718	82-36
2	Boston Bruins	485-188-115	.688	69-43
3	Philadelphia Flyers	393-244-151	.595	51-44
4	New York Rangers	387-278-123	.569	44-38
5	Chicago Blackhawks	379-273-136	.567	38-45
6	Buffalo Sabres	332-251-129	.557	22-27
7	New York Islanders	252-200-104	.547	33-26
8	Toronto Maple Leafs	334-324-130	.506	22-36
9	Atlanta Flames	233-228-95	.504	1-12
10	Pittsburgh Penguins	300-353-135	.466	15-21

Stanley Cup champions: •Boston (1970); •Montreal (1971); •Boston (1972); •Montreal (1973); •Philadelphia (1974, 1975); •Montreal (1976–79).
Note: Three of the above were expansion teams. Buffalo played its first season in 1970–71, and Atlanta and the N.Y. Islanders in 1972–73.

Winningest NHL Teams of the 1960s

	Team	Regular Season		Playoff
		Record	Pct.	Record
1	Montreal Canadiens	384-201-125	.629	62-30
2	Toronto Maple Leafs	343-250-117	.565	39-38
3	Chicago Blackhawks	334-251-125	.558	35-43
4	St. Louis Blues	64-56-30	.527	16-14
5	Detroit Red Wings	294-300-116	.496	29-32
6	Philadelphia Flyers	51-67-32	.447	3-8
7	New York Rangers	257-338-115	.443	4-16
8	Los Angeles Kings	55-75-20	.433	7-11
9	Minn. North Stars	45-75-30	.400	7-7
10	Boston Bruins	228-376-106	.396	6-8

Stanley Cup champions: •Montreal (1960); •Chicago (1961); •Toronto (1962–64); •Montreal (1965, 1966); •Toronto (1967); •Montreal (1968, 1969).
Note: The NHL doubled in size from 6 to 12 teams for the 1967-68 season, adding the Los Angeles Kings, Oakland Seals, Minnesota North Stars, Philadelphia Flyers, Pittsburgh Penguins, and St. Louis Blues.

Winningest NHL Teams of the 1950s

Only 6 teams played the entire decade in the league.

	Team	Regular Season		Playoff
		Record	Pct.	Record
1	Detroit Red Wings	362-208-130	.610	42-34
2	Montreal Canadiens	354-216-130	.599	64-39
3	Toronto Maple Leafs	277-283-140	.496	18-29
4	Boston Bruins	268-289-143	.485	24-37
5	New York Rangers	250-312-138	.456	11-17

Stanley Cup champions: •Detroit (1950); •Toronto (1951); •Detroit (1952); •Montreal (1953); •Detroit (1954, 1955); •Montreal (1956–59).

Winningest NHL Teams of the 1940s

Only 6 teams played the entire decade in the league.

	Team	Regular Season		Playoff
		Record	Pct.	Record
1	Toronto Maple Leafs	253-196-75	.554	52-31
2	Detroit Red Wings	244-197-83	.545	39-47
3	Montreal Canadiens	249-203-72	.544	30-23
4	Boston Bruins	244-198-82	.544	27-36
5	Chicago Blackhawks	196-260-68	.439	7-16

Stanley Cup champions: •N.Y. Rangers (1940); •Boston (1941); •Toronto (1942); •Detroit (1943); •Montreal (1944); •Toronto (1945); •Montreal (1946); •Toronto (1947–49).

Winningest NHL Teams of the 1930s

	Team	Regular Season		Playoff
		Record	Pct.	Record
1	Boston Bruins	261-151-60	.617	18-22
2	Toronto Maple Leafs	230-172-70	.561	27-30
3	New York Rangers	216-174-82	.544	23-20
4	Montreal Maroons*	183-176-65	.508	10-16
5	Montreal Canadiens	199-193-80	.506	16-17

*The Maroons folded after the 1937–38 season.
Stanley Cup champions: •Montreal Canadiens (1930, 1931); •Toronto (1932); •N.Y. Rangers (1933); •Chicago (1934); •Montreal Maroons (1935); •Detroit Red Wings (1936, 1937); •Chicago (1938); •Boston (1939).

Winningest WHA Teams (1972–79)

The World Hockey Association (WHA) rivaled the NHL from 1972 through 1979 when it folded. Four WHA teams—Edmonton Oilers, Hartford Whalers, Quebec Nordiques, and Winnipeg Jets—were absorbed by the NHL after the 1978-79 season.

	Team	Regular Season		Playoff
		Record	Pct.	Record
1	Houston Aeros	285-170-19	.621	44-27
2	Winnipeg Jets	302-227-26	.568	48-22
3	Quebec Nordiques	295-237-24	.552	26-26
4	Minn. Fighting Saints I	124-102-8	.547	13-15
5	New Eng. Whalers	281-236-38	.541	37-30
6	Minn. Fighting Saints II	169-162-25	.510	7-15
7	San Diego Mariners	184-191-20	.491	12-16
8	Edmonton Oilers	259-273-24	.487	9-23
9	Phoenix Roadrunners	106-114-18	.483	3-7
10	Cincinnati Stingers	142-164-15	.466	1-6

WHA champions: •New England (1973); •Houston (1974, 1975); •Winnipeg (1976); •Quebec (1977); •Winnipeg (1978, 1979).
Franchise moves and name changes: •Edmonton—originally the Alberta Oilers in first WHA season (1972-73); •Houston—Aeros folded after 1977-78 season; •Minnesota I—Fighting Saints folded after 1974-75 season; •Minnesota II—original Cleveland Crusaders moved to Minnesota after 1975-76 season and became the second franchise named the Fighting Saints; •New England—Whalers played first WHA season (1972-73) in Boston (1972-73) then moved to Hartford; •San Diego—originally New York Raiders renamed the Golden Blades in 1973-74, then moved to New Jersey and became the Knights before moving to San Diego and becoming the Mariners in 1974-75.

All-Time Career Leaders

NHL regular-season career leaders through the 1997-97 season; asterisks (*) indicate players active in 1996–97.

Most Points

NHL games only; listed with goals (G) and assists (A).

Points	Player	Yrs.	G	A	Last Year
2,705	Wayne Gretzky*	18	862	1,843	active
1,850	Gordie Howe	26	801	1,049	1980
1,771	Marcel Dionne	18	731	1,040	1989
1,590	Phil Esposito	18	717	873	1981
1,552	Mark Messier*	18	575	977	active
1,494	Mario Lemieux*	12	613	881	1997
1,467	Stan Mikita	22	541	926	1980
1,444	Paul Coffey*	17	381	1,063	active
1,425	Bryan Trottier	18	524	901	1994
1,409	Dale Hawerchuk*	16	518	891	1997
1,376	Jari Kurri*	16	596	780	active
1,369	John Bucyk	23	556	813	1978
1,363	Ray Bourque*	18	362	1,001	active
1,353	Guy Lafleur	17	560	793	1991
1,347	Ron Francis*	16	403	944	active

Combined NHL–WHA Career Points

Including service in World Hockey Association (1972–79); listed with goals (G) and assists (A)

Points	Player	Yrs.	G	A	Last Year
2,815	Wayne Gretzky*#	19	908	1,907	active
2,358	Gordie Howe#	32	975	1,383	1980
1,808	Bobby Hull#	23	913	895	1980
1,771	Marcel Dionne	18	731	1,040	1989
1,590	Phil Esposito	18	717	873	1981
1,563	Mark Messier*#	19	576	987	active
1,494	Mario Lemieux*	12	613	881	1997
1,467	Stan Mikita	22	541	926	1980
1,444	Paul Coffey*	17	381	1,063	active
1,425	Bryan Trottier	18	524	901	1994
1,409	Dale Hawerchuk*	16	518	891	1997
1,376	Jari Kurri*	16	596	780	active
1,369	John Bucyk	23	556	813	1978

#Active in both WHA and NHL. Hull played 7 years in WHA; Howe, 6; and Gartner, Gretzky and Messier, 1 each.

Most Goals

No.	Player
862	Wayne Gretzky*
801	Gordie Howe
731	Marcel Dionne
717	Phil Esposito
696	Mike Gartner*
613	Mario Lemieux*
610	Bobby Hull
596	Jari Kurri*
586	Dino Ciccarelli*
575	Mark Messier*
573	Mike Bossy
560	Guy Lafleur
556	John Bucyk
548	Michel Goulet
544	Maurice Richard

Most Assists

No.	Player
1,843	Wayne Gretzky*
1,063	Paul Coffey*
1,049	Gordie Howe
1,040	Marcel Dionne
1,001	Ray Bourque*
977	Mark Messier*
944	Ron Francis*
926	Stan Mikita
901	Bryan Trottier
891	Dale Hawerchuk*
881	Mario Lemieux*
873	Phil Esposito
865	Denis Savard*
852	Bobby Clarke
825	Alex Delvecchio

Most Penalty Minutes

Min.	Player
3,966	Dave Williams
3,343	Dale Hunter*
3,146	Tim Hunter*
3,078	Marty McSorley*
3,043	Chris Nilan
2,653	Bob Probert*
2,574	Willi Plett
2,469	Rick Tocchet*
2,457	Basil McRae*
2,362	Pat Verbeek*
2,360	Scott Stevens*
2,359	Jay Wells*
2,340	Joey Kocur*
2,327	Dave Manson*
2,302	Garth Butcher

Most Years

Yrs.	Player
26	Gordie Howe#
24	Alex Delvecchio
24	Tim Horton
23	John Bucyk
22	Stan Mikita
22	Doug Mohns
22	Dean Prentice

#Including 6 seasons in the WHA brings Howe's total to 32 years.

Most Years—Goaltenders

No.	Player
21	Terry Sawchuk
21	Gump Worsley
18	Four players tied.

Gordie Howe and a young Wayne Gretzky (11 years old) met at a hockey dinner in Toronto in 1972.

Best Goals-Against Averages

Based on at least 200 games played. This category has been split into two parts, one covering the period from the NHL's inaugural 1917–18 season through 1966–67, the other beginning with the 1967–68 season when the league increased from 6 to 12 teams.

Avg.	Goaltender	Gm.	Min.	GA	Last Year
1917–18 to 1966–67					
1.91	George Hainsworth	465	29,415	937	1937
1.92	Alex Connell	417	26,030	830	1937
2.02	Chuck Gardiner	316	19,687	664	1934
2.04	Lorne Chabot	411	25,309	861	1937
2.08	Tiny Thompson	553	34,174	1,183	1940
2.17	Dave Kerr	426	26,519	960	1941
Since 1967–68 Season					
2.24	Ken Dryden	397	23,352	870	1979
2.25	Martin Brodeur*	235	13,259	497	active
2.38	Jacques Plante	837	49,533	1,965	1973
2.40	Dominik Hasek*	278	15,866	635	active
2.51	Glenn Hall	906	53,464	2,239	1971
2.52	Terry Sawchuk	971	57,114	2,401	1970
2.52	Johnny Bower	549	32,016	1,347	1970

Most Games
No.	Player
1,767	Gordie Howe
1,549	Alex Delvecchio
1,540	John Bucyk
1,446	Tim Horton
1,411	Harry Howell
1,410	Norm Ullman

Most Games—Goaltenders
No.	Player
971	Terry Sawchuk
906	Glenn Hall
886	Tony Esposito
862	Gump Worsley
837	Jacques Plante

Most Wins
No.	Player
435	Terry Sawchuk
434	Jacques Plante
423	Tony Esposito
407	Glenn Hall
355	Rogie Vachon
354	Andy Moog*
353	Grant Fuhr*
349	Patrick Roy*
335	Gump Worsley
332	Harry Lumley
305	Billy Smith
302	Turk Broda
301	Mike Vernon*
295	Tom Barrasso*
293	Mike Liut

Most Losses
No.	Player
353	Gump Worsley
351	Gilles Meloche
337	Terry Sawchuk
327	Glenn Hall
324	Harry Lumley
307	Tony Esposito
291	Rogie Vachon
284	Greg Millen
272	Don Beaupre*
271	Mike Liut
261	Cesare Maniago
256	Eddie Johnston
256	John Vanbiesbrouck*
250	Grant Fuhr*
249	Kelly Hrudey*

Most Shutouts
No.	Player
103	Terry Sawchuk
94	George Hainsworth
84	Glenn Hall
82	Jacques Plante
81	Alex Connell
81	Tiny Thompson
76	Tony Esposito
73	Lorne Chabot
71	Harry Lumley
66	Roy Worters
62	Turk Broda
58	John Roach
57	Clint Benedict
55	Bernie Parent
54	Eddie Giacomin

Current Career Leaders

Active NHL regular season career leaders through the 1996–97 season.
Note that Mario Lemieux and Denis Savard retired before start of 1997–98 season.

Wayne Gretzky scores against Buffalo on the way to a 92-goal season in 1981–82.

The Great One

In addition to most goals, assists, and points, Wayne Gretzky holds career records for most scoring titles (10), most hat tricks (49), most seasons with 40 or more goals (12), most seasons with 60 or more goals (5), most seasons with 100 or more assists (11), and most seasons with 100 or more points (15).

Most Points

Listed with goals (G) and assists (A).

Points	Player	Yrs.	G	A	First Year
2,705	Wayne Gretzky	18	862	1,843	1979
1,552	Mark Messier	18	575	977	1979
1,494	Mario Lemieux	12	613	881	1984
1,444	Paul Coffey	17	381	1,063	1980
1,409	Dale Hawerchuk	16	518	891	1981
1,376	Jari Kurri	16	596	780	1980
1,363	Ray Bourque	18	362	1,001	1979
1,347	Ron Francis	16	403	944	1982
1,340	Steve Yzerman	14	539	801	1983
1,338	Denis Savard	17	473	865	1980
1,308	Mike Gartner	18	696	612	1979
1,179	Bernie Nicholls	16	469	710	1982
1,160	Dino Ciccarelli	17	586	574	1981
1,123	Doug Gilmour	14	368	755	1983
1,064	Dave Andreychuk	15	503	561	1983

Most Goals

No.	Player
862	Wayne Gretzky
696	Mike Gartner
613	Mario Lemieux
596	Jari Kurri
586	Dino Ciccarelli
575	Mark Messier
539	Steve Yzerman
527	Brett Hull
518	Dale Hawerchuk
503	Dave Andreychuk
502	Joe Mullen
473	Denis Savard
469	Bernie Nicholls
462	Brian Bellows
462	Luc Robitaille

Most Assists

No.	Player
1,843	Wayne Gretzky
1,063	Paul Coffey
1,001	Ray Bourque
977	Mark Messier
944	Ron Francis
891	Dale Hawerchuk
881	Mario Lemieux
865	Denis Savard
801	Steve Yzerman
797	Larry Murphy
780	Jari Kurri
755	Doug Gilmour
738	Adam Oates
710	Bernie Nicholls
705	Phil Housley

Most Penalty Minutes

Min.	Player
3,343	Dale Hunter
3,146	Tim Hunter
3,078	Marty McSorley
2,653	Bob Probert
2,469	Rick Tocchet
2,457	Basil McRae
2,362	Pat Verbeek
2,360	Scott Stevens
2,359	Jay Wells
2,340	Joey Kocur
2,327	Dave Manson
2,301	Shane Churla
2,268	Craig Berube
2,174	Ulf Samuelsson
2,118	Ken Daneyko

Most Years

No.	Player
18	Ray Bourque
18	Mike Gartner
18	Wayne Gretzky
18	Kevin Lowe
18	Brad McCrimmon
18	Mark Messier
18	Jay Wells

Most Years—Goaltenders

No.	Player
17	Don Beaupre
17	Andy Moog
16	Grant Fuhr
15	John Vanbiesbrouck

Most Games

No.	Player
1,372	Mike Gartner
1,335	Wayne Gretzky
1,315	Larry Murphy
1,290	Ray Bourque
1,272	Mark Messier
1,263	Dale Hunter
1,247	Kevin Lowe
1,222	Brad McCrimmon
1,211	Paul Coffey

Most Games—Goaltenders

No.	Player
747	Grant Fuhr
671	Andy Moog
667	Don Beaupre
657	John Vanbiesbrouck
652	Patrick Roy

Most Wins

No.	Player
354	Andy Moog
353	Grant Fuhr
349	Patrick Roy
301	Mike Vernon
295	Tom Barrasso
288	John Vanbiesbrouck
268	Don Beaupre
267	Kelly Hrudey
265	Ron Hextall
223	Bill Ranford
207	Kirk McLean
204	Ed Belfour
198	Ken Wregget
184	Curtis Joseph
182	Mike Richter

Most Losses

No.	Player
272	Don Beaupre
256	John Vanbiesbrouck
250	Grant Fuhr
249	Kelly Hrudey
243	Bill Ranford
220	Ken Wregget
218	Tom Barrasso
213	Kirk McLean
203	Patrick Roy
192	Andy Moog
190	Ron Hextall
186	Sean Burke
179	Mike Vernon
160	Glenn Healy
157	Jon Casey

Most Shutouts

No.	Player
37	Patrick Roy
31	Ed Belfour
25	Andy Moog
25	John Vanbiesbrouck
23	Tom Barrasso
22	Martin Brodeur
20	Grant Fuhr
20	Dominik Hasek
19	Ron Hextall
19	Kirk McLean
18	Mike Richter
17	Don Beaupre
17	Darren Puppa
16	Jon Casey
16	Bob Essensa
16	Kelly Hrudey

Best Goals-Against Averages

Based on at least 200 games played; goals against (GA).

Avg.	Goaltender	Gm.	Min.	GA	First Year
2.25	Martin Brodeur	235	13,259	497	1992
2.40	Dominik Hasek	278	15,866	635	1991
2.68	Ed Belfour	428	24,436	1,090	1989
2.72	Patrick Roy	652	37,921	1,722	1985
2.88	Felix Potvin	297	17,298	831	1992
2.91	Guy Hebert	254	14,220	689	1992
2.93	Mike Richter	352	20,016	978	1990
3.04	Darren Puppa	385	21,423	1,086	1986
3.06	Curtis Joseph	386	22,012	1,121	1990
3.06	Rick Tabaracci	218	11,524	588	1989
3.06	Ron Hextall	539	30,827	1,574	1986
3.13	Mike Vernon	562	32,192	1,679	1983
3.14	John Vanbiesbrouck	657	37,432	1,959	1982
3.14	Chris Terreri	343	18,876	988	1987
3.15	Mark Fitzpatrick	253	14,241	747	1989

Buffalo's Dominik Hasek, the NHL's Most Valuable Player in 1996-97, was the first goaltender to win the award since Jacques Plante of Montreal was honored in 1962.

Single-Season Leaders

Mario Lemieux of Pittsburgh retired in 1997 after winning his sixth scoring championship in ten seasons.

Most Points

Pts.	Player/Team	Season	G	A
215	Wayne Gretzky, Edm.	1985-86	52	163
212	Wayne Gretzky, Edm.	1981-82	92	120
208	Wayne Gretzky, Edm.	1984-85	73	135
205	Wayne Gretzky, Edm.	1983-84	87	118
199	Mario Lemieux, Pitt.	1988-89	85	114
196	Wayne Gretzky, Edm.	1982-83	71	125
183	Wayne Gretzky, Edm.	1986-87	62	121
168	Mario Lemieux, Pitt.	1987-88	70	98
168	Wayne Gretzky, L.A.	1988-89	54	114
164	Wayne Gretzky, Edm.	1980-81	55	109
163	Wayne Gretzky, L.A.	1990-91	41	122
161	Mario Lemieux, Pitt.	1995-96	69	92
160	Mario Lemieux, Pitt.	1992-93	69	91
155	Steve Yzerman, Det.	1988-89	65	90
152	Phil Esposito, Bos.	1970-71	76	76

Most Goals

No.	Player/Team	Season
92	Wayne Gretzky, Edm.	1981-82
87	Wayne Gretzky, Edm.	1983-84
86	Brett Hull, St.Louis	1990-91
85	Mario Lemieux, Pitt.	1988-89
76	Phil Esposito, Bos.	1970-71
76	Alexander Mogilny, Buf.	1992-93
76	Teemu Selanne, Win.	1992-93
73	Wayne Gretzky, Edm.	1984-85
72	Brett Hull, St.Louis	1989-90
71	Wayne Gretzky, Edm.	1982-83
71	Jari Kurri, Edm.	1984-85
70	Brett Hull, St.Louis	1991-92
70	Mario Lemieux, Pitt.	1987-88
70	Bernie Nichols, L.A.	1988-89
69	Three tied.	

Most Assists

No.	Player/Team	Season
163	Wayne Gretzky, Edm.	1985-86
135	Wayne Gretzky, Edm.	1984-85
125	Wayne Gretzky, Edm.	1982-83
122	Wayne Gretzky, L.A.	1990-91
121	Wayne Gretzky, Edm.	1986-87
120	Wayne Gretzky, Edm.	1981-82
118	Wayne Gretzky, Edm.	1983-84
114	Wayne Gretzky, L.A.	1988-89
114	Mario Lemieux, Pitt.	1988-89
109	Wayne Gretzky, Edm.	1987-88
109	Wayne Gretzky, Edm.	1980-81
102	Wayne Gretzky, L.A.	1989-90
102	Bobby Orr, Bos.	1970-71
98	Mario Lemieux, Pitt.	1987-88
97	Adam Oates, Bos.	1992-93

Most Goals by a Rookie

No.	Player/Team	Season
76	Teemu Selanne, Win.	1992-93
53	Mike Bossy, N.Y. Islanders	1977-78
51	Joe Nieuwendyk, Calg.	1987-88
45	Dale Hawerchuk, Win.	1981-82
45	Luc Robitaille, L.A.	1986-87
44	Rick Martin, Buf.	1971-72
44	Barry Pederson, Bos.	1981-82

Most Goals by a Defenseman

No.	Player/Team	Season
48	Paul Coffey, Edm.	1985-86
46	Bobby Orr, Bos.	1974-75
40	Paul Coffey, Edm.	1983-84
39	Doug Wilson, Chi.	1981-82
37	Bobby Orr, Bos.	1970-71, 1971-72
37	Paul Coffey, Edm.	1984-85

Most Penalty Minutes

Min.	Player/Team	Season
472	Dave Schultz, Phila.	1974-75
409	Paul Baxter, Pitt.	1981-82
408	Mike Peluso, Chi.	1991-92
405	Dave Schultz, L.A.-Pitt.	1977-78
399	Marty McSorley, L.A.	1992-93
398	Bob Probert, Det.	1987-88
382	Basil McRae, Min.	1987-88
377	Joey Kocur, Det.	1985-86
375	Tim Hunter, Calg.	1988-89
371	Gino Odjick, Van.	1996-97
370	Steve Durbano, Pitt.-KC	1975-76
370	Gino Odjick, Van.	1992-93
365	Basil McRae, Min.	1988-89
361	Tim Hunter, Calg.	1986-87
358	Three players tied.	

Most Wins

No.	Player/Team	Season
47	Bernie Parent, Phila.	1973-74
44	Terry Sawchuk, Det.	1950-51
44	Terry Sawchuk, Det.	1951-52
44	Bernie Parent, Phila.	1974-75
43	Ed Belfour, Chi.	1990-91
43	Tom Barrasso, Pitt.	1992-93
42	Jacques Plante, Mon.	1955-56
42	Jacques Plante, Mon.	1961-62
42	Ken Dryden, Mon.	1975-76
42	Mike Richter, NYR	1993-94
41	Ken Dryden, Mon.	1976-77
41	Ed Belfour, Chi.	1992-93
40	Six players tied.	

Most Shutouts

No.	Goaltender/Team	Season
1917–18 to 1942–43		
22	George Hainsworth, Mon.	1928-29
15	Alex Connell, Ott.	1925-26
15	Alex Connell, Ott.	1927-28
15	Hal Winkler, Bos.	1927-28
14	George Hainsworth, Mon.	1926-27
Since 1943-44 Season		
15	Tony Esposito, Chi.	1969-70
13	Harry Lumley, Tor.	1953-54
12	Terry Sawchuk, Det.	1951-52
12	Terry Sawchuk, Det.	1953-54
12	Terry Sawchuk, Det.	1954-55
12	Glenn Hall, Det.	1955-56
12	Bernie Parent, Phila.	1973-74
12	Bernie Parent, Phila.	1974-75
11	Six players tied.	

Best Goals-Against Averages

Based on at least 30 games played. Goals-per-game average determined by games played through 1942-43 season and by minutes played since then.

Avg.	Goaltender/Team	Season	Gm.	GA
1917–18 to 1942–43				
0.98	George Hainsworth, Mon.	1928-29	44	43
1.09	George Hainsworth, Mon.	1927-28	44	48
1.17	Alex Connell, Ott.	1925-26	36	42
1.18	Tiny Thompson, Bos.	1928-29	44	52
1.21	Roy Worters, N.Y. Amer.	1928-29	38	46
Since 1943–44 Season				
1.77	Tony Esposito, Chi.	1971-72	48	82
1.77	Al Rollins, Tor.	1950-51	40	70
1.86	Harry Lumley, Tor.	1953-54	69	128
1.86	Jacques Plante, Mon.	1955-56	64	119
1.88	Martin Brodeur, N.J.	1996-97	67	120
1.88	Jacques Plante, Tor.	1970-71	40	73
1.89	Bernie Parent, Phila.	1973-74	73	136
1.90	Terry Sawchuk, Det.	1951-52	70	133
1.90	Terry Sawchuk, Det.	1952-53	63	120
1.93	Terry Sawchuk, Det.	1953-54	67	129

Goaltender Tony Esposito of the Chicago Blackhawks.

Single-Game Leaders

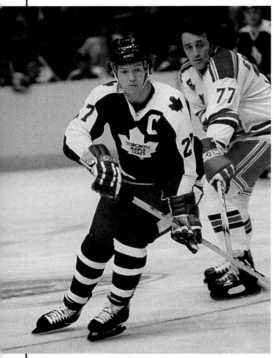

Darryl Sittler played in 1,096 games in 15 NHL seasons, but he'll be best remembered for the game against Boston on February 7, 1976, when he scored 10 points.

Most Points
Listed with goals (G) and assists (A).

Pts.	Player/Team	Opponent	G	A	Date
10	Darryl Sittler, Toronto	Boston	6	4	2/7/76
8	Maurice Richard, Montreal	Detroit	5	3	12/28/44
8	Bert Olmstead, Montreal	Chicago	4	4	1/9/54
8	Tom Bladon, Philadelphia	Cleveland	4	4	12/11/77
8	Bryan Trottier, N.Y. Islanders	N.Y. Rangers	5	3	12/23/78
8	Peter Stastny, Quebec	Washington	4	4	2/22/81
8	Anton Stastny, Quebec	Washington	3	5	2/22/81
8	Wayne Gretzky, Edmonton	New Jersey	3	5	11/19/83
8	Wayne Gretzky, Edmonton	Minnesota	4	4	1/4/84
8	Paul Coffey, Edmonton	Detroit	2	6	3/14/86
8	Mario Lemieux, Pittsburgh	St. Louis	2	6	10/15/88
8	Mario Lemieux, Pittsburgh	New Jersey	5	3	12/31/88
8	Bernie Nicholls, Los Angeles	Toronto	2	6	12/1/88

Most Goals

No.	Player/Team/Opponent/Date
7	Joe Malone, Quebec vs. Toronto (1/31/20)
6	Newsy Lalonde, Montreal vs. Toronto (1/10/20)
6	Joe Malone, Quebec vs. Ottawa (3/10/20)
6	Corb Denneny, Toronto vs. Hamilton (1/26/21)
6	Cy Denneny, Ottawa vs. Hamilton (3/7/21)
6	Syd Howe, Detroit vs. N.Y. Rangers (2/3/44)
6	Red Berenson, St. Louis vs. Philadelphia (11/7/68)
6	Darryl Sittler, Toronto vs. Boston (11/7/76)

Most Assists

No.	Player/Team/Opponent/Date
7	Billy Taylor, Detroit vs. Chicago (3/16/47)
7	Wayne Gretzky, Edmonton vs. Washington (2/15/80)
7	Wayne Gretzky, Edmonton vs. Chicago (12/11/85)
7	Wayne Gretzky, Edmonton vs. Quebec (2/14/86)
6	Twenty-two players tied.

Most Penalty Minutes

No.	Player/Team/Opponent/Date
67	Randy Holt, Los Angeles vs. Philadelphia (3/11/79)
55	Frank Bathe, Philadelphia vs. Los Angeles (3/11/79)
51	Russ Anderson, Pittsburgh vs. Edmonton (1/19/80)

Note: In the Kings-Flyers game of Mar. 11, 1979, Holt's penalties included 1 minor, 3 majors, 2 10-minute misconducts and 3 game misconducts, while Bathe was sent to the showers with 3 majors, 2 10-minute misconducts and 2 game misconducts.

Most Goals—One Game
Two teams combined.

No.	Final Score/Date
21	Montreal 14, Toronto 7 (1/10/20)
21	Edmonton 12, Chicago 9 (12/11/85)
20	Edmonton 12, Minnesota 8 (1/4/84)
20	Toronto 11, Edmonton 9 (1/8/86)
19	Six games tied.

Most Career Hat Tricks
Three or more goals in one game.

No.	Player	Last Year
49	Wayne Gretzky	active
39	Mike Bossy	1987
39	Mario Lemieux	1997
32	Phil Esposito	1981
28	Bobby Hull	1980
28	Marcell Dionne	1989

Head Coaches

Asterisks (*) indicate head coaches active at start of 1997–98 season.

Best Winning Percentages
Regular season only; at least 250 NHL victories.

Pct.	Head Coach	Yrs.	Record	Last Year
.659	Scotty Bowman*	25	1,105-460-263	active
.634	Toe Blake	13	500-255-159	1968
.616	Glen Sather	11	464-268-110	1994
.612	Fred Shero	10	390-225-119	1981
.601	Don Cherry	6	250-153-77	1980
.599	Tommy Ivan	9	288-174-111	1957
.586	Mike Keenan	12	470-318-99	1996
.580	Pat Burns*	8	307-211-83	active
.577	Terry Murray	8	281-198-58	1997
.577	Emile Francis	13	393-273-112	1983
.571	Billy Reay	16	542-385-175	1977
.571	Bryan Murray	12	467-337-112	1993
.563	Al Arbour#	22	779-576-246	1994
.559	Dick Irvin	26	690-521-226	1956

#Served a 5-game suspension as New York Islanders' coach in 1994 and is not credited with the team's 2-1-2 record during that period.

Toe Blake coaching the Montreal Canadiens. Under his leadership, the team won eight Stanley Cup titles. As a player, he had captained the team to two previous cup wins.

Most Wins
Through 1996–97 season; not including playoffs.

Wins	Head Coach	Yrs.
1,013	Scotty Bowman*	25
779	Al Arbour	22
690	Dick Irvin	26
542	Billy Reay	16
500	Toe Blake	13
470	Mike Keenan	12
467	Bryan Murray	12
464	Glen Sather	11
423	Jack Adams	21
395	Punch Imlach	15
393	Emile Francis	13
390	Fred Shero	10
384	Bob Berry	11
382	Sid Abel	16

Most Playoff Wins
Through 1997 Stanley Cup playoffs.

Wins	Head Coach	Cup Titles
178	Scotty Bowman*	7
123	Al Arbour	4
100	Dick Irvin	4
91	Mike Keenan	1
89	Glen Sather	4
82	Toe Blake	8
61	Fred Shero	2
57	Billy Reay	0
55	Jacques Demers	1
53	Pat Burns*	0
53	Pat Quinn	0
52	Jack Adams	2
49	Hap Day	5
47	Jacques Lemaire*	1

Most Wins by Active Coaches
Regular season only; through 1996–97.

Wins	Head Coach	Yrs.
1,013	Scotty Bowman, Detroit	25
307	Pat Burns, Boston	6
284	Terry Crisp, Tampa Bay	8
246	Brian Sutter, Calgary	7
227	Pierre Page, Anaheim	7
199	Jacques Lemaire, New Jersey	6
182	Jim Schoenfeld, Phoenix	8
126	Marc Crawford, Colorado	3
120	Ron Wilson, Washington	4
110	Darryl Sutter, San Jose	3
107	Jacques Martin, Ottawa	4
101	Colin Campbell, N.Y. Rangers	3
98	Rick Bowness, N.Y. Islanders	7
76	Doug MacLean, Florida	2

Home Ice

Biggest NHL Arenas

Seats	Home Ice	Home Team
21,300	Greensboro Coliseum	Carolina Hurricanes
21,273	Molson Centre	Montreal Canadiens
20,500	United Center	Chicago Blackhawks
20,000	MCI Center	Washington Capitals
19,758	Ice Palace	Tampa Bay Lightning
19,500	Marine Midland Arena	Buffalo Sabres
19,500	CoreStates Center	Philadelphia Flyers
19,275	Joe Louis Arena	Detroit Red Wings
19,260	Kiel Center	St. Louis Blues
19,040	Continental Airlines Arena	New Jersey Devils
18,840	Canadian Airlines Saddledome	Calgary Flames
18,500	Corel Centre	Ottawa Senators
18,422	General Motors Place	Vancouver Canucks

Recently renamed: Canadian Airlines Saddledome (originally Olympic Saddledome, 1983-95); Continental Airlines Arena (originally Meadowlands Arena, 1981-96); Corel Center (originally The Palladium, 1996).
Note: The Greensboro (N.C.) Coliseum Arena was gutted and rebuilt before reopening in 1992.

Oldest NHL Arenas

Opened	Home Ice	Home Team
1931	Maple Leaf Gardens	Toronto Maple Leafs
1959	Greensboro Coliseum	Carolina Hurricanes
1961	Civic Arena	Pittsburgh Penguins
1967	Great Western Forum	Los Angeles Kings
1968	Madison Square Garden	New York Rangers
1972	Veterans' Coliseum	New York Islanders

Newest NHL Arenas

Opened	Home Ice	Home Team
1997	MCI Center	Washington Capitals
1996	Marine Midland Arena	Buffalo Sabres
1996	Molson Centre	Montreal Canadiens
1996	Corel Centre	Ottawa Senators
1996	CoreStates Center	Philadelphia Flyers
1996	Ice Palace	Tampa Bay Lightning

Smallest NHL Arenas

Seats	Home Ice	Home Team
14,703	Miami Arena	Miami Panthers
15,746	Maple Leaf Gardens	Toronto Maple Leafs
16,005	Great Western Forum	Los Angeles Kings
16,061	McNichols Arena	Colorado Avalanche
16,210	America West Arena	Phoenix Coyotes
16,297	Veterans' Coliseum	New York Islanders
16,924	Reunion Arena	Dallas Stars
17,099	Edmonton Coliseum	Edmonton Oilers
17,174	Arrowhead Pond	Anaheim Mighty Ducks
17,181	Civic Arena	Pittsburgh Penguins
17,190	San Jose Arena	San Jose Sharks
17,565	FleetCenter	Boston Bruins
18,200	Madison Square Garden	New York Rangers

Recently renamed: Great Western Forum (originally The Forum, 1967-90); Edmonton Coliseum (originally Northlands Coliseum, 1974-94); Arrowhead Pond (originally Anaheim Arena, 1993).

Maple Leaf Gardens is a prominent part of the Conn Smythe Trophy, which is named aftrer the late Toronto owner, coach, and general manager and given each year to the MVP of the Stanley Cup playoffs. The arena was built in 165 days in 1931 for $1.5 million.

Awards

Most Popular Retired Numbers

Through 1996–97 regular season.

Jersey No.	Persons Honored
9	Johnny Bucyk (Bruins), Clark Gillies (Islanders), Gordie Howe (twice—Red Wings and Hurricanes), Bobby Hull (twice—Blackhawks and Coyotes); Lanny McDonald (Flames), and Maurice Richard (Canadiens).
7	Bill Barber (Flyers), Phil Esposito (Bruins), Rod Gilbert (N.Y. Rangers), Yvan Labre (Capitals), Ted Lindsay (Red Wings), Rick Martin (Sabres), and Howie Morenz (Canadiens).
1	Eddie Giacomin (N.Y. Rangers), Glenn Hall (Blackhawks), Bernie Parent (Flyers), Jacques Plante (Canadiens), and Terry Sawchuk (Red Wings).
2	Doug Harvey (Canadiens), Tim Horton (Sabres), Rick Ley (Hurricanes), and Eddie Shore (Bruins).
3	Bob Gassoff (Blues), Al Hamilton (Oilers), and Lionel Hitchman (Bruins).
4	Barry Ashbee (Flyers), Jean Beliveau (Canadiens), and Bobby Orr (Bruins).
5	Bill Barilko (Maple Leafs), Dit Clapper (Bruins), and Denis Potvin (Islanders).
8	Frank Finnigan (Senators), Bill Goldsworthy (Stars), and Barclay Plager (Blues).
16	Bobby Clarke (Flyers), Marcel Dionne (Kings), and Henri Richard (Canadiens).

Goaltenders Who Have Been Named MVP

Through 1996–97 regular season.

Season	Player/Team
1928-29	Roy Worters, N.Y. Americans
1949-50	Chuck Rayner, N.Y. Rangers
1953-54	Al Rollins, Chicago
1961-62	Jacques Plante, Montreal
1996-97	Dominik Hasek, Buffalo

Most Frequent Most Valuable Players

Through 1996–97 regular season.

No.	Player/Team/MVP Years
9	Wayne Gretzky, Edmonton and Los Angeles, 1980-87, 1989
6	Gordie Howe, Detroit, 1952, 1953, 1957, 1958, 1960, 1963
4	Eddie Shore, Boston, 1933, 1935, 1936, 1938
3	Bobby Clarke, Philadelphia, 1973, 1975, 1976
3	Mario Lemieux, Pittsburgh, 1988, 1993, 1996
3	Howie Morenz, Montreal, 1928, 1931, 1932
3	Bobby Orr, Boston, 1970-72

Positions: All are centers except right wing Howe and defensemen Orr and Shore.
Note: The Cecil Hart Memorial Trophy for regular season MVP has been awarded by the NHL since 1924.

Bobby Hull in 1962; his no. 9 has been retired twice.

Rookies of the Year Who Became MVPs

First Year	Player/Position	First MVP
1952	Bernie Geoffrion, RW	1961
1967	Bobby Orr, D	1970
1976	Bryan Trottier, C	1979
1985	Mario Lemieux, C	1988

Note: The Calder Memorial Trophy for regular season Rookie of the Year has been given out by the NHL since 1933. Wayne Gretzky was the Rookie of the Year in the World Hockey Assn. for the 1978-79 season. He joined the NHL the following year.

Most Individual Trophies Won in a Career

Through 1996–97 regular season.

No.	Player	Trophies
25	Wayne Gretzky	Ross (10), Hart (9), Lady Byng (4), Conn Smythe (2)
16	Bobby Orr	Norris (8), Hart (3), Ross (2), Smythe (2), Calder (1)
13	Mario Lemieux	Ross (6), Hart (3), Smythe (2), Calder (1), Masterton (1)
12	Gordie Howe	Hart (6), Ross (6)
8	Stan Mikita	Ross (8), Hart (2), Lady Byng (2)
8	Jacques Plante	Vezina (7), Hart (1)
7	Frank Boucher	Lady Byng (7)
7	Ken Dryden	Vezina (5), Calder (1), Smythe (1)
7	Phil Esposito	Ross (5), Hart (2)
7	Doug Harvey	Norris (7)
6	Ray Bourque	Norris (6), Calder (1)
6	Guy Lafleur	Ross (3), Hart (2), Smythe (1)
5	Seven players tied.	

NHL Trophies: •Calder—Rookie of the Year; •Hart—Regular season Most Valuable Player; •Lady Byng—Sportsmanship, ability, and gentlemanly conduct; •Masterton—Perseverance, ability, and dedication to hockey; •Norris—Best defenseman; •Ross—Regular season scoring champion; •Smythe—Playoffs' Most Valuable Player; and •Vezina—Best goaltender.

Miscellaneous

Most Regular-Season Points

Since 1917–18 season.

Pts.	Team/Record	Season
132	Montreal Canadiens,* 60-8-12	1976-77
131	Detroit Red Wings, 62-13-7	1995-96
129	Montreal Canadiens,* 59-10-11	1977-78
127	Montreal Canadiens,* 58-11-11	1975-76
121	Boston Bruins, 57-14-7	1970-71
120	Montreal Canadiens,* 52-10-16	1972-73
119	Four teams tied.	

*Went on to win Stanley Cup.
Note: NHL wins equal 2 points and a tie 1 point.

Fewest Regular-Season Points

Based on at least 70 games in the season.

Pts.	Team/Record	Season
21	Washington Capitals, 8-67-5	1974-75
24	Ottawa Senators, 10-70-4	1992-93
24	San Jose Sharks, 11-71-2	1992-93
30	New York Islanders, 12-60-6	1972-73
31	Quebec Nordiques, 12-61-7	1989-90
31	Chicago Blackhawks, 12-51-7	1953-54

Highest-Scoring Games

Most goals, both teams combined.

Goals	Final Score/Date
21	Montreal 14, Toronto 7, Jan. 10, 1920
21	Edmonton 12, Chicago 9, Dec. 11, 1985
20	Edmonton 12, Minnesota 8, Jan. 4, 1984
20	Toronto 11, Edmonton 9, Jan. 8, 1986
19	Six games tied.

Longest Winning Streaks

Single season; regular-season games only.

Gm.	Team	Dates
17	Pittsburgh	3/9/93 to 4/10/93
15	N.Y. Islanders	1/21/82 to 2/20/82
14	Boston	12/3/29 to 1/9/30
13	Boston	2/23/71 to 3/20/71
13	Philadelphia	10/19/85 to 11/17/85

Longest Losing Streaks

Single season; regular-season games only

Gm.	Team	Dates
17	Washington	2/18/75 to 3/26/75
17	San Jose	1/4/93 to 2/12/93
15	Phila. Quakers	11/29/30 to 1/8/31
14	Kansas City	12/30/75 to 1/29/76
14	Detroit	2/24/82 to 3/25/82
14	Quebec	10/21/90 to 11/19/90
14	Ottawa	3/2/93 to 4/7/93

Best One-Season Team Turnarounds

Not including the strike-interrupted 1994-95 season of 48 games; based on increases in the number of points scored.

Swing	Team	Points Records
+58 pts	San Jose	24 in 1992-93 82 in 1993-94
+52 pts	Quebec	52 in 1991-92 104 in 1992-93
+48 pts	Winnipeg	32 in 1980-81 80 in 1981-82
+40 pts	Boston	44 in 1966-67 84 in 1967-68
+38 pts	Detroit	40 in 1985-86 78 in 1986-87
+38 pts	Dallas	66 in 1995-96 104 in 1996-97

Longest Undefeated Streaks

Single season; regular-season games only, including ties.

Gm.	Team/Record	Dates
35	Philadelphia, 25-0-10	10/14/79 to 1/6/80
28	Montreal, 23-0-5	12/18/77 to 2/23/78
23	Boston, 15-0-8	12/22/40 to 2/23/41
23	Philadelphia, 17-0-6	1/29/76 to 3/18/76

Longest Winless Streaks

Single season; regular-season games only.

Gm.	Team/Record	Dates
30	Winnipeg, 0-23-7	10/19/80 to 12/20/80
27	Kansas City, 0-21-6	2/12/76 to 4/4/76
25	Washington, 0-22-3	11/29/75 to 1/21/76

Goaltenders Who Have Scored Goals

Regular season and playoffs.

Date	Player/Game
11/28/79	Billy Smith, NY Islanders vs. Colorado
12/8/87	Ron Hextall, Philadelphia vs. Boston
4/11/89	Ron Hextall, Philadelphia vs. Washington*
3/6/96	Chris Osgood, Detroit vs. Hartford
4/17/97	Martin Brodeur, New Jersey vs. Montreal*

*In playoffs.
Note: Hextall, Osgood, and Brodeur scored their goals on rink-length shots through traffic. Smith, however, got his goal without taking a shot. It came about on a delayed penalty against New York during which Colorado lifted its goaltender in favor of an extra skater. Smith made a save, the rebound came to the Rockies' Rob Ramage, and Ramage, attempting a pass back to the blue line, inadvertently sent the puck out of the Islanders' defensive zone and into his own unattended net. As the last New York player to touch the puck, Smith got credit for the goal—the first by a goaltender in NHL history.

GOLF

Tiger Woods, the 1997 Masters champion, with caddie Mike (Fluff) Cowan.

The Grand Slam

Bobby Jones at the British Open, 1930.

The Impregnable Quadrilateral

In golf history there have been two recognized Grand Slams. The first, dubbed "the impregnable quadrilateral" by sportswriter Grantland Rice, was attained only once, when 28-year-old Atlanta amateur Bobby Jones won the British Amateur on June 1, 1930 the British Open on June 20, the U.S. Open on July 12, and the U.S. Amateur on Sept. 27. The second Grand Slam, which has never been completed, consists of the Masters, U.S. Open, British Open, and PGA Championship. It was recognized in 1960 when a charismatic 30-year-old named Arnold Palmer started the season with victories at the Masters and the U.S. Open. Golf writers seized the opportunity to point out that he was chasing a "modern" Grand Slam, but Palmer finished second at the British and seventh at the PGA. Only one golfer, Ben Hogan, has won three of the four, and that was in 1953 before the modern slam had gained worldwide acceptance.

Most Major Championship Titles

Golf's major professional championships are the British Open (first played in 1860), U.S. Open (1895), PGA Championship (1916), and the Masters (1934). Totals include 1997 results.

Wins	Player	British Open	U.S. Open	PGA	Masters	Last Major
18	Jack Nicklaus*	3	4	5	6	1986
11	Walter Hagen	4	2	5	0	1929
9	Ben Hogan	1	4	2	2	1953
9	Gary Player	3	1	2	3	1978
8	Tom Watson*	5	1	0	2	1983
7	Bobby Jones	3	4	0	0	1930
7	Arnold Palmer	2	1	0	4	1964
7	Gene Sarazen	1	2	3	1	1935
7	Sam Snead	1	0	3	3	1954
7	Harry Vardon	6	1	DNP	DNP	1914
6	Nick Faldo*	3	0	0	3	1996
6	Lee Trevino	2	2	2	0	1984
5	Seve Ballesteros	3	0	0	2	1988
5	James Braid	5	0	DNP	DNP	1910
5	Byron Nelson	0	1	2	2	1945
5	J.H. Taylor	5	0	DNP	DNP	1913
5	Peter Thomson	5	0	0	0	1965

*Made the cut in at least one major in 1997.
DNP—Did not play in tournament.

Most Frequent Runners-up

Totals include 1997 results.

No.	Player	British Open	U.S. Open	PGA	Masters	Majors Played
19	Jack Nicklaus	7	4	4	4	148
10	Arnold Palmer	1	4	3	2	131
8	Greg Norman	1	2	2	3	68
8	Sam Snead	0	4	2	2	105
7	J.H. Taylor	6	1	DNP	DNP	27
7	Tom Watson	1	2	1	3	92
6	Ben Hogan	0	2	0	4	54
6	Byron Nelson	0	1	3	2	33
6	Gary Player	0	2	2	2	134
6	Harry Vardon	4	2	DNP	DNP	26

DNP—Did not play in tournament.

Players Who Have Won All 4 Majors
Listed with the first or only year in which each title was won.

Player	British Open	U.S. Open	PGA	Masters
Ben Hogan	1953	1948	1946	1951
Jack Nicklaus	1966	1962	1963	1963
Gary Player	1959	1965	1962	1961
Gene Sarazen	1932	1922	1922	1935

Players Who Have Won 3 of 4 Majors
Through 1997; listed with the first or only year in which each title was won
and the best finish in the missing championship ("T" indicates a tie).

Player	British Open	U.S. Open	PGA	Masters
Tommy Armour	1931	1927	1930	T-8th, 1937
Jim Barnes	1925	1921	1916	DNP
Ray Floyd	T-2nd, 1978	1986	1969	1976
Walter Hagen	1922	1914	1921	T-11th, 1936
Byron Nelson	5th, 1937	1939	1940	1937
Arnold Palmer	1961	1960	2nd*	1958
Sam Snead	1946	2nd#	1942	1949
Lee Trevino	1971	1968	1974	10th†
Tom Watson	1975	1982	T-2nd, 1978‡	1977

*Palmer tied for 2nd in the PGA Championship in 1964, 1968, and 1970.
#Snead lost to Lew Worsham in a playoff for the U.S. Open title in 1947 and finished or tied for 2nd in 1937, 1949, and 1953.
†Trevino tied for 10th at The Masters in 1975 and 1985.
‡Watson and Jerry Pate lost to John Mahaffey in a playoff for the 1978 PGA Championship.

CALENDAR YEAR

Players Who Have Won 2 of 4 Majors

Year	Player	Majors Won	Year	Player	Majors Won
1994	Nick Price	British Open, PGA	1962	Arnold Palmer	Masters, Brit. Open
1990	Nick Faldo	Masters, Brit. Open	1960	Arnold Palmer	Masters, U.S. Open
1982	Tom Watson	U.S., Brit. Open	1956	Jack Burke Jr.	Masters, PGA
1980	Jack Nicklaus	U.S. Open, PGA	1951	Ben Hogan	Masters, U.S. Open
1977	Tom Watson	Masters, Brit. Open	1949	Sam Snead	Masters, PGA
1975	Jack Nicklaus	Masters, PGA	1948	Ben Hogan	U.S. Open, PGA
1974	Gary Player	Masters, Brit. Open	1941	Craig Wood	Masters, U.S. Open
1972	Jack Nicklaus	Masters, U.S. Open	1932	Gene Sarazen	U.S., Brit. Open
1971	Lee Trevino	U.S., Brit. Open	1926	Bobby Jones	U.S., Brit. Open
1966	Jack Nicklaus	Masters, Brit. Open	1924	Walter Hagen	Brit. Open, PGA
1963	Jack Nicklaus	Masters, PGA	1922	Gene Sarazen	U.S. Open, PGA

Players Who Have Won 2 of 4 Majors
Through 1997.

British Open & U.S. Open
Tony Jacklin, Bobby Jones, Johnny Miller, Ted Ray, Harry Vardon

British Open & PGA
John Daly, Jock Hutchison, Nick Price, Denny Shute, Payne Stewart

British Open & Masters
Seve Ballesteros, Nick Faldo, Sandy Lyle

U.S. Open & PGA
Julius Boros, Olin Dutra, David Graham, Hubert Green, Larry Nelson

U.S. Open & Masters
Billy Casper, Ralph Guldahl, Cary Middlecoff, Craig Wood, Fuzzy Zoeller

PGA & Masters
Jack Burke Jr., Doug Ford, Henry Picard

Hogan's Hat Trick
Ben Hogan (above), was severely injured in early 1949 in a car accident, sustaining extensive damage to his legs. The thirty-six-year-old Texan struggled through a painful, seventeen-month recuperation, and on June 11, 1950, his legs wrapped in bandages, he completed one of the great comebacks in sports history by winning his second U.S. Open. The following year Hogan won the Masters and repeated at the Open, and in 1953, he topped himself, becoming the only golfer to win three of the four majors in one year—the Masters, U.S. Open, and British Open. The PGA Championship that July conflicted with the playing dates at the British Open.

The Masters

Arnold Palmer (left), Jack Nicklaus (center) and Tiger Woods have won the Masters championship a combined 11 times.

Youngest Winners

Age	Player	Year	Score
21 yrs., 104 days	Tiger Woods	1997	270*
23 yrs., 4 days	Seve Ballesteros	1980	275
23 yrs., 76 days	Jack Nicklaus	1963	286
25 yrs., 59 days	Byron Nelson	1937	283
25 yrs., 77 days	Jack Nicklaus	1965	271

*Tournament record.

Oldest Winners

Age	Player	Year	Score
46 yrs., 82 days	Jack Nicklaus	1986	279
43 yrs., 88 days	Ben Crenshaw	1995	274
42 yrs., 159 days	Gary Player	1978	277
41 yrs., 320 days	Sam Snead	1954	289*
40 yrs., 242 days	Ben Hogan	1953	274

*Playoff: Snead, 78 days older than Ben Hogan, shot 70 in 18-hole playoff to defeat Hogan by 1 stroke.

The Tournament

Called the Augusta National Invitational from 1934 to 1937, the Masters is the only major professional golf championships that is by invitation only and is played on same the course each year—the Augusta National near Atlanta. Both the course and the tournament were the handiwork of Bobby Jones, a native Georgian who had retired from competitive golf at the height of his powers in 1930. The following year Jones and several friends bought a former tree nursery covering 365 acres and commissioned famed Scottish architect Alister Mackenzie to help design and construct its unique 18-hole layout. Jones, who came out of retirement to play in the inaugural Masters in 1934 (he tied for 13th), died in 1971.

Most Wins

No.	Player	Years
6	Jack Nicklaus	1986, 1975, 1972, 1966*, 1965, 1963
4	Arnold Palmer	1964, 1962,* 1960, 1958
3	Jimmy Demaret	1950, 1947, 1940
3	Nick Faldo	1996, 1990,* 1989*
3	Gary Player	1978, 1974, 1961
3	Sam Snead	1954,* 1952, 1949
2	Seve Ballesteros	1983, 1980
2	Ben Crenshaw	1995, 1984
2	Ben Hogan	1953, 1951
2	Bernhard Langer	1993, 1985
2	Byron Nelson	1942,* 1937
2	Horton Smith	1936, 1934
2	Tom Watson	1981, 1977

*Won playoff.

Most Frequent Runners-up

Players who have finished 2nd or tied for 2nd more than once.

No.	Player	Years
4	Ben Hogan	1955, 1954*, 1946, 1942*
4	Jack Nicklaus	1981, 1977, 1971, 1964
4	Tom Weiskopf	1975, 1974, 1972, 1969
3	Ray Floyd	1992, 1990*, 1985
3	Tom Kite	1997, 1986, 1983
3	Johnny Miller	1981, 1975, 1971
3	Greg Norman	1996, 1987*, 1986
3	Tom Watson	1984, 1979*, 1978
2	Twelve players tied#	

* Lost playoff.
#Seve Ballesteros (1987,* 1985), Harry Cooper (1938, 1936), Ben Crenshaw (1983, 1976), Ralph Guldahl (1938, 1937), Lloyd Mangrum (1949, 1940), Cary Middlecoff (1959, 1948), Byron Nelson (1947, 1941), Arnold Palmer (1965, 1961), Gary Player (1965, 1962*), Sam Snead (1957, 1939), Ken Venturi (1960, 1956), and Craig Wood (1935,* 1934).

Lowest Score for 18 Holes

Par at Augusta National Golf Club is 72.

Total	Player	Round	Year	Final Place
63	Nick Price	3rd	1986	5th
63	Greg Norman	1st	1996	2nd
64	Lloyd Mangrum	1st	1940	2nd
64	Jack Nicklaus	3rd	1965	Won
64	Maurice Bembridge	4th	1974	T-9th
64	Hale Irwin	4th	1975	T-4th
64	Gary Player	4th	1978	Won
64	Miller Barber	2nd	1979	T-12th
64	Greg Norman	4th	1988	T-5th
64	Mike Donald	1st	1990	47th
64	Jay Haas	2nd	1995	T-3rd

Lowest 72-Hole Totals

Par over 4 rounds at Augusta National is 288.

Total	Player	Rounds	Year
270	Tiger Woods	70-66-65-69	1997
271	Jack Nicklaus	67-71-64-69	1965
271	Ray Floyd	65-66-70-70	1976
274	Ben Hogan	70-69-66-69	1953
274	Ben Crenshaw	70-67-69-68	1995
275	Seve Ballesteros	66-69-68-72	1980
275	Fred Couples	69-67-69-70	1992
275	Davis Love III*	69-69-71-66	1995

*Runner-up.

Wire-to-Wire Winners

Led or tied for lead from start to finish since first Masters in 1934.

Year	Winner	Year	Winner
1980	Seve Ballesteros	1947	Jimmy Demaret
1976	Ray Floyd*	1946	Herman Kaiser
1972	Jack Nicklaus*	1941	Craig Wood*
1964	Arnold Palmer	1934	Horton Smith
1960	Arnold Palmer*		

*Outright leader after every round.

Widest Margins of Victory

Shots	Winner/Score	Runner-up	Year
12	Tiger Woods, 270	Tom Kite	1997
9	Jack Nicklaus, 271	Arnold Palmer, Gary Player	1965
8	Ray Floyd, 271	Ben Crenshaw	1976
7	Cary Middlecoff, 279	Ben Hogan	1955
6	Arnold Palmer, 276	Dave Marr, Jack Nicklaus	1964

Most Top-5 Finishes

No.	Player	1st	2nd	3rd	4th	5th
15	Jack Nicklaus	6	4	2	2	1
9	Ben Hogan	2	4	0	3	0
9	Arnold Palmer	4	2	1	2	0
9	Sam Snead	3	2	3	1	0
8	Gary Player	3	2	1	0	2
8	Tom Watson	2	3	1	1	1

Jack Nicklaus became the oldest player to win the Masters in 1986 when he fired a final round 65 to beat Tom Kite and Greg Norman by 1 shot—at age 46.

United States Open

Sam Snead (left) and
Ben Hogan in 1953.

The Tournament

The United States Open Championship was first played in 1895, 35 years after the inaugural British Open. British-born golfers won the first 16 U.S. Opens, a situation that wasn't remedied until 1911 when Johnny McDermott of the Atlantic City (N.J.) Country Club won a three-way playoff for the title in Chicago. At age 19, McDermott remains the Open's youngest champion. Two years later, 20-year-old American amateur Francis Ouimet defeated British pros Harry Vardon and Ted Ray in a memorable playoff at Ouimet's home course in Brookline, MA. Administered by the U.S. Golf Association (USGA), the Open has been held at 47 different golf clubs across the country.

Youngest Winners

Age	Player	Year	Score
19 yrs., 318 days	John McDermott	1911	307*
20 yrs., 135 days	Francis Ouimet	1913	304*
20 yrs., 138 days	Gene Sarazen	1922	288
20 yrs., 356 days	John McDermott	1912	294
21 yrs., 47 days	Willie Anderson	1901	331*
22 yrs., 147 days	Jack Nicklaus	1962	283*

*Playoffs: •Anderson shot 85 in 18-hole playoff to defeat Alex Smith (86); •McDermott shot 80 in 18-hole playoff to defeat Mike Brady (82) and George Simpson (85); •Ouimet, an amateur, shot 72 in 18-hole playoff to defeat Harry Vardon (77) and Ted Ray (78); •Nicklaus shot 71 in 18-hole playoff to defeat Arnold Palmer (74).

Oldest Winners

Age	Player	Year	Score
45 yrs., 15 days	Hale Irwin	1990	280*
43 yrs., 284 days	Ray Floyd	1986	279
43 yrs., 138 days	Ted Ray	1920	295
43 yrs., 112 days	Julius Boros	1963	293*
40 yrs., 304 days	Ben Hogan	1953	283

*Playoffs: •Boros shot 70 in 18-hole playoff to defeat Jacky Cupit (73) and Arnold Palmer (76); •Irwin defeated Mike Donald, 3-4, on first extra hole after they each shot 74 in an 18-hole playoff.

Most Wins

No.	Player	Years
4	Willie Anderson	1905, 1904, 1903,* 1901
4	Ben Hogan	1953, 1951, 1950,* 1948
4	Bobby Jones	1930, 1929,* 1926, 1923*
4	Jack Nicklaus	1980, 1972, 1967, 1962*
3	Hale Irwin	1990,* 1979, 1974
2	Julius Boros	1963,* 1952
2	Billy Casper	1966,* 1959
2	Ernie Els	1997, 1994
2	Ralph Guldahl	1938, 1937
2	Walter Hagen	1919,* 1914
2	John McDermott	1912, 1911*
2	Cary Middlecoff	1956, 1949
2	Andy North	1985, 1978
2	Gene Sarazen	1932, 1922
2	Alex Smith	1910,* 1906
2	Curtis Strange	1989, 1988*
2	Lee Trevino	1968, 1971*

*Won playoff.

Most Frequent Runners-up

Players who have finished 2nd or tied for 2nd more than once.

No.	Player	Years
4	Bobby Jones	1928,* 1925,* 1924, 1922
4	Jack Nicklaus	1982, 1971,* 1968, 1960
4	Arnold Palmer	1967, 1966,* 1963,* 1962*
4	Sam Snead	1953, 1949, 1947,* 1937,
3	Alex Smith	1905, 1901,* 1898
2	Nineteen players tied.#	

* Lost playoff.
#Chip Beck (1989, 1986), Mike Brady (1919,* 1911*), Harry Cooper (1936, 1927*), Bobby Cruickshank (1932, 1923*), Al Geiberger (1976, 1969), Ben Hogan (1956, 1955*), Jock Hutchison (1920, 1916), Tom McNamara (1912, 1909), Colin Montgomerie (1997, 1994*), Gil Nicholls (1907, 1904), Greg Norman (1995, 1984*), Gary Player (1979, 1958), Bob Rosburg (1969, 1959), Gene Sarazen (1940,* 1934), Denny Shute (1941, 1939*), Macdonald Smith (1930, 1910*), Willie Smith (1908,* 1906), Harry Vardon (1920, 1913*), and Tom Watson (1987, 1983).

Lowest Score for 18 Holes

Total	Player	Round	Year	Final Place
63	Johnny Miller	4th	1973	Won
63	Jack Nicklaus	1st	1980	Won
63	Tom Weiskopf	1st	1980	37th
64	Lee Mackey Jr.	1st	1950	T-25th
64	Tommy Jacobs	2nd	1964	2nd
64	Rives McBee	2nd	1966	T-13th
64	Ben Crenshaw	3rd	1981	T-11th
64	Loren Roberts	3rd	1994	T-2nd

Playing sites: 1994—Oakmont (PA); 1981—Merion (PA); 1980—Baltusrol (NJ); 1973—Oakmont (PA); 1966—Olympic (CA); 1964—Congressional (MD); 1950—Merion (PA).

Lowest 72-Hole Totals

Total	Player	Rounds	Year
272	Jack Nicklaus	63-71-70-68	1980
272	Lee Janzen	67-67-69-69	1993
273	David Graham	68-68-70-69	1981
274	Isao Aoki*	68-68-68-70	1980
274	Payne Stewart*	70-66-68-70	1993
275	Jack Nicklaus	71-67-72-65	1967
275	Lee Trevino	69-68-69-69	1968

*Runner-up
Playing sites: 1993—Baltusrol (NJ); 1981—Merion (PA); 1980—Baltusrol (NJ); 1968—Oak Hill (NY); 1967—Baltusrol (NJ).

Wire-to-Wire Winners
Led or tied for lead from start to finish, after the Open went to 72 holes in 1898.

Year	Winner
1991	Payne Stewart
1980	Jack Nicklaus
1977	Hubert Green
1972	Jack Nicklaus
1970	Tony Jacklin*
1958	Tommy Bolt
1953	Ben Hogan*
1921	Jim Barnes*
1916	Chick Evans
1914	Walter Hagen*
1906	Alex Smith

*Outright leader after every round.

Widest Margins of Victory

Shots	Winner/Score	Runner-up	Year
11	Willie Smith, 315	3-way tie for 2nd	1899
9	Jim Barnes, 289	Walter Hagen, Fred McLeod	1921
7	Fred Herd, 328	Alex Smith	1898
7	Alex Smith, 295	Willie Smith	1906
7	Tony Jacklin, 281	Dave Hill	1970

Most Top-5 Finishes

No.	Player	1st	2nd	3rd	4th	5th
11	Jack Nicklaus	4	4	1	2	0
11	Willie Anderson	4	1	1	2	3
10	Ben Hogan	4	2	2	1	1
10	Walter Hagen	2	1	1	4	2
10	Arnold Palmer	1	4	1	1	3
9	Gene Sarazen	2	2	3	1	1

Most Frequent Playing Sites

No.	Golf Course	Location	Years
7	Baltusrol CC	Springfield, NJ	1993, 1980, 1967, 1954, 1936, 1915, 1903
7	Oakmont CC	Oakmont, PA	1994, 1983, 1973, 1962, 1953, 1935, 1927
6	Oakland Hills CC	Bloomfield Hills, MI	1996, 1985, 1961, 1951, 1937, 1924

Note: Four other courses have been the tournament venue four times each—Inverness (OH), Merion (PA), Myopia Hunt (MA), and Winged Foot (NY).

Jack Nicklaus on his way to winning the 1962 U.S. Open at the age of 22.

British Open

Tom Watson holds up his 5th British Open trophy in 1983.

Most Wins

No.	Player	Years
6	Harry Vardon	1914, 1911,* 1903, 1899, 1898, 1896*
5	James Braid	1910, 1908, 1906, 1905, 1901
5	J.H. Taylor	1913, 1909, 1900, 1895, 1894
5	Peter Thomson	1965, 1958,* 1954-56
5	Tom Watson	1983, 1982, 1980, 1977, 1975*
4	Walter Hagen	1929, 1928, 1924, 1922
4	Bobby Locke	1957, 1952, 1950, 1949*
4	Tom Morris Sr.	1867, 1864, 1862, 1861
4	Tom Morris Jr.	1872, 1868-70
4	Willie Park Sr.	1875, 1866, 1863, 1960
3	Jamie Anderson	1877-79
3	Seve Ballesteros	1988, 1984, 1979
3	Henry Cotton	1948, 1937, 1934
3	Nick Faldo	1992, 1990, 1987
3	Robert Ferguson	1880-82
3	Bobby Jones	1930, 1927, 1926
3	Jack Nicklaus	1978, 1970,* 1966
3	Gary Player	1974, 1968, 1959
2	Six players tied.#	

* Won playoff.
#Harold Hilton (1897, 1892), Bob Martin (1885, 1876*), Greg Norman (1993, 1986), Arnold Palmer (1962, 1961), Willie Park Jr. (1889*, 1887), and Lee Trevino (1972, 1971).

Most Frequent Runners-up

Players who finished second or tied for second more than once.

No.	Player	Years
7	Jack Nicklaus	1979, 1977, 1976, 1972, 1968, 1967, 1964
6	J.H. Taylor	1914, 1904-7, 1896*
4	James Braid	1909, 1904, 1902, 1897
4	Willie Fernie	1891, 1890, 1884, 1882
4	Alexander Herd	1920, 1910, 1895, 1892
4	Willie Park Sr.	1867, 1865, 1862, 1861
4	Harry Vardon	1912, 1900-02
3	Four players tied.#	
2	Twenty players tied.†	

* Lost playoff.
# Andrew Kirkaldy (1891, 1889,* 1879), Tom Morris Sr. (1869, 1863, 1860), Dai Rees (1961, 1954, 1953), David Strath (1876,* 1872, 1870), and Peter Thomson (1957, 1953, 1952).
† Jimmy Adams (1938, 1936), Jamie Anderson (1881, 1873), Johnny Bulla (1946, 1939), Tony Cerda (1953, 1951), Bob Charles (1969, 1968), Ben Crenshaw (1979, 1978), Bob Kirk (1878, 1870), Bernhard Langer (1984, 1981), Peter Oosterhuis (1982, 1974), Nick Price (1988, 1982), Ted Ray (1925, 1913), Doug Sanders (1970,* 1966), Archie Simpson (1890, 1885), Macdonald Smith (1932, 1930), Payne Stewart (1990, 1985), Fred Stranahan (1953, 1947), Dave Thomas (1966, 1958*) and Flory Van Donck (1959, 1956).

Youngest Winners

Age	Player	Year	Score
17 yrs., 156 days	Tom Morris Jr.	1868	157
18 yrs., 149 days	Tom Morris Jr.	1869	154
19 yrs., 148 days	Tom Morris Jr.	1870	149
21 yrs., 24 days	Willie Auchterlonie	1893	322
21 yrs., 146 days	Tom Morris Jr.	1872	166
22 yrs., 103 days	Seve Ballesteros	1979	283

Oldest Winners

Age	Player	Year	Score
46 yrs., 96 days	Tom Morris Sr.	1867	170
44 yrs., 92 days	Roberto de Vicenzo	1967	278
44 yrs., 41 days	Harry Vardon	1914	306
43 yrs., 86 days	Tom Morris Sr.	1864	167
42 yrs., 97 days	J.H. Taylor	1913	304

Lowest Score for 18 Holes

Total	Player	Round	Year	Final Place
63	Mark Hayes	2nd	1977	T-8th
63	Isao Aoki	3rd	1980	T-7th
63	Greg Norman	2nd	1986	Won
63	Paul Broadhurst	3rd	1990	T-12th
63	Jodie Mudd	4th	1991	T-4th
63	Nick Faldo	2nd	1993	2nd

Playing sites: 1993—Sandwich; 1991—Birkdale; 1990—St. Andrews; 1986—Turnberry; 1980—Muirfield; 1977—Turnberry.

Lowest 72-Hole Totals

Total	Player	Rounds	Year
267	Greg Norman	66-68-69-64	1993
268	Tom Watson	68-70-65-65	1977
268	Nick Price	69-66-67-66	1994
269	Jack Nicklaus*	68-70-65-66	1977
269	Nick Faldo*	69-63-70-67	1993
269	Jesper Parnevik*	68-66-68-67	1994
270	Nick Faldo	67-65-67-71	1990
270	Bernhard Langer†	67-66-70-67	1993
271	Tom Watson	68-70-64-69	1980
271	Fuzzy Zoeller†	71-66-64-70	1994
271	Tom Lehman	67-67-64-73	1996

*Runner-up. †Third place.
Playing sites: 1996—Lytham; 1994—Turnberry; 1993—Sandwich; 1990—St. Andrews; 1980—Muirfield; 1977—Turnberry.

Wire-to-Wire Winners

Year	Winner	Year	Winner
1974	Gary Player	1908	James Braid*
1973	Tom Weiskopf*	1903	Harry Vardon
1971	Lee Trevino	1900	J.H. Taylor*
1934	Henry Cotton*	1899	Harry Vardon
1932	Gene Sarazen*	1894	J.H. Taylor*
1927	Bobby Jones*	1893	Willie Auchterlonie*
1912	Ted Ray*		

*Outright leader after every round.

Widest Margins of Victory

Shots	Winner/Score	Runner-up	Year
13	Tom Morris Sr., 163	Willie Park	1862
12	Tom Morris Jr., 149	Bob Kirk	1870
8	J.H. Taylor, 309	Harry Vardon	1900
8	James Braid, 291	Tom Ball	1908
8	J.H. Taylor, 304	Ted Ray	1913

Most Top-5 Finishes

No.	Player	1st	2nd	3rd	4th	5th
16	J.H. Taylor	5	6	1	2	2
16	Jack Nicklaus	3	7	3	2	1
15	Harry Vardon	6	4	2	0	3
15	James Braid	5	4	2	0	4
10	Peter Thomson	5	3	1	0	1

Most Frequent Playing Sites

No.	Golf Course	Location	First Used	Last Used
25	St. Andrews	Scotland	1873	1995
24	Prestwick	Scotland	1860	1925
14	Muirfield	Scotland	1892	1992
12	Sandwich	England	1894	1993
10	Hoylake	England	1897	1967

The Tournament

In addition to being golf's oldest major championship, the British Open is the only one that is traditionally played on seaside links, limiting the number of available courses to just 14. The first Open Championship was held in 1860 with 8 entrants playing 3 rounds over the 12 holes of the Prestwick Club in Ayrshire, Scotland. Led by professional Walter Hagen and amateur Bobby Jones, American golfers dominated the Open from 1921 to 1933, but U.S. participation dropped off after World War II. Ben Hogan's victory in 1953 marked the only time he ever entered the tournament. Arnold Palmer's consecutive victories in 1961 and 1962 revived American interest, and the Yanks have won 17 more titles since then.

PGA Championship

The PGA Championship was a match-play tournament from 1916 to 1957 and has been stroke play since then.

Twenty-year-old champion Gene Sarazen, 1922.

The Tournament

Soon after the formation of the Professional Golfers' Association of America (PGA) in January 1916, an annual all-professional match-play tournament was established to showcase the best golfers in America. Walter Hagen, the first American-born champion, held the title five times between 1921 and 1927. Match play, which had set the PGA Championship apart from the Masters and the two Opens, was surrendered in 1958 with the emerging power of television. Since then the PGA has been a stroke-play championship and the last of the four majors played each year.

Youngest Winners

Age	Player	Year	Score
20 yrs., 172 days	Gene Sarazen	1922	4 &3*
20 yrs., 223 days	Tom Creavy	1931	2 &1*
21 yrs., 214 days	Gene Sarazen	1923	1 up (38)*
23 yrs., 181 days	Jack Nicklaus	1963	279
24 yrs., 201 days	Johnny Revolta	1935	5 & 4*

*Match play finals: •Creavy defeated Denny Shute; •Revolta defeated Tommy Armour; •Sarazen defeated Emmet French in 1922 and Walter Hagen in 1923 on the 2nd extra hole after they finished the first 36 holes even.

Oldest Winners

Age	Player	Year	Score
48 yrs., 140 days	Julius Boros	1968	281
45 yrs., 97 days	Jerry Barber	1961	277*
44 yrs., 262 days	Lee Trevino#	1984	273
40 yrs., 202 days	Jack Nicklaus	1980	274
39 yrs., 338 days	Ray Floyd	1982	272

*Playoff: Barber shot 67 in 18-hole playoff to defeat Don January (68).
#Trevino was 4 strokes better and 4 years younger than runner-up Gary Player, who would have been the tournament's oldest winner ever at 48 years and 292 days.

Most Wins

Match-play and stroke-play eras combined.

No.	Player	Years
5	Walter Hagen	1924-27, 1921
5	Jack Nicklaus	1980, 1975, 1973, 1971, 1963
3	Gene Sarazen	1933, 1923,* 1922
3	Sam Snead	1951, 1949, 1942
2	Jim Barnes	1919, 1916
2	Leo Diegel	1929, 1929
2	Ray Floyd	1982, 1969
2	Ben Hogan	1948, 1946
2	Byron Nelson	1945, 1940
2	Larry Nelson	1987,* 1981
2	Gary Player	1972, 1962
2	Nick Price	1994, 1992
2	Paul Runyan	1938, 1934*
2	Denny Shute	1937,* 1936
2	Dave Stockton	1976, 1970
2	Lee Trevino	1984, 1974

*Won playoff.

Most Frequent Runners-up

Match-play and stroke-play eras combined.

No.	Player	Years
4	Jack Nicklaus	1983, 1974, 1965, 1964
3	Billy Casper	1971, 1965, 1958
3	Byron Nelson	1944, 1941,* 1939*
3	Arnold Palmer	1970, 1968, 1964
3	Lanny Wadkins	1987,* 1984, 1982
2	Nine players tied.#	

*Lost playoff.
#Jim Barnes (1924, 1921), Andy Bean (1989, 1980), Walter Burkemo (1954, 1951), Bruce Crampton (1975, 1973), Chick Harbert (1952, 1947), Don January (1976, 1961*), Greg Norman (1993,* 1986), Gary Player (1984, 1969), and Sam Snead (1940, 1938).

Lowest Score for 18 Holes

After the PGA switched to stroke play in 1958.

Total	Player	Round	Year	Final Place
63	Bruce Crampton	2nd	1975	2nd
63	Ray Floyd	1st	1982	Won
63	Gary Player	2nd	1984	T-2nd
63	Vijay Singh	2nd	1993	4th
63	Brad Faxon	4th	1995	5th
63	Michael Bradley	1st	1995	T-54th

Lowest 72-Hole Totals

After the PGA switched to stroke play in 1958.

Total	Player	Rounds	Year
267*	Steve Elkington	68-67-68-64	1995
267*	Colin Montgomerie	68-67-67-65	1995
269#	Ernie Els	66-65-66-72	1995
269#	Jeff Maggert	66-69-65-69	1995
269	Nick Price	67-65-70-67	1994
269	Davis Love III	66-71-66-66	1997

*Elkington beat Montgomerie on 1st extra hole of playoff.
#Els and Maggert finished in a tie for third.

Wire-to-Wire Winners

Led or tied for lead from start to finish; after the PGA was switched to stroke play in 1958.

Year	Winner	Year	Winner
1983	Hal Sutton*	1969	Ray Floyd
1982	Ray Floyd*	1964	Bobby Nichols*
1971	Jack Nicklaus*		

*Outright leaders after every round.

Most Frequent Playing Sites

No.	Golf Course	Location	Years
3	Firestone CC	Akron, OH	1975, 1966, 1960
3	Oakmont CC	Oakmont, PA	1978, 1951, 1922
3	Southern Hills CC	Tulsa, OK	1994, 1982, 1970

Note: 7 other courses have been the tournament venue twice each—Cherry Hills (CO), Inverness (OH), Oakland Hills (MI), Olympia Fields (IL), PGA National (FL), Riviera (CA), and Shoal Creek (AL).

Widest Margins of Victory

Shots	Winner/Score	Runner-up	Year
Stroke Play (since 1958)			
7	Jack Nicklaus (274)	Andy Bean	1980
6	Nick Price (269)	Corey Pavin	1994
5	Davis Love III (269)	Justin Leonard	1997
Match-Play Final (1916–57)			
8 &7	Paul Runyan	Sam Snead	1938
7 &6	Ben Hogan	Mike Turnesa	1948
7 &6	Sam Snead	Walter Burkemo	1951

Most Top-5 Finishes

No.	Player	1st	2nd	3rd	4th	5th
Stroke Play (since 1958)						
14	Jack Nicklaus	5	4	3	2	0
6	Billy Casper	0	3	1	1	1
6	Gary Player	2	2	1	1	0
5	Greg Norman	0	2	0	2	1
5	Lanny Wadkins	1	3	1	0	0
Match Play Quarterfinals* (1916–57)						
12	Gene Sarazen	3	1	3	0	5
9	Walter Hagen	5	1	2	0	1
9	Sam Snead	3	2	0	0	4
9	Byron Nelson	2	3	1	0	3
7	Horton Smith	0	0	1	0	6

*The two semifinal round losers tied for third place and the four quarterfinal round losers tied for fifth. No one finished fourth.

Most Matches Played

No.	Player
82	Gene Sarazen
64	Sam Snead
51	Denny Shute
50	Walter Hagen
47	Vic Ghezzi
45	Byron Nelson
43	Horton Smith
41	Ed Dudley
40	Claude Harmon

Most Matches Won

Record	Player
57-25	Gene Sarazen
50-14	Sam Snead
40-10	Walter Hagen
37-8	Byron Nelson
35-16	Denny Shute
27-6	Walter Burkemo
27-20	Vic Ghezzi
26-14	Claude Harmon
26-17	Horton Smith

PGA All-Time Leaders

Lowest Scores for 18 Holes

Total	Player/Tournament	Round	Under Par
59	Al Geiberger (1977 Memphis Classic)	2nd	-13
59	Chip Beck (1991 Las Vegas Invitational)	3rd	-13
60	Ten players tied.		

Lowest Scores for First 54 Holes

Total	Player/Tournament	Rounds	Under Par
189	John Cook (1996 St. Jude Classic)	64-62-63	-24
191	Gay Brewer (1967 Pensacola Open)	66-64-61	-25
191	Johnny Palmer (1954 Texas Open)	65-62-64	-22
192	Mike Souchak (1955 Texas Open)	60-68-64	-21
192	Bob Gilder (1982 Westchester Classic)	64-63-65	-18

Lowest Scores for First 36 Holes

Total	Player/Tournament	Rounds	Under Par
126	Tommy Bolt (1954 Virginia Beach Open)	64-62	-12
126	Paul Azinger (1989 Texas Open)	64-62	-14
126	John Cook (1996 St. Jude Classic)	64-62	-16
126	Rick Fehr (1996 Las Vegas Invitational)	64-62	-18

Lowest 72-Hole Totals

Total	Player/Tournament	Rounds	Under Par
257	Mike Souchak (1955 Texas Open)	60-68-64-65	-27
258	Donnie Hammond (1989 Texas Open)	65-64-65-64	-22
258	John Cook (1996 St. Jude Classic)	64-62-63-69	-26
259	Five players tied.		

All-Time Career Wins
PGA Tour events only.

Wins	Player	Turned Pro
81	Sam Snead	1934
70	Jack Nicklaus	1961
63	Ben Hogan	1931
60	Arnold Palmer	1954
52	Byron Nelson	1932
51	Billy Casper	1954
40	Walter Hagen	1912
40	Cary Middlecoff	1947
38	Gene Sarazen	1920
36	Lloyd Mangrum	1929
33	Tom Watson*	1971
32	Horton Smith	1926
31	Harry Cooper	1923
31	Jimmy Demaret	1927
30	Leo Diegel	1916

*PGA Tour regular in 1997.
Note: The PGA Tour did not make the British Open an official tour event until 1995, hence the career victory totals listed above do not include British Open titles won by the following players: Watson (5 times); Hagen (4); Nicklaus (3); Norman and Palmer (2 each); Hogan, Price, Sarazen and Snead (1 each).

Current Career Leaders
PGA Tour events only through Sept. 28, 1997.

Wins	Player	Turned Pro
33	Tom Watson	1971
21	Lanny Wadkins	1971
19	Ben Crenshaw	1973
19	Tom Kite	1972
18	Greg Norman	1976
17	Curtis Strange	1976
15	Nick Price	1977
14	Mark O'Meara	1980
14	Corey Pavin	1982
12	Fred Couples	1980
12	Craig Stadler	1975
11	Paul Azinger	1981
11	Wayne Levi	1973
11	Davis Love III	1985
11	Phil Mickelson	1992

Most Wins in a Calendar Year
PGA Tour events only; through Sept. 28, 1997.

Wins	Player	Year
18	Byron Nelson	1945
13	Ben Hogan	1946
11	Sam Snead	1950
10	Ben Hogan	1948
9	Paul Runyan	1933

Byron Nelson set a PGA record of 18 victories in 1945, thanks to an 11-tournament winning streak that has never been challenged.

Most Consecutive Victories
In events sanctioned by the PGA Tour.

Wins	Player	Dates	Tournaments
11	Byron Nelson	3/11/45 to 8/4/45	Miami Four-Ball, Charlotte Open, Greensboro Open, Durham Open, Atlanta Open, Montreal Open, Philadelphia Inquirer Invitational, Chicago Victory National Open, PGA Championship (Dayton), Tam O'Shanter Open (Chicago) and Canadian Open (Toronto). Streak ended August 19 at Memphis Invitational where Nelson finished 4th behind winning amateur Fred Haas.
6	Ben Hogan	6/12/48 to 8/22/48	U.S. Open (Los Angeles) Inverness Round Robin (Toledo), Motor City Open (Northville, MI), Reading Open, Western Open (Buffalo), Denver Open. Streak ended August 29 at Utah Invitational Open in Salt Lake City where Hogan finished 9th behind winner Lloyd Mangrum.
5*	Ben Hogan	4/12/53 to 7/10/53	Masters, Pan American Open (Mexico City), Colonial National Invitational (Ft. Worth), U.S. Open (Oakmont), British Open (Carnoustie). Streak ended January 31, 1954 at Thunderbird Invitational in Palm Springs, CA, where Hogan finished 7th behind winner Fred Haas Jr.

*Includes the British Open, which at the time was not an official PGA Tour event.

Youngest Winners

Age	Player	Tournament
19 yrs., 318 days	John McDermott	1911 U.S. Open
20 yrs., 5 days	Gene Sarazen	1922 Southern Open
20 yrs., 46 days	Chick Evans*	1910 Western Open
20 yrs., 135 days	Francis Ouimet*	1913 U.S. Open
20 yrs., 138 days	Gene Sarazen	1922 U.S. Open

*Amateur
Note: Tiger Woods was 20 years, 281 days old when he won his first tournament, the 1996 Las Vegas Invitational.

Oldest Winners

Age	Player	Tournament
52 yrs., 312 days	Sam Snead	1965 Greater Greensboro Open
51 yrs., 222 days	Art Wall	1975 Greater Milwaukee Open
51 yrs., 98 days	Jim Barnes	1937 Long Island Open
51 yrs., 36 days	John Barnum	1962 Cajun Classic
49 yrs., 186 days	Ray Floyd	1992 Doral-Ryder Open

Note: In 1974, Sam Snead placed 2nd in the Los Angeles Open and 3rd in the PGA Championship at age 62. He also shot his age twice (66 and 67) in the 2nd and 4th rounds of the 1979 Quad Cities Open.

Youngest to Win 5 PGA Tournaments

Age	Player	Tournaments
20 yrs., 305 days	Horton Smith	•1928—Oklahoma City Open and Catalina Island Open; •1929—Berkeley Open, Pensacola Open, and Florida Open (Smith won 5 more tournaments in 1929).
21 yrs., 139 days	Tiger Woods	•1996—Las Vegas Invitational and Disney Classic; •1997—Mercedes Championships, Masters, and Byron Nelson Classic. (Through September 28, Woods had also won the 1997 Western Open).
23 yrs., 76 days	Jack Nicklaus	•1962—U.S. Open, Seattle World's Fair Open, and Portland Open; •1963—Palm Springs Classic and Masters (Nicklaus won 3 more tournaments in 1963, including his 2nd major at the PGA Championship).
23 yrs., 140 days	Gene Sarazen	•1922—Southern (Spring) Open, U.S. Open, and PGA Championship; •1923—PGA Championship; •1925—Metropolitan Open.
23 yrs., 224 days	Paul Runyan	•1930—North & South Open and New Jersey Open; •1931—Metropolitan PGA and Westchester Open; 1932—Gasparilla Open Match Play.

The Ryder Cup

In 1927, British seed merchant and golf enthusiast Samuel Ryder presented a trophy for competition between professional golfers of Great Britain and the United States. The Ryder Cup Matches, which now consist of foursome (two-man teams in alternate shot), four-ball (two-man teams in best ball), and singles matches played over three days, debuted at Worcester (MA) Country Club with the U.S. team winning, 9½ points to 2½. The Ryder Cup, which is contested for prestige rather than prize money, has taken place biennially since 1927; four matches between 1939 and 1945 were canceled because of World War II. Trailing badly in the series, 18 to 3 with one draw, the British team was expanded in 1979 to include all of Europe. This infusion of talent revived the rivalry, and since then the Americans hold a slim lead of 5 matches to 4 with 1 draw. The next match will be held at The Country Club in Brookline, MA (September 24–26, 1999).

Bernhard Langer of the victorious 1997 European team helped clinch the cup with 3 wins.

Results of Last 10 Matches

Year	Winner	Loser	Site
1997	Europe 14½	USA 13½	Valderrama GC, Sotogrande, Spain
1995	Europe 14½	USA 13½	Oak Hill CC, Rochester, NY
1993	USA 15	Europe 13	The Belfry, Sutton Coldfield, England
1991	USA 14½	Europe 13½	Ocean Course, Kiawah Island, SC
1989	Europe 14*	USA 14	The Belfry, Sutton Coldfield, England
1987	Europe 15	USA 13	Muirfield Village GC, Dublin, OH
1985	Europe 16½	USA 11½	The Belfry, Sutton Coldfield, England
1983	USA 14½	Europe 13½	PGA Nat'l., Palm Beach Gardens, FL
1981	USA 18½	Europe 9½	Walton Health GC, Surrey England
1979	USA 17	Europe 11	Greenbrier, W. Sulphur Springs, WV

*Holder retains possession of cup when final score is a draw.

All-Time Individual Winning Percentages

Based on at least 10 matches played through 1997 Ryder Cup and percentage figured by dividing number of total points by matches played.

United States

Pct.	Player	Matches Played	Record	Total Points
.900	Gardner Dickinson	10	9-1-0	9
.818	J.C. Snead	11	9-2-0	9
.818	Tony Lema	11	8-1-2	9
.808	Sam Snead	13	10-2-1	10½
.750	Tom Weiskopf	10	7-2-1	7½
.731	Dow Finsterwald	13	9-3-1	9½
.731	Larry Nelson	13	9-3-1	9½
.719	Arnold Palmer	32	22-8-2	23
.708	Gene Sarazen	12	7-2-3	8½
.700	Hale Irwin	20	13-5-2	14
.700	Tom Watson	15	10-4-1	10½
.688	Julius Boros	16	9-3-4	11
.667	Lee Trevino	30	17-7-6	20

Note: Walter Hagen, who was the playing captain for the U.S. team in the first 5 Ryder Cup meetings with Great Britain from 1927 to 1935, had a record of 7-1-1 in 9 matches.

Europe

Pct.	Player	Matches Played	Record	Total Points
.620	Jose-Maria Olazabal*	25	14-8-3	15½
.608	Seve Ballesteros	37	20-12-5	22½
.583	Colin Montgomerie*	18	9-6-3	10½
.554	Peter Oosterhuis	28	14-11-3	15½
.545	Costantino Rocca*	11	6-5-0	6
.545	Jose Maria Canizares	11	5-4-2	6
.543	Nick Faldo*	46	23-19-4	25
.539	Bernhard Langer*	38	18-15-5	20½
.532	Ian Woosnam*	31	14-12-5	16½
.500	Bernard Gallacher	31	13-13-5	15½
.500	Howard Clark	15	7-7-1	7½
.500	Ken Bousfield	10	5-5-0	5
.486	Tony Jacklin	35	13-14-8	17

*Played on 1997 Ryder Cup team.

All-Time Matches Played

United States		Europe	
No.	Player	No.	Player
37	Billy Casper	46	Nick Faldo
34	Lanny Wadkins	40	Neil Coles
32	Arnold Palmer	38	Bernhard Langer
30	Ray Floyd	37	Seve Ballesteros
30	Lee Trevino	36	Christy O'Connor Sr.
28	Tom Kite	35	Tony Jacklin
28	Jack Nicklaus	31	Bernard Gallacher
27	Gene Littler	31	Ian Woosnam
20	Fred Couples	30	Peter Alliss
20	Hale Irwin	28	Peter Oosterhuis
20	Curtis Strange	28	Sam Torrance
16	Julius Boros	27	Bernard Hunt
16	Payne Stewart	25	Brian Barnes
15	Tom Watson	24	Brian Huggett
14	Paul Azinger	24	Mark James

From left, European captain Seve Ballesteros of Spain with players Nick Faldo of England, Colin Montgomerie of Scotland, and Jose Marie Olazabal of Spain after winning their second straight Ryder Cup on September 28, 1997.

All-Time Matches Won

United States		Europe	
No.	Player	No.	Player
22	Arnold Palmer	23	Nick Faldo
20	Billy Casper	20	Seve Ballesteros
20	Lanny Wadkins	18	Bernhard Langer
17	Jack Nicklaus	14	Peter Oosterhuis
17	Lee Trevino	14	Jose-Maria Olazabal
15	Tom Kite	14	Ian Woosnam
14	Gene Littler	13	Bernard Gallacher
13	Hale Irwin	13	Tony Jacklin
12	Ray Floyd	12	Neil Coles
10	Sam Snead	11	Christy O'Connor Sr.
10	Tom Watson	10	Peter Alliss
9	Julius Boros	10	Brian Barnes
9	Gardner Dickinson	9	Colin Montgomerie
9	Dow Finsterwald	8	Brian Huggett
9	Larry Nelson	8	Mark James
9	J.C. Snead	7	Four players tied.

Matches Won, 1991–97
Based on the 4 Ryder Cup meetings of the 1990s.

United States		Europe	
No.	Player	No.	Player
8	Corey Pavin	9	Colin Montgomerie
7	Fred Couples	8	Bernhard Langer
5	Paul Azinger	7	Seve Ballesteros
5	Ray Floyd	7	Nick Faldo
5	Davis Love III	7	Jose-Marie Olazabal
5	Payne Stewart	7	Ian Woosnam
5	Lanny Wadkins	6	Costantino Rocca
4	Jeff Maggert	3	Peter Baker
4	Phil Mickelson	3	David Gilford
3	Chip Beck	3	Mark James
3	Tom Lehman	3	Per-Urik Johansson
3	Loren Roberts	3	Sam Torrance
2	Five players tied.	2	Three players tied.

Senior PGA Tour

Chi Chi Rodriguez at the Olympia Fields, Illinois, Seniors Open, June 27, 1997.

Most Career Wins

Senior events only; through September 28, 1997.

Wins	Player	Joined Sr. Tour
27	Lee Trevino	1989
24	Miller Barber	1981
23	Bob Charles	1986
22	Don January	1980
22	Chi Chi Rodriguez	1985
20	Bruce Crampton	1985
18	Jim Colbert	1991
18	Mike Hill	1989
18	Gary Player	1985
17	George Archer	1989
14	Ray Floyd	1992
14	Dave Stockton	1991
11	Jim Dent	1989
11	Dale Douglass	1986
11	Hale Irwin	1995
11	Orville Moody	1984
11	Bob Murphy	1993
11	Peter Thomson	1982

Most Senior Major Championships

The Senior Tour's major tournaments are the PGA Seniors' Championship (first played in 1937), U.S. Senior Open (1980), Senior Players Championship (1983), and the Tradition (1989).

No.	Player	PGA Sr.	U.S. Open	Senior Players	Tradition	Last Major
8	Jack Nicklaus	1	2	1	4	1996
6	Gary Player	3	2	1	0	1990
6	Sam Snead	6	0	0	0	1973
5	Miller Barber	1	3	1	0	1985
5	Arnold Palmer	2	1	2	0	1985
4	Lee Trevino	2	1	0	1	1994
3	Ray Floyd	1	0	1	1	1996
3	Al Watrous	3	0	0	0	1957
3	Eddie Williams	3	0	0	0	1946
2	Billy Casper	0	1	1	0	1988
2	Hale Irwin	2	0	0	0	1997
2	Orville Moody	0	1	1	0	1989
2	Chi Chi Rodriguez	1	0	1	0	1987
2	Dave Stockton	0	0	2	0	1996

Most Wins in a Calendar Year

Senior events only; through September. 28, 1997.

Wins	Player	Year
9	Peter Thomson	1985
7	Bruce Crampton	1986
7	Hale Irwin	1997
7	Chi Chi Rodriguez	1987
7	Lee Trevino	1990
6	Don January	1983
6	Lee Trevino	1994
5	Bob Charles	1988
5	Bob Charles	1989
5	Mike Hill	1991
5	Gary Player	1988
5	Dave Stockton	1993
5	Lee Trevino	1992
5	Jim Colbert	1996
4	Miller Barber	1984
4	Jim Colbert	1995
4	Bob Murphy	1995

Most Combined Wins on PGA, Senior Tours*

Through September 28, 1997.

Wins	Player	Turned Pro
88	Sam Snead	1934
83	Jack Nicklaus	1961
72	Arnold Palmer	1954
58	Billy Casper	1954
56	Lee Trevino	1960
42	Gary Player	1953
37	Gene Littler	1954
35	Miller Barber	1958
35	Ray Floyd	1961
34	Bruce Crampton	1953
31	Hale Irwin	1968
30	Chi Chi Rodriguez	1960
29	George Archer	1964
29	Bob Charles	1960

*Includes all British Opens and all PGA Seniors' Championships before formation of Senior Tour in 1980.

Women's LPGA Tour

Most Major Championships

The LPGA Tour's major tournaments are the U.S. Women's Open (first played 1946), LPGA Championship (1955), du Maurier Classic (1979), and Nabisco Dinah Shore (1983). The first two majors for women professionals have been discontinued—the Western Open (1930-67) and Titleholders Championship (1937-72). Totals include 1997 results.

No.	Player	Western Open	Titleholders	U.S. Open	LPGA	du Maurier	Dinah Shore
15	Patty Berg	7	7	1	0	DNP	DNP
13	Mickey Wright	3	2	4	4	DNP	DNP*
11	Louise Suggs	4	4	2	1	DNP	DNP
10	Babe Zaharias	4	3	3	DNP	DNP	DNP
8	Betsy Rawls	2	0	4	2	DNP	DNP#
6	Pat Bradley	DNP	DNP	1	1	3	1
6	Betsy King	DNP	DNP	2	1	0	3
6	Patty Sheehan	DNP	DNP	2	3	0	1
6	Kathy Whitworth	1	2	0	3	0	0
5	Amy Alcott	DNP	DNP	1	0	1	3

*Wright won the Colgate Dinah Shore in 1973 but retired before the event became an LPGA major in 1983.
#Rawls played in the tournament but had also retired by 1983.
DNP—Did not play in the tournament.
Note: No woman golfer has ever won four major titles in the same year. Three players, however, have won three majors—Pat Bradley in 1986 (won Shore and LPGA, tied for 5th in U.S. Open, and won du Maurier); Mickey Wright in 1961 (won Titleholders, placed 3rd in Western Open, and won U.S. Open and LPGA), and Babe Zaharias in 1950 (won only three majors available: Titleholders, Western Open, and U.S. Open). Nancy Lopez, while she ranks 6th in career victories with 47, has only three major titles—all at the LPGA Championship (1989, 1985, and 1978).

Most Career Wins

LPGA events only; through September 28, 1997.

Wins	Player	Joined LPGA
88	Kathy Whitworth	1958
82	Mickey Wright	1955
57	Patty Berg	1950
55	Betsy Rawls	1951
50	Louise Suggs	1950
48	Nancy Lopez*	1977
42	JoAnne Carner	1970
42	Sandra Haynie	1961
38	Carol Mann	1960
35	Patty Sheehan*	1980
32	Beth Daniel*	1979
31	Pat Bradley*	1974
31	Betsy King*	1977
31	Babe Zaharias	1950
29	Amy Alcott*	1975
29	Jane Blalock	1969

*Tour regular in 1997.

Current Career Leaders

LPGA events only; through September 28, 1997.

Wins	Player	Joined LPGA
48	Nancy Lopez	1977
35	Patty Sheehan	1980
32	Beth Daniel	1979
31	Pat Bradley	1974
31	Betsy King	1977
29	Amy Alcott	1975
21	Sandra Palmer	1964
18	Hollis Stacy	1974
16	Jan Stephenson	1974
15	Laura Davies	1987
15	Juli Inkster	1983
15	Sally Little	1971
14	Dottie Pepper	1987
11	Jane Geddes	1983
10	Annika Sorenstam	1993

Babe Didrikson Zaharias, who helped found the Ladies Professional Golf Association in 1950.

Miscellaneous

PGA Tour Winners Who Turn 50 in the Next 10 Years
And become eligible for the Senior PGA Tour.

•**1998** (born 1948): Bobby Cole (May 11), Bruce Fleisher (October 16), John Mahaffey (May 9), and Peter Oosterhuis (May 3).

•**1999** (born 1949): George Burns (July 29), Forrest Fezler (September 23), Mark Hayes (July 12), Lon Hinkle (July 17), Barry Jaeckel (February 14), Tom Kite (December 9), Doug Tewell (August 27), Jim Thorpe (February 1), Howard Twitty (January 15), Lanny Wadkins (December 5), and Tom Watson (September 4).

•**2000** (born 1950): Rex Caldwell (May 5), Bob Gilder (December 31), Andy North (March 9), and Jim Simons (May 15).

•**2001** (born 1951): Danny Edwards (June 14), Morris Hatalsky (November 10), Bruce Lietzke (July 18), Roger Maltbie (June 30), Mark McCumber (September 7), Mac O'Grady (April 26), Mark Pfeil (July 18), Don Pooley (August 27), Tom Purtzer (December 5), and Fuzzy Zoeller (November 11).

•**2002** (born 1952): Dave Barr (March 1), Ben Crenshaw (January 11), Dan Halldorson (April 2), Gary Koch (November 21), Bill Kratzert (June 29), Wayne Levi (February 22), and Mark Lye (November 13).

•**2003** (born 1953): Andy Bean (March 13), Ed Fiori (April 21), Jay Haas (December 2), Jerry Pate (September 16), Craig Stadler (June 2), and D.A. Weibring (May 25).

•**2004** (born 1954): Brad Bryant (December 11), Keith Fergus (March 3), Peter Jacobsen (March 4), Mike Reid (July 1), and Ron Streck (July 17).

•**2005** (born 1955): Bill Britton (November 13), Mike Donald (July 11), Scott Hoch (November 24), Greg Norman (February 10), Dan Pohl (April 1), Loren Roberts (June 24), Tom Sieckmann (January 14), Tony Sills (December 5), Scott Simpson (September 17), Curtis Strange (January 30), Mike Sullivan (January 1), and Denis Watson (October 18).

•**2006** (born 1956): Chip Beck (September 12), David Edwards (April 18), Fred Funk (June 14), Kenny Knox (August 15), Mike Nicolette (December 7), Jack Renner (July 6), and Tim Simpson (May 6).

•**2007** (born 1957): Fulton Allem (September 15), Seve Ballesteros (April 9), Phil Blackmar (September 22), John Cook (October 2), Nick Faldo (July 18), Wayne Grady (July 26), Donnie Hammond (April 1), Bernhard Langer (August 27), Tim Norris (November 20), Mark O'Meara (January 13), David Ogrin (December 31), Nick Price (January 28), Clarence Rose (December 8), Jeff Sluman (September 11), Payne Stewart (January 30), and Mark Wiebe (September 13).

SENIOR PGA TOUR

Youngest Winners

Age	Player	Tournament
50 yrs., 11 days	Gil Morgan	1996 Ralphs Classic
50 yrs., 14 days	George Archer	1989 Southwest Classic
50 yrs., 16 days	Ray Floyd	1992 GTE North Classic
50 yrs., 18 days	Dale Douglass	1986 Vantage Invitational
50 yrs., 23 days	John Bland	1995 Ralphs Classic

Note: Jack Nicklaus turned 50 on January 21, 1990, but delayed his Senior Tour debut until the 1990 Tradition (March 29-April 1). He won at age 50 years, 70 days.

Oldest Winners

Age	Player	Tournament
63 yrs., 0 days	Mike Fetchick	1985 Hilton Head Invit'l.
61 yrs., 249 days	Jimmy Powell	1996 Brickyard Crossing
61 yrs., 92 days	Roberto De Vicenzo	1984 Commemorative
60 yrs., 227 days	Bob Charles	1996 Kaanapali Classic
60 yrs., 187 days	Jimmy Powell	1995 First America Classic

Note: Arnold Palmer was 59 years, 8 days old when he won his last Senior Tour title, the 1988 Crestar Classic.

LPGA TOUR

Youngest Winners

Age	Player	Tournament
18 yrs., 14 days	Marlene Hagge	1952 Sarasota Open
19 yrs., 1 day	Amy Alcott	1975 Orange Blossom Classic
19 yrs., 6 days	Sandra Haynie	1962 Austin Open
20 yrs., 67 days	Brandie Burton	1992 Ping/Welch's
21 yrs., 20 days	Mickey Wright	1956 Jacksonville Open

Note: Karrie Webb was 21 years, 31 days old when she won her first tournament, the 1996 HealthSouth Inaugural; and Nancy Lopez was 21 years, 51 days old when she won her first, the 1978 Bent Tree Classic.

Oldest Winners

Age	Player	Tournament
46 yrs., 164 days	JoAnne Carner	1985 Safeco Classic
45 yrs., 227 days	Kathy Whitworth	1985 United Bank Classic
45 yrs., 11 days	Sandra Palmer	1986 Mayflower Classic
44 yrs., 171 days	Betsy Rawls	1972 GAC Classic
44 yrs., 96 days	Patty Berg	1962 Muskogee Open

Note: Two-time LPGA Player of the Year Pat Bradley was 43 years, 304 days old when she won the 1995 HealthSouth Inaugural.

TENNIS

Pete Sampras in 1997, winning his fourth Wimbledon singles title in five years.

Men's Grand Slam

The Tennis Grand Slam is made up of the national championships of England (first played at Wimbledon in 1877), the United States (1881), Australia (1905), and France (1925). The Open era, which allowed professionals to participate in the four majors for the first time, dawned in 1968 at the French Open (FRA), Wimbledon(WIM), and the U.S. Open (US), and a year later at the Australian Open (AUS).

All-Time Leading Winners of Major Championships

Players with the most singles (S), doubles (D), and mixed doubles (M) titles in all four grand slam tournament; totals include 1997 results.

Total Titles	Player/Country	First/Last*	Wimbledon S-D-M	US S-D-M	Australian S-D-M	French S-D-M	Overall S-D-M
28	Roy Emerson, AUS	1959-71	2-3-0	2-4-0	6-3-0	2-6-0	12-16-0
25	John Newcombe, AUS	1965-76	3-6-0	2-3-1	2-5-0	0-3-0	7-17-1
22	Frank Sedgman, AUS	1949-52	1-3-2	2-2-2	2-2-2	0-2-2	5-9-8
21	Bill Tilden, USA	1913-30	3-1-0	7-5-4	DNP	0-0-1	10-6-5
20	Rod Laver, AUS	1959-71	4-1-2	2-0-0	3-4-0	2-1-1	11-6-3
19	John Bromwich, AUS	1938-50	0-2-2	0-3-1	2-8-1	0-0-0	2-13-4
19	Neale Fraser, AUS	1957-62	1-2-1	2-3-3	0-3-1	0-3-0	3-11-5
18	Jean Borotra, FRA	1925-36	2-3-1	0-0-1	1-1-1	1-5-2	4-9-5
18	Ken Rosewall, AUS	1953-72	0-2-0	2-2-1	4-3-0	2-2-0	8-9-1
18	Fred Stolle, AUS	1962-69	0-2-3	1-3-2	0-3-1	1-2-0	2-10-6
17	Jack Crawford, AUS	1929-35	1-1-1	0-0-0	4-4-3	1-1-1	6-6-5
17	John McEnroe, USA	1977-92	3-5-0	4-4-0	0-0-0	0-0-1	7-9-1
17	Adrian Quist, AUS	1936-50	0-2-0	0-1-0	3-10-0	0-1-0	3-14-0
16	Laurie Doherty, GBR	1897-1906	5-8-0	1-2-0	DNP	DNP	6-10-0
15	Henri Cochet, FRA	1926-32	2-2-0	1-0-1	DNP	4-3-2	7-5-3
15	Bob Hewitt, AUS/SAF	1961-79	0-5-2	0-1-1	0-2-1	0-1-2	0-9-6
15	Vic Seixas, USA	1952-56	1-0-4	1-2-3	0-1-0	0-2-1	2-5-8

*First and last years player won a major championship.
DNP—Did not play in tournament.

Career Grand Slam Winners

Only 4 men have won all 4 major singles titles at least once in their careers.

Player/Country	WIM	US	AUS	FRA
Don Budge, USA	2	2	1	1
Roy Emerson, AUS	2	2	6	2
Rod Laver, AUS	4	2	3	2
Fred Perry, GBR	3	3	1	1

Australia's Rod Laver with his 1962 U.S. Open trophy. He won the Grand Slam as an amateur that year and again as a professional in 1969.

Grand Slam Singles Winners

Don Budge, United States (age 23)—1938
Australian final: beat John Bromwich, AUS, 6-4, 6-2, 6-1
French final: beat Rod Menzel, CZE, 6-3, 6-2, 6-4
Wimbledon final: beat Bunny Austin, GBR, 6-1, 6-0, 6-3
United States final: beat Gene Mako, USA, 6-3, 6-8, 6-2, 6-1

Rod Laver, Australia (age 24)—1962
Australian final: beat Roy Emerson, AUS, 8-6, 0-6, 6-4, 6-4
French final: beat Roy Emerson, 3-6, 2-6, 6-3, 9-7, 6-2
Wimbledon final: beat Marty Mulligan, AUS, 6-2, 6-2, 6-1
United States final: beat Roy Emerson, 6-2, 6-4, 5-7, 6-4

Rod Laver, Australia (age 31)—1969
Australian final: beat Andres Gimeno, SPA, 6-3, 6-4, 7-5
French final: beat Ken Rosewall, AUS, 6-4, 6-3, 6-4
Wimbledon final: beat John Newcombe, AUS, 6-4, 5-7, 6-4, 6-4
United States final: beat Tony Roche, AUS, 7-9, 6-1, 6-2, 6-2

Key: ARG, Argentina; AUS, Australia; AUT, Austria; BEL, Belgium; BRA, Brazil; CRO, Croatia; CZE, Czechoslovakia; FRA, France; GBR, Great Britain; GER, Germany; HUN, Hungary; IND, India; ITA, Italy; NOR, Norway; ROM, Romania; SAF, South Africa; SPA, Spain; SWE, Sweden; SWI, Switzerland; YUG, Yugoslavia.

Most Major Singles Titles

Total	Player/Country	WIM	US	AUS	FRA	Last Major
12	Roy Emerson, AUS	2	2	6	2	1967
11	Bjorn Borg, SWE	5	0	0	6	1981
11	Rod Laver, AUS	4	2	3	2	1969
10	Pete Sampras, USA*	4	4	2	0	1997
10	Bill Tilden, USA	7	3	DNP	0	1930
8	Jimmy Connors, USA	2	5	1	0	1983
8	Ivan Lendl, CZE/USA	0	3	2	3	1990
8	Fred Perry, GBR	3	3	1	1	1936
8	Ken Rosewall, AUS	0	2	4	2	1972
7	Henri Cochet, FRA	2	1	DNP	4	1932
7	Rene Lacoste, FRA	2	2	DNP	3	1929
7	Bill Larned, USA	0	7	DNP	DNP	1911
7	John McEnroe, USA	3	4	0	0	1984
7	John Newcombe, AUS	3	2	2	0	1975
7	Willie Renshaw, GBR	7	DNP	DNP	DNP	1889
7	Dick Sears, USA	0	7	DNP	DNP	1887

*Played in at least one major in 1997.
DNP—Did not play in tournament.

Most Grand Slam Singles Finals

With won-lost records for each Grand Slam tournament.

Finals	Player/Country	WIM W-L	US W-L	AUS W-L	FRA W-L	Overall Record
19	Ivan Lendl, CZE/USA	0-2	3-5	2-2	3-2	8-11
17	Rod Laver, AUS	4-2	2-2	3-1	2-1	11-6
16	Bjorn Borg, SWE	5-1	0-4	0-0	6-0	11-5
16	Ken Rosewall, AUS	0-4	2-2	4-1	2-1	8-8
15	Roy Emerson, AUS	2-0	2-1	6-1	2-1	12-3
15	Bill Tilden, USA	3-0	7-3	DNP	0-2	10-5
15	Jimmy Connors, USA	2-4	5-2	1-1	0-0	8-7
12	Pete Sampras, USA*	4-0	4-1	2-1	0-0	10-2
12	Jack Crawford, AUS	1-1	0-1	4-3	1-1	6-6
11	John McEnroe, USA	3-2	4-1	0-0	0-1	7-4
11	Stefan Edberg, SWE	2-1	2-0	2-3	0-1	6-5
10	Fred Perry, GBR	3-0	3-0	1-1	1-1	8-2
10	Henri Cochet, FRA	2-1	1-1	0-0	4-1	7-3
10	Rene Lacoste, FRA	2-1	2-0	0-0	3-2	7-3
10	John Newcombe, AUS	3-1	2-1	2-1	0-0	7-3
10	Mats Wilander, SWE	0-0	1-1	3-1	3-1	7-3
10	Boris Becker, GER*	3-4	1-0	2-0	0-0	6-4
10	Jean Borotra, FRA	2-3	0-1	1-0	1-2	4-6

*Played in at least one major in 1997.
DNP—Did not play in tournament.

The Grand Slam of Tennis

In 1938, eight years after Bobby Jones won golf's first Grand Slam (see page 136), 23-year-old Californian Don Budge, made tennis history by becoming the first player to sweep the national championships of Australia, France, England, and the United States in one year. Since then, only one man—Rod Laver—and three women—Maureen Connolly, Margaret Smith Court, and Steffi Graf—have been able to duplicate Budge's feat. Laver is the only player to win the Grand Slam twice, once as an amateur in 1962 and again as a professional in 1969. Like Budge, Laver turned pro at age 24, but unlike Budge and other pioneering pros from Bill Tilden to Pancho Gonzales, Laver got a second chance at the slam with the advent of Open tennis in 1968. The line between amateurs and pros was abolished and prize money was offered in the four major tournaments, and a year later, Laver, at age 31, won them all again.

Winners of 3 Major Singles Titles in 1 Year

Mats Wilander, SWE
(1988 Australian, French, U.S.)

Jimmy Connors, USA*
1974 (Australian, Wimbledon, U.S.)

Roy Emerson, AUS
1964 (Australian, Wimbledon, U.S.)

Ashley Cooper, AUS
1958 (Australian, Wimbledon, U.S.)

Lew Hoad, AUS
1956 (Australian, French, Wimbledon)

Tony Trabert, USA
1955 (French, Wimbledon, U.S.)

Fred Perry, GBR
1934 (Australian, Wimbledon, U.S.)

Jack Crawford, AUS
1933 (Australian, French, Wimbledon)

*Connors was not allowed to compete in the 1974 French Open because he had signed to play World Team Tennis in the United States. European tennis officials, afraid that WTT was a threat to their summer clay court tournaments, banned all WTT players (including Billie Jean King and Evonne Goolagong, among others).
Note: Hoad in 1956 and Crawford in 1933 lost their bid to complete the Grand Slam in the last slam event, the U.S. National Championship (the U.S. Open after 1967). Both lost in the final, Hoad to Ken Rosewall (in 4 sets after winning the first) and Crawford to Fred Perry (after leading 2 sets to 1).

Women's Grand Slam

The Tennis Grand Slam is made up of the national championships of England (first played by women at Wimbledon in 1884), the United States (1887), Australia (1922), and France (1925). The Open Era, which allowed professionals to participate in the four majors for the first time, dawned in 1968 at the French Open (FRA), Wimbledon (WIM), and the U.S. Open (US), and a year later at the Australian Open (AUS).

All-Time Leading Winners of Major Championships

Players with the most singles (S), doubles (D), and mixed doubles (M) titles in all four grand slam tournaments. Totals include 1997 results.

Total Titles	Player/Country	First/Last*	Wimbledon S-D-M	U.S. S-D-M	Australian S-D-M	French S-D-M	Overall S-D-M
62	Margaret Smith Court, AUS	1960-75	3-2-5	5-5-8	11-8-2	5-4-4	24-19-19
56	Martina Navratilova, CZE/USA	1974-95	9-7-3	4-9-2	3-8-0	2-7-2	18-31-7
39	Billie Jean Moffitt King, USA	1961-81	6-10-4	4-5-4	1-0-1	1-1-2	12-16-11
37	Margaret Osborne duPont, USA	1941-60	1-5-1	3-13-9	DNP	2-3-0	6-21-10
35	Louise Brough, USA	1942-57	4-5-4	1-12-4	1-1-0	0-3-0	6-21-8
35	Doris Hart, USA	1948-55	1-4-5	2-4-5	1-1-2	2-5-3	6-14-15
31	Helen Wills Moody, USA	1923-38	8-3-1	7-4-2	DNP	4-2-0	19-9-3
26	Elizabeth Ryan, USA	1914-34	0-12-7	0-1-2	DNP	0-4-0	0-17-9
22	Steffi Graf, GER	active	7-1-0	5-0-0	4-0-0	5-0-0	21-1-0
22	Pam Shriver, USA	1981-91	0-5-0	0-5-0	0-7-0	0-4-1	0-21-1
21	Darlene Hard, USA	1958-69	0-4-3	2-6-0	DNP	1-3-2	3-13-5
21	Suzanne Lenglen, FRA	1919-26	6-6-3	0-0-0	DNP	2-2-2	8-8-5
21	Chris Evert, USA	1974-86	3-1-0	6-0-0	2-0-0	7-2-0	18-3-0
20	Nancye Wynne Bolton, AUS	1935-52	0-0-0	0-0-0	6-10-4	0-0-0	6-10-4
19	Maria Bueno, BRA	1958-68	3-5-0	4-4-0	0-1-0	0-1-1	7-11-1
19	Thelma Coyne Long, AUS	1936-58	0-0-0	0-0-0	2-12-4	0-0-1	2-12-5

*First and last years player won a major championship.
DNP—Did not play in tournament.

Career Grand Slam Winners

Eight women have won all 4 major singles titles at least once in their careers.

Player/Country	WIM	US	AUS	FRA
Maureen Connolly, USA	3	3	1	2
Margaret Smith Court, AUS	3	5	11	5
Chris Evert, USA	3	6	2	7
Shirley Fry, USA	1	1	1	1
Steffi Graf, GER	7	5	4	5
Doris Hart, USA	1	2	1	2
Billie Jean King, USA	6	4	1	1
Martina Navratilova, USA	9	4	3	2

Margaret Court Smith possessed a 24-5 win-loss record in Grand Slam singles finals.

Grand Slam Singles Winners

Steffi Graf, West Germany (age 18)—1988
Australian final: beat Chris Evert, USA, 6-1, 7-6 (7-3)
French final: beat Natalia Zvereva, USSR, 6-0, 6-0
Wimbledon final: beat Martina Navratilova, USA, 5-7, 6-2, 6-1
United States final*: beat Gabriela Sabatini, ARG, 6-3, 3-6, 6-1

Margaret Smith Court, Australia (age 28)—1970
Australian final: beat Kerry Melville, AUS, 6-3, 6-1
French final: beat Helga Niessen, W.GER, 6-2, 6-4
Wimbledon final: beat Billie Jean King, USA, 14-12, 11-9
United States final: beat Rosie Casals, USA, 6-2, 2-6, 6-1

Maureen Connolly, United States (age 18)—1953
Australian final: beat Julie Simpson, USA, 6-3, 6-2
French final: beat Doris Hart, USA, 6-2, 6-4
Wimbledon final: beat Doris Hart, 8-6, 7-5
United States final: beat Doris Hart, 6-2, 6-4

*Less than a month after winning the 1988 U.S. Open, Graf achieved a unique "Golden Slam," beating Sabatini, 6-3, 6-3, in the women's singles final at the Summer Olympics in Seoul, South Korea.

Most Major Singles Titles

Total	Player/Country	WIM	US	AUS	FRA	Last Major
24	Margaret Smith Court, AUS	3	5	11	5	1973
21	Steffi Graf, GER*	7	5	4	5	1996
19	Helen Wills Moody, USA	8	7	DNP	4	1938
18	Chris Evert, USA	3	6	2	7	1986
18	Martina Navratilova, CZE/USA	9	4	3	2	1990
12	Billie Jean King, USA	6	4	1	1	1975
9	Maureen Connolly, USA	3	3	1	2	1954
9	Monica Seles, YUG/USA*	0	2	4	3	1996
8	Suzanne Lenglen, FRA	6	0	DNP	2	1926
8	Molla Mallory, NOR/USA#	0	8	DNP	0	1926
7	Maria Bueno, BRA	3	4	0	0	1966
7	Dorothea Chambers, GBR#	7	0	DNP	DNP	1914
7	Evonne Goolagong, AUS#	2	0	4	1	1980

*Played in at least one major in 1997. DNP—Did not play in tournament.
#Full name (including maiden name): Molla Bjurstedt Mallory, Dorothea Douglass Chambers, and Evonne Goolagong Cawley.
Note: Suzanne Lenglen won the French Championships singles title six times, but only twice after 1925 when the tournament was opened to players from outside France.

Most Grand Slam Singles Finals
With won-lost records for each Grand Slam tournament

Finals	Player/Country	WIM W-L	US W-L	AUS W-L	FRA W-L	Overall Record
34	Chris Evert, USA	3-7	6-3	2-4	7-2	18-16
32	Martina Navratilova, USA	9-3	4-4	3-3	2-4	18-14
29	Margaret Smith Court, AUS	3-2	5-1	11-1	5-1	24-5
29	Steffi Graf, GER*	7-1	5-3	4-1	5-3	21-8
22	Helen Wills Moody, USA	8-1	7-2	DNP	4-0	19-3
19	Evonne Goolagong, AUS	2-3	0-4	4-4	1-1	7-12
18	Billie Jean King, USA	6-3	4-2	1-1	1-0	12-6
18	Doris Hart, USA	1-3	2-5	1-1	2-3	6-12
15	Helen Jacobs, USA	1-4	4-4	DNP	0-2	5-10
14	Louise Brough, USA	4-3	1-5	1-0	0-0	6-8
13	Monica Seles, YUG/USA*	0-1	2-2	4-0	3-1	9-4
13	Maria Bueno, BRA	3-2	4-2	0-1	0-1	7-6
13	Blanche Hillyard, GBR	6-7	DNP	DNP	DNP	6-7
11	Molla Mallory, USA	0-1	8-2	DNP	DNP	8-3
11	Dorothea Chambers, GBR	7-4	0-0	DNP	DNP	7-4
11	Charlotte Sterry, GBR	5-6	DNP	DNP	DNP	5-6
11	A. Sanchez Vicario, SPA*	0-2	1-1	0-2	2-3	3-8

*Played in at least one major in 1997. DNP—Did not play in tournament.
Note: Helen Wills Moody entered 22 grand slam singles tournaments from 1922-35, reached every final, and won 19. She also won 126 of 129 matches, losing only to Molla Mallory (1922 U.S. Nationals), Kitty McKane (1924 Wimbledon), and Helen Jacobs (1933 U.S. Nationals).

Winners of 3 Major Singles Titles in 1 Year

Martina Hingis, SWI
1997 (Australian, Wimbledon, U.S.)

Monica Seles, YUG/USA
1991 (Australian, French, U.S.)
1992 (Australian, French, U.S.)

Steffi Graf, GER
1989 (Australian, Wimbledon, U.S.)
1993 (French, Wimbledon, U.S.)*
1995 (French, Wimbledon, U.S.)
1996 (French, Wimbledon, U.S.)

Martina Navratilova, AUS
1983 (Wimbledon, U.S., Australian)*
1984 (French, Wimbledon, U.S.)

Billie Jean King, USA
1972 (French, Wimbledon, U.S.)

Margaret Smith Court, AUS
1962 (Australian, French, U.S.)
1965 (Australian, Wimbledon, U.S.)
1969 (Australian, French, U.S.)
1973 (Australian, French, U.S.)

Helen Wills Moody, USA
1928 (French, Wimbledon, U.S.)
1929 (French, Wimbledon, U.S.)

*The Grand Slam must be accomplished during the calendar year to count. Graf and Navratilova have completed noncalendar year Grand Slams—Graf winning 1993 French Open, Wimbledon, and U.S. Open and 1994 Australian Open; and Navratilova taking 1983 Wimbledon, U.S. Open, and Australian Open (then a December tournament), and 1984 French Open.
Note: None of the seven players listed above came into the U.S. National Championship (the U.S. Open after 1967) needing to win the title to complete the Grand Slam in one year.

The Brief But Brilliant Career of Maureen Connolly

In 1953, at age 18, Maureen Connolly became the first women to complete the tennis Grand Slam when she captured the world's four major national tournaments. Less than a year later—two weeks after winning a third straight Wimbledon title—her career was over, ended when a horse she was riding collided with a cement-mixer truck. "Little Mo" broke her right leg, severing all the calf muscles. Dissatisfied with the progress of her rehabilitation, she retired on Feb. 22, 1955. From 1951 to 1954, she had entered nine majors and won them all, with a match record of 50-0.

Wimbledon

MEN

Youngest Singles Champions

Age	Player/Country	Year
17 yrs., 227 days	Boris Becker, W.GER	1985
18 yrs., 226 days	Boris Becker, W.GER	1986
19 yrs., 174 days	Wilfred Baddeley, GBR	1891
19 yrs., 243 days	Sidney Wood, USA	1931
20 yrs., 27 days	Bjorn Borg, SWE	1976

Oldest Singles Champions

Age	Player/Country	Year
41 yrs., 183 days	Arthur Gore, GBR	1909
40 yrs., 171 days	Arthur Gore, GBR	1908
37 yrs., 145 days	Bill Tilden, USA	1930
36 yrs., 235 days	Norman Brookes, AUS	1914
36 yrs., 53 days	Herbert Lawford, GBR	1887

Note: Ken Rosewall never won Wimbledon, but played in 4 singles finals—the first and fourth coming 20 years apart. He was 19 years, 243 days old, when he lost to Jaroslav Drobny in 1954, and was 39 years, 246 days old, when he lost to Jimmy Connors in 1974.

Most Overall Titles
Including singles, doubles, and mixed doubles.

Total	Player	Singles	Doubles	Mixed
13	Laurie Doherty	5	8	0
12	Willie Renshaw	7	5	0
12	Reggie Doherty	4	8	0
9	John Newcombe	3	6	0
8	John McEnroe	3	5	0
8	Tony Wilding	4	4	0

Fred Perry in 1934. No British player has won the Wimbledon men's singles title since Perry won three straight from 1934 to 1936.

Most Singles Titles

No.	Player	Years
7	Willie Renshaw	1889, 1881-86
5	Bjorn Borg	1976-80
5	Laurie Doherty	1902-06
4	Reggie Doherty	1897-1900
4	Rod Laver	1969, 1968, 1962, 1961
4	Pete Sampras	1997, 1993-95
4	Tony Wilding	1910-13
3	Wilfred Baddeley	1895, 1892, 1891
3	Boris Becker	1989, 1986, 1985
3	Arthur Gore	1909, 1908, 1901
3	John McEnroe	1984, 1983, 1981
3	John Newcombe	1971, 1970, 1967
3	Fred Perry	1934-36
3	Bill Tilden	1930, 1921, 1920
2	Twelve players tied.*	

*Jean Borotra (1926, 1924), Norman Brookes (1914, 1907), Don Budge (1938, 1937), Henri Cochet (1929, 1927), Jimmy Connors (1982, 1974), Stefan Edberg (1990, 1988), Roy Emerson (1965, 1964), John Hartley (1880, 1879), Lew Hoad (1957, 1956), Rene Lacoste (1928, 1925), Gerald Patterson (1922, 1919), and Joshua Pim (1894, 1893).

Most Frequent Singles Runners-up

No.	Player	Years
5	Arthur Gore	1912, 1910, 1907, 1902, 1899
4	Boris Becker	1995, 1991, 1990, 1988
4	Jimmy Connors	1984, 1978, 1977, 1975
4	Herbert Lawford	1888, 1884-86
4	Ernest Renshaw	1889, 1887, 1883, 1882
4	Ken Rosewall	1974, 1970, 1956, 1954
3	Wilfred Baddeley	1896, 1894, 1893
3	Jean Borotra	1929, 1927, 1925
3	Frank Riseley	1906, 1904, 1903
3	Fred Stolle	1963-65
3	Gottfried von Cramm	1935-37
2	Ten players tied.*	

*Bunny Austin (1938, 1932), Roper Barrett (1911, 1908), Jaroslav Drobny (1952, 1949), Goran Ivanisevic (1994, 1992), Rod Laver (1960, 1959), Ivan Lendl (1987, 1986), John McEnroe (1982, 1980), Ilie Nastase (1976, 1972), Kurt Neilsen (1955, 1953), and Joshua Pim (1892, 1891).

Most Singles Titles

No.	Player	Years
9	Martina Navratilova	1990, 1982-87, 1979, 1978
8	Helen Wills Moody	1938, 1935, 1933, 1932, 1927-30
7	Dorothea Chambers*	1914, 1913, 1911, 1910, 1906, 1904, 1903
7	Steffi Graf	1996, 1995, 1991-93, 1989, 1988
6	Blanche Hillyard*	1900, 1899, 1897, 1894, 1889, 1886
6	Billie Jean King	1975, 1973, 1972, 1966-68
6	Suzanne Lenglen	1925, 1919-23
5	Lottie Dod	1891-93, 1888, 1887
5	Charlotte Sterry*	1908, 1901, 1898, 1896, 1895
4	Louise Brough	1955, 1948-50
3	Maria Bueno	1964, 1960, 1959
3	Maureen Connolly	1952-54
3	Margaret Smith Court	1970, 1965, 1963
3	Chris Evert	1981, 1976, 1974
2	Five players tied.#	

*Full names (including maiden names): Dorothea Douglass Chambers; Blanche Bingley Hillyard; Charlotte Cooper Sterry.
#Evonne Goolagong Cawley (1980, 1971), Althea Gibson (1958, 1957), Dorothy Round (1937, 1934), May Sutton (1907, 1905), and Maud Watson (1885, 1884).

Martina Navratilova winning her eighth of nine Wimbledon singles titles in 1987. Her nineteen overall titles, including doubles and mixed doubles, rank her second only to Billie Jean King, who won twenty.

Youngest Singles Champions

Age	Player/Country	Year
15 yrs., 286 days	Lottie Dod, GBR	1887
16 yrs., 278 days	Martina Hingis, SWI	1997
16 yrs., 301 days	Lottie Dod, GBR	1888
17 yrs., 292 days	Maureen Connolly, USA	1952
18 yrs., 286 days	May Sutton, USA	1905

Note: Steffi Graf was 19 years, 18 days old, when she won her first Wimbledon title in 1988.

Most Frequent Singles Runners-up

No.	Player	Years
7	Chris Evert	1985, 1984, 1982, 1978-80, 1973
7	Blanche Hillyard*	1901, 1891-93, 1888, 1887, 1885
6	Charlotte Sterry*	1912, 1904, 1902, 1900, 1899, 1897
5	Helen Jacobs	1938, 1935, 1934, 1932, 1929
4	Dorothea Chambers*	1920, 1919, 1907, 1905
3	Louise Brough	1954, 1952, 1946
3	Lili de Alvarez	1926-28
3	Evonne Goolagong*	1976, 1975, 1972
3	Doris Hart	1953, 1948, 1947
3	Billie Jean King*	1970, 1969, 1963
3	Martina Navratilova	1994, 1989, 1988
2	Ten players tied.#	

*Full names (including maiden names): Blanche Bingley Hillyard; Charlotte Cooper Sterry; Dorothea Douglass Chambers; Evonne Goolagong Cawley; Billy Jean Moffitt King.
#Dora Boothby (1911, 1910), Maria Bueno (1966, 1965), Margaret Smith Court (1971, 1964), Margaret Osborne duPont (1950, 1949), Darlene Hard (1959, 1957), Hana Mandlikova (1986, 1981), Agnes Morton (1909, 1908), Jana Novotna (1997, 1994), Elizabeth Ryan (1930, 1921), and Arantxa Sanchez Vicario (1996, 1995).

Oldest Singles Champions

Age	Player/Country	Year
37 yrs., 274 days	Charlotte Sterry, GBR	1908
36 yrs., 247 days	Blanche Hillyard, GBR	1900
35 yrs., 304 days	Dorthea Chambers, GBR	1914
33 yrs., 262 days	Martina Navratilova, USA	1990
33 yrs., 29 days	Ethel Larcombe, GBR	1912

Most Overall Titles
Including singles, doubles, and mixed doubles.

Total	Player	Singles	Doubles	Mixed
20	Billie Jean King	6	10	4
19	Martina Navratilova	9	7	3
19	Elizabeth Ryan	0	12	7
15	Suzanne Lenglen	6	6	3
13	Louise Brough	4	5	4

Note: Helen Wills Moody collected 12 overall titles (8 singles, 3 doubles, 1 mixed) and Margaret Smith Court has 10 (3 singles, 2 doubles, 5 mixed).

United States Open

MEN

Seven-time U.S. Open champion Bill Tilden.

Most Singles Titles

No.	Player	Years
7	Bill Larned	1907-11, 1902, 1901
7	Dick Sears	1881-87
7	Bill Tilden	1929, 1920-25
5	Jimmy Connors	1983, 1982, 1978, 1976, 1974
4	John McEnroe	1984, 1979-81
4	Pete Sampras	1996, 1995, 1993, 1990
4	Bob Wrenn	1897, 1896, 1894, 1893
3	Oliver Campbell	1890-92
3	Ivan Lendl	1985-87
3	Fred Perry	1936, 1934, 1933
3	Mal Whitman	1898-1900
2	Twenty players tied.*	

Don Budge (1938, 1937), Stefan Edberg (1992, 1991), Roy Emerson (1964, 1961), Neale Fraser (1960, 1959), Pancho Gonzales (1949, 1948), Bill Johnston (1919, 1915), Jack Kramer (1947, 1946), Rene Lacoste (1927, 1926), Rod Laver (1969, 1962), Maurice McLoughlin (1913, 1912), Lindley Murray (1918, 1917), John Newcombe (1973, 1967), Frank Parker (1945, 1944), Bobby Riggs (1941, 1939), Ken Rosewall (1970, 1956), Frank Sedgman (1952, 1951), Henry Slocum (1889, 1888), Tony Trabert (1955, 1953), Ellsworth Vines (1932, 1931), and Dick Williams (1916, 1914).

Youngest Singles Champions

Age	Player/Country	Year
19 yrs., 28 days	Pete Sampras, USA	1990
19 yrs., 190 days	Oliver Campbell, USA	1890
19 yrs., 312 days	Dick Sears, USA	1881
19 yrs., 344 days	Bob Wrenn, USA	1893
19 yrs., 349 days	Ellsworth Vines, USA	1931

Note: Pancho Gonzales was 20 years, 133 days old, when he won his first National Championship in 1948.

Oldest Singles Champions

Age	Player/Country	Year
38 yrs., 247 days	Bill Larned, USA	1911
37 yrs., 238 days	Bill Larned, USA	1910
36 yrs., 240 days	Bill Larned, USA	1909
36 yrs., 216 days	Bill Tilden, USA	1929
35 yrs., 326 days	Ken Rosewall, AUS	1970

Most Frequent Singles Runners-up

No.	Player	Years
6	Bill Johnston	1922-25, 1920, 1916
5	Ivan Lendl	1989, 1988, 1982-84
4	Bjorn Borg	1981, 1980, 1978, 1976
3	Fred Hovey	1896, 1893, 1892
3	Maurice McLoughlin	1915, 1914, 1911
3	Bill Tilden	1927, 1919, 1918
3	Beals Wright	1908, 1906, 1901
2	Fifteen players tied.*	

*Andre Agassi (1995, 1990), Bill Clothier (1909, 1904), Jimmy Connors (1977, 1975), Frank Hunter (1929, 1928), Wallace Johnson (1921, 1912), Jan Kodes (1973, 1971), Bill Larned (1903, 1900), Rod Laver (1961, 1960), Frank Parker (1947, 1942), Tony Roche (1970, 1969), Ken Rosewall (1955, 1974), Vic Seixas (1953, 1951), Henry Slocum (1890, 1887), Bill Talbert (1945, 1944), and Howard Taylor (1888, 1884).

Most Overall Titles
Including singles, doubles, and mixed doubles

Total	Player	Singles	Doubles	Mixed
16	Bill Tilden	7	5	4
13	Dick Sears	7	6	0
8	Neale Fraser	2	3	3
8	George Lott	0	5	3
8	John McEnroe	4	4	0
8	Bill Talbert	0	4	4

Most Singles Titles

No.	Player	Years
8	Molla Bjurstedt Mallory	1926, 1920-22, 1915-18
7	Helen Wills Moody	1931, 1927-29, 1923-25
6	Chris Evert	1982, 1980, 1975-78
5	Margaret Smith Court	1973, 1969-70, 1965, 1962
5	Steffi Graf	1996, 1995, 1993, 1989, 1988
4	Pauline Betz	1946, 1942-44
4	Mario Bueno	1966, 1964, 1963, 1959
4	Helen Jacobs	1932-35
4	Billie Jean King	1974, 1972, 1971, 1967
4	Alice Marble	1938-40, 1936
4	Bessie Moore	1905, 1903, 1901, 1896
4	Martina Navratilova	1987, 1986, 1984, 1983
4	Hazel Wightman*	1919, 1909-11
3	Four players tied.#	
2	Eight players tied.†	

*Full name (including maiden name): Hazel Hotchkiss Wightman.
#Juliette Atkinson (1898, 1897, 1895), Mary Browne (1912-14), Maureen Connolly (1951-53), and Margaret Osborne duPont (1948-50).
†Tracy Austin (1981, 1979), Mabel Cahill (1892, 1891), Sarah Palfrey Cooke (1945, 1941), Darlene Hard (1961, 1960), Doris Hart (1955, 1954), Althea Gibson (1958, 1957), Monica Seles (1992, 1991) and Bertha Townsend (1889, 1888).

Most Frequent Singles Runners-up

No.	Player	Years
5	Louise Brough	1957, 1954, 1948, 1943, 1942
5	Doris Hart	1953, 1952, 1950, 1949, 1946
4	Evonne Goolagong*	1973-76
4	Helen Jacobs	1940, 1939, 1936, 1928
4	Bessie Moore	1904, 1902, 1897, 1892
4	Martina Navratilova	1991, 1989, 1985, 1981
3	Chris Evert	1984, 1983, 1979
3	Steffi Graf	1994, 1990, 1987
2	Seventeen players tied.#	

*Full name (including maiden name): Evonne Goolagong Cawley.
#Pauline Betz (1945, 1941), Rosie Casals (1971, 1970), Sarak Palfrey Fabyan Cooke (1935, 1934), Margaret Osborne duPont (1947, 1944), Darlene Hard (1962, 1958), Ann Haydon Jones (1967, 1961), Marion Jones (1903, 1898), Billie Jean Moffitt King (1968, 1965), Molla Bjurstedt Mallory (1924, 1923), Hana Mandlikova (1982, 1980), Helen Wills Moody (1933, 1922), Louise Hammond Raymond (1916, 1910), Nancy Richey (1969, 1966), Monica Seles (1996, 1995), Helena Sukova (1993, 1986), Maud Barger Wallach (1909, 1906) and Marion Zinderstein (1920, 1919).

Molla Mallory won the first of her eight U.S. titles at age 31.

Youngest Singles Champions

Age	Player/Country	Year
16 yrs., 271 days	Tracy Austin, USA	1979
16 yrs., 342 days	Martina Hingis, SWI	1997
16 yrs., 353 days	Maureen Connolly, USA	1951
17 yrs., 279 days	Monica Seles, YUG	1991
17 yrs., 316 days	Helen Wills, USA	1923

Oldest Singles Champions

Age	Player/Country	Year
42 yrs., 170 days	Molla Mallory, USA	1926
38 yrs., 166 days	Molla Mallory, USA	1922
38 yrs., 64 days	Maud Wallach, USA	1908
37 yrs., 167 days	Molla Mallory, USA	1921
36 yrs., 203 days	Molla Mallory, USA	1920

Most Overall Titles

Including singles, doubles, and mixed doubles.

Total	Player	Singles	Doubles	Mixed
25	Margaret duPont*	3	13	9
18	Margaret Smith Court	5	5	8
17	Louise Brough	1	12	4
16	Hazel H. Wightman*	4	6	6
15	Sarah Palfrey Cooke*	2	9	4
15	Martina Navratilova	4	9	2

*Full names (including maiden names): Margaret Osborne duPont; Hazel Hotchkiss Wightman; Sarah Palfrey Fabyan Cooke.

Australian Open
<u>MEN</u>

Ken Rosewall in 1954. Almost twenty years separate his first and last singles titles at the Australia Open.

Most Singles Titles

No.	Player	Years
6	Roy Emerson	1963-67, 1961
4	Jack Crawford	1935, 1931-33
4	Ken Rosewall	1972, 1971, 1955, 1953
3	James Anderson	1925, 1924, 1922
3	Rod Laver	1969, 1962, 1960
3	Adrian Quist	1948, 1940, 1936
3	Mats Wilander	1988, 1984, 1983
3	Pat O'Hara Wood	1923, 1920, 1914
2	Thirteen players tied.*	

*Boris Becker (1996, 1991), John Bromwich (1946, 1939), Ashley Cooper (1958, 1957), Jim Courier (1993, 1992), Stefan Edberg (1987, 1985), Rod Heath (1910, 1905), Johan Kriek (1982, 1981), Ivan Lendl (1990, 1989), John Newcombe (1975, 1973), Pete Sampras (1997, 1994), Frank Sedgman (1950, 1949), Guillermo Vilas (1979, 1978), and Tony Wilding (1909, 1906).

Youngest Singles Champions

Age	Player/Country	Year
18 yrs., 76 days	Ken Rosewall, AUS	1953
18 yrs., 111 days	Mats Wilander, SWE	1983
18 yrs., 323 days	Stefan Edberg, SWE	1985
19 yrs., 109 days	Mats Wilander, SWE	1984
20 yrs., 77 days	John Bromwich, AUS	1939

Oldest Singles Champions

Age	Player/Country	Year
37 yrs., 61 days	Ken Rosewall, AUS	1972
36 yrs., 132 days	Ken Rosewall, AUS	1971
33 yrs., 353 days	Horrie Rice, AUS	1907
33 yrs., 11 days	Norman Brookes, AUS	1911
32 yrs., 110 days	Pat O'Hara Wood, AUS	1923

Most Frequent Singles Runners-up

No.	Player	Years
5	John Bromwich	1947-49, 1938, 1937
3	Arthur Ashe	1971, 1967, 1966
3	Jack Crawford	1940, 1936, 1934
3	Stefan Edberg	1993, 1992, 1990
3	Neale Fraser	1960, 1959, 1957
3	Harry Hopman	1930-32
3	Gerald Patterson	1925, 1922, 1914
3	Horace Rice	1915, 1911, 1910
2	Eight players tied.*	

*Mal Anderson (1972, 1958), Pat Cash (1988, 1987), Steve Denton (1982, 1981), Ivan Lendl (1991, 1983), Ken McGregor (1951, 1950), Harry Parker (1913, 1907), Bob Schlesinger (1929, 1924), and Fred Stolle (1965, 1964).

Most Overall Titles
Including singles, doubles, and mixed doubles.

Total	Player	Singles	Doubles	Mixed
13	Adrian Quist	3	10	0
11	John Bromwich	2	8	1
11	Jack Crawford	4	4	3
9	Roy Emerson	6	3	0
8	John Newcombe	2	5	1

Harry Hopman's Kangaroos
Australia's Harry Hopman, who won seven major doubles titles as a player, went on to gain lasting fame as his country's Davis Cup captain. From 1939 to 1967, Hopman guided the Aussies to 16 cup titles and coached many of the greatest players in tennis history, including John Bromwich, Adrian Quist, Lew Hoad, Ken Rosewall, Rod Laver, and Roy Emerson. He later became a teaching pro in the U.S., where he coached John McEnroe, among other future American stars.

Most Wins

No.	Player	Years
11	Margaret Smith Court	1973, 1969-71, 1960-66
6	Nancye Wynne Bolton	1951, 1946-48, 1940, 1937
5	Daphne Akhurst	1928-30, 1926, 1925
4	Evonne Goolagong*	1977 (Dec.), 1974-76
4	Steffi Graf	1994, 1988-90
4	Monica Seles	1996, 1991-93
3	Joan Hartigan	1936, 1934, 1933
3	Martina Navratilova	1985, 1983, 1981
2	Coral Buttsworth	1932, 1931
2	Chris Evert	1984, 1982
2	Thelma Coyne Long	1954, 1952
2	Hana Mandlikova	1987, 1980
2	Mall Molesworth	1923, 1922
2	Mary Carter Reitano	1959, 1956

*Full name (including maiden name)—Evonne Goolagong Cawley.
Note: There were two Australian Opens in 1977—one in January and a second in December.

Most Frequent Singles Runners-up

No.	Player	Years
6	Esna Boyd	1928, 1922-26
4	Chris Evert	1988, 1985, 1981, 1974
4	Jan Lehane	1960-63
4	Thelma Coyne Long	1956, 1955, 1951, 1940
3	Evonne Goolagong*	1971-73
3	Martina Navratilova	1987, 1982, 1975
2	Six players tied.#	

*Full name (including maiden name): Evonne Goolagong Cawley.
#Nancye Wynne Bolton (1949, 1936), Mary Joe Fernandez (1992, 1990), Sylvia Lance Harper (1930, 1927), Helena Sukova (1989, 1984), Lesley Turner (1967, 1964), and Arantxa Sanchez Vicario (1995, 1994).

Local Girl Makes Good

Australia's Margaret Smith won her first Grand Slam championship, the 1960 Australian singles title, at age 17. By the time she retired as Margaret Smith Court in 1977, she had become the greatest Grand Slam champion in tennis history, with 62 championships. No other player—man or woman—has won more major singles titles (24) or mixed doubles titles (19). And no one else has won the Grand Slam in both singles (1970) and doubles (with countryman Ken Fletcher in 1963).

Youngest Singles Champions

Age	Player/Country	Year
16 yrs., 117 days	Martina Hinges, SWI	1997
17 yrs., 54 days	Monica Seles, YUG	1991
17 yrs., 200 days	Margaret Smith, AUS	1960
18 yrs., 53 days	Monica Seles, YUG	1992
18 yrs., 122 days	Maureen Connolly, USA	1953

Oldest Singles Champions

Age	Player/Country	Year
35 yrs., 110 days	Thelma Coyne Long, AUS	1954
33 yrs., 233 days	Nancye Wynne Bolton, AUS	1951
33 yrs., 104 days	Thelma Coyne Long, AUS	1952
30 yrs., 228 days	Nancye Wynne Bolton, AUS	1948
30 yrs., 169 days	Margaret Smith Court, AUS	1973

Most Overall Titles
Including singles, doubles, and mixed doubles.

Total	Player	Singles	Doubles	Mixed
21	Margaret Smith Court	11	8	4
20	Nancye Wynne Bolton	6	10	4
18	Thelma Coyne Long	2	12	4
14	Daphne Akhurst	5	5	4
11	Martina Navratilova	3	8	0

Note: Mixed doubles matches were not played at the Australian Open from 1970 to 1986.

Four-time champion Monica Seles, winning her first title in 1991.

French Open

MEN

Bjorn Borg in 1981. He won six titles in eight years beginning in 1974 .

Most Singles Titles

No.	Player	Years
6	Bjorn Borg	1978-81, 1975, 1974
4	Henri Cochet	1932, 1930, 1928, 1926
3	Rene Lacoste	1929, 1927, 1925
3	Ivan Lendl	1987, 1986, 1984
3	Mats Wilander	1988, 1985, 1982
2	Twelve players tied.*	

*Sergi Bruguera (1994, 1993), Jim Courier (1992, 1991), Jaroslav Drobny (1952, 1951), Roy Emerson (1967, 1963), Jan Kodes (1971, 1970), Rod Laver (1969, 1962), Frank Parker (1949, 1948), Nicola Pietrangeli (1960, 1959), Ken Rosewall (1968, 1953), Manuel Santana (1964, 1961), Tony Trabert (1955, 1954), and Gottfried von Cramm (1936, 1934).

Youngest Singles Champions

Age	Player/Country	Year
17 yrs., 109 days	Michael Chang, USA	1989
17 yrs., 288 days	Mats Wilander, SWE	1982
18 yrs., 10 days	Bjorn Borg, SWE	1974
18 yrs., 209 days	Ken Rosewall, AUS	1953
19 yrs., 9 days	Bjorn Borg, SWE	1975

Most Frequent Singles Runners-up

No.	Player	Years
3	Jaroslav Drobny	1950, 1948, 1946
3	Guillermo Vilas	1982, 1978, 1975
2	Eleven players tied.*	

*Andre Agassi (1991, 1990), Luis Ayala (1960, 1958), Jean Borotra (1929, 1925), Sven Davidson (1956, 1955), Rene Lacoste (1928, 1926), Ivan Lendl (1985, 1981), Nicola Pietrangeli (1964, 1961), Tony Roche (1967, 1965), Eric Sturgess (1951, 1947), Bill Tilden (1930, 1927), and Mats Wilander (1987, 1983).

Oldest Singles Champions

Age	Player/Country	Year
34 yrs., 306 days	Andres Gimeno, SPA	1972
33 yrs., 219 days	Ken Rosewall, AUS	1968
33 yrs., 127 days	Frank Parker, USA	1949
32 yrs., 291 days	Jean Borotra, FRA	1931
32 yrs., 70 days	Marcel Barnard, FRA	1946

The Four Musketeers

The singular fame that came to Frenchwoman Suzanne Lenglen in the 1920s (see page 165) was exceeded in short order by a quartet of male compatriots, who claimed 38 majors individually or in pairs from 1924 to 1932. More importantly, the Four Musketeers—(below, from left) Henri Cochet, Jean Borotra, Rene Lacoste, and Jacques Brugnon—also teamed to capture the Davis Cup for the first time in 1927 and successfully defended it for five straight years after that.

Most Overall Titles
Including singles, doubles, and mixed doubles.

Total	Player	Singles	Doubles	Mixed
9	Henri Cochet	4	3	2
8	Jean Borotra	1	5	2
8	Roy Emerson	2	6	0
7	Jacques Brugnon	0	5	2
6	Bjorn Borg	6	0	0

Most Singles Titles

No.	Player	Years
7	Chris Evert	1986, 1985, 1983, 1980, 1979, 1975, 1974
5	Margaret Smith Court	1973, 1970, 1969, 1964, 1962
5	Steffi Graf	1996, 1995, 1993, 1988, 1987
4	Helen Wills Moody	1932, 1928-30
3	Monica Seles	1990-92
3	Hilde Sperling	1935-37
2	Ten players tied.*	

*Maureen Connelly (1954, 1953), Margaret Osborne duPont (1949, 1946), Doris Hart (1952, 1950), Ann Haydon Jones (1966, 1961), Suzanne Lenglen (1926, 1925), Simone Passemard Mathieu (1939, 1938), Margaret Scriven (1934, 1933), Martina Navratilova (1984, 1982), Lesley Turner (1965, 1963), and Arantxa Sanchez Vicario (1994, 1989).

Note: Suzanne Lenglen won four additional French national singles titles from 1920 to 1923, before the tournament was opened to foreigners in 1925.

Most Frequent Singles Runners-up

No.	Player	Years
6	Simone Mathieu	1935-37, 1933, 1932, 1929
4	Martina Navratilova	1985-87, 1975
3	Steffi Graf	1992, 1990, 1989
3	Doris Hart	1953, 1951, 1947
3	Ann Haydon Jones	1969, 1968, 1963
3	Arantxa Sanchez Vicario	1996, 1995, 1991
2	Seven players tied.*	

*Chris Evert (1984, 1973), Shirley Fry (1952, 1948), Helen Jacobs (1934, 1930), Mima Jausovec (1983, 1978), Dorothy Head Knode (1957, 1955), Yola Ramirez (1961, 1960), and Lesley Turner (1967, 1962).

The Great Lenglen

At the 1920 Olympics in Antwerp, a gate keeper at the tennis stadium stopped gold medalist Suzanne Lenglen and asked to see her ticket. Indignant, the 21-year-old Lenglen replied, "I? I am the great Lenglen." She was right. From 1919 to 1925, she won 15 Wimbledon titles in singles and doubles. The biggest match of her career came at the height of her fame in 1926 at a tournament in Cannes where she met 20-year-old Helen Wills and beat the three-time U.S. national champion, 6-3, 8-6. Scalpers reportedly sold 5-franc seats for 1,000 francs. Those who couldn't buy a seat watched from perches in nearby trees and on rooftops. Realizing that she was the top box-office draw in tennis, Lenglen turned pro at age 27 and toured the United States, earning $100,000.

Seven-time French Open champion Chris Evert, 1982.

Youngest Singles Champions

Age	Player/Country	Year
16 yrs., 189 days	Monica Seles, YUG	1990
17 yrs., 174 days	Arantxa Sanchez Vicario, SPA	1989
17 yrs., 188 days	Monica Seles, YUG	1991
17 yrs., 357 days	Steffi Graf, W.GER	1987
18 yrs., 103 days	Christine Truman, GBR	1959

Oldest Singles Champions

Age	Player/Country	Year
33 yrs., 279 days	Suzi Kormoczi, HUN	1958
31 yrs., 180 days	Nelly Landry, FRA	1948
31 yrs., 168 days	Chris Evert, USA	1986
31 yrs., 157 days	Simone Mathieu, FRA	1939
31 yrs., 95 days	Margaret duPont, USA	1949

Most Overall Titles
Including singles, doubles, and mixed doubles.

Total	Player	Singles	Doubles	Mixed
13	Margaret Smith Court	5	4	4
11	Doris Hart	2	5	4
11	Martina Navratilova	2	7	2
10	Simone Mathieu	2	6	2
9	Françoise Durr	1	5	3

The Davis Cup

Don Budge, 1936. He led the United States to consecutive Davis Cup titles in 1937 and 1938 before turning pro.

Team Championships
From 1900 through 1996.

No.	Country	Championship Years
31	United States	1995, 1992, 1990, 1982, 1981, 1979, 1978, 1968-72, 1963, 1958, 1954, 1946-49, 1938, 1937, 1920-26, 1913, 1902, 1900
26	Australia	1986, 1983, 1977, 1973, 1964-67, 1959-62, 1955-57, 1950-53, 1939, 1919, 1914, 1911, 1907-09
9	Great Britain	1933-36, 1912, 1903-06
8	France	1996, 1991, 1927-32
5	Sweden	1994, 1987, 1985, 1984, 1975
3	Germany	1993, 1989, 1988
1	Czechoslovakia	1980
1	Italy	1976
1	South Africa	1974*

*Won Davis Cup in walkover after finalist India refused to play in protest over South Africa's apartheid policy.
Note: Germany was known as West Germany from 1949 until reunification in 1990.

Most Cups Won by U.S. Players

No.	Player	Last Cup
7	Bill Johnston	1926
7	Stan Smith	1979
7	Bill Tilden	1926
5	Bob Lutz	1979
5	John McEnroe	1992
4	Vinnie Richards	1926
4	Ted Schroeder	1949
4	Dick Williams	1926
3	Arthur Ashe	1970
3	Gardnar Malloy	1949
2	Thirteen players tied.*	

*Andre Agassi, Don Budge, Jim Courier, Dwight Davis, Peter Fleming, Jack Kramer, Gene Mako, Frank Parker, Pete Sampras, Bill Talbert, Erik van Dillen, Holcombe Ward, and Malcolm Whitman.

Most Cups Won by Non-U.S. Players

No.	Player/Country	Last Cup
8	Roy Emerson, AUS	1967
6	Jean Borotra, FRA	1932
6	Norman Brookes, AUS	1919
6	Henri Cochet, FRA	1932
5	Rod Laver, AUS	1973
4	Bunny Austin, GBR	1936
4	Jacques Brugnon	1932
4	Laurie Doherty, GBR	1906
4	Reggie Doherty, GBR	1906
4	Neale Fraser, AUS	1962
4	Pat Hughes, GBR	1936
4	John Newcombe, AUS	1973
4	Fred Perry, GBR	1936
4	Tony Roche, AUS	1977
4	Tony Wilding, AUS	1914

The Davis Cup

Dwight Davis, a 20-year-old Harvard student and leading American tennis player at the turn of the century, conceived the idea of a regularly scheduled team competition between the United States and the British Isles. In 1900 he donated the sterling silver punchbowl that was originally called the International Lawn Tennis Challenge Trophy. From 1900 to 1971, the defending champion automatically qualified for the final, or Challenge Round, to meet the winner of a preliminary tournament of up to 64 teams. Qualifying rules changed in 1972 when defenders were required to join the preliminaries, and again in 1981 with the creation of the World Group of 16 countries that are eligible to play for the cup each year. In 1997 the field, including zonal competition, was a record 127 nations. Professionals affiliated with national federations were first allowed to play in 1969, then all players were welcomed in 1973. Unlike golf's Ryder Cup, prize money was introduced in the Davis Cup in 1981.

Best Winning Percentages—U.S. Players
Based on at least 20 matches played overall in all rounds; through 1996.

Pct.	Player	Overall Record	Singles	Doubles	Years	First Year
.909	Ham Richardson	20-2	17-1	3-1	7	1952
.906	John Van Ryn	29-3	7-1	22-2	8	1929
.862	Don Budge	25-4	19-2	6-2	4	1935
.857	Bill Johnston	18-3	14-3	4-0	8	1920
.855	John McEnroe	59-10	41-8	18-2	12	1978
.846	Andre Agassi	22-4	22-4	0-0	7	1988
.833	Stan Smith	35-7	15-4	20-3	11	1968
.829	Bill Tilden	34-7	25-5	9-2	11	1920
.824	Arthur Ashe	28-6	27-5	1-1	10	1963
.818	George Lott	18-4	7-4	11-0	6	1928
.800	Clark Graebner	16-4	11-2	5-2	4	1965
.771	Tony Trabert	27-8	16-5	11-3	5	1951
.763	Chuck McKinley	29-9	16-6	13-3	6	1960
.735	Dennis Ralston	25-9	14-5	11-4	7	1960
.727	Wilmer Allison	32-12	18-10	14-2	8	1928

Best Winning Percentages—Non-U.S. Players
Based on at least 20 matches won overall in all rounds; through 1996.

Pct.	Player	Overall Record	Singles	Doubles	Years	First Year
.905	Bob Hewitt, SAF	38-4	22-3	16-1	5	1967
.895	Roy Emerson, AUS	34-4	21-2	13-2	9	1959
.893	Frank Sedgman, AUS	25-3	16-3	9-0	4	1949
.865	Fred Perry, GBR	45-7	34-4	11-3	6	1931
.860	Jaroslav Drobny, CZE	37-6	24-4	13-2	4	1946
.833	Rod Laver, AUS	20-4	16-4	4-0	5	1959
.833	Frew McMillan, SAF	25-5	2-0	23-5	11	1965
.820	Boris Becker, GER	50-11	36-3	14-8	9	1985
.812	Gottfried von Cramm, GER	82-19	58-10	24-9	9	1932
.804	Bjorn Borg, SWE	45-11	37-3	8-8	7	1972
.800	Balazs Taroczy, HUN	76-19	50-12	26-7	14	1973
.791	Guy Forget, FRA	38-10	17-7	21-3	11	1984
.784	Rene Lacoste, FRA	40-11	32-8	8-3	6	1923
.768	Adrian Quist, AUS	43-13	24-10	19-3	9	1933
.767	Manuel Santana, SPA	92-28	69-17	23-11	14	1958

Most Career Wins
All players, all rounds; singles and doubles combined.

Record	Player/Country
120-44	Nicola Pietrangeli, ITA
109-37	Ilie Nastase, ROM
92-28	Manuel Santana, SPA
82-19	Gottfried von Cramm, GER
80-25	Alex Metreveli, RUS
76-19	Balazs Taroczy, HUN
74-44	Tomas Koch, BRA
71-49	Jacques Brichant, BEL
70-39	Ion Tiriac, ROM
69-28	Ramanathan Krishnan, IND
68-41	Jose Edison Mandarino, BRA
67-35	Wilhelm Bungert, GER
66-36	Ulf Schmidt, SWE
66-36	Philippe Washer, BEL
64-27	Jan-Erik Lundqvist, SWE
64-36	Adriano Panatta, ITA

Arthur Ashe in 1975.
He won Davis Cup championships
three times as a player and twice as
captain of the American team.

Miscellaneous

All-Time Open Era Leaders
From 1968 through 1997 U.S. Open; asterisk (*) indicates players active in 1997.

Most Singles Titles

MEN		WOMEN	
No.	**Player/Country**	**No.**	**Player/Country**
109	Jimmy Connors, USA	167	Martina Navratilova, CZE/USA
94	Ivan Lendl, CZE/USA	157	Chris Evert, USA
77	John McEnroe, USA	103	Steffi Graf, GER*
62	Bjorn Borg, SWE	88	Evonne Goolagong Cawley, AUS
62	Guillermo Vilas, ARG	79	Margaret Smith Court, AUS
57	Ilie Nastase, ROM	67	Billie Jean King, USA
49	Boris Becker, GER*	55	Virginia Wade, GBR
49	Pete Sampras, USA*	40	Monica Seles, YUG/USA*
47	Rod Laver, AUS	37	Helga Masthoff, GER
44	Thomas Muster, AUT*	31	Olga Morozova, USSR
41	Stefan Edberg, SWE	31	Conchita Martinez, SPA*
39	Stan Smith, USA	29	Tracy Austin, USA
34	Andre Agassi, USA*	27	Hana Mandlikova, CZE
33	Arthur Ashe, USA	27	Gabriela Sabatini, ARG
33	Mats Wilander, SWE*	25	Nancy Richey, USA

Current Most Singles Titles

MEN		WOMEN	
No.	**Player/Country**	**No.**	**Player/Country**
49	Boris Becker, GER	103	Steffi Graf, GER
49	Pete Sampras, USA	40	Monica Seles, YUG/USA
44	Thomas Muster, AUT	31	Conchita Martinez, SPA
34	Andre Agassi, USA	24	Arantxa Sanchez Vicario, SPA
33	Mats Wilander, SWE	17	Jana Novotna, CZE
31	Michael Chang, USA	14	Zina Garrison, USA
20	Jim Courier, USA	11	Lindsay Davenport, USA
19	Goran Ivanisevic, YUG/CRO	10	Martina Hingis, SWI
18	Michael Stich, GER	10	Anke Huber, GER
15	Emilio Sanchez, SPA	10	Lori McNeil, USA
14	Sergi Bruguera, SPA	10	Helena Sukova, CZE
13	Four players tied.	8	Mary Pierce, FRA
		7	Three players tied.

THE FED CUP

Final Round Appearances
From 1963 through 1996.

No.	Country	Record
23	United States	15-8
17	Australia	7-10
7	Spain	4-3
6	Czechoslovakia	5-1
6	Germany	2-4
4	Great Britain	0-4
2	South Africa	1-1
2	Soviet Union*	0-2
1	Holland	0-1

*In 1988 and 1990 before breakup of USSR.
Note: Germany was known as West Germany from 1949 until reunification in 1990.

Members of Most Cup-Winning Teams

No.	Player/Country	Last Cup
8	Chris Evert, USA	1989
7	Rosie Casals, USA	1981
7	Billie Jean King, USA	1979
4	Margaret Court, AUS	1971
4	Conchita Martinez, SPA	1995
4	Helena Sukova, CZE	1988
4	A. Sanchez Vicario, SPA	1995

The Fed Cup

The Federation Cup is an annual international competition for women, similar to the men's Davis Cup. It was an amateurs-only event when it debuted in 1963 as part of the International Tennis Federation's 50th anniversary and became an open event in 1969. From 1963 to 1994 the competition involved eight teams playing one-day, best-of-three match series at one site in one week. In 1995 the name was shortened to Fed Cup and the format expanded to three rounds of best-of-five match series over three days like the Davis Cup.

All-Time U.S. gold medalist Carl Lewis winning his fourth straight long jump title in 1996.

Winter Games

Summer Games

THE WINTER GAMES

Olympic Sites

The 1st Winter Olympic Games were staged by the International Olympic Committee (IOC) in 1924 at Chamonix in the French Alps.

Year	Host City	Events	Nations
1998	Nagano, JPN (Feb. 7–22)	68	83*
1994#	Lillehammer, NOR	61	67
1992	Albertville, FRA	57	63
1988	Calgary, CAN	46	57
1984	Sarajevo, YUG	39	49
1980	Lake Placid, New York	38	37
1976	Innsbruck, AUT	37	37
1972	Sapporo, JPN	35	35
1968	Grenoble, FRA	35	37
1964	Innsbruck, AUT	34	36
1960	Squaw Valley, California	27	30
1956	Cortina, ITA	24	32
1952	Oslo, NOR	22	30
1948	St. Moritz, SWI	22	28
1944	Not held (World War II)	—	—
1940	Not held (World War II)	—	—
1936	Garmisch-Partenkirchen, GER	17	28
1932	Lake Placid, New York	14	17
1928	St. Moritz, SWI	13	25
1924	Chamonix, FRA	14	16

* As of October 1, 1997.

#After sharing the four-year Olympic cycle with the Summer Games from 1924 to 1992, the Winter Games were moved ahead two years in 1994. The Winter and Summer Olympics now alternate every two years.

Note: The Winter Games will be held in the United States for a record fourth time in 2002 when Salt Lake City will serve as host (Feb. 9-24). France has held the games three times, while Austria, Japan, Norway, and Switzerland have each hosted twice.

All-Time Medal Standings

Countries listed with gold, silver, and bronze medals won through 1994.

	Country	G	S	B	Total
1	Norway	73	77	64	214
2	Soviet Union (1956-88)*	78	57	59	194
3	United States	53	56	37	146
4	Austria	36	48	44	128
5	Finland	36	45	42	123
6	East Germany (1956-88)	43	39	36	118
7	Sweden	39	26	34	99
8	Switzerland	27	29	29	85
9	Italy	25	21	21	67
10	Canada	19	20	25	64
11	Germany (1928-36, 92–)#	23	21	17	61
12	West Germany (1952-88)	18	20	19	57
13	France	16	16	21	53
14	Holland	14	19	17	50
15	Czechoslovakia (1924-92)†	2	8	16	26
16	Russia (1994–)	12	8	4	24
17	Unified Team (1992)	9	6	8	23
	Great Britain	7	4	12	23
19	Japan	3	8	8	19
20	South Korea	6	2	2	10

*The Soviet Union made its Winter Olympic debut in 1956 and played a dominant role until the breakup of the USSR in 1991. Russia and fourteen other former Soviet republics competed together as the Unified Team (UT) in 1992, but have all fielded independent teams since then.

#Because of its aggressor status in two world wars, Germany was barred from the Olympics in 1920 and 1924, and again in 1948. From 1952 to 1964, Communist East Germany and non-Communist West Germany officially competed under one flag. The two countries entered separate teams from 1968 until reunification in 1990.

†Czechoslovakia ceased to exist as a single state in 1993 and became two nations—the Czech Republic and Slovakia—in time for the 1994 Winter Games.

Combined Totals: Soviet Union, Russia, and Unified Team (99 gold medals, 71 silver, 71 bronze for a total of 241); Germany, East Germany, and West Germany (84 gold, 80 silver, 72 bronze for 236). Neither the Czech Republic nor Slovakia won any medals in 1994.

Opening ceremonies at Lillehammer in 1994, where host country Norway added to its domination of the Winter Games by winning 26 medals.

All-Time Medal Leaders

Most Medals

No.	Athlete/Country	Sport	G-S-B	Olympic Games
	MEN			
9	Sixten Jernberg, SWE	Cross-country	4-3-2	3 (1956-64)
8	Bjorn Dählie, NOR	Cross-country	5-3-0	2 (1992-94)
7	Clas Thunberg, FIN	Speed Skating	5-1-1	2 (1924-28)
7	Ivar Ballangrud, NOR	Speed Skating	4-2-1	3 (1928-36)
7	Veikko Hakulinen, FIN	Cross-country	3-3-1	3 (1952-60)
7	Eero Mäntyranta, FIN	Cross-country	3-2-2	3 (1960-68)
7	Bogdan Musiol, E.GER/GER	Bobsled	1-5-1	4 (1980-92)
6	Gunde Svan, SWE	Cross-country	4-1-1	2 (1984-88)
6	Vegard Ulvang, NOR	Cross-country	3-2-1	3 (1988-94)
6	Johan Gröttumsbraten, NOR	Nordic	3-1-2	3 (1924-32)
6	Wolfgang Hoppe, E.GER/GER	Bobsled	2-3-1	4 (1984-94)
6	Eugenio Monti, ITA	Bobsled	2-2-2	4 (1956-68)
6	Roald Larsen, NOR	Speed Skating	0-2-4	2 (1924-28)
5	Twelve tied.*			
	WOMEN			
10	Raisa Smetanina, USSR/UT	Cross-country	4-5-1	5 (1976-92)
9	Lyubov Egorova, UT/RUS	Cross-country	6-3-0	2 (1992-94)
8	Galina Kulakova, USSR	Cross-country	4-2-2	4 (1968-80)
8	Karin Kania, E.GER	Speed Skating	3-4-1	3 (1980-88)
7	Marja-Liisa Kirvesniemi, FIN	Cross-country	3-0-4	6 (1976-94)
7	Andrea Ehrig, E.GER	Speed Skating	1-5-1	4 (1976-88)
6	Lydia Skoblikova, USSR	Speed Skating	6-0-0	2 (1960-64)
6	Bonnie Blair, USA	Speed Skating	5-0-1	4 (1984- 94)
6	Manuela Di Centa, ITA	Cross-country	2-2-2	3 (1988-94)
6	Elena Valbe, UT/RUS	Cross-country	2-0-4	2 (1992-94)

*Including U.S. speed skater Eric Heiden, who won 5 gold medals in 1980.

Most Gold Medals

No.	Athlete/Country	Sport
	MEN	
5	Bjorn Dählie, NOR	CC
5	Eric Heiden, USA	SS
5	Clas Thunberg, FIN	SS
4	Sixten Jernberg, SWE	CC
4	Ivar Ballangrud, NOR	SS
4	Gunde Svan, SWE,	CC
4	Yevgeny Grishin, USSR	SS
4	Johann Olav Koss, NOR	SS
4	Matti Nykänen, FIN	SJ
4	Aleksandr Tikhonov, USSR	B
4	Nikolai Zimyatov, USSR	CC
4	Thomas Wassberg, SWE	CC
	WOMEN	
6	Lyubov Egorova, UT/RUS	CC
6	Lydia Skoblikova, USSR	SS
5	Bonnie Blair, USA	SS
4	Galina Kulakova, USSR	CC
4	Raisa Smetanina,USSR/UT	CC
3	Karin Kania, E.GER	SS
3	Anfisa Reztsova,USSR/UT	B/CC
3	Vreni Schneider, SWI	AS
3	Marja-Liisa Kirvesniemi, FIN	CC
3	Claudia Boyarskikh, USSR	CC
3	Sonja Henie, NOR	FS
3	Irina Rodnina, USSR	FS
3	Yvonne van Gennip, HOL	SS

Key: AS (Alpine skiing); B (Biathlon); BS (Bobsled); BS/C (Bobsled and Cresta); CC (Cross-country skiing); FS (Figure Skating); IH (Ice hockey); L (Luge); SJ (Ski jumping); SS (Speed skating).For a key to country name abbreviations, see page 177.

Norwegian cross-country skiers Bjorn Dählie (left) and Vegard Ulvang in 1992.

All-Time U.S. Medal Leaders

Eddie Eagan, captain of the Yale boxing team in 1919, won Olympic gold as a boxer and a bobsleder.

Most Gold Medals

No.	Athlete	Sport
MEN		
5	Eric Heiden	Speed Skating
3	Irving Jaffee	Speed Skating
2	Dick Button	Figure Skating
2	Eddie Eagan	Bobsled/Boxing
2	Billy Fiske	Bobsled
2	Cliff Gray	Bobsled
2	Jack Shea	Speed Skating
WOMEN		
5	Bonnie Blair	Speed Skating
2	Cathy Turner	Speed Skating
2	Andrea Mead Lawrence	Alpine Skiing

Eagan's Unique Double

Eddie Eagan of the United States is the only athlete to win gold medals in both the Summer and Winter Olympics. His Summer Games victory came first in 1920 when, at age 22, he captured the Light Heavyweight boxing title at Antwerp. Twelve years later, he was a member of driver Billy Fiske's winning four-man bobsled team at Lake Placid.

Two other athletes have won medals in both Olympics. Norway's Jacob Tullin Thams won gold in the Large Hill Ski Jump at Chaminox in 1924 and silver in 8-meter yachting at Berlin in 1936. Germany's Christa Luding-Rothenburger earned four speed skating sprint medals—gold in 1984, gold and silver in 1988, and bronze in 1992—and took a silver medal as a cyclist in 1988 in the Match Sprint. Her 1988 double makes her the only athlete to win medals in both Olympic games in the same year.

Most Medals: Women

No.	Athlete	Sport	G-S-B
6	Bonnie Blair	SS	5-0-1
4	Cathy Turner	SS	2-1-1
4	Dianne Holum	SS	1-2-1
3	Sheila Young	SS	1-1-1
3	Leah Poulos Mueller	SS	0-3-0
3	Beatrix Loughran	FS	0-2-1
3	Amy Peterson	SS	0-2-1
2	Andrea Mead Lawrence	AS	2-0-0
2	Tenley Albright	FS	1-1-0
2	Gretchen Fraser	AS	1-1-0
2	Carol Heiss	FS	1-1-0
2	Diann Roffe-Steinrotter	AS	1-1-0
2	Anne Henning	SS	1-0-1
2	Penny Pitou	AS	0-2-0
2	Nancy Kerrigan	FS	0-1-1
2	Jean Saubert	AS	0-1-1
2	Nikki Ziegelmeyer	SS	0-1-1

Most Medals: Men

No.	Athlete	Sport	G-S-B
5	Eric Heiden	SS	5-0-0
3	Irving Jaffee*	SS	3-0-0
3	Pat Martin	BS	1-2-0
3	John Heaton	BS/C	0-2-1
2	Dick Button	FS	2-0-0
2	Eddie Eagan	BS	2-0-0
2	Billy Fiske	BS	2-0-0
2	Cliff Gray	BS	2-0-0
2	Jack Shea	SS	2-0-0
2	Billy Cleary	IH	1-1-0
2	Jennison Heaton	BS/C	1-1-0
2	John Mayasich	IH	1-1-0
2	Terry McDermott	SS	1-1-0
2	Dick Meredith	IH	1-1-0
2	Tommy Moe	AS	1-1-0
2	Weldy Olson	IH	1-1-0
2	Dick Rodenheiser	IH	1-1-0
2	David Jenkins	FS	1-0-1
2	Stan Benham	BS	0-2-0
2	Herb Drury	IH	0-2-0
2	Eric Flaim	SS	0-2-0
2	Frank Synott	IH	0-2-0
2	John Garrison	IH	0-1-1

*While the I.O.C. credits Jaffee with only the 5,000- and 10,000-meter gold medals from 1932, most Olympic historians agree he also won the 10,000 in 1928 when he turned in the fastest time before the race was canceled because of thawing ice.

Key

AS (Alpine skiing); B (Biathlon); BS (Bobsled); BS/C (Bobsled and Cresta); CC (Cross-country skiing); FS (Figure Skating); IH (Ice hockey); L (Luge); SJ (Ski jumping); SS (Speed skating).

The Soviet Union's medals include those won by the Unified Team (UT) in 1992 (after the breakup of the USSR in 1991), but not those won by Russia in 1994. Germany's medals include those won by East Germany and West Germany from 1968 to 1988.

Gold-medal figure skater Peggy Fleming (center) of the United States in 1968.

Most Figure Skating Medals

Men's and women's singles, pairs, and ice dancing.

No.	Country	G	S	B
37	United States	11	12	14
29	Soviet Union/UT	13	10	6
20	Austria	7	9	4
20	Germany*	7	7	6
17	Canada	2	6	9

*Including East and West Germany.
Note: Figure skating was an Olympic sport at the Summer Games in 1908 and again in 1920.

Most Luge Medals

Men's single and 2-seater, and women's single.
Includes men's cresta competition in 1928 and 1948 at St. Moritz.

No.	Country	G	S	B
51	Germany*	19	16	1
13	Austria	3	5	5
12	Italy	6	3	3
6	Soviet Union	1	2	3
3	United States	1	2	0

*Including East and West Germany.
Note: The U.S. has never won a medal in the luge; all three American medals came in the cresta, or skeleton event, at the two St. Moritz Olympics (1928 and 1948). In the cresta, sliders ride sleds on their stomachs rather than on their backs.

Most Bobsled Medals

Including 2-man and 4-man events
(5-man sleds were used in 1928).

No.	Country	G	S	B
28	Germany*	9	10	9
25	Switzerland	9	8	8
14	United States	5	4	5
10	Italy	3	4	3
3	Austria	1	2	0
3	Great Britain	1	1	1
3	Soviet Union	1	0	2

*Including East and West Germany.

Most Nordic Skiing Medals

Men's and women's cross-country, plus men's ski jumping and nordic combined.

No.	Country	G	S	B
108	Norway	38	41	29
90	Finland	28	31	31
81	Soviet Union/UT	29	25	27
53	Sweden	21	16	16
29	Germany*	13	6	10

*Including East and West Germany.

Most Speed Skating Medals

Including short-track speed skating, which became a medal sport in 1992.

No.	Country	G	S	B
76	Norway	24	28	24
61	Soviet Union/UT	24	17	20
52	United States	24	17	11
51	Germany*	18	18	15
47	Holland	13	17	17

*Including East and West Germany.

Most Alpine Skiing Medals

Men's and women's downhill, slalom, giant slalom, super giant slalom, and alpine combined.

No.	Country	G	S	B
67	Austria	21	23	23
47	Switzerland	16	17	14
35	France	11	11	13
26	United States	9	13	4
27	Germany*	10	11	6

*Including East and West Germany.

Most Ice Hockey Medals

No.	Country	G	S	B
12	Canada	6	4	2
10	Soviet Union/UT	8	1	1
9	United States	2	6	1
8	Czechoslovakia	0	4	4
7	Sweden	1	2	4

Note: Men's ice hockey was introduced as an Olympic event at the 1920 Summer Games. NHL players will be allowed to compete in 1998.

Wolfgang Hoppe driving the four-man German bobsled to a silver medal in 1992.

All-Time Single Olympics Leaders

Bonnie Blair, 1980.

Most Individual U.S. Medals

No.	Athlete	G-S-B	Year
	MEN		
5	Eric Heiden	5-0-0	1980
2	Irving Jaffee	2-0-0	1932
2	Jack Shea	2-0-0	1932
2	Jennison Heaton	1-1-0	1928
2	Tommy Moe	1-1-0	1994
2	Stan Benham	0-2-0	1952
2	Pat Martin	0-2-0	1952
	WOMEN		
3	Sheila Young	1-1-1	1976
2	Andrea Mead Lawrence	2-0-0	1952
2	Bonnie Blair	2-0-0	1992
2	Bonnie Blair	2-0-0	1994
2	Gretchen Fraser	1-1-0	1948
2	Dianne Holum	1-1-0	1972
2	Cathy Turner	1-1-0	1992
2	Bonnie Blair	1-0-1	1988
2	Anne Henning	1-0-1	1972
2	Cathy Turner	1-0-1	1994
2	Penny Pitou	0-2-0	1960
2	Leah Mueller	0-2-0	1980
2	Jean Saubert	0-1-1	1964
2	Dianne Holum	0-1-1	1968
2	Amy Peterson	0-0-2	1994

Sports: •Men—Speed skating (Heiden, Jaffee, and Shea); Bobsled (Benham and Martin); Bobsled and Cresta (Heaton); Alpine (Moe). •Women—Alpine skiing (Fraser, Lawrence, Pitou, and Saubert); the rest are speed skaters.

Most National Medals

No.	Country	Year	G-S-B
29	Soviet Union	1988	11-9-9
27	Soviet Union	1976	13-6-8
26	Norway	1994	10-11-5
26	Germany	1992	10-10-6
25	Soviet Union	1964	11-8-6
25	East Germany	1988	9-10-6
24	East Germany	1984	9-9-6
24	Germany	1994	9-7-8
23	Russia	1994	11-8-4
23	East Germany	1980	9-7-7

Note: In 1990-91, East and West Germany reunified and sent a single team to the 1992 Winter Games. The Soviet Union competed as the Unified Team in 1992 and as Russia and 14 other independent states in 1994.

Most U.S. Medals

No.	Location	Year	G-S-B
13	Lillehammer, NOR	1994	6-5-2
12	Lake Placid, USA	1932	6-4-2
12	Lake Placid, USA	1980	6-4-2
11	Oslo, NOR	1952	4-6-1
11	Albertville, FRA	1992	5-4-2
10	Squaw Valley, USA	1960	3-4-3
10	Innsbruck, AUT	1976	3-3-4
9	St. Moritz, SWI	1948	3-4-2
8	Sapporo, JPN	1972	3-2-3
8	Sarajevo, YUG	1984	4-4-0

Note: While the U.S. won exactly the same number of gold, silver, and bronze medals at Lake Placid in 1932 and 1980, the competition was stiffer the second time around. In 1932, there were 17 competing nations, 252 athletes (231 men and 21 women) and 14 medal events; in 1980, there were 37 nations represented by 1,072 athletes (839 men and 233 women) and 38 medal events.

Most Individual Medals

No.	Athlete/Country	G-S-B	Year
	MEN		
5	Eric Heiden, USA	5-0-0	1980
5	Clas Thunberg, FIN	3-1-1	1924
5	Roald Larsen, NOR	0-2-3	1924
4	Ivar Ballangrud, NOR	3-1-0	1936
4	Bjorn Dählie, NOR	3-1-0	1992
4	Vegard Ulvang, NOR	3-1-0	1992
4	Bjorn Daehlie, NOR	2-2-0	1994
4	Gunde Svan, SWE	2-1-1	1984
4	Sixten Jernberg, SWE	1-2-1	1956
3	Forty-one tied.		
	WOMEN		
5	Lyubov Egorova, UT	3-2-0	1992
5	Manuela Di Centa, ITA	2-2-1	1994
5	Elena Valbe, UT	1-0-4	1992
4	Lydia Skoblikova, USSR	4-0-0	1964
4	Lyubov Egorova, RUS	3-1-0	1994
4	Marja-Liisa Hämäläinen, FIN	3-0-1	1984
4	Karin Enke, E.GER	2-2-0	1984
4	Tatiana Averina, USSR	2-0-2	1976
3	Twenty tied.		

Sports: •Men—speed skating (Heiden, Thunberg, Larsen, and Ballangrud); the rest are cross-country skiers. •Women—speed skating (Skoblikova, Enke, and Averina); the rest are cross-country skiers.

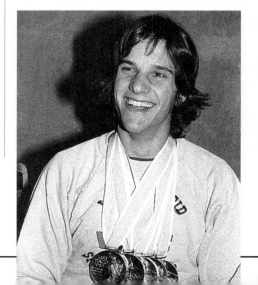

Eric Heiden with the five speed-skating gold medals he won in the 1980 games. Bonnie Blair (above) also won five gold medals but in three separate Olympics.

Miscellaneous

Sonja Henie in 1928 with the first of her three gold medals.

U.S. Figure Skating Medalists

The United States has won 31 individual figure skating medals in the Olympics, 18 by women and 13 by men.

WOMEN

Year	Gold
1992	Kristi Yamaguchi
1976	Dorothy Hamill
1968	Peggy Fleming
1960	Carol Heiss
1956	Tenley Albright

Year	Silver
1994	Nancy Kerrigan
1984	Rosalyn Sumners
1980	Linda Fratianne
1956	Carol Heiss
1952	Tenley Albright
1924	Beatrix Loughran

Year	Bronze
1992	Nancy Kerrigan
1988	Debi Thomas
1972	Janet Lynn
1960	Barbara Ann Roles
1932	Maribel Vinson
1928	Beatrix Loughran
1920	Theresa Weld

MEN

Year	Gold
1988	Brian Boitano
1984	Scott Hamilton
1960	David Jenkins
1956	Hayes Alan Jenkins
1952	Dick Button
1948	Dick Button

Year	Silver
1992	Paul Wylie
1968	Tim Wood
1956	Ronnie Robertson

Year	Bronze
1980	Charles Tickner
1964	Scotty Allen
1956	David Jenkins
1952	Jim Grogan

Note: Peggy Fleming (1968) is the only figure skater ever to win the Associated Press Athlete of the Year award.

Sonja Henie's "Three-peat"

Norway's Sonja Henie was only 11 years old when she competed in her first Winter Olympics in 1924. finishing eighth. Four years later, she won the gold medal and then became the only women's three-time singles champion with repeat victories in 1932 and '36. She also won 10 straight world titles from 1927 to 1936, after which she turned professional, established the first touring ice skating show, signed a film contract with 20th Century Fox, and became a very wealthy movie star. Her claim as the youngest skater ever to win the world championship was erased on March 22, 1997, by 14-year-old American Tara Lipinski, who was a month younger than Henie had been in 1927.

Most Alpine Skiing Medals in a Single Olympics

All skiers listed won 3 medals.

Year	Athlete/Country	G-S-B
	MEN	
1968	Jean Claude Killy, FRA	3-0-0
1956	Toni Sailer, AUT	3-0-0
1948	Henri Oreiller, FRA	2-0-1
	WOMEN	
1980	Hanni Wenzel, LIE	2-1-0
1976	Rosi Mittermaier, W.GER	2-1-0
1952	Annemarie Buchner, GER	0-1-2

Most All-Time Alpine Medals by U.S. Skiers

No.	Athlete/Country	G-S-B
	MEN	
2	Tommy Moe	1-1-0
2	Phil Mahre	1-1-0
	WOMEN	
2	Andrea Mead Lawrence	2-0-0
2	Gretchen Fraser	1-1-0
2	Diann Roffe-Steinrotter	1-1-0
2	Penny Pitou	0-2-0
2	Jean Saubert	0-0-2

Note: The all-time leaders in career Alpine medals are Alberto Tomba of Italy (3-2-0) and Vreni Schneider of Switzerland (3-1-1) with 5 each.

Years U.S. Hockey Teams Have Won Medals

Year	Gold	Silver	Bronze
1980	USA	USSR	SWE
1972	USSR	USA	CZE
1960	USA	Canada	USSR
1956	USSR	USA	Canada
1952	Canada	USA	SWE
1936	Britain	Canada	USA
1932	Canada	USA	GER
1924	Canada	USA	Britain
1920	Canada	USA	CZE

Note: Both gold medals came at home—Squaw Valley in 1960 and Lake Placid in 1980.

THE SUMMER GAMES

Olympic Sites

Year	Host City	Events	Nations
2000	Sydney, AUS (Sept. 16-Oct. 1)	TBA	TBA
1996	Atlanta, Georgia	271	197
1992	Barcelona, SPA	257	172
1988	Seoul, S.KOR	237	160
1984	Los Angeles, California	221	140
1980	Moscow, USSR	203	81
1976	Montreal, CAN	198	88
1972	Munich, GER	195	122
1968	Mexico City, MEX	172	113
1964	Tokyo, JPN	163	93
1960	Rome, ITA	150	83
1956	Melbourne, AUS	151	72
1952	Helsinki, FIN	149	69
1948	London, GBR	136	59
1944	Not held (World War II)	—	—
1940	Not held (World War II)	—	—
1936	Berlin, GER	129	49
1932	Los Angeles, California	116	37
1928	Amsterdam, HOL	109	46
1924	Paris, FRA	126	44
1920	Antwerp, BEL	154	29
1916	Not held (World War I)	—	—
1912	Stockholm, SWE	102	28
1908	London, GBR	109	22
1906	Athens, GRE*	78	20
1904	St. Louis, Missouri	94	13
1900	Paris, FRA	87	26
1896	Athens, GRE	43	14

* Although the International Olympic Committee does not recognize the 1906 Intercalated Games in Athens because they did not take place in the four-year cycle established in 1896, most record books do include these tenth-anniversary games.
Note: On September 5, 1997, the IOC voted 66–41 to accept Athens' bid to host the 2004 Summer Games (August 13–29). Rome was runner-up on the fourth ballot.

All-Time Medal Standings

Countries listed with gold, silver, and bronze medals won through 1996.

	Country	G	S	B	Total
1	United States	832	634	553	2,019
2	USSR (1952-88)*	395	319	296	1,010
3	Great Britain	169	223	218	610
4	France	175	179	206	560
5	Sweden	132	151	174	457
6	Italy	166	135	144	445
	East Germany (1956-88)	159	150	136	445
8	Hungary	142	129	155	426
9	Germany (1896-1936, 1992–)#	124	121	134	379
10	West Germany (1952-88)	77	104	120	301
11	Finland	99	80	113	292
	Australia	86	85	121	292
13	Japan	92	89	97	278
14	Romania	63	77	99	239
15	Poland	50	67	110	227
16	Canada	48	78	90	216
17	Holland	49	58	81	188
18	Bulgaria	43	76	63	182
19	Switzerland	46	69	59	174
20	China	52	63	49	164

*The Soviet Union made its Olympic debut in 1952 and played a dominant role until the collapse of Communism and the breakup of the USSR in 1991. Russia and the 14 other former Soviet republics competed together as the Unified Team (UT) in 1992, but have all fielded independent teams since then.
#Because of its aggressor status in two world wars, Germany was barred from the Olympics in 1920 and 1924, and again in 1948. From 1952 to 1964, Communist East Germany and non-Communist West Germany officially competed under one flag. The two countries entered separate teams from 1968 until reunification in 1990. Combined Totals: Soviet Union, Russia and Unified Team (466 gold medals, 381 silver, 343 bronze for a total of 1,190); Germany, East Germany and West Germany (360 gold, 375 silver, 390 bronze for 1,125).

In 1894 French educator Baron Pierre de Coubertin proposed reviving the ancient Olympic Games (776 B.C. to 393 A.D.). Two years later, the games of the first Olympiad of the modern era were held in Athens, Greece, where 311 athletes from 14 nations gathered to compete. On September 5, 1997, the International Olympic Committee (IOC) announced that the Summer Games will return to Athens in 2004, when over 16,000 athletes are expected to compete from August 13 to August 29.

All-Time Medal Winners

Most Medals

No.	Athlete/Country	Sport	G-S-B	Olympic Games
	MEN			
15	Nikolai Andrianov, USSR	Gymnastics	7-5-3	3 (1972-80)
13	Boris Shakhlin, USSR	Gymnastics	7-4-2	3 (1956-64)
13	Edoardo Mangiarotti, ITA	Fencing	6-5-2	5 (1936-60)
13	Takashi Ono, JPN	Gymnastics	5-4-4	4 (1952-64)
12	Paavo Nurmi, FIN	Track & Field	9-3-0	3 (1920-28)
12	Sawao Kato, JPN	Gymnastics	8-3-1	3 (1968-76)
11	Mark Spitz, USA	Swimming	9-1-1	2 (1968-72)
11	Matt Biondi, USA	Swimming	8-2-1	3 (1984-92)
11	Viktor Chukarin, USSR	Gymnastics	7-3-1	2 (1952-56)
11	Carl Osburn, USA	Shooting	5-4-2	3 (1912-24)
10	Ray Ewry, USA	Track & Field	10-0-0	4 (1900-08)
10	Carl Lewis, USA	Track & Field	9-1-0	4 (1984-96)
10	Aládár Gerevich, HUN	Fencing	7-1-2	6 (1932-60)
10	Akinori Nakayama, JPN	Gymnastics	6-2-2	2 (1968-72)
10	Aleksandr Dityatin, USSR	Gymnastics	3-6-1	2 (1976-80)
	WOMEN			
18	Larissa Latynina, USSR	Gymnastics	9-5-4	3 (1956-64)
11	Vera Cáslavská, CZE	Gymnastics	7-4-0	3 (1960-68)
10	Ágnes Keleti, HUN	Gymnastics	5-3-2	2 (1952-56)
10	Polina Astaknova, USSR	Gymnastics	5-2-3	3 (1956-64)
9	Nadia Comaneci, ROM	Gymnastics	5-3-1	2 (1976-80)
9	Lyudmila Tourischeva, USSR	Gymnastics	4-3-2	3 (1968-76)
8	Kornelia Ender, E.GER	Swimming	4-4-0	2 (1972-76)
8	Dawn Fraser, AUS	Swimming	4-4-0	3 (1956-64)
8	Shirley Babashoff, USA	Swimming	2-6-0	2 (1972-76)
8	Sofia Muratova, USSR	Gymnastics	2-2-4	2 (1956-60)
8	Margit Korondi, HUN	Gymnastics	2-2-4	2 (1952-56)

Most Gold Medals

No.	Athlete/Country
	MEN
10	Ray Ewry, USA*
9	Carl Lewis, USA
9	Paavo Nurmi, FIN
9	Mark Spitz, USA
8	Matt Biondi, USA
8	Sawao Kato, JPN
7	Nikolai Andrianov, USSR
7	Viktor Chukarin, USSR
7	Aládár Gerevich, HUN
7	Boris Shakhlin, USSR
	WOMEN
9	Larissa Latynina, USSR
7	Vera Cáslavská, CZE
6	Kristin Otto, E.GER#
5	Ágnes Keleti, HUN
5	Polina Astaknova, USSR
5	Nadia Comaneci, ROM
5	Krisztina Egerszegi, HUN†
5	Jenny Thompson, USA

*Ewry won his medals in the standing high jump, standing long jump, and standing triple jump. These events were discontinued by 1920.

#Otto, a swimmer, won all 6 of the races she entered in 1988.

†Egerszegi, a swimmer, won 7 overall medals (5-1-1) in 3 Olympics from 1988 to 1996.

Key: ARG, Agentina; AUS, Australia; AUT, Austria; BEL, Belgium; BRA, Brazil; CAN, Canada; CHN, China; CRO, Croatia; CZE, Czechoslovakia; FIN, Finland; FRA, France; GBR, Great Britain; GER, Germany; GRE, Greece; HOL, Holland; HUN, Hungary; IND, India; ITA, Italy; JPN, Japan; KOR, Korea; LIE, Lichtenstein; MEX, Mexico; NOR, Norway; ROM, Romania; RUS, Russia; SAF, South Africa; SPA, Spain; SWE, Sweden; SWI, Switzerland; UT, Unified Team; YUG, Yugoslavia.

All-time individual medals winner Nikolai Andrianov of the USSR winning the gold medal in the rings event in 1976.

All-Time U.S. Medal Winners

Mark Spitz in Munich in 1972, where he won seven of his nine career gold medals.

Most Gold Medals

MEN

No.	Athlete	Sport
10	Ray Ewry	Track/Field
9	Carl Lewis	Track/Field
9	Mark Spitz	Swimming
8	Matt Biondi	Swimming
5	Charles Daniels	Swimming
5	Morris Fisher	Shooting
5	Anton Heida	Gymnastics
5	Tom Jager	Swimming
5	Alfred Lane	Shooting
5	Willis Lee	Shooting
5	Carl Osburn	Shooting
5	Don Schollander	Swimming
5	Martin Sheridan	Track/Field
5	Johnny Weissmuller	Swimming
4	Harrison Dillard	Track/Field
4	Archie Hahn	Track/Field
4	Marcus Hurley	Cycling
4	Alvin Kraenzlein	Track/Field
4	Jim Lightbody	Track/Field
4	Greg Louganis	Diving
4	John Naber	Swimming
4	Al Oerter	Track/Field
4	Jon Olsen	Swimming
4	Jesse Owens	Track/Field
4	Meyer Prinstein	Track/Field
4	Mel Sheppard	Track/Field
4	Lloyd Spooner	Shooting

WOMEN

No.	Athlete	Sport
5	Jenny Thompson	Swimming
4	Evelyn Ashford	Track/Field
4	Janet Evans	Swimming
4	Pat McCormick	Diving
4	Amy Van Dyken	Swimming
3	Melissa Belote	Swimming
3	Ethelda Bleibtrey	Swimming
3	Valerie Briscoe	Track/Field
3	Tracy Caulkins	Swimming
3	Gail Devers	Track/Field
3	Florence Griffith Joyner	Track/Field
3	Nicole Haislett	Swimming
3	Nancy Hogshead	Swimming
3	Jackie Joyner-Kersee	Track/Field
3	Helen Madison	Swimming
3	Angel Martino	Swimming
3	Mary T. Meagher	Swimming
3	Debbie Meyer	Swimming
3	Sandra Neilson	Swimming
3	Martha Norelius	Swimming
3	Wilma Rudolph	Track/Field
3	Carrie Steinseifer	Swimming
3	Sharon Stouder	Swimming
3	Wyomia Tyus	Track/Field
3	Chris von Saltza	Swimming

Most Medals

MEN

No.	Athlete	G-S-B
11	Mark Spitz	9-1-1
11	Matt Biondi*	8-2-1
11	Carl Osburn	5-4-2
10	Ray Ewry	10-0-0
10	Carl Lewis	9-1-0
9	Martin Sheridan	5-3-1
8	Charles Daniels	5-1-2
7	Tom Jager#	5-1-1
7	Willis Lee	5-1-1
7	Lloyd Spooner	4-1-2

WOMEN

No.	Athlete	G-S-B
8	Shirley Babashoff	2-6-0
7	Shannon Miller	2-2-3
6	Jenny Thompson	5-1-0
6	Jackie Joyner-Kersee	3-1-2
6	Angel Martino	3-0-3
5	Evelyn Ashford	4-1-0
5	Janet Evans	4-1-0
5	Florence Griffith Joyner	3-2-0
5	Mary T. Meagher†	3-1-1
5	Gwen Torrence	3-1-1
5	Mary Lou Retton	1-2-2

*Biondi's total includes one gold medal as a preliminary race member of an eventual first-place relay team.
#Jager's total includes 3 gold medals as a preliminary race member of 3 eventual first-place relay teams.
†Meagher's total includes one silver medal as a preliminary race member of an eventual second-place relay team.

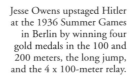

Jesse Owens upstaged Hitler at the 1936 Summer Games in Berlin by winning four gold medals in the 100 and 200 meters, the long jump, and the 4 x 100-meter relay.

Sport-by-Sport National Medal Winners

The USSR's medals include those won by the Unified Team (UT) in 1992 (after the breakup of the USSR in 1991), but not those won by Russia in 1996. Germany's medals include those won by East Germany and West Germany from 1968 to 1988.

Most Track & Field Medals
Men and women.

No.	Country	G	S	B
694	United States	299	217	178
245	Germany	67	86	92
214	USSR/Unified Team	71	66	77
172	Great Britain	43	72	57
113	Finland	48	35	30
87	Sweden	17	25	45
60	Australia	17	19	24
56	France	13	21	22
52	Canada	14	15	23
52	Italy	16	13	23

Most Swimming Medals
Men and women; not including diving or synchronized swimming.

No.	Country	G	S	B
401	United States	178	130	93
176	Germany	53	60	63
123	Australia	39	37	47
69	USSR/Unified Team	18	24	27
62	Great Britain	14	22	26
59	Hungary	23	20	16
45	Japan	15	18	12
38	Canada	7	13	18
36	Holland	9	13	14
31	Sweden	7	12	12

Most Diving Medals
Men and women.

No.	Country	G	S	B
127	United States	46	40	41
26	Germany	8	10	8
21	Sweden	6	8	7
17	USSR	4	6	7
19	China	9	6	4

Most Gymnastics Medals
Men and women; not including rhythmic gymnastics.

No.	Country	G	S	B
200	USSR/Unified Team	81	72	47
86	Japan	27	28	31
77	United States	26	23	28
70	Germany	19	21	30
50	Romania	16	14	20
48	Switzerland	16	19	13
39	Hungary	13	12	14
35	Czechoslovakia	12	13	10
30	Italy	13	8	9
27	China	9	12	6

Most Boxing Medals

No.	Country	G	S	B
102	United States	47	21	34
53	USSR/Unified Team	14	20	19
45	Great Britain	12	10	23
43	Poland	8	9	26
44	Germany	11	14	19
41	Cuba	23	13	5
39	Italy	14	12	13
24	Argentina	7	7	10
22	Romania	1	8	13
19	South Africa	6	4	9
19	Hungary	10	2	7

Most Tennis Medals
Men and women.

No.	Country	G	S	B
36	Great Britain	14	11	11
26	United States	14	4	8
19	France	8	5	6
9	Greece	1	5	3
9	Germany	3	3	3

U.S. diver Greg Louganis in 1988. He won four gold medals and a silver in three Olympics.

Most Basketball Medals
Men and women.

No.	Country	G	S	B
18	United States	14	2	2
13	USSR	5	4	4
8	Yugoslavia	1	5	2
4	Brazil	0	1	3
2	Four tied.			

Note: The U.S. men's team has won 11 of 14 gold medals since 1936, while the women's team has won 3 of 6 since 1976.

All-Time Single-Olympics Winners

Matt Biondi at the Seoul Olympics in 1988.

Most National Medals

No.	Country	Year	G-S-B
244	United States	1904	78-84-82
195	USSR	1980	80-69-46
174	United States	1984	83-61-30
138	Great Britain	1908	54-46-38
132	USSR	1988	55-31-46
126	East Germany	1980	47-37-42
125	USSR	1976	49-41-35
112	Unified Team	1992	45-38-29
108	United States	1992	37-34-37
107	United States	1968	45-28-34

Note: With the fall of communism in Eastern Europe, 1990–91, East and West Germany reunified and sent a single team to the 1992 Summer Games, while the USSR competed as the Unified Team in 1992 and as Russia and 14 other independent states in 1996.

Most Individual Medals: Men

No.	Athlete/Country	Sport	G	S	B	Year
8	Aleksandr Dityatin, USSR	Gymnastics	3	4	1	1980
7	Mark Spitz, USA	Swimming	7	0	0	1972
7	Willis Lee, USA	Shooting	5	1	1	1920
7	Matt Biondi, USA	Swimming	5	1	1	1988
7	Boris Shakhlin, USSR	Gymnastics	4	2	1	1960
7	Nikolai Andrianov, USSR	Gymnastics	4	2	1	1976
7	Lloyd Spooner, USA	Shooting	4	1	2	1920
7	Mikhail Voronin, USSR	Gymnastics	2	4	1	1968
6	Vitaly Scherbo, UT	Gymnastics	6	0	0	1992
6	Anton Heida, USA	Gymnastics	5	1	0	1904
6	Hubert van Innis, BEL	Archery	4	2	0	1920
6	Ville Ritola, FIN	Track/Field	4	2	0	1924
6	Viktor Chukarin, USSR	Gymnastics	4	2	0	1956
6	Carl Osburn, USA	Shooting	4	1	1	1920
6	Akinori Nakayama, JPN	Gymnastics	4	1	1	1968
6	Louis Richardet, SWI	Shooting	3	3	0	1906
6	Hermann Weingartner, GER	Gymnastics	3	2	1	1896
6	George Eyser, USA	Gymnastics	3	2	1	1904
6	Li Ning, CHN	Gymnastics	3	2	1	1984
6	Konrad Frey, GER	Gymnastics	3	1	2	1936
6	Takashi Ono, JPN	Gymnastics	3	1	2	1960
6	Burton Downing, USA	Cycling	2	3	1	1904
6	Alexi Nemov, RUS	Gymnastics	2	1	3	1996

Most U.S. Medals

No.	Location/Year	G-S-B
244	St. Louis, 1904	78-84-82
174	Los Angeles, 1984	83-61-30
108	Barcelona, 1992	37-34-37
107	Mexico City, 1968	45-28-34
103	Los Angeles, 1932	41-32-30
101	Atlanta, 1996	44-32-25
99	Paris, 1924	45-27-27
95	Antwerp, 1920	41-27-27
94	Seoul, 1988	36-31-27
94	Montreal, 1976	34-35-25
94	Munich, 1972	33-31-30

Note: The U.S. totals were abnormally high at St. Louis in 1904 because only 11 nations attended and 500 of the 681 athletes competing were Americans. At Los Angeles in 1984, the USSR, East Germany, Cuba, and 11 other Communist countries stayed home to retaliate for the American-led boycott of the 1980 Summer Games in Moscow after the Soviet invasion of Afghanistan.

Four or More Gold Medals

No.	Athlete/Country	Year
MEN		
7	Mark Spitz, USA	1972
6	Vitaly Scherbo, UT	1992
5	Anton Heida, USA	1904
5	Willis Lee, USA	1920
5	Nedo Nadi, ITA	1920
5	Paavo Nurmi, FIN	1924
5	Matt Biondi, USA	1988
4	Karl Schuman, GER	1896
4	Alvin Kraenzlein, USA	1900
4	Marcus Hurley, USA	1904
4	Hubert van Innis, BEL	1920
4	Lloyd Spooner, USA	1920
4	Carl Osburn, USA	1920
4	Ville Ritola, FIN	1924
4	Jesse Owens, USA	1936
4	Viktor Chukarin, USSR	1956
4	Boris Shakhlin, USSR	1960
4	Don Schollander, USA	1964
4	Akinori Nakayama, JPN	1968
4	Nikolai Andrianov, USSR	1976
4	John Naber, USA	1976
4	Carl Lewis, USA	1984
WOMEN		
6	Kristin Otto, E.GER	1988
4	Ágnes Keleti, HUN	1956
4	Vera Cáslavská, CZE	1968
4	Larissa Latynina, USSR	1956
4	Kornelia Ender, E.GER	1976
4	Ecaterina Szabó, ROM	1984
4	Fanny Blankers-Koen, HOL	1948
4	Amy Van Dyken, USA	1996

Sports: •Men—Archery (van Innis); Cycling (Hurley); Fencing (Nadi); Gymnastics (Andrianov, Chukarin, Heida, Nakayama, Scherbo, and Shakhlin); Shooting (Lee, Osburn, and Spooner); Swimming (Biondi, Naber, Schollander, and Spitz); Track & Field (Lewis, Kraenzlein, Nurmi, Owens, and Ritola); Wrestling & Gymnastics (Schuman).•Women—Gymnastics (Caslavska, Keleti, Latynina, and Szabo); Swimming (Ender, Otto, and Van Dyken); Track & Field (Blankers-Koen).

Shannon Miller performing her floor excercise at the Barcelona Olympics in 1992.

Most Individual Medals: Women

No.	Athlete/Country	Sport	G	S	B	Year
7	Maria Gorokhovskaya, USSR	Gymnastics	2	5	0	1952
6	Kristin Otto, E.GER	Swimming	6	0	0	1988
6	Ágnes Keleti, HUN	Gymnastics	4	2	0	1956
6	Vera Cáslavská, CZE	Gymnastics	4	2	0	1968
6	Larissa Latynina, USSR	Gymnastics	4	1	1	1956
6	Larissa Latynina, USSR	Gymnastics	3	2	1	1960
6	Daniela Silivas, ROM	Gymnastics	3	2	1	1988
6	Larissa Latynina, USSR	Gymnastics	2	2	2	1964
6	Margit Korondi, HUN	Gymnastics	1	1	4	1952
5	Kornelia Ender, E.GER	Swimming	4	1	0	1976
5	Ecaterina Szabó, ROM	Gymnastics	4	1	0	1984
5	Shane Gould, AUS	Swimming	3	1	1	1972
5	Nadia Comaneci, ROM	Gymnastics	3	1	1	1976
5	Karin Janz, E.GER	Gymnastics	2	2	1	1972
5	Ines Diers, E.GER	Swimming	2	2	1	1980
5	Shirley Babashoff, USA	Swimming	1	4	0	1976
5	Mary Lou Retton, USA	Gymnastics	1	2	2	1984
5	Shannon Miller, USA	Gymnastics	0	2	3	1992

Note: Larissa Latynina is the only athlete to win 6 medals in 3 separate Olympics (1956, 1960, and 1964).

Miscellaneous

World's Best Athletes: U.S. Decathlon Champions

Americans have won 11 of 19 gold medals in the Olympic decathlon since 1912; world record (WR), Olympic record (OR).

Year	Winner	Points*
1996	Dan O'Brien	8,824
1976	Bruce Jenner	8,634 WR
1968	Bill Toomey	8,158 OR
1960	Rafer Johnson	7,901 OR
1956	Milt Campbell	7,565 WR
1952	Bob Mathias	7,580 WR
1948	Bob Mathias	6,628
1936	Glenn Morris	7,254 WR
1932	Jim Bausch	6,735 WR
1924	Harold Osborn	6,476 WR
1912	Jim Thorpe	6,564 WR

*Point totals before 1996 have been refigured based on adjusted tables approved in 1985 by the International Amateur Track Federation.
Note: The decathlon consists of 10 events staged over 2 days—(in order) 100 meters, long jump, shot put, high jump, 400 meters, 110-meter hurdles, discus, pole vault, javelin, and 1,500 meters.

The Greatest Athlete in the World

A two-time college football All-America at Carlisle (Pa.) Institute, Jim Thorpe was the standout performer at the 1912 Summer Games in Stockholm, easily winning the decathlon and the five-event pentathlon (discontinued after 1924). "You, sir," said Sweden's King Gustav V at the medal ceremony, "are the greatest athlete in the world." To which the 24-year-old Native American is said to have replied shyly, "Thanks, King." A year later, with the full backing of American Olympic officials, the International Olympic Committee stripped Thorpe of his medals and erased his records when it was learned he had played minor league baseball for $25 a week in 1910. After a long campaign to reverse the decision, the I.O.C. finally agreed in 1983 to restore the medals and records, 30 years after Thorpe's death. Thorpe, who played major league baseball and pro football after the Olympics, was voted the greatest athlete of the first half of the century in a 1950 Associated Press poll of U.S. sportswriters.

Most Wins in Men's Basketball

Based on at least 15 games played in men's competition since 1936; listed with number of appearances in Olympic tournaments.

Pct.	Country	App.	W	L
.980	United States	13	100	2
.807	USSR/Unified Team	10	67	16
.773	Yugoslavia	9	58	17
.688	Lithuania	2	11	5
.625	Croatia	2	10	6
.586	Italy	10	41	29
.564	Brazil	12	57	44
.556	Argentina	3	10	8
.548	Mexico	7	23	19
.537	Uruguay	7	29	25

Note: The United States won 62 consecutive games from 1936, the year basketball was introduced at the Olympics, to 1972, when it lost a bitterly controversial gold medal final to the USSR, 51-50. The Soviets won on a lay-up when three seconds were put back on the clock after the game had originally ended with the Americans ahead, 50-49. The U.S. team refused the silver medal.

Jim Thorpe, the 1912 decathlon champion, was named the "Greatest Athlete of the Half Century" by the Associated Press in 1950.

Basketball Champions in College, Olympics, and the Pros

Only 7 men and 1 woman have played on championship teams in NCAA Division I, the Olympics, and either the National Basketball Association or Women's NBA.

MEN

Quinn Buckner
NCAA—Indiana (1976)
Olympics—Montreal (1976)
NBA—Boston Celtics (1984)

Magic Johnson
NCAA—Michigan State (1979)
Olympics—Barcelona (1992)
NBA-- L.A. Lakers (5 times)

K.C. Jones
NCAA—San Francisco (1955)
Olympics—Melbourne (1956)
NBA—Boston Celtics (8 times)

Michael Jordan
NCAA—North Carolina (1982)
Olympics—Los Angeles (1984)
and Barcelona (1992)
NBA—Chicago Bulls (5 times)

Clyde Lovellette
NCAA—Kansas (1952)
Olympics—Helsinki (1952)
NBA—Minneapolis Lakers (1954) and Boston Celtics (2 times).

Jerry Lucas
NCAA—Ohio State (1960)
Olympics—Rome (1960)
NBA—New York Knicks (1973)

Bill Russell
NCAA—San Francisco (1955, 1956)
Olympics—Melbourne (1956)
NBA—Boston Celtics (11 times)

WOMEN

Sheryl Swoopes
NCAA—Texas Tech (1993)
Olympics—Atlanta (1996)
WNBA—Houston Comets (1997)

TRACK&FIELD

World, Olympic,
& American
Records:
Men   184
Women   186

American track star
Michael Johnson
breaking 200-meter
world record at the
1996 Olympics.

SWIMMING

World, Olympic &
American Records:
Men   189
Women   191

Janet Evans of the U.S.
set three freestyle world
records before retiring
in 1996.

TRACK & FIELD
World, Olympic, & American Records

Donovan Bailey of Canada setting a new world record in the 100 meters at the 1996 Atlanta Olympics. On June 1, 1997, in Toronto, Bailey defeated 200-meter world record holder Michael Johnson of the U.S. in a match race over 150 meters. Bailey's time was 14.99 seconds.

Running
All distances are in meters.

Event	Record	Time	Holder/Country	Date	Location
100m	World	9.84	Donovan Bailey, CAN	7/27/96	Atlanta, GA
	Olympic	9.84	Donovan Bailey, CAN	7/27/96	Atlanta, GA
	American	9.85	Leroy Burrell	7/6/94	Lausanne, SWI
200m	World	19.32	Michael Johnson, USA	8/1/96	Atlanta, GA
	Olympic	19.32	Michael Johnson, USA	8/1/96	Atlanta, GA
	American	19.32	Michael Johnson	8/1/96	Atlanta, GA
400m	World	43.29	Butch Reynolds, USA	8/17/88	Zurich, SWI
	Olympic	43.49	Michael Johnson, USA	7/29/96	Atlanta, GA
	American	43.29	Butch Reynolds	8/17/88	Zurich, SWI
800m	World	1:41.11*	Wilson Kipketer, DEN	8/24/97	Cologne, GER
	Olympic	1:42.58	Vebjorn Rodal, NOR	7/31/96	Atlanta, GA
	American	1:42.60	Johnny Gray	8/28/85	Koblenz, W.GER
1,500m	World	3:27.37	Noureddine Morceli, ALG	7/12/95	Nice, FRA
	Olympic	3:32.53	Sebastian Coe, GBR	8/11/84	Los Angeles, CA
	American	3:29.77	Sydney Maree	8/25/85	Cologne, W.GER
1 mile (1,609m)	World	3:44.39	Noureddine Morceli, ALG	9/5/93	Rieti, ITA
	Olympic	—	not an Olympic event	—	—
	American	3:47.69	Steve Scott	7/7/82	Oslo, NOR
5,000m	World	12:39.74*	Daniel Komen, KEN	8/22/97	Brussels, BEL
	Olympic	13:05.59	Said Aouita, MOR	8/11/84	Los Angeles, CA
	American	12:58.21	Bob Kennedy	8/14/96	Zurich, SWI
10,000m	World	26:27.85*	Paul Tergat, KEN	8/22/97	Brussels, BEL
	Olympic	27:07.34	Haile Gebrselassie, ETH	7/29/96	Atlanta, GA
	American	27:20.56	Mark Nenow	9/5/86	Brussels, BEL
Marathon#	World	2:06:50	Belayneh Dinsamo, ETH	4/17/88	Rotterdam, HOL
	Olympic	2:09.21	Carlos Lopes, POR	8/12/84	Los Angeles, CA
	American	2:10.04	Pat Petersen	4/23/89	London, GBR
	American	2:08.52†	Alberto Salazar	4/19/82	Boston, MA

#Since marathon road courses are all different and lack the uniformity of oval tracks laid out for runners, the fastest marathon times are officially recognized as "bests" rather than "records." The marathon is 26 miles, 385 yards (or 42,195 meters).
†Former American record, officially stricken from record books in 1990 when the Boston Marathon was found to be in violation of new TAC (The Athletics Congress, now USA Track and Field) rule limiting drop of elevation, distance between start and finish lines, and average prevailing wind.

Relays

Event	Record	Time	Country/Team	Date	Location
4 x 100m	World	37.40	USA (Mike Marsh, Leroy Burrell, Dennis Mitchell, Carl Lewis)	8/8/92	Barcelona, SPA
	World=	37.40	USA (Jon Drummond, Andre Cason, Dennis Mitchell, Leroy Burrell)	8/21/93	Stuttgart, GER
	Olympics	37.40	USA (Mike Marsh, Leroy Burrell, Dennis Mitchell, Carl Lewis)	8/8/92	Barcelona, SPA
	American	37.40	The two U.S. world record holders listed above.		
4 x 400m	World	2:54.29	USA (Andrew Valmon, Quincy Watts, Butch Reynolds, Michael Johnson)	8/22/93	Stuttgart, GER
	Olympic	2:55.74	USA (Andrew Valmon, Quincy Watts, Michael Johnson, Steve Lewis)	8/8/92	Barcelona, SPA
	American	2:54.29	USA (Andrew Valmon, Quincy Watts, Butch Reynolds, Michael Johnson)	8/22/93	Stuttgart, GER

Hurdles

Event	Record	Time	Holder/Country	Date	Location
110m	World	12.91	Colin Jackson, GBR	8/20/93	Stuttgart, GER
	Olympic	12.95	Allen Johnson, USA	7/29/96	Atlanta, GA
	American	12.92	Roger Kingdom	6/23/96	Zurich, SWI
	American=	12.92	Allen Johnson	6/23/96	Atlanta, GA
400m	World	46.78	Kevin Young, USA	8/6/92	Barcelona, SPA
	Olympic	46.78	Kevin Young, USA	8/6/92	Barcelona, SPA
	American	46.78	Kevin Young	8/6/92	Barcelona, SPA

Note: The hurdles are 3 feet, 6 inches high over 110 meters and 3 feet over 400 meters. There are 10 hurdles in both races.

Steeplechase

Event	Record	Time	Holder/Country	Date	Location
3,000m	World	7:55.72*	Bernard Barmasai, KEN	8/24/97	Cologne, GER
	Olympic	8:05.51	Julius Kariuki, KEN	9/30/88	Seoul, S.KOR
	American	8:09.17	Henry Marsh	8/28/85	Koblenz, GER

Note: The steeplechase course consists of 28 hurdles (3 feet high) and 7 water jumps (12 feet long).

Field Events
All height and distance marks are in feet.

Event	Record	Mark	Holder/Country	Date	Location
High Jump	World	8-0½	Javier Sotomayor, CUB	7/27/93	Salamanca, SPA
	Olympic	7-10	Charles Austin, USA	7/28/96	Atlanta, GA
	American	7-10½	Charles Austin	8/7/91	Zurich, SWI
Pole Vault	World	20-2#	Sergey Bubka, UKR	2/21/93	Donyetsk, UKR
	Olympic	19-5¼†	Jean Galfione, FRA	8/2/96	Atlanta, GA
	Olympic=	19-5¼	Igor Trandenkov, RUS	8/2/96	Atlanta, GA
	Olympic=	19-5¼	Andrei Tivontchik, GER	8/2/96	Atlanta, GA
	American	19-7½	Lawrence Johnson	5/25/96	Knoxville, TN

#Indoor record. Bubka also holds the outdoor record of 20 feet, 1¾ inches set on July 31, 1994, at Sestriere, Italy.
†In Atlanta, Galfione reached 19 feet, 5¼ inches first and won the gold medal on fewer misses.

Sergey Bubka of the Ukraine, the only pole vaulter to clear 20 feet or more.

Men's Field Events (continued)

Event	Record	Mark	Holder/Country	Date	Location
Long Jump	World	29-4½	Mike Powell, USA	8/30/91	Tokyo, JPN
	Olympic	29-2½	Bob Beamon, USA	10/18/68	Mexico City, MEX
	American	29-4½	Mike Powell	8/30/91	Tokyo, JPN
Triple Jump	World	60-0¼	Jonathan Edwards, GBR	8/7/95	Goteborg, SWE
	Olympic	57-10½	Mike Conley, USA	8/3/92	Barcelona, SPA
	American	59-4½	Kenny Harrison	7/27/96	Atlanta, GA
Shot Put	World	75-10¼	Randy Barnes, USA	5/20/90	Los Angeles, CA
	Olympic	73-8¾	Ulf Timmermann, E.GER	9/23/88	Seoul, S.KOR
	American	75-10¼	Randy Barnes	5/20/90	Los Angeles, CA
Discus	World	243-0	Jurgen Schult, E.GER	6/6/86	Neubrandenburg, E.GER
	Olympic	227-8	Lars Riedel, GER	7/31/96	Atlanta, GA
	American	237-4	Ben Plucknett	7/7/81	Stockholm, SWE
Hammer	World	284-7	Yuri Sedykh, USSR	8/30/86	Stuttgart, W.GER
	Olympic	278-2	Sergy Litinov, USSR	9/26/88	Seoul, S.KOR
	American	270-9	Lance Deal	9/7/96	Milan, ITA
Javelin	World	323-1	Jan Zelezny, CZE	5/25/96	Jena, GER
	Olympic	294-2	Jan Zelezny, CZE	8/8/92	Barcelona, SPA
	American	285-10	Tom Pukstys	5/25/97	Jena, GER

Note: International weights for men—discus (4.41 lbs.); hammer (16 lbs.); javelin (1.76 lbs.); shot (16 lbs.).

Decathlon

Events	Record	Pts.	Holder/Country	Date	Location
10	World	8,891	Dan O'Brien, USA	9/5/92	Talence, FRA
	Olympic	8,847	Daley Thompson, GBR	8/9/84	Los Angeles, CA
	American	8,891	Dan O'Brien	9/5/92	Talence, FRA

World record: O'Brien's times and marks, in order, over two days of competition: •First day—100m (10.43 seconds), Long Jump (26-6¼), Shot (54-9¼), High Jump (6-9½), and 400m (48.51); •Second day—110m Hurdles (13.98), Discus (159-4), Pole Vault (16-4¾), Javelin (205-4), and 1,500m (4:42.10).
Olympic record: Daley's times and marks, in order, over two days of competition: •First day—100m (10.44 seconds), Long Jump (26-3½), Shot (51-7), High Jump (6-8), and 400m (46.97); •Second day—110m Hurdles (14.33), Discus (152-9), Pole Vault (16-4¾), Javelin (214-0), and 1,500m (4:35.00).

WOMEN

All records listed are as of September 1, 1997; equal sign (=) indicates equaled record; asterisk (*) indicates record set in 1997.

Running

All distances are in meters.

Event	Record	Time	Holder/Country	Date	Location
100m	World	10.49	Florence Griffith Joyner, USA	7/16/88	Indianapolis, IN
	Olympic	10.62	Florence Griffith Joyner, USA	9/24/88	Seoul, S.KOR
	American	10.49	Florence Griffith Joyner	7/16/88	Indianapolis, IN

Florence Griffith Joyner after setting the Olympic record in the 100 meters in a preliminary heat at the 1988 Olympics. Her record still stands a decade later.

Event	Record	Time	Holder/Country	Date	Location
200m	World	21.34	Florence Griffith Joyner, USA	9/29/88	Seoul, S.KOR
	Olympic	21.34	Florence Griffith Joyner, USA	9/29/88	Seoul, S.KOR
	American	21.34	Florence Griffith Joyner	9/29/88	Seoul, S.KOR
400m	World	47.60	Marita Koch, CZE	10/6/85	Canberra, AUS
	Olympic	48.65	Olga Bryzgina, USSR	9/26/88	Seoul, S.KOR
	American	48.83	Valerie Brisco	8/6/84	Los Angeles, CA
800m	World	1:53.28	Jarmila Kratochvilova, CZE	7/26/83	Munich, W.GER
	Olympic	1:53.42	Nadezhda Olizarenko, USSR	7/27/80	Moscow, USSR
	American	1:56.78*	Jearl Miles-Clark	8/22/97	Brussels, BEL
1,500m	World	3:50.46	Qu Yunxia, CHN	9/11/93	Beijing, CHN
	Olympic	3:53.96	Paula Ivan, ROM	10/1/88	Seoul, S.KOR
	American	3:57.12	Mary Slaney	7/26/83	Stockholm, SWE
1 mile (1,609m)	World	4:12.56	Svetlana Masterkova, RUS	8/14/96	Zurich, SWI
	Olympic	—	not an Olympic event	—	—
	American	4:16.71	Mary Slaney	8/21/85	Zurich, SWI
3,000m	World	8:06.11	Wang Junxia, CHN	9/13/93	Beijing, CHN
	Olympic	—	No longer an Olympic event#	—	—
	American	8:25.83	Mary Slaney	9/7/85	Rome, ITA
5,000m	World	14:36.45	Fernanda Ribeiro, POR	7/22/95	Hechtel, BEL
	Olympic	14:59.88	Wang Junxia, CHN	7/28/96	Atlanta, GA
	American	14:56.04	Amy Randolph	7/8/96	Stockholm, SWE
10,000m	World	29:31.78	Wang Junxia, CHN	9/8/93	Beijing, CHN
	Olympic	31:05.21	Olga Bondarenko, USSR	9/30/88	Seoul, S.KOR
	American	31:19.89	Lynn Jennings	8/7/92	Barcelona, SPA
Marathon†	World	2:21:06	Ingrid Kristiansen, NOR	4/21/85	London, GBR
	Olympic	2:24:52	Joan Benoit, USA	8/5/84	Los Angeles, CA
	American	2:21:21	Joan Benoit	10/20/85	Chicago, IL

Joan Benoit celebrating her victory in the first women's Olympic marathon. It was run at the 1984 Summer Games in Los Angeles.

#The 3,000-meter race (1984–92) was discontinued after the Barcelona Olympics in favor of the 5,000 meters.
†Since marathon road courses are all different and lack the uniformity of oval tracks laid out for runners, the fastest marathon times are officially recognized as "bests" rather than "records." The marathon distance is 26 miles, 385 yards (42,195m).

Relays

Event	Record	Time	Country/Team	Date	Location
4x100m	World	41.37	E.GER (Silke Gladisch, Sabine Rieger, Ingrid Auerswald, Marlies Gohr)	10/6/85	Canberra, AUS
	Olympic	41.60	E.GER (Romy Muller, Barbel Wockel, Ingrid Auerswald, Marlies Gohr)	8/1/80	Moscow, USSR
	American	41.47*	USA (Chryste Gaines, Marion Jones, Inger Miller, Gail Devers)	8/9/97	Athens, GRE
4x400m	World	3:15.17	USSR (Tatiana Ledovskaya, Olga Nazarova, Maria Pinigina, Olga Bryzgina)	10/1/88	Seoul, S.KOR
	Olympic	3:15.17	USSR (Tatiana Ledovskaya, Olga Nazarova, Maria Pinigina, Olga Bryzgina)	10/1/88	Seoul, S.KOR
	American	3:15.51	USA (Denean Howard-Hill, Diane Dixon, Valerie Brisco, Florence Griffith Joyner)	10/1/88	Seoul, S.KOR

The Heptathlon

The heptathlon belongs to Jackie Joyner-Kersee. She set the World, Olympic, and American records at the Seoul Olympics on Sept. 24, 1988, completing the 7 events over 2 days of competition with a total of 7,291 points. Her record-making times and marks, in order, are: •First day—100m Hurdles (12.69), High Jump (6-1¼), Shot (51-10), and 200m (22.56); •Second day—Long Jump (23-10¼), Javelin (149-10), and 800m (2:08.51).

Jackie Joyner-Kersee, who set four world records in the heptathlon and one in the long jump from 1986 to 1988.

Hurdles

Event	Record	Time	Holder/Country	Date	Location
	World	12.21	Yordanka Donkova, BUL	8/20/88	Stara Zagora, BUL
100m	Olympic	12.38	Yordanka Donkova, BUL	9/30/88	Seoul, S.KOR
	American	12.46	Gail Devers	8/20/93	Stuttgart, GER
	World	52.61	Kim Batten, USA	8/11/95	Goteborg, SWE
400m	Olympic	53.17	Debbie Flintoff-King, AUS	9/28/88	Seoul, S.KOR
	American	52.61	Kim Batten, USA	8/11/95	Goteborg, SWE

Note: The hurdles are 3 feet, 6 inches high over 110 meters and 3 feet over 400 meters. There are 10 hurdles in both races.

Field Events
All height and distance marks are in feet.

Event	Record	Mark	Holder/Country	Date	Location
	World	6-10¼	Stefka Kostadinova, BUL	8/30/87	Rome, ITA
High Jump	Olympic	6-8	Louise Ritter, USA	9/30/88	Seoul, S.KOR
	American	6-8	Louise Ritter, USA	7/9/88	Austin, TX
	American =	6-8	Louise Ritter, USA	9/30/88	Seoul, S.KOR
	World	14-11*	Emma George, AUS	2/20/97	Melbourne, AUS
Pole Vault	Olympic	—	not an Olympic event	—	–
	American	14-7¼*	Stacy Dragila	5/10/97	Modesto, CA
	World	24-8¼	Galina Chistyakova, USSR	6/11/88	Leningrad, USSR
Long Jump	Olympic	24-3¼	Jackie Joyner-Kersee, USA	9/29/88	Seoul, S.KOR
	American	24-7	Jackie Joyner-Kersee, USA	5/22/94	New York, NY
	World	50-10¼	Inessa Kravets, UKR	8/10/95	Goteborg, SWE
Triple Jump	Olympic	50-3½	Inessa Kravets, UKR	7/31/96	Atlanta, GA
	American	47-3½	Sheila Hudson	7/8/96	Stockholm, SWE
	World	74-3	Natalya Lisovskaya, USSR	6/7/87	Moscow, USSR
Shot Put	Olympic	73-6¼	Ilona Slupianek, E.GER	7/24/80	Moscow, USSR
	American	66-2½	Ramona Pagel	6/25/88	San Diego, CA
	World	252-0	Gabriele Reinsch, E.GER	7/9/88	Neubrandenburg, E.GER
Discus	Olympic	237-2½	Martina Hellman, E.GER	9/29/88	Seoul, S.KOR
	American	216-10	Carol Cady	5/31/86	San Jose, CA
	World	239-10*	Olga Kuzenkova, RUS	6/22/97	Munich, GER
Hammer	Olympic	—	not an Olympic event	—	—
	American	210-8*	Dawn Ellerbe	4/19/97	Walnut, CA
	World	262-5	Petra Felke, E.GER.	9/9/88	Potsdam, E.GER
Javelin	Olympic	245-0	Petra Felke, E.GER.	9/26/88	Seoul, S.KOR
	American	227-5	Kate Schmidt	9/10/77	Furth, W.GER

Note: International weights for women—discus (2.21 lbs.); hammer (16 lbs.); javelin (1.32 lbs.); shot (8.81 lbs.).

SWIMMING
World, Olympic & American Records

<u>MEN</u>

All records listed are as of September 1, 1997; all distances are in meters; asterisk (*) indicates a record set in 1997.

Freestyle

Event	Record	Time	Holder/Country	Date	Location
	World	21.81	Tom Jager, USA	3/24/90	Nashville, TN
50m	Olympic	21.91	Aleksandr Popov, UT	7/30/92	Barcelona, SPA
	American	21.81	Tom Jager	3/24/90	Nashville, TN
	World	48.21	Aleksandr Popov, RUS	6/18/94	Monte Carlo, MON
100m	Olympic	48.63	Matt Biondi, USA	9/22/88	Seoul, S.KOR
	American	48.42	Matt Biondi	8/10/88	Austin, TX
	World	1:46.69	Giorgio Lamberti, ITA	8/15/89	Bonn, W.GER
200m	Olympic	1:46.70	Yevgeny Sadovyi, UT	7/26/92	Barcelona, SPA
	American	1:47.72	Matt Biondi	8/8/88	Austin, TX
	World	3:43.80	Kieren Perkins, AUS	9/9/94	Rome, ITA
400m	Olympic	3:45.00	Yevgeny Sadovyi, UT	7/29/92	Barcelona, SPA
	American	3:48.06	Matt Cetlinski	8/11/88	Austin, TX
	World	7:46.00#	Kieren Perkins, AUS	8/24/94	Victoria, CAN
800m	Olympic	—	not an Olympic event	—	—
	American	7:52.45	Sean Killion	7/27/87	Clovis, CA
	World	14:41.66	Kieren Perkins, AUS	8/24/94	Victoria, CAN
1,500m	Olympic	14:43.48	Kieren Perkins, AUS	7/31/92	Barcelona, SPA
	American	15:01.51	George DiCarlo	6/30/84	Indianapolis, IN

Split time.

Backstroke

Event	Record	Time	Holder/Country	Date	Location
	World	53.86#	Jeff Rouse, USA	7/31/92	Barcelona, SPA
100m	Olympic	53.98	Mark Tewksbury, CAN	7/30/92	Barcelona, SPA
	American	53.86#	Jeff Rouse	7/31/92	Barcelona, SPA
	World	1:56.57	Martin Zubero, SPA	11/23/91	Tuscaloosa, AL
200m	Olympic	1:58.47	Martin Zubero, SPA	7/28/92	Barcelona, SPA
	American	1:57.87*	Lenny Krayzelburg	8/12/97	Fukuoka, JPN

#Record set on leadoff split of medley relay race.

Australia's Kieren Perkins at the 1996 Summer Games in Atlanta. He set three world freestyle records in 1994 and is the two-time defending Olympic champion at 1,500 meters.

Gary Hall celebrates after helping the U.S. men's 4 x 100-meter freestyle relay team set a new Olympic record at the 1996 Summer Games in Atlanta.

Breaststroke

Event	Record	Time	Holder/Country	Date	Location
100m	World	1:00.60	Fred deBurghgraeve, BEL	7/20/96	Atlanta, GA
	Olympic	1:00.60	Fred deBurghgraeve, BEL	7/20/96	Atlanta, GA
	American	1:00.77	Jeremy Linn	7/20/96	Atlanta, GA
200m	World	2:10.16	Mike Barrowman, USA	7/29/92	Barcelona, SPA
	Olympic	2:10.16	Mike Barrowman, USA	7/29/92	Barcelona, SPA

Butterfly

Event	Record	Time	Holder/Country	Date	Location
100m	World	52.27	Denis Pankratov, RUS	7/24/96	Atlanta, GA
	Olympic	52.27	Denis Pankratov, RUS	7/24/96	Atlanta, GA
	American	52.76*	Neil Walker	8/12/97	Fukuoka, JPN
200m	World	1:55.22	Denis Pankratov, RUS	6/14/95	Canet, FRA
	Olympic	1:56.26	Melvin Stewart, USA	7/30/92	Barcelona, SPA
	American	1:55.69	Melvin Stewart	1/12/91	Perth, AUS

Individual Medley

Event	Record	Time	Holder/Country	Date	Location
200m	World	1:58.16	Jani Sievinen, FIN	9/11/94	Rome, ITA
	Olympic	1:59.91	Atilla Czene, HUN	7/25/96	Atlanta, USA
	American	2:00.11	David Wharton	8/20/89	Tokyo, JPN
400m	World	4:12.30	Tom Dolan, USA	9/6/94	Rome, ITA
	Olympic	4:14.23	Tamas Darnyi, HUN	7/27/92	Barcelona, SPA
	American	4:12.30	Tom Dolan	9/6/94	Rome, ITA

Freestyle Relays

Event	Record	Time	Country/Team	Date	Location
4x100m	World	3:15.11	USA (David Fox, Joe Hudepohl, Jon Olsen, Gary Hall)	8/12/95	Atlanta, GA
	Olympics	3:15.41	USA (Jon Olsen, Josh Davis, Bradley Schumacher, Gary Hall)	7/23/96	Atlanta, GA
	American	3:15.11	USA (David Fox, Joe Hudepohl, Jon Olsen, Gary Hall)	8/12/95	Atlanta, GA
4x200m	World	7:11.95	UT (Dmitri Lepikov, Vladimir Pychenko, Veniamin Tayanovich, Yevgeny Sadovyi)	7/27/92	Barcelona, SPA
	Olympic	7:11.95	UT (Dmitri Lepikov, Vladimir Pychenko, Veniamin Tayanovich, Yevgeny Sadovyi)	7/27/92	Barcelona, SPA
	American	7:12.51	USA (Troy Dalbey, Matt Cetlinski, Doug Gjertsen, Matt Biondi)	9/21/88	Seoul, S.KOR

Medley Relay

Event	Record	Time	Country/Team	Date	Location
4x100m	World	3:34.84	USA (Jeff Rouse, Jeremy Linn, Mark Henderson, Gary Hall)	7/26/96	Atlanta, GA
	Olympics	3:34.84	USA (Jeff Rouse, Jeremy Linn, Mark Henderson, Gary Hall)	7/26/96	Atlanta, GA
	American	3:34.84	USA (Jeff Rouse, Jeremy Linn, Mark Henderson, Gary Hall)	7/26/96	Atlanta, GA

WOMEN

All records listed are as of September 1, 1997; all distances are in meters; no new records were set in 1997.

Freestyle

Event	Record	Time	Holder/Country	Date	Location
	World	24.51	Le Jingyi, CHN	9/11/94	Rome, ITA
50m	Olympic	24.79	Yang Wenyi, CHN	7/31/92	Barcelona, SPA
	American	24.87	Amy Van Dyken	7/26/96	Atlanta, GA
	World	54.01	Le Jingyi, CHN	9/5/94	Rome, ITA
100m	Olympic	54.64	Zhuang Yong, CHN	7/26/92	Barcelona, SPA
	American	54.48	Jenny Thompson	3/1/92	Indianapolis, IN
	World	1:56.78	Franziska Van Almsick, GER	9/6/94	Rome, ITA
200m	Olympic	1:57.65	Heike Friedrich, E.GER	9/21/88	Seoul, S.KOR
	American	1:57.90	Nicole Haislett	7/27/92	Barcelona, SPA
	World	4:03.85	Janet Evans, USA	9/22/88	Seoul, S.KOR
400m	Olympic	4:03.85	Janet Evans, USA	9/22/88	Seoul, S.KOR
	American	4:03.85	Janet Evans, USA	9/22/88	Seoul, S.KOR
	World	8:16.22	Janet Evans, USA	8/20/89	Tokyo, JPN
800m	Olympic	8:20.20	Janet Evans, USA	9/24/88	Seoul, S.KOR
	American	8:16.22	Janet Evans, USA	8/20/89	Tokyo, JPN
	World	15:52.10	Janet Evans, USA	3/26/88	Orlando, FL
1,500m	Olympic	—	not an Olympic event	—	—
	American	15:52.10	Janet Evans, USA	3/26/88	Orlando, FL

Backstroke

Event	Record	Time	Holder/Country	Date	Location
	World	1:00.16	He Cihong, CHN	9/10/94	Rome ITA
100m	Olympic	1:00.68	Krisztina Egerszegi, HUN	7/28/92	Barcelona, SPA
	American	1:00.82*	Lea Loveless	7/30/92	Barcelona, SPA
	World	2:06.62	Krisztina Egerszegi, HUN	8/26/91	Athens, GRE
200m	Olympic	2:07.06	Krisztina Egerszegi, HUN	7/31/92	Barcelona, SPA
	American	2:08.60	Betsy Mitchell	6/27/86	Orlando, FL

*Record set on leadoff split of medley relay race.

Breaststroke

Event	Record	Time	Holder/Country	Date	Location
	World	1:07.02	Penny Heyns, SAF	7/21/96	Atlanta, GA
100m	Olympic	1:07.02	Penny Heyns, SAF	7/21/96	Atlanta, GA
	American	1:08.09	Amanda Beard	7/21/96	Atlanta, GA
	World	2:24.76	Rebecca Brown, AUS	3/16/94	Queensland, AUS
200m	Olympic	2:26.65	Kyoko Iwasaki, JPN	7/27/92	Barcelona, SPA
	American	2:25.35	Anita Nall	3/2/92	Indianapolis, IN

Amy Van Dyken, American record holder and 1996 Olympic 50-meter freestyle champion.

Mary T. Meagher at the Summer Olympics in Los Angeles in 1994 where she won both gold medals in the butterfly events, setting the Olympic record at 200 meters that still stands.

Butterfly

Event	Record	Time	Holder/Country	Date	Location
	World	57.93	Mary T. Meagher, USA	8/16/81	Brown Deer, WI
100m	Olympic	58.62	Qian Hong, CHN	7/29/92	Barcelona, SPA
	American	57.93	Mary T. Meagher	8/16/81	Brown Deer, WI
	World	2:05.96	Mary T. Meagher, USA	8/13/81	Brown Deer, WI
200m	Olympic	2:06.90	Mary T. Meagher, USA	8/4/84	Los Angeles, CA
	American	2:05.96	Mary T. Meagher	8/13/81	Brown Deer, WI

Individual Medley

Event	Record	Time	Holder/Country	Date	Location
	World	2:11.65	Lin Li, CHN	7/28/92	Barcelona, SPA
200m	Olympic	2:11.65	Lin Li, CHN	7/28/92	Barcelona, SPA
	American	2:11.91	Summer Sanders	7/28/92	Barcelona, SPA
	World	4:36.10	Petra Schneider, E.GER	8/1/82	Guayaquil, ECU
400m	Olympic	4:36.29	Petra Schneider, E.GER	7/26/80	Moscow, USSR
	American	4:37.58	Summer Sanders	7/26/92	Barcelona, SPA

Freestyle Relays

Event	Record	Time	Country/Team	Date	Location
	World	3:37.91	CHN (Le Jingyi, Shan Ying, Le Ying, Bin Lu)	9/7/94	Rome, ITA
4x100m	Olympics	3:39.29	USA (Angel Martino, Amy Van Dyken, Catherine Fox, Jenny Thompson)	7/22/96	Atlanta, GA
	American	3:39.29	USA (Angel Martino, Amy Van Dyken, Catherine Fox, Jenny Thompson)	7/22/96	Atlanta, GA
	World	7:55.47	E.GER (Manuella Stellmach, Astrid Strauss, Anke Mohring, Heike Friedrich)	8/18/87	Strasbourg, FRA
4x200m	Olympic	7:59.87	USA (Trina Jackson, Cristina Teuscher, Sheila Taormina, Jenny Thompson)	7/25/96	Atlanta, GA
	American	7:59.87	USA (Trina Jackson, Cristina Teuscher, Sheila Taormina, Jenny Thompson)	7/25/96	Atlanta, GA

Medley Relay

Event	Record	Time	Country/Team	Date	Location
	World	4:01.67	CHN (He Cihong, Dai Guohong, Liu Limin, Le Jingyi)	9/10/94	Rome, ITA
4x100m	Olympics	4:02.54	USA (Lea Loveless, Anita Nall, Christine Ahmann-Leighton, Jenny Thompson)	7/26/96	Atlanta, GA
	American	4:02.54	USA (Lea Loveless, Anita Nall, Christine Ahmann-Leighton, Jenny Thompson)	7/26/96	Atlanta, GA

The First Woman to Swim the English Channel

Gertrude Ederle of New York went to the 1924 Summer Olympics as the world record holder in the 100-meter freestyle with a time of 1:12.8. She won three medals in Paris but astonished the world two years later when, at age 19, she became the first woman to swim the English Channel. Noting that Ederle had attempted the Channel swim in 1925 but had quit when she became seasick, the *London Daily News* ridiculed her second effort in a chauvinistic editorial that concluded: "Even the most uncompromising champion of the rights and capacities of women must admit that in contests of physical skill, speed and endurance, they must remain forever the weaker sex." They were proved wrong however, when, starting off from France just after 7 a.m. on August 6, 1926, Ederle reached the English coast 14 hours and 31 minutes later—almost two hours faster than the previous record set by a man. Her time stood as the standard for women until 1964.

SOCCER

John Harkes (left), U.S. national team captain, playing against Mexico in the World Cup qualifier on April 20, 1997. The game ended in a 2-2 draw.

The World Cup

Maldino Romario (right) led Brazil past Italy in the 1994 World Cup final.

All-Time Champions
Only six countries have won the World Cup since 1930.

Cups	Country	Cup Finals	Championship Years
4	Brazil	5	1994, 1970, 1962, 1958
3	Italy	5	1982, 1938, 1934
3	Germany*	6	1990, 1974, 1954
2	Argentina	4	1986, 1978
2	Uruguay	2	1950, 1930
1	England	1	1966

*Competed in finals as Germany (1930-38, 1994) and West Germany (1954-90). Losses in cup final: •three—Germany (1986, 1982, 1966); •two—Argentina (1990, 1930), Czechoslovakia (1962, 1934), Holland (1978, 1974), Hungary (1954, 1938), and Italy (1994, 1970); •one—Brazil (1950) and Sweden (1958).

The Trophy
The first World Cup trophy, named in honor of FIFA's first president Jules Rimet, was retired in 1970 after Brazil won it three times. The second trophy, known simply as the World Cup, has been won twice by Argentina, in 1978 and 1986, and by West Germany (now Germany) in 1974 and 1990.

Host Countries
Including the 1998 tournament scheduled for France (June 10–July 12), the 16 World Cups since 1930 have been held in 13 countries.

Continent	Country	Years as Host	Site of Final
Europe	France	1998, 1938	Paris
	Italy	1990, 1934	Rome
	England	1966	London
	Spain	1986	Madrid
	Sweden	1958	Stockholm
	Switzerland	1954	Berne
	West Germany	1974	Munich
North America	Mexico	1986, 1970	Mexico City
	United States	1994	Pasadena
South America	Argentina	1978	Buenos Aires
	Brazil	1950	Rio de Janeiro
	Chile	1962	Santiago
	Uruguay	1930	Montevideo

Note: The World Cup will be played in Asia for the first time in 2002 when Japan and South Korea share the duties of host country. The cup final will be held in Tokyo.

Most Final Four Appearances
Listed with 1st through 4th place finishes.

App.	Country	1st	2nd	3rd	4th
9	Germany	3	3	2	1
8	Brazil	4	1	2	1
7	Italy	3	2	1	1
4	Argentina	2	2	0	0
4	Uruguay	2	0	0	2
4	Sweden	0	1	2*	1
3	France	0	0	2	1
2	England	1	0	0	1
2	Czech Republic	0	2	0	0
2	Holland	0	2	0	0
2	Hungary	0	2	0	0
2	Poland	0	0	2	0
2	Yugoslavia	0	0	1	1

*One of Sweden's 3rd-place finishes came in 1950 when no consolation game was played and the Swedes tied for 3rd with Spain, the tournament's other semifinal round loser. The only other World Cup without a consolation game was in 1930 when the United States and Yugoslavia shared 3rd.

The World Cup
Founded by the Federation Internationale de Football Association (FIFA), the World Cup championship tournament has been held 15 times at 4-year intervals since 1930. It was canceled in 1942 and 1946 due to World War II. Uruguay, whose national soccer team had won consecutive Olympic championships in 1924 and 1928, was selected to host the first World Cup, an event coinciding with the country's centennial anniversary of constitutional government. Thirteen countries participated and the home team won. Through the qualifying rounds of 1997, a record 170 countries competed for 30 of 32 berths at the 16th World Cup tournament scheduled for France from June 10 to July 12, 1998. Host country France and defending champion Brazil are the only automatic qualifiers.

All-Time World Cup Top 30

Ranking table based on points earned through 1994 final tournament. Listed with appearances in final tournament, games played, overall record, and total points (2 points for a win, 1 for a tie).

	Country	App.	Gm.	Record	Pts.
1	Brazil	15	73	49-11-13	111
2	Germany*	13	73	42-15-16	100
3	Italy	13	61	35-12-14	84
4	Argentina	11	52	26-17-9	61
5	England	9	41	18-11-12	48
6	Spain	9	37	15-13-9	39
7	Russia#	8	34	16-12-6	38
	Uruguay	8	37	15-14-8	38
9	Sweden	9	38	14-15-9	37
10	France	9	34	15-14-5	35
	Yugoslavia	8	33	14-12-7	35
12	Hungary	9	32	15-14-3	33
13	Poland	5	25	13-7-5	31
14	Holland	6	25	11-8-6	28
15	Czech Republic†	8	30	11-14-5	27
16	Austria	6	26	12-12-2	26
17	Belgium	9	29	9-16-4	22
	Mexico	10	33	7-18-8	22
19	Chile	6	21	7-11-3	17
20	Romania	6	17	6-7-4	16
21	Switzerland	7	22	6-13-3	15
22	Scotland	7	20	4-10-6	14
23	Bulgaria	6	23	3-13-7	13
24	Portugal	2	9	6-3-0	12
25	Peru	4	15	4-8-3	11
	Northern Ireland	3	13	3-5-5	11
27	Cameroon	3	11	3-4-4	10
	Paraguay	4	11	3-4-4	10
29	United States	5	14	4-9-1	9
30	Ireland	2	9	1-3-5	7

*Includes appearances as West Germany (1954–90).
#Includes appearances as Soviet Union (1958–90).
†Includes appearances as Czechoslovakia (1934–90)

Jose Basualdo of Argentina (left) heads the ball away from West Germany's Lothar Matthaus during the 1990 World Cup final in Rome. The West Germans won, 1-0.

The 10 Biggest Upsets

All games played in first round of the final tournament.

Year	Final Score	Host Country
1994	USA 2, Colombia 1	USA
1994	Saudi Arabia 1, Belgium 0	USA
1990	Cameroon 1, Argentina 0	Italy
1986	Morocco 3, Portugal 1	Mexico
1982	Algeria 2, West Germany 1	Spain
1966	North Korea 1, Italy 0	England
1958	No. Ireland 1, Czechoslovakia 0	Sweden
1950	USA 1, England 0	Brazil
1938	Cuba 2, Romania 1*	France
1938	Switzerland 4, Germany 2*	France

*Both victories came in replays after overtime draws. In the first games, Cuba tied Romania 3-3 and Switzerland tied Germany 1-1.

Highest-Scoring Games

Through 1994 World Cup; listed with leader and score at halftime.

Goals	Final Score	Year	Halftime
12	Austria 7, Switzerland 5	1954	AUT, 5-4
11	Hungary 10, El Salvador 1	1982	HUN, 3-0
11	Hungary 8, West Germany 3	1954	HUN, 3-1
11	Brazil 6, Poland 5 OT*	1938	BRA, 3-1
10	France 7, Paraguay 3	1958	Tie, 2-2
9	Hungary 9, South Korea 0	1954	HUN, 4-0
9	Yugoslavia 9, Zaire 0	1974	YUG, 6-0
9	West Germany 7, Turkey 2	1954	W.GER, 3-1
9	Argentina 6, Mexico 3	1930	ARG, 3-0
9	France 6, West Germany 3	1958	FRA, 3-1

*Regulation time ended with a 4-4 tie, after which Brazil outscored Poland, 2-1, in overtime. Leónidas of Brazil and Poland's Ernest Willimowski scored 4 goals each.

World Cup All-Time Leaders

Most World Cup Appearances
Through 1994.

Total	Player/Country	First Year	Last Year
5	Antonio Carbajal, Mexico	1950	1966
4	Diego Maradona, Argentina	1982	1994
4	Pelé, Brazil	1958	1970
4	Gianni Rivera, Italy	1962	1974
4	Pedro Rocha, Uruguay	1962	1974
4	Djalma Santos, Brazil	1954	1966
4	Karl-Heinz Schnellinger, W.Germany	1958	1970
4	Uwe Seeler, W.Germany	1958	1970
4	Wladislaw Zmuda	1974	1986

Most Games
Through 1994 World Cup.

Gm.	Player/Country	First Year	Last Year
21	Diego Maradona, Argentina	1982	1994
21	Uwe Seeler, W.Germany	1958	1970
21	Wladislaw Zmuda, Poland	1974	1986
20	Gregorz Lato, Poland	1974	1982
19	Berti Vogts, W.Germany	1970	1978
19	Wolfgang Overath, W.Germany	1966	1974
19	Karl-Heinz Rummenigge, W.Germany	1978	1986
19	Lothar Matthäus, Germany*	1986	1994

*West Germany became Germany after national reunification in 1990.
Note: Diego Maradona, who failed a random drug test after Argentina's second game of the 1994 World Cup, was suspended for the remainder of the tournament by the Argentine soccer federation.

Most Goals in One Tournament
Through 1994 World Cup.

Goals	Player/Country	Gm.	Year
13	Just Fontaine, France	6	1958
11	Sandor Kocsis, Hungary	5	1954
10	Gerd Müller, West Germany	6	1970
9	Ademir, Brazil	6	1950
9	Eusebio, Portugal	6	1966

Pelé of Brazil (10) scored 12 goals in four World Cups.

Most Career Goals
Through 1994 World Cup.

Goals	Player/Country	Years Played
14	Gerd Müller, W.Ger.	1974, 1970
13	Just Fontaine, France	1958
12	Pelé, Brazil	1970, 1966, 1962, 1958
11	Sandor Kocsis, Hungary	1954
10	Teofilo Cubillas, Peru	1978, 1970
10	Gregorz Lato, Poland	1982, 1978, 1974
10	Gary Lineker, England	1990, 1986
10	Helmut Rahn, W.Ger.	1958, 1954
9	Ademir, Brazil	1950
9	Eusebio, Portugal	1966
9	Jairzinho, Brazil	1974, 1970
9	Leónidas, Brazil	1938, 1934
9	Paolo Rossi, Italy	1982, 1978
9	Heinz-Karl Rummenigge, W.Ger.	1986, 1982, 1978
9	Uwe Seller, W.Ger.	1970, 1966, 1962, 1958
9	Vavà, Brazil	1962, 1958

Most Career Goals by Players Who Played in World Cup '94

Goals	Player/Country	Years Played
8	Jürgen Klinsmann, Germany	1994, 1990
8	Diego Maradona, Argentina	1994, 1990, 1986, 1982
7	Robert Baggio, Italy	1994, 1990
7	Rudi Völler, Germany	1994, 1990, 1986
6	Lothar Matthäus, Germany	1994, 1990, 1986
6	Oleg Salenko, Russia	1994
6	Hristo Stoichkov, Bulgaria	1994

All-Time World Cup Team

A pre-1994 World Cup poll of 991 international soccer writers from 109 countries chose 22 players and 3 coaches for an all-time team. They are listed with positions—defense (D), forward (F), goalkeeper (G), and midfield (M)—as well as number of appearances and the last World Cup in which they played.

Votes	Player/Country	Pos.	App.	Last Year
991	Pelé, Brazil	F	4	1970
954	Franz Beckenbauer, W.Germany	D/M	3	1974
911	Johan Cruyff, Holland	M/F	1	1974
907	Diego Maradona, Argentina	F	3	1990*
872	Michel Platini, France	M	3	1986
862	Garrincha, Brazil	F	3	1966
850	Bobby Charlton, England	F	3	1970
814	Bobby Moore, England	D	3	1970
727	Lothar Matthäus, W.Germany	M	2	1990*
705	Gerd Müller, W.Germany	F	2	1974
659	Ferenc Puskas, Hungary	F	1	1954
642	Eusebio, Portugal	F	1	1966
641	Lev Yashin, Soviet Union	G	3	1966
588	Djalma Santos, Brazil	D	4	1966
549	Robert Rivelino, Brazil	F	3	1978
538	Paolo Rossi, Italy	F	2	1982
535	Mario Kempes, Argentina	F	3	1982
522	Didi, Brazil	M	3	1962
495	Paul Breitner, W.Germany	D/M	2	1982
484	Daniel Passarella, Argentina	D	2	1982
483	Jairzinho, Brazil	F	3	1974
478	Gordon Banks, England	G	2	1970

Votes	Coach/Country	Years	Won Cup
596	Franz Beckenbauer, W.Germany	1990, 1986	1990
429	Cesar Luis Menotti, Argentina	1982, 1978	1978
429	Mario Zagalo, Brazil	1974, 1970	1970

*Also played in 1994 World Cup.

West German captain Franz Beckenbauer (left) with World Cup in 1974.

United States in World Cup

The USA has qualified for 5 of the 15 World Cup tournaments since 1930 and compiled an overall record of 4-9-1 in 14 games.

Year	Summary
1994	**Record:** 1-2-1 (eliminated in 2nd round). **1st Round** (3-game round robin): USA 1, Switzerland 1; USA 2, Colombia 1; Romania 1, USA 0. **2nd Round** (knockout): Brazil 1, USA 0. **Scoring:** 3 goals—Ernie Stewart, Eric Wynalda, and an "own goal" kicked in by Colombia defender Andres Escobar.
1990	**Record:** 0-3 (eliminated in 1st round). **1st Round** (3-game round robin): Czechoslovakia 5, USA 1; Italy 1, USA 0; Austria 2, USA 1. **Scoring:** 2 goals—Paul Caligiuri and Bruce Murray.
1950	**Record:** 1-2 (eliminated in 1st Round). **1st Round** (3-game round robin): Spain 3, USA 1; USA 1, England 0; Chile 5, USA 2. **Scoring:** 4 goals—Joe Gaetjens, Joe Maca, John Souza and Frank Wallace. Gaetjens had the goal against England.
1934	**Record:** 0-1 (eliminated in 1st round). **1st Round** (knockout): Italy 7, USA 1. **Scoring:** 1 goal—Buff Donelli.
1930	**Record:** 2-1 (eliminated in semifinals). **1st Round** (2-game round robin): USA 3, Belgium 0; USA 3, Paraguay 0. **Semifinals** (knockout): Argentina 6, USA 1. **Scoring:** 7 goals—Bert Patenaude 3, Bart McGhee 2, James Brown, and Thomas Florie.

Pelé, Zagalo, and Beckenbauer

Pelé, the brilliant Brazilian forward who would later become a pro soccer pioneer in the United States, is the only player in World Cup history to play on three championship teams. He was only 17 years old when he helped lead Brazil to its first World Cup title in Sweden in 1958. They repeated in Chile in 1962 and won a third time in Mexico in 1970. Mario Zagalo, Pelé's teammate for all three of those championships, played left wing on the 1958 and 1962 teams and then stepped up to coach the 1970 squad, which has been called the strongest national side ever. Zagalo held the distinction of being the only man to win World Cups as both a player and a coach until West Germany's Franz Beckenbauer came along. Beckenbauer, an attacking sweeper, captained the West Germans to victory in 1974. He then took over as coach in 1984 and reached two consecutive World Cup finals against Argentina—losing (3-2) in 1986 and winning (1-0) in 1990.

U.S. National Teams

MEN

Most Appearances

Against international competition,
including the World Cup qualifiers.

No.	Player	Pos.	Years
121	Marcelo Balboa	D	1988–
113	Paul Caligiuri	D	1984-96
93	Bruce Murray	M	1985-93
93	Cobi Jones	M	1992–
89	Alexi Lalas	D	1990–
89	Tony Meola	G	1988-94
87	Eric Wynalda	F	1990–
84	Desmond Armstrong	D	1987-94
81	John Harkes	M	1987–

Most Goals

Against international competition, including the
World Cup; listed with position and number of games.

Goals	Player	Pos.	Gm.
31	Eric Wynalda*	F	87
21	Bruce Murray	M	93
16	Joe-Max Moore*	M/F	56
16	Hugo Perez	M	79
13	Frank Klopas	F	45

*Active in 1997.

Team Record in 1990s

Against international competition, including World
Cup tournaments (1990, 1994) and all games
through Oct. 3, 1997).

Year	Gm.	Record	GF	GA
1997	15	3-6-6	15	19
1996	16	10-4-2	28	19
1995	14	5-6-3	20	18
1994	27	7-9-11	30	28
1993	34	10-13-11	45	44
1992	21	6-11-4	21	27
1991	18	8-5-5	22	15
1990	24	8-13-2	29	34
Total	169	57-67-44	210	204

United States in Women's World Cup

The FIFA Women's World Championship has been played every four years since 1991, when the United States won the first title in China. Norway won the second cup at Sweden in 1995.

1995 in Sweden

Record: 4-1-1 (won 3rd place)
1st round (3-game round robin): USA 3, China 3; USA 2, Denmark 0; USA 4, Australia 1.
Quarterfinals: USA 4, Japan 0.
Semifinals: Norway 1, USA 0.
3rd Place: USA 2, China 0.
Scoring: 15 goals— Kristine Lilly 3, Tiffeny Milbrett 3, Tisha Venturini 3, Mia Hamm 2, Joy Fawcett, Julie Foudy, Debbie Keller, and Carla Overbeck 1 each.

Note: Norway defeated Germany, 2-0, in World Cup final.

1991 in China

Record: 6-0 (won championship)
1st round (3-game round robin): USA 3, Sweden 2; USA 5, Brazil 0; USA 3, Japan 0.
Quarterfinals: USA 7, Taiwan 0;
Semifinals: USA 5, Germany 2
Final: USA 2, Norway 1
Scoring: 25 goals— Michelle Akers 10, Carin Jennings 6, April Heinrichs 4, Mia Hamm 2, Joy Biefeld, Julie Foudy, and Wendy Gebauer 1 each.

WOMEN

Most Appearances

In international competition.

No.	Player	Pos.	Years
133	Kristine Lilly	M	1987–
130	Mia Hamm	F	1987–
117	Carin Gabarra	F	1987-96
109	Michelle Akers	F	1985-96
108	Julie Foudy	M	1988–
101	Joy Fawcett	D	1987-96
100	Carla Overbeck	D	1988-96
82	Tisha Venturini	M	1992–
76	Tiffeny Milbrett	F	1991–

Most Goals

In international competition, including the World Cup.

Goals	Player	Pos.	Gm.
92	Michelle Akers	F	109
78	Mia Hamm*	F	130
53	Carin Gabarra	F	117
51	Kristine Lilly*	M	133
38	April Heinrichs	F	47
31	Tiffeny Milbrett*	F	76
31	Tisha Venturini*	M	82
19	Julie Foudy*	M	108
15	Joy Fawcett	D	101

*Active in 1997.

Team Record in 1990s

Against international competition, including the 1991 and 1995 World Cup tournaments and all games through Sept. 1, 1997; listed with goals for (GF) and goals against (GA).

Year	Gm.	Record	GF	GA	Year	Gm.	Record	GF	GA
1997	12	12-0-0	54	6	1992	2	0-2-0	3	7
1996	24	21-1-2	80	17	1991	28	21-6-1	122	22
1995	23	19-2-2	82	16	1990	6	6-0-0	26	3
1994	13	12-1-0	59	6	Total	125	104-16-5	480	84
1993	17	13-4-0	54	7					

The Kentucky Derby, 1997. Silver Charm (6), with jockey Gary Stevens aboard, was the winner.

The Triple Crown

Eddie Arcaro in 1947.

Jockeys With Most Wins in Triple Crown Races

Listed with last year as active jockey, and wins in Kentucky Derby (K), Preakness (P), and Belmont (B).

Wins	Jockey/Last Year	K/P/B
17	Eddie Arcaro (1961)	5-6-6
11	Bill Shoemaker (1990)	4-2-5
9	Bill Hartack (1974)	5-3-1
9	Earl Sande (1947)	3-1-5
8	Pat Day (active)	1-5-2
8	Jim McLaughlin (1892)	1-1-6
6	Angel Cordero Jr. (1992)	3-2-1
6	Charley Kurtsinger (1939)	2-2-2
6	Chris McCarron (active)	2-2-2
6	Ron Turcotte (1978)	2-2-2

Trainers With Most Wins in Triple Crown Races

Wins	Trainer	K/P/B
13	Sunny Jim Fitzsimmons	3-4-6
12	R.W. Walden	1-7-4
11	James Rowe Sr.	2-1-8
10	D. Wayne Lukas	3-4-3
9	Max Hirsch	3-2-4
9	Ben A. Jones	6-2-1
8	Woody Stephens	2-1-5
7	Sam Hildreth	0-0-7
7	Jimmy Jones	2-4-1
6	T.J. Healy	0-5-1
6	Lucien Laurin	2-1-3

The Eleven Winners

Turf writer Charles Hatton of the *Daily Racing Form* coined the term "Triple Crown" in 1930 while covering Gallant Fox's sweep of the Kentucky Derby, Preakness Stakes, and Belmont Stakes.

Year	Horse	Jockey	Trainer	Owner
1978	Affirmed	Steve Cauthen	Laz Barrera	Harbor View Farm
1977	Seattle Slew	Jean Cruguet	Billy Turner	Karen Taylor
1973	Secretariat	Ron Turcotte	Lucien Laurin	Meadow Stable
1948	Citation	Eddie Arcaro	Ben A. Jones	Calumet Farm
1946	Assault	Warren Mehrtens	Max Hirsch	King Ranch
1943	Count Fleet	Johnny Longden	Don Cameron	Mrs. J.D. Hertz
1941	Whirlaway	Eddie Arcaro	Ben A. Jones	Calumet Farm
1937	War Admiral	Charley Kurtsinger	George Conway	Samuel Riddle
1935	Omaha	Willie Saunders	J.E. Fitzsimmons	Belair Stud
1930	Gallant Fox*	Earl Sande	J.E. Fitzsimmons	Belair Stud
1919	Sir Barton	Johnny Loftus	H. Guy Bedwell	J.K.L. Ross

*Gallant Fox is the only Triple Crown winner to sire another one—Omaha, who won in 1935. Both horses were trained by J.E. (Sunny Jim) Fitzsimmons and bred in Kentucky by Belair Stud.
Note: The Kentucky Derby is held every year on the first Saturday in May at Churchill Downs in Louisville, Ky. The Preakness Stakes is two weeks later at Pimlico Race Course in Baltimore, and the Belmont Stakes is three weeks after that at Belmont Park in New York. The three races are for three-year-old thoroughbreds only.

The Near Misses

Thirteen horses have won both the Kentucky Derby and the Preakness only to lose in the Belmont.

Year	Horse	Jockey	Belmont Finish	Winner/Margin
1997	Silver Charm	Gary Stevens	2nd	Touch Gold (¾ of a length)
1989	Sunday Silence	Pat Valenzuela	2nd	Easy Goer (8 lengths)
1987	Alysheba	Chris McCarron	4th	Bet Twice (14)
1981	Pleasant Colony	Jorge Velasquez	3rd	Summing (neck)
1979	Spectacular Bid	Ron Franklin	3rd	Coastal (3¼)
1971	Canonero II	Gustavo Avila	4th	Pass Catcher (¾)
1969	Majestic Prince	Bill Hartack	2nd	Arts and Letters (5½)
1968	Forward Pass*	Ismael Valenzuela	2nd	Stage Door Johnny (1½)
1966	Kauai King	Don Brumfield	4th	Amberoid (2½)
1964	Northern Dancer	Bill Hartack	3rd	Quadrangle (2)
1961	Carry Back	Johnny Sellers	7th	Sherluck (2¼)
1958	Tim Tam	Ismael Valenzuela	2nd	Cavan (6)
1944	Pensive	Conn McCreary	2nd	Bounding Home (½)

*Declared winner of the Kentucky Derby when postrace tests resulted in the disqualification of Dancer's Image.

KENTUCKY DERBY

Fastest Winning Times

Over 1¼-mile distance at Churchill Downs since 1896.

Time	Horse	Year
1:59 2/5	Secretariat	1973
2:00	Northern Dancer	1964
2:00 1/5	Spend A Buck	1985
2:00 2/5	Decidedly	1962
2:00 3/5	Proud Clarion	1967

Fastest Fractions

Fraction	Time	Horse/Year
1/4 mile	0:21 4/5	Top Avenger, 1981
1/2 mile	0:45 1/5	Top Avenger, 1981
3/4 mile	1:09 3/5	Spend A Buck, 1985
1 mile	1:34 4/5	Spend A Buck, 1985

Most Mounts in the Derby

Listed with 1st, 2nd, and 3rd place finishes.

No.	Jockey	1	2	3
26	Bill Shoemaker	4	3	4
21	Eddie Arcaro	5	3	2
19	Laffit Pincay Jr.*	1	4	2
17	Angel Cordero Jr.	3	1	0
15	Pat Day*	1	3	2
14	Chris McCarron*	2	3	0
14	Jorge Velasquez*	1	1	2
14	Mack Garner	1	0	1
13	Johnny Adams	0	2	0
13	Don Brumfield	1	0	1

*Active in 1997.
Derby riding spans: Adams (1939-57), Arcaro (1935-61), Brumfield (1966-87), Cordero (1968-91), Day (1982-97), Garner (1916-35), McCarron (1976-96), Pincay (1971-94), Shoemaker (1952-88), Velasquez (1969-96).

Extra Point

In 1978 Alydar finished second behind Affirmed in all three Triple Crown races. The runner-up lost by 1¼ lengths in the Derby, a neck in the Preakness, and a head in the Belmont Stakes.

PREAKNESS STAKES

Fastest Winning Times

Over 1³⁄₁₆-mile distance at Pimlico Race Course since 1925.

Time	Horse	Year
1:53 2/5	Tank's Prospect	1985
1:53 2/5	Louis Quatorze	1996
1:53 3/5	Gate Dancer	1984
1:53 3/5	Summer Squall	1990
1:53 4/5	Sunday Silence	1989

Note: Secretariat, the fastest horse ever in both the Kentucky Derby and Belmont, won the 1973 Preakness in 1:54 2/3, the 10th-fastest time in race history.

Fastest Fractions

Fraction	Time	Horse/Year
1/4 mile	0:22 2/5	Flag Raiser, 1965 Fight Over, 1984 Eternal Prince, 1985
1/2 mile	0:45	Bold Forbes, 1976
1/4 mile	1:09	Bold Forbes, 1976
1 mile	1:34 1/5	Chief's Crown, 1985 Sunday Silence, 1989

Most Mounts

Listed with 1st, 2nd, and 3rd place finishes

No.	Jockey	1	2	3
15	Eddie Arcaro	6	2	4
12	Bill Shoemaker	2	4	1
12	Angel Cordero Jr.	2	1	4
12	Chris McCarron*	2	2	2
11	Pat Day*	5	3	0
11	Bill Hartack	3	1	0
11	Jorge Velasquez*	1	2	1
10	Pony McAtee	1	2	1
10	Braulio Baeza	0	3	2
9	Clarence Kummer	2	1	1
9	George Woolf	1	0	2

*Active in 1997.
Preakness riding spans: Arcaro (1935-59), Baeza (1961-76), Cordero (1971-90), Day (1983-96), Hartack (1954-74), Kummer (1918-28), McAtee (1916-31), McCarron (since 1977), Shoemaker (1954-86), Velasquez (1971-96), Woolf (1935-45).

BELMONT STAKES

Fastest Winning Times

Over 1½-mile distance at Belmont Park since 1926.

Time	Horse	Year
2:24*	Secretariat	1973
2:26	Easy Goer	1989
2:26	A.P. Indy	1992
2:26 2/5	Risen Star	1988
2:26 4/5	Affirmed	1978
2:26 4/5	Tabasco Cat	1994

*World record for a mile-and-a-half on a dirt track.

Fastest Fractions

Fraction	Time	Horse/Year
1/4 mile	0:23	Another Review, 1991
1/2 mile	0:46 1/5	Secretariat, 1973
3/4 mile	1:09 4/5	Secretariat, 1973
1 mile	1:34 1/5	Secretariat, 1973
1 1/4 mi.	1:59	Secretariat, 1973

Most Mounts

Listed with 1st, 2nd, and 3rd place finishes.

No.	Jockey	1	2	3
22	Eddie Arcaro	6	3	2
21	Angel Cordero Jr.	1	2	4
14	Braulio Baeza	3	2	0
13	Laffit Pincay Jr.*	3	3	0
13	Jorge Velasquez*	0	1	5
11	Bill Shoemaker	5	1	1
11	Eric Guerin	2	2	1
11	Eddie Maple*	2	0	1
11	Jerry Bailey*	1	1	1
10	Pat Day*	2	1	1
10	Jean Cruguet*	1	0	2

*Active in 1997.
Belmont riding spans: Arcaro (1938-60), Baeza (1961-75), Bailey (1982-97), Cordero (1967-91), Cruguet (1970-92), Day (1976-97), Guerin (1944-60), Maple (1974-96), Pincay (1973-93), Shoemaker (1957-86), Velasquez (1969-97).

The Breeders' Cup

Established in 1984 as the one-day season-ending championship of Thoroughbred racing, this consists of 7 championship races: the Juvenile (1¹⁄₁₆ miles for 2-year-old colts and geldings), Juvenile Fillies (1¹⁄₁₆ miles for 2-year-old fillies), and Distaff (1⅛ miles for fillies and mares, 3-year-olds and up); and the Sprint (6 furlongs), Mile (on grass), Turf (1½ miles in grass), and Classic (1¼ miles), all for 3-year-olds and up. The 14th Breeder's Cup championship was scheduled for November 8, 1997 at Hollywood Park in Los Angeles.

Most Money Won by Horses
Listed with 1st, 2nd, and 3rd place finishes.

Earnings ($)	Horse/Starts	1-2-3
2,133,000	Alysheba (3)	1-1-1
2,080,000	Alphabet Soup (1)	1-0-0
2,040,000	Cigar (2)	1-0-1
1,710,000	Unbridled (2)	1-0-1
1,688,000	Black Tie Affair (3)	1-0-1
1,560,000	A.P. Indy (1)	1-0-0
1,560,000	Arcangues (1)	1-0-0
1,560,000	Concern (1)	1-0-0
1,350,000	Ferdinand (1)	1-0-0
1,350,000	Proud Truth (1)	1-0-0
1,350,000	Skywalker (2)	1-0-0
1,350,000	Sunday Silence (1)	1-0-0
1,350,000	Theatrical (3)	1-1-0
1,350,000	Wild Again (1)	1-0-0
1,040,000	Five horses tied.	

Most Mounts
Listed with 1st, 2nd, and 3rd place finishes.

No.	Jockey	1	2	3
72	Chris McCarron	7	11	6
69	Pat Day	8	13	7
60	Laffit Pincay Jr.	7	4	9
58	Eddie Delahoussaye	7	3	5
57	Gary Stevens	4	10	7
48	Angel Codero Jr.	4	7	7
41	Jose Santos	5	1	4
38	Jerry Bailey	6	3	3
32	Pat Valenzuela	6	0	1
31	Mike Smith	6	3	2
27	Pat Eddery	2	3	3
25	Craig Perret	3	2	1
19	Cash Asmussen	0	0	3
18	Jorge Velasquez	2	5	1
17	Randy Romero	2	0	1

Most Starters Saddled by Trainers
Listed with 1st, 2nd, and 3rd place finishes.

No.	Trainer	1	2	3
104	D. Wayne Lukas	13	16	11
39	Shug McGaughey	7	8	1
26	Andre Fabre	2	4	5
26	Bobby Frankel	0	4	3
24	Chas. Whittingham	2	2	3
22	Scotty Schulhofer	2	2	4
21	Ron McAnally	4	2	2
19	Bill Mott	3	3	2
19	Francois Boutin	3	0	2
16	Michael Stoute	1	1	2
16	LeRoy Jolley	2	1	0
15	Neil Drysdale	5	2	0
14	Jack Van Berg	1	3	3
12	James Day	1	2	1
10	Gary Jones	0	2	1

Miscellaneous

All-Time Money-Winning Horses
Horses stabled in the United States and ranked by career earnings through September 1, 1997, according to the *Daily Racing Form*.

Horse/Year Foaled	Sts.	1	2	3	Earnings ($)
Cigar, 1991	33	19	4	5	9,999,815
Alysheba, 1984	26	11	8	2	6,679,242
John Henry, 1975	83	39	15	9	6,597,947
Best Pal, 1988	47	18	11	4	5,668,245
Sunday Silence, 1986	14	9	5	0	4,968,554
Easy Goer, 1986	20	14	5	1	4,873,770
Unbridled, 1987	24	8	6	6	4,489,475
Spend A Buck, 1982	15	10	3	2	4,220,689
Creme Fraiche, 1982	64	17	12	13	4,024,727
Devil His Due, 1989	41	11	12	3	3,920,405

All-Time Winning Jockeys
Ranked by career wins through September 1, 1997, according to *The American Racing Manual* and *Thoroughbred Racing Communications* (TRC).

Wins	Jockey	Career	Earnings ($)
8,833	Bill Shoemaker	1949-90	123,375,524
8,547	Laffitt Pincay Jr.*	1967–	196,047,999
7,134	David Gall*	1957–	23,379,948
7,057	Angel Cordero Jr.	1965-95	164,561,227
7,002	Pat Day*	1972–	183,379,672
6,789	Jorge Velasquez*	1964–	125,450,916
6,518	Chris McCarron*	1976–	210,995,379
6,433	Sandy Hawley*	1968–	87,965,873
6,388	Larry Snyder	1960-94	47,207,289

*Active in 1997.

NASCAR 204   Indy Car 208   Formula One 208

Jeff Gordon in car number 24 winning the 1997 Daytona 500 ahead of Hendrick Motorsports teammates Terry Labonte (5) and Ricky Craven (far left).

NASCAR

The National Association for Stock Car Auto Racing.

Richard Petty after winning the 1983 Winston 500 at the Talladega, Alabama, Superspeedway.

All-Time Driver Wins

Through October 5, 1997; listed with career span, 2nd and 3rd place finishes, and number of times driver was top qualifier (Pole)

Wins	Driver	Career	2nd	3rd	Pole
200	Richard Petty	1958-92	155	102	127
105	David Pearson	1960-86	89	44	113
84	Bobby Allison	1961-88	86	71	57
84	Darrell Waltrip*	1972–	58	62	59
83	Cale Yarborough	1957-88	59	46	70
70	Dale Earnhardt*	1975–	62	54	22
54	Lee Petty	1949-64	48	50	18
50	Ned Jarrett	1953-66	37	38	36
50	Junior Johnson	1953-66	18	23	47
48	Herb Thomas	1949-62	25	19	38
47	Rusty Wallace*	1989–	32	23	18
46	Buck Baker	1949-76	56	52	44
40	Bill Elliott	1976–	26	24	48
39	Tim Flock	1949-61	19	15	39
37	Bobby Isaac	1961-76	37	27	50

* Active in 1997

All-Time Pole Winners

Through October 5, 1997

No.	Driver
127	Richard Petty
113	David Pearson
70	Cale Yarborough
59	Darrell Waltrip*
57	Bobby Allison
50	Bobby Isaac
49	Bill Elliott*
47	Junior Johnson
44	Buck Baker
40	Buddy Baker
39	Tim Flock
38	Herb Thomas
37	Fireball Roberts
36	Geoff Bodine*
36	Ned Jarrett
36	Rex White
35	Mark Martin*
33	Fred Lorenzen
30	Fonty Flock

Current Pole Winners

Through October 5, 1997.

No.	Driver
59	Darrell Waltrip
49	Bill Elliott
36	Geoff Bodine
35	Mark Martin
26	Terry Labonte
23	Ricky Rudd
22	Dale Earnhardt
20	Ken Schrader
18	Ernie Irvan
18	Rusty Wallace
16	Jeff Gordon
14	Dave Marcis
9	Bobby Labonte
9	Sterling Marlin
8	Kyle Petty
7	Morgan Shepherd
6	Dale Jarrett
5	Brett Bodine
5	Ted Musgrave

Current Driver Wins

Through October 5, 1997; listed with driver's first year, 2nd and 3rd place finishes, and number of times driver was top qualifier (Pole)

Wins	Driver	First Year	2nd	3rd	Pole
84	Darrell Waltrip*	1972	58	62	59
70	Dale Earnhardt*	1975	62	54	22
47	Rusty Wallace*	1989	32	23	18
40	Bill Elliott	1976	27	24	49
29	Jeff Gordon	1992	13	13	16
22	Mark Martin	1981	31	34	35
19	Ricky Rudd	1975	24	28	23
18	Terry Labonte	1978	40	34	26
18	Geoff Bodine	1979	17	26	35
15	Ernie Irvan	1987	21	7	18
14	Dale Jarrett	1984	12	15	6
8	Kyle Petty	1979	5	13	8

Most Wins at Daytona 500
Since 1959, when the first race was held at Daytona International Speedway
at Daytona Beach, FL.

No.	Driver	Year/Car
7	Richard Petty	1981, Buick; 1979, Oldsmobile; 1974, Dodge*; 1973, Dodge; 1971, Plymouth; 1966, Plymouth*; 1964, Plymouth
4	Cale Yarborough	1984, Chevrolet; 1983, Pontiac; 1977, Chevrolet; 1968, Mercury
3	Bobby Allison	1988, Buick; 1982, Buick; 1978, Ford
2	Bill Elliott	1987, Ford; 1985, Ford
2	Dale Jarrett	1996, Ford; 1993, Chevrolet
2	Sterling Marlin	1995, Chevrolet; 1994, Chevrolet

*Shortened races: 1974 (450 miles due to national energy crisis); 1966 (495 miles due to rain).

Fastest Daytona 500 Winners
Average speed in 200-lap race.

MPH	Driver	Car	Year
177.602	Buddy Baker	Olds Cutlass	1980
176.263	Bill Elliott	Ford Thunderbird	1987
172.265	Bill Elliott	Ford Thunderbird	1985
169.651	Richard Petty	Buick Regal	1981

Fastest Daytona 500 Qualifiers
Average speed over two laps.

MPH	Driver	Car	Year
210.364	Bill Elliott	Ford Thunderbird	1987
205.114	Bill Elliott	Ford Thunderbird	1985
205.039	Bill Elliott	Ford Thunderbird	1986
201.848	Cale Yarborough	Chevy Monte Carlo	1984

Winners From the Pole

Year	Driver
1987	Bill Elliott
1985	Bill Elliott
1984	Cale Yarborough
1980	Buddy Baker
1968	Cale Yarborough
1966	Richard Petty
1962	Fireball Roberts

Most 2nd Place Finishes

No.	Driver
4	Dale Earnhardt
4	Cale Yarborough
3	Bobby Allison
3	Terry Labonte
2	Three drivers tied.

Most Winston Cup Championships
Originally the Grand National Championship (1949–70);
sponsored by R.J. Reynolds Tobacco Co. since 1971.

No.	Driver	Years/Cars
7	Richard Petty	1979, Chevy; 1975, Dodge; 1974, Dodge; 1972, Plymouth; 1971, Plymouth; 1967, Plymouth; 1964, Plymouth
7	Dale Earnhardt	1994, 1993, 1991, 1990, 1987, 1986, 1980 (all Chevys)
3	David Pearson	1969, Ford; 1968, Ford; 1966, Dodge
3	Lee Petty	1959, Plymouth; 1958, Olds; 1954, Chrysler
3	Darrell Waltrip	1985, Chevy; 1982, Buick; 1981, Buick
3	Cale Yarborough	1978, Olds; 1977, Chevy; 1976, Chevy
2	Buck Baker	1957, Chevy; 1956, Chrysler
2	Tim Flock	1955, Chrysler; 1952, Hudson
2	Ned Jarrett	1965, Ford; 1961, Chevy
2	Terry Labonte	1996, Chevy; 1984, Chevy
2	Herb Thomas	1953, Hudson; 1951, Hudson
2	Joe Weatherly	1963, Ford/Mercury; 1962, Pontiac

Winners of Brickyard 400
Held annually since 1994 at Indianapolis Motor Speedway.

Year	Winner/Car	Fastest Qualifier/MPH
1997	Ricky Rudd, Ford	Ernie Irvan, 177.736
1996	Dale Jarrett, Ford	Jeff Gordon, 176.419
1995	Dale Earnhardt, Chevy	Jeff Gordon, 172.536
1994	Jeff Gordon, Chevy	Rick Mast, 172.414

Miscellaneous Daytona 500 Items

Item	Driver	Year
Youngest winner	Jeff Gordon (25 yrs, 196 days)	1997
Oldest winner	Bobby Allison (50 yrs, 73 days)	1988
Closest margin of victory	Lee Petty over Johnny Beaucam (2 feet)	1959
Widest margin of victory	Richard Petty over Bobby Isaac (2 laps)	1973

Extra Point
Seven-time Winston Cup champion Dale Earnhardt has won just about everything in his 23 years as a NASCAR driver, but he has yet to win the circuit's biggest race, the Daytona 500. In 19 tries, he has placed in the Top Five 10 times, including 4 second-place finishes in 1984, 1993, 1995, and 1996.

Indy Car

All-time Indy-car champion A.J. Foyt in 1967, after winning the Indianapolis 500 for the third time.

All-Time Driver Wins

Through October 5, 1997; listed with career span, 2nd and 3rd place finishes, and number of times driver was top qualifier (Pole), based on totals since 1930.

Wins	Driver	Career	2nd	3rd	Pole
67	A.J. Foyt	1957-92	29	24	53
52	Mario Andretti	1964-94	56	33	67
39	Al Unser	1964-93	31	28	27
36	Michael Andretti*	1983–	20	18	30
35	Bobby Unser	1955-81	31	18	49
31	Al Unser Jr.*	1982–	27	20	7
29	Rick Mears	1976-92	22	24	38
27	Johnny Rutherford	1962-89	19	14	23
26	Rodger Ward	1950-66	11	10	11
25	Gordon Johncock	1965-91	25	26	20
24	Bobby Rahal*	1982–	37	26	18
24	Ralph DePalma	1909-33	7	5	0
23	Tommy Milton	1916-27	19	14	0
22	Tony Bettenhausen	1941-61	13	3	14
22	Emerson Fittipaldi	1984-96	21	22	17
20	Earl Cooper	1911-27	13	4	0
19	Jimmy Murphy	1919-24	8	9	0
19	Jimmy Bryan	1951-60	6	6	3

* Active in 1997.
Also raced on Formula One circuit in Europe: •Mario Andretti (128 races between 1968 and 1982; won 12 races, 18 poles, and 1978 driving championship); •Michael Andretti (13 races in 1993, placed in Top 6 three times); •Fittipaldi (144 races between 1970 and 1980; won 14 races, 6 poles, and driving titles in 1972 and 1974).

Current Driver Wins

Through October 5, 1997; listed with driver's first year, 2nd and 3rd place finishes, and number of times driver was top qualifier (Pole).

Wins	Driver	First Year	2nd	3rd	Pole
36	Michael Andretti	1983	20	18	30
31	Al Unser Jr.	1982	27	20	7
24	Bobby Rahal	1982	37	26	18
13	Scott Tracy	1991	9	7	11
8	Alex Zanardi	1996	3	2	10
5	Jimmy Vasser	1992	5	5	4
3	Mark Blundell	1933	2	0	0
3	Andre Ribeiro	1995	0	1	2
2	Gil de Ferran	1995	5	6	4
2	Scott Pruett	1988	3	7	3
2	Greg Moore	1996	4	2	0
1	Maurico Gugelmin	1993	4	2	3
1	Adrian Fernandez	1993	0	2	0

All-Time Pole Winners
Through October 5, 1997

No.	Driver
67	Mario Andretti
53	A.J. Foyt
49	Bobby Unser
38	Rick Mears
30	Michael Andretti
27	Al Unser
23	Johnny Rutherford
20	Gordon Johncock
19	Rex Mays
19	Danny Sullivan

Current Pole Winners
Through October 5, 1997.

No.	Driver
30	Michael Andretti
18	Bobby Rahal
11	Scott Tracy
10	Alez Zanardi
7	Al Unser Jr.
4	Gil de Ferran
4	Jimmy Vasser
3	Bryan Herta
3	Scott Pruett
3	Raul Boesel

Extra Point

A.J. (Anthony Joseph) Foyt is the only driver to win all four of auto racing's most prestigeous races—the Indianapolis 500, the Daytona 500, the 24 Hours of Le Mans, and the 24 Hours of Daytona. A four-time Indy champion, Foyt won NASCAR's biggest race in 1972. He teamed with Dan Gurney to win at Le Mans in 1967 and shared the Daytona endurance title with three other drivers in 1983 and 1985.

Most Wins at Indianapolis 500

No.	Driver	Years/Chassis
4	A.J. Foyt	1977, Coyote; 1967, Coyote; 1964, Watson; 1961, Trevis
4	Rick Mears	1991, Penske; 1988, Penske; 1984, March; 1979, Penske
4	Al Unser	1987, March; 1978, Lola; 1971, P.J. Colt; 1970, P.J. Colt
3	Louis Meyer	1936, Stevens; 1933, Miller; 1928, Miller
3	Mauri Rose	1948, Deidt; 1947, Deidt; 1941, Wetteroth
3	Johnny Rutherford	1980, Chaparral; 1976, McLaren*; 1974, McLaren
3	Wilber Shaw	1940, Maserati; 1939, Maserati; 1937; Shaw
3	Bobby Unser	1981, Penske; 1975, Eagle*; 1968, Eagle
2	Seven drivers tied.#	

* Rain-shortened races: 1976 (255 miles), 1975 (435 miles).
# Emerson Fittipaldi (1993, 1989), Gordon Johncock (1982, 1973—rain-shortened to 332 ½ miles), Arie Luyendyk (1997, 1990), Tommy Milton (1923, 1921), Al Unser Jr. (1994, 1992), Bill Vukovich (1954, 1953), Rodger Ward (1962, 1959).

Winners From the Pole

Year	Driver	Year	Driver
1997	Arie Luyendyk	1970	Al Unser
1994	Al Unser Jr.	1963	Parnelli Jones
1991	Rick Mears	1956	Pat Flaherty
1988	Rick Mears	1953	Bill Vukovich
1981	Bobby Unser	1938	Floyd Roberts
1980	Johnny Rutherford	1930	Billy Arnold
1979	Rick Mears	1923	Tommy Milton
1976	Johnny Rutherford	1922	Jimmy Murphy

Fastest Indianapolis 500 Winners
Average speed over 200 laps.

MPH	Driver	Chassis/Engine	Year
185.981	Arie Luyendyk	Lola, Chevrolet	1990
176.457	Rick Mears	Penske, Chevrolet	1991
170.722	Bobby Rahal	March, Cosworth	1986
167.581	Emerson Fittipaldi	Penske, Chevrolet	1989
163.612	Rick Mears	March, Cosworth	1984

Fastest Indianapolis 500 Qualifiers
Average speed over 4 laps.

MPH	Driver	Chassis/Engine	Year
233.718	Scott Brayton*	Lola, Menard	1996
233.100	Tony Stewart	Lola, Menard	1996
232.882	Davy Jones	Lola, Mercedes	1996
232.684	Eliseo Salazar	Lola, Cosworth	1996
232.482	Roberto Guerrero	Lola, Buick	1992

*Brayton was killed in a crash during practice 9 days before the race.
Note: Due to a power struggle between Tony George, president of the fledgling Indy Racing League of Indianapolis Motor Speedway, and the team owners who control Championship Auto Racing Teams (CART), the best-known Indy car drivers boycotted the Indy 500 in 1996 and 1997.

Miscellaneous Indianapolis 500 Items

Item	Driver	Year
Youngest winner	Troy Ruttman (22 yrs, 80 days)	1952
Oldest winner	Al Unser (47 yrs, 360 days)	1987
1st woman driver	Janet Guthrie (29th place)	1977
Closest margin of victory	Al Unser Jr. over Scott Goodyear (43 thousandths of a second)	1992
Widest margin of victory	Jules Goux over Spencer Wishart (13 minutes, 8 seconds)	1913

Most CART Driving Championships
Officially the PPG Industries Championship Auto Racing Teams (CART) Indy Car World Series championship since 1979.
Also includes annual winners when the Indy car circuit was sanctioned by the AAA (1909–55) and the U.S. Auto Club (1956–78).

No.	Driver	Years	No.	Driver	Years
7	A.J. Foyt	1978, 1975, 1967, 1964, 1963, 1961, 1960	3	Rick Mears	1982, 1981, 1979
4	Mario Andretti	1984, 1969, 1966, 1965	3	Louie Meyer	1933, 1929, 1928
3	Jimmy Bryan	1957, 1956, 1954	3	Bobby Rahal	1992, 1987, 1986
3	Earl Cooper	1917, 1915, 1913	3	Al Unser	1985, 1983, 1970
3	Ted Horn	1946-48	2	Twelve drivers tied.	

Formula One

Lotus teammates Graham Hill (left) and Jim Clark in 1967 take cover using an improvised shelter in the rain.

Most World Driving Championships
Since the 1950 formation of Formula One circuit.

No.	Driver	Years/Constructors
5	Juan Manuel Fangio	1957, Maserati; 1956, Ferrari; 1955, Mercedes; 1954, Mercedes*; 1951, Alfa Romeo
4	Alain Prost	1993, Williams; 1989, 1986, and 1985, McLaren
3	Jack Brabham	1966, Brabham; 1960 and 1959, Cooper
3	Jackie Stewart	1973 and 1971, Tyrrell; 1969, Matra
3	Niki Lauda	1984, McLaren; 1977 and 1975, Ferrari
3	Nelson Piquet	1987, Williams; 1983 and 1981, Brabham
3	Ayrton Senna	1991, 1990, and 1988, McLaren
2	Alberto Ascari	1953 and 1952, Ferrari
2	Graham Hill	1968, Lotus; 1962, BRM
2	Jim Clark	1965 and 1963, Lotus
2	Emerson Fittipaldi	1974, McLaren; 1972, Lotus
2	Michael Schumacher	1995 and 1994, Benetton

*Fangio drove the first 2 races of the 1955 season in a Maserati and the last 6 races in a Mercedes.

Extra Point
Formula One, or Grand Prix, cars are manufactured according to a formula limiting engine size and body design and imposed by the Federation Internationale de Automobile (FIA). The F-1 circuit in 1997 included 12 races in Europe, 2 in South America, and 1 each in Australia, Canada, and Japan. All events are held on road courses.

All-Time Driver Wins
Through October 5, 1997; listed with career span, 2nd and 3rd place finishes, and number of times driver was top qualifier (Pole).

Wins	Driver	Career	2nd	3rd	Pole
51	Alain Prost	1980-93	35	20	33
41	Ayrton Senna*	1984-94	23	16	65
31	Nigel Mansell	1980-95	17	11	32
27	Jackie Stewart	1965-73	11	5	17
26	Michael Schumacher#	1991–	17	10	17
25	Jim Clark*	1960-68	1	6	33
25	Niki Lauda	1971-85	20	9	24
24	Juan Manuel Fangio	1950-58	10	1	28
23	Nelson Piquet	1978-91	20	17	24
21	Damon Hill#	1992–	15	5	20
16	Stirling Moss	1951-61	5	3	16
14	Jack Brabham	1955-70	10	7	13
14	Emerson Fittipaldi	1970-80	13	8	6
14	Graham Hill	1958-75	15	7	13
13	Alberto Ascari*	1950-55	4	0	14
12	Mario Andretti	1968-82	2	5	18
12	Alan Jones	1975-86	7	5	6
12	Carlos Reutemann	1972-82	13	20	6

* Killed racing: Jim Clark during a Formula 2 race at Hockenheim, West Germany (April 7, 1968); Alberto Ascari during a private practice run at Monza, Italy (May 26, 1955); Ayrton Senna during the San Marino Grand Prix at Imola, Italy (May 1, 1994). # Active in 1997.
Home countries: Argentina (Fangio, Reutemann); Australia (Brabham, Jones); Austria (Lauda); Brazil (Fittipaldi, Piquet, Senna); France (Prost); Germany (Schumacher); Great Britain (Clark, D.Hill, G.Hill, Mansell, Moss, Stewart); Italy (Ascari); USA (Andretti).

Current Driver Wins
Through October 5, 1997; listed with driver's first year, 2nd and 3rd place finishes, and number of times driver was top qualifier (Pole).

Wins	Driver	First Year	2nd	3rd	Poles
26	Michael Schumacher	1991	17	10	17
21	Damon Hill	1992	15	5	20
11	Jacques Villeneuve	1996	5	2	11
10	Gerhard Berger	1984	16	21	12
3	David Coulthard	1994	7	4	5
2	Johnny Herbert	1989	1	3	0

Home countries: Austria (Berger); Canada (Villeneuve); Germany (Schumacher); Great Britain (Coulthard, Herbert, Hill).

MISCELLANEOUS

Susan Butcher, four-time winner of the Iditarod Trail Sled Dog Race.

Money

Highest-Paid Football Players

As of October 1, 1997; average salary based on generally accepted reports of money in contract (not including incentives) divided by length of contract (years).

Player/Team/Position	Years	First Year	Avg. Salary Per Year ($)*
Steve Young, 49ers, QB	6	1997	7,500,000
Brett Favre, Packers, QB	7	1997	6,750,000
Troy Aikman, Cowboys, QB	8	1994	6,250,000
Mark Brunell, Jaguars, QB	5	1997	6,100,000
Drew Bledsoe, Patriots, QB	7	1995	6,000,000
Emmitt Smith, Cowboys, RB	8	1996	6,000,000
Dan Marino, Dolphins, QB	3	1996	5,960,000
John Elway, Broncos, QB	3	1996	5,900,000
Barry Sanders, Lions, RB	6	1997	5,760,000
Neil O'Donnell, Jets, QB	5	1996	5,000,000
Deion Sanders, Cowboys, DB	7	1995	5,000,000

*Annual salary figures include signing bonuses. Aikman ($11 million), Bledsoe ($11.5 million), Brunell ($10 million), Elway ($6.2 million), Favre ($12 million), Marino ($5.8 million), O'Donnell ($7 million), B. Sanders ($11.75 million), D. Sanders ($13 million), Smith ($10.5 million), Young (none). NFL contracts are not guaranteed.

Highest-Paid Baseball Players

As of October 1, 1997; average salary based on generally accepted reports of money in contract (not including incentives) divided by length of contract (years).

Player/Team/Position	Years	First Year	Avg. Salary Per Year ($)
Greg Maddux, Braves, P	5	1998	11,500,000
Barry Bonds, Giants, OF	2	1999	11,450,000*
Albert Belle, White Sox, OF	5	1997	11,000,000
Sammy Sosa, Cubs, OF	4	1998	10,625,000
Gary Sheffield, Marlins, OF	6	1998	10,167,000
Mark McGwire, Cardinals, 1B	3	1998	9,500,000
Ken Griffey Jr., Mariners, OF	4	1997	8,500,000
Tom Glavine, Braves, P	4	1998	8,500,000
Ivan Rodriguez, Rangers, C	5	1998	8,400,000
Roger Clemens, Blue Jays, P	3	1997	8,250,000
Frank Thomas, White Sox, 1B	4	1998	7,981,000
John Smoltz, Braves, P	4	1997	7,750,000

*Bonds' current 6-year contract was signed in 1993 and averages $7,292,000 through 1998.

Atlanta Braves' owner Ted Turner can afford to pay his pitching staff top dollar—and does.

Richest Owners in U.S. Sports

Net worth (in billions of dollars), according to *Forbes Magazine* (October 13, 1997).

Owner	Properties	Net Worth ($)
Paul Allen	Trail Blazers (NBA), Seahawks (NFL)	17.0
Phil Knight	Nike	5.4
Philip Anschutz	Kings (NHL)	5.2
Rupert Murdoch	Fox network, purchasing Dodgers (MLB)	3.9
Ted Turner	Braves (MLB), Hawks (NBA), TBS, TNT, and CNN networks	3.5
Micky Arison	Family-owned Heat (NBA)	2.7
Richard DeVos	Magic (NBA)	2.4
Preston Tisch	50% of Giants (NFL)	2.4
Wayne Huizenga	Dolphins (NFL), Marlins (MLB), Panthers (NHL), Pro Player Stadium	1.7
Williams Davison	Pistons (NBA)	1.5
William Clay Ford	Lions (NFL)	1.4
Hiroshi Yamauchi*	Mariners (MLB)	1.2

*Yamauchi is a Japanese citizen; worth according to *Forbes Magazine* (July 28, 1997).

Highest-Paid Basketball Players

As of October 1, 1997; average salary based on generally accepted reports of money in contract (not including incentives) divided by length of contract (years).

Player/Team/Position	Years	First Year	Avg. Salary Per Year ($)
Michael Jordan, Bulls, G	1	1997-98	31,000,000*
Kevin Garnett, Timberwolves, F	6	1998-99	20,500,000
Shaquille O'Neal, Lakers, C	7	1996-97	17,343,000
Patrick Ewing, Knicks, C	4	1997-98	16,250,000
Alonzo Mourning, Heat, C	7	1996-97	15,000,000
Juwan Howard, Wizards, F	7	1996-97	14,714,000
Hakeem Olajuwon, Rockets, C	5	1996-97	13,400,000
Rasheed Wallace, Blazers, C/F	6	1998-99	13,333.000
Gary Payton, Sonics, G	7	1996-97	12,143,000
David Robinson, Spurs, C	6	1995-96	11,800,000
Dikembe Mutombo, Nuggets, C	5	1996-97	11,200,000
Bryant Reeves, Grizzlies, C	6	1998-99	10,817,000
Reggie Miller, Pacers, G	3	1996-97	9,000,000

*Jordan can receive another $1.5 million if he is the regular season MVP and $1.5 million more if the Bulls win the NBA title.

Highest-Paid Hockey Players

As of October 2, 1997; average salary based on generally accepted reports of money in contract (not including incentives) divided by length of contract (years).

Player/Team/Position	Years	First Year	Avg. Salary Per Year ($)
Joe Sakic, Avalanche, C	3	1997–98	7,000,000
Mark Messier, Canucks, C	3	1997–98	6,667,000
Wayne Gretzky, Rangers, C	2	1997-98	6,250,000
Steve Yzerman, Red Wings,C	4	1996–97	4,935,000
Pavel Bure, Canucks, F	5	1994-95	4,900,000
Patrick Roy, Avalanche, G	3	1996-97	4,673,000
Pat LaFontaine, Rangers, C	5	1994-95	4,420,000
Scott Stevens, Devils, D	4	1994-95	4,265,000
Dominik Hasek, Sabres, G	3	1996-97	4,067,000
Jeremy Roenick, Coyotes, C	5	1996-97	4,000,000
Peter Forsberg, Avalanche,C	3	1996-97	3,930,000
Jaromir Jagr, Penguins, F	5	1994-95	3,920,000
Eric Lindros, Flyers, C	5	1993-94	3,864,000

Note: List does not include free agents Sergei Federov (Red Wings), Paul Kariya (Ducks), and Alexander Mogilny (Canucks), who are expected to sign big contracts early in the 1997–98 season.

Values of Sports Franchises

According to *Financial World* (June 17, 1997). Estimated total market value (in millions of dollars) of clubs based on gate receipts, radio and TV revenue, stadium or arena income, operating income, player salaries, and other expenses.

Top 15 NFL Teams

Team	Value ($)
Dallas Cowboys	320
St. Louis Rams	243
Miami Dolphins	242
Carolina Panthers	240
Jacksonville Jaguars	239
Baltimore Ravens	235
San Francisco 49ers	218
New York Giants	211
Oakland Raiders	210
Philadelphia Eagles	209
Chicago Bears	204
Kansas City Chiefs	204
Buffalo Bills	200
Washington Redskins	200
New Orleans Saints	199

Top 15 NBA Teams

Team	Value ($)
New York Knicks	250
Phoenix Suns	220
Chicago Bulls	214
Los Angeles Lakers	211
Detroit Pistons	202
Cleveland Cavaliers	180
Portland Trail Blazers	179
Utah Jazz	163
Orlando Magic	156
San Antonio Spurs	156
Boston Celtics	155
Houston Rockets	154
Toronto Raptors	138
New Jersey Nets	137
Seattle SuperSonics	137

Top 15 Baseball Teams

Team	Value ($)
New York Yankees	241
Baltimore Orioles	207
Atlanta Braves	199
Colorado Rockies	184
Los Angeles Dodgers	178
Cleveland Indians	175
Texas Rangers	174
Boston Red Sox	172
Chicago Cubs	165
Toronto Blue Jays	155
Chicago White Sox	149
New York Mets	144
St. Louis Cardinals	134
San Francisco Giants	128
Florida Marlins	123

Top 15 NHL Teams

Team	Value ($)
Chicago Blackhawks	151
New York Rangers	147
Detroit Red Wings	146
Boston Bruins	130
Philadelphia Flyers	128
Toronto Maple Leafs	105
Anaheim Ducks	104
San Jose Sharks	104
Pittsburgh Penguins	96
St. Louis Blues	95
Montreal Canadiens	95
Vancouver Canucks	91
Washington Capitals	85
Los Angeles Kings	83
Colorado Avalanche	81

Movies

Sylvester Stallone (left) and Burgess Meredith teamed up as fighter Rocky Balboa and his trainer Mickey in the first three Rocky films. The original, released in 1976, is one of only two sports movies to win the Academy Award for Best Picture.

Top-Grossing Contemporary Sports Movies
Total domestic revenue earned in North America as of October 1, 1997, by films released since 1970.

	Title/Year Released	Sport	Domestic Gross ($)
1	Jerry Maguire (1996)	General	153,620,822
2	Rocky 4 (1985)	Boxing	127,873,716
3	Rocky 3 (1982)	Boxing	122,823,192
4	Rocky (1976)	Boxing	117,235,147
5	A League of Their Own (1992)	Baseball	107,439,000
6	Rocky 2 (1979)	Boxing	99,911,904
7	Space Jam (1996)	Basketball	90,384,232
8	Days of Thunder (1990)	Stock Cars	82,663,996
9	White Men Can't Jump (1992)	Basketball	71,969,454
10	Cool Runnings (1993)	Bobsled	68,856,263
11	Field of Dreams (1989)	Baseball	63,648,094
12	Chariots of Fire (1981)	Olympics	62,471,886
13	Tin Cup (1996)	Golf	53,888,896
14	Rookie of the Year (1993)	Baseball	53,133,660
15	The Main Event (1979)	Boxing	52,000,000*
16	The Mighty Ducks (1992)	Hockey	50,727,056
17	Bull Durham (1988)	Baseball	50,346,467
18	Angels in the Outfield (1994)	Baseball	50,236,831
19	Caddyshack (1980)	Golf	50,000,000*
20	Major League (1989)	Baseball	49,793,054
21	The Bad News Bears (1976)	Baseball	48,000,000*
22	The Natural (1984)	Baseball	47,951,979
23	The Longest Yard (1974)	Football	47,000,000*
24	Mighty Ducks 2 (1994)	Hockey	45,610,410
25	Rocky 5 (1990)	Boxing	40,100,303
26	Happy Gilmore (1996)	Golf	38,648,864
27	North Dallas Forty (1979)	Football	34,000,000*
28	The Sandlot (1993)	Baseball	31,709,974
29	Eddie (1996)	Basketball	31,388,164
30	Major League 2 (1994)	Baseball	30,616,359

* Gross estimated from theatrical film rentals.
Note: List does not include The Karate Kid (1984, $90,815,558), Karate Kid 2 (1986, $115,103,979), and Karate Kid 3 (1989, $38,956,288).
Source: Exhibitor Relations Co., Inc.

Sports Movies Nominated for Best Picture
Through 1997 Academy Awards ceremony.

Year	Nominee	Director
1996	Jerry Maguire	Cameron Crowe
1981	Chariots of Fire*	Hugh Hudson
1980	Raging Bull	Martin Scorsese
1979	Breaking Away	Peter Yates
1978	Heaven Can Wait	Warren Beatty and Buck Henry
1976	Rocky*	John Avildsen
1961	The Hustler	Robert Rossen
1942	The Pride of the Yankees	Sam Wood
1941	Here Comes Mr. Jordan	Alexander Hall
1932	The Champ	King Vidor

* Won Academy Award for Best Picture.

Most Emmy Awards for Best Sportscaster

Studio hosts, play-by-play, and analysts.

No.	Sportscaster/Network
11	John Madden, CBS (9)/Fox (2)
9	Jim McKay, ABC
8	Bob Costas, NBC
4	Dick Enberg, NBC
3	Al Michaels, ABC
2	Keith Jackson, ABC

Note: Jim McKay has won four other Emmys, two for writing, one for news commentary during the 1972 Olympic massacre, and a life achievement award.

Most Sportscaster-of-the-Year Awards

Voted on annually since 1959 by the National Sportscasters and Sportswriters Association.

No.	Sportscaster/Network
6	Bob Costas, NBC
5	Chris Berman, ESPN
5	Keith Jackson, ABC
4	Lindsey Nelson, CBS/NBC
4	Chris Schenkel, ABC
3	Dick Enberg, NBC
3	Al Michaels, ABC
3	Vin Scully, NBC/CBS
2	Curt Gowdy, NBC
2	Ray Scott, CBS

Pulitzer Prize–Winning Sports Columnists

The Pulitzer Prizes for journalism have been presented since 1917. The prize for commentary was introduced in 1970. There is no separate sportswriting award.

Year	Columnist/Newspaper
1990	Jim Murray, *Los Angeles Times*
1981	Dave Anderson, *New York Times*
1976	Red Smith, *New York Times*
1956	Arthur Daley, *New York Times*

Note: Daley won his award for General Reporting.

All-Time Highest-Rated TV Programs

According to Nielson Media Research, half of the Top 20 most-watched television programs of all time have been Super Bowl games. Programs are listed with rating points and audience share.

	Program	Episode or Game	Date	Rtg.	Share
1	M*A*S*H (series)	Final episode (CBS)	2/28/83	60.2	77%
2	Dallas (series)	"Who Shot J.R.?" (CBS)	11/21/80	53.3	76
3	Roots (mini-series)	Part 8 (ABC)	1/30/77	51.1	71
4	Super Bowl XVI	49ers 26, Bengals 21 (CBS)	1/24/82	49.1	73
5	Super Bowl XVII	Redskins 27, Dolphins 17 (NBC)	1/30/83	48.6	69
6	Winter Olympics	Women's Figure Skating (CBS)	2/23/94	48.5	64
7	Super Bowl XX	Bears 46, Patriots 10 (NBC)	1/26/86	48.3	70
8	Gone With the Wind	Part 1 of movie (NBC)	11/7/76	47.7	65
9	Gone With the Wind	Part 2 of movie (NBC)	11/8/76	47.4	64
10	Super Bowl XII	Cowboys 27, Broncos 10 (CBS)	1/15/78	47.2	67
11	Super Bowl XIII	Steelers 35, Cowboys 31 (NBC)	1/21/79	47.1	74
12	Bob Hope Special	1970 Christmas Show (NBC)	1/15/70	46.6	64
13	Super Bowl VIII	Raiders 38, Redskins 9 (CBS)	1/22/84	46.4	71
	Super Bowl XIX	49ers 38, Dolphins 16 (ABC)	1/20/85	46.4	63
15	Super Bowl XIV	Steelers 31, Rams 19 (CBS)	1/20/80	46.3	67
16	Super Bowl XXX	Cowboys 27, Steelers 17 (NBC)	1/28/96	46.0	68
17	ABC Theater movie	"The Day After" (ABC)	11/20/83	46.0	62
18	Roots (mini-series)	Part 6 (ABC)	1/28/77	45.9	66
19	The Fugitive (series)	Final episode (ABC)	8/29/67	45.9	72
20	Super Bowl XXI	Giants 39, Broncos 20 (CBS)	1/25/87	45.8	66

Note: Nielsen estimates that 138,488,000 viewers watched some portion of Super Bowl XXX, an all-time TV record for a single event on a single network.

Most Sportswriter-of-the-Year Awards

Voted on annually since 1959 by the National Sportscasters and Sportswriters Association.

No.	Sportswriter/Publication
14	Jim Murray, *Los Angeles Times*
6	Frank Deford, *Sports Illustrated*
5	Rick Reilly, *Sports Illustrated*
5	Red Smith, *N.Y. Herald Tribune*
4	Will Grimsley, Associated Press
3	Peter Gammons, *Boston Globe*

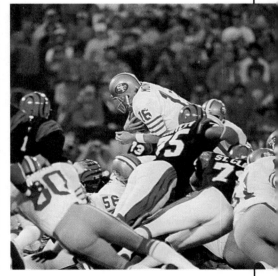

Super Bowl XVI remains the highest-rated sports event ever seen on American television.

Boxing

Underdog Muhammad Ali tags champion George Foreman in their 1974 title fight.

All-Time Heavyweight Upsets

Date	Winner/Age	Favorite/Age	KO/Decision	Location
11/9/96	Evander Holyfield, 34	Mike Tyson, 30	TKO 11 (0:37)	Las Vegas
11/5/94	George Foreman, 45	Michael Moorer, 26	KO 10 (2:03)	Las Vegas
2/10/90	Buster Douglas, 29	Mike Tyson, 23	KO 10 (1:23)	Tokyo
9/21/85	Michael Spinks, 29	Larry Holmes, 35	Unanimous, 15	Las Vegas
2/15/78	Leon Spinks, 24	Muhammad Ali, 36	Split, 15	Las Vegas
10/30/74	Muhammad Ali, 32	George Foreman, 25	KO 8 (2:58)	Zaire
2/25/64	Cassius Clay, 22	Sonny Liston, 31	TKO 7*	Miami Beach
6/26/59	Ingemar Johansson, 26	Floyd Patterson, 24	TKO 3 (2:03)	New York
7/18/51	Jersey Joe Wolcott, 37	Ezzard Charles, 30	KO 7 (0:55)	Pittsburgh
6/19/36	Max Schmeling, 30	Joe Louis, 22	KO 12 (2:29)	New York
6/13/35	James J. Braddock, 29	Max Baer, 26	Unanimous, 15	L.I. City, NY
9/23/26	Gene Tunney, 29	Jack Dempsey, 31	Unanimous, 15	Philadelphia
4/5/15	Jess Willard, 33	Jack Johnson, 37	KO 26 (1:26)	Havana, Cuba
9/7/1892	James J. Corbett, 26	John L. Sullivan, 33	KO 21 (1:30)	New Orleans

*Liston failed to answer the bell for Round 7.
Note: Cassius Clay announced after the Liston fight that he had changed his name to Muhammad Ali.

Most Times Named
Fighter of the Year
Since 1928, according to *The Ring*.

No.	Fighter	Last Year
5	Muhammad Ali	1978
4	Joe Louis	1941
3	Joe Frazier	1971
3	Rocky Marciano	1955
2	Thirteen fighters tied.*	

*Ezzard Charles, George Foreman, Marvin Hagler, Thomas Hearns, Evander Holyfield, Ingemar Johansson, Sugar Ray Leonard, Tommy Loughran, Floyd Patterson, Sugar Ray Robinson, Barney Ross, Dick Tiger, Mike Tyson.

Youngest and Oldest World Champions
The youngest fighter to win a world title was Wilfred Benitez, who was 17 years, 176 days old when he beat defending WBA junior welterweight champion Antonio Cervantes in 1976. George Foreman became the oldest fighter to win a world title when, at 45 years, 299 days old, he knocked out Michael Moorer to win the heavyweight title in 1994.

Most Career Knockouts
All weight divisions.

No.	Fighter/Weight Div.	Career
131	Archie Moore, LH	1936-63
125	Young Stribling, H	1921-33
124	Billy Bird, W	1920-48
117	Sam Langford, H	1902-26
114	George Odwel, W	1930-45
109	Sugar Ray Robinson, M	1940-65
103	Sandy Saddler, F	1944-56
101	Henry Armstrong, W	1931-45
99	Jimmy Wilde, F	1910-23
93	Len Wickwar, LH	1928-47
85	Joe Gans, L	1891-1909
85	Fritzie Zivic, W	1931-49

Key: F (featherweight), H (heavyweight), L (lightweight), LH (light heavyweight), M (middleweight), W (welterweight).

Most Consecutive Fights
Without a Loss
All weight divisions.

No.	Fighter/Weight Div.	Streak
97	Packey McFarland, L	1905-15
94	Fred Dyer, W	1908-12
93	Pedro Carrasco, L	1964-71
91	Sugar Ray Robinson, M	1943-51
90	Julio Cesar Chavez, JW	1980-93
83	Jimmy Wilde, F	1911-14
82	Carlos Monzon, M	1964-77
73*	Willie Pep, F	1943-48
65	Nino Benvenuti, M	1961-65
63*	Willie Pep, F	1940-43

*Two different unbeaten streaks.
Key: F (featherweight), H (heavyweight), JW (Junior Welterweight), L (lightweight), M (middleweight), W (welterweight).

Etcetera

Athletes Most Frequently on the Cover of *Sports Illustrated*

Ten covers or more through October 6, 1997.

Total	Athlete	1997
41	Michael Jordan	4
34	Muhammad Ali	0
27	Kareem Abdul-Jabbar	0
23	Magic Johnson	0
23	Jack Nicklaus	0
19	Larry Bird	0
17	Pete Rose	0
14	Wayne Gretzky	0
14	Arnold Palmer	0
14	Mike Tyson	2
14	Bill Walton	0
13	Sugar Ray Leonard	0
13	Joe Montana	0
13	Patrick Ewing	1
12	Mickey Mantle	0
10	Reggie Jackson	0
10	John McEnroe	0
10	Emmitt Smith	0

Most Wins in the Tour de France

Since the first race held in 1903.

No.	Cyclist	Last Win
5	Jacques Anquetil, France	1964
5	Bernard Hinault, France	1985
5	Miguel Indurain, Spain	1995
5	Eddy Merckx, Belgium	1974
3	Louison Bobet, France	1955
3	Greg Lemond, U.S.	1990
3	Philippe Thys, Belgium	1920
2	Eleven cyclists tied.	

Note: The Tour de France is the world's premier annual cycling event, covering approximately 2,300 miles in France and neighboring countries over three weeks in June and July.

America's Top Jock Schools

According to *Sports Illustrated* (April 18, 1997). Colleges listed with number of varsity and intramural sports during 1996–97 school year.

	School	Varsity Sports	Intra- murals
1	UCLA	21	18
2	Notre Dame	25	22
3	Stanford	33	19
4	Texas	20	29
5	Florida	20	19
6	Michigan	16	19
7	North Carolina	25	26
8	Penn State	29	16
9	Nebraska	22	22
10	Princeton	38	38
11	Southern Cal	20	28
12	Arizona	18	11
13	Ohio State	21	31
14	Virginia	22	24
15	Wisconsin	22	25

Also in the Top 25 were: 16. Tennessee, 17. Iowa, 18. California, 19. Indiana, 20. Alabama, 21. Georgia, 22. Michigan St., 23. Brigham Young, 24. Syracuse, and 25. Duke.

Note: The SI survey evaluated all 305 NCAA Division I men's basketball schools, weighing criteria such as national championships won, athlete graduation rates, rivalries, bands, and mascots, among other things.

Most Wins in the Iditarod Trail Sled Dog Race

Since the first race held in 1973.

No.	Musher	Last Win
5	Rick Swenson	1991
4	Susan Butcher	1990
3	Martin Buser	1997
2	Jeff King	1996
2	Rick Mackey	1983

Note: The Iditarod Trail Sled Dog Race covers 1,155 miles from Anchorage to Nome, Alaska, every March. The record is 9 days, 2 hours, 42 minutes, 19 seconds, set by Doug Swingley and his dogs in 1995.

Most Popular Participation Sports in the U.S.

Activities that Americans seven years old and older took part in at least once in 1996.

	Sport	Millions
1	Exercise walking	73.3
2	Swimming	60.2
3	Bicycle riding	53.3
4	Exercising with equipment	47.8
5	Fishing	45.6
6	Overnight camping	44.7
7	Bowling	42.9
8	Pool/Billiards	34.5
9	Basketball	33.3
10	Boating (motor/power)	28.8
11	Hiking	26.5
12	In-line skating	25.5
13	Aerobic exercising	24.1
14	Golf	23.1
15	Running/Jogging	22.2
16	Dart throwing	21.3
17	Softball	19.9
18	Hunting with firearms	19.3
19	Volleyball	18.5
20	Target shooting	15.7
21	Roller skating	15.1
22	Baseball	14.8
23	Soccer	13.9
24	Touch football	11.6
25	Backpacking	11.5
	Tennis	11.5
27	Mountain biking (on road)	11.3
	Step aerobics	11.3
29	Alpine skiing	10.5
30	Calisthenics	10.1

Note: The population of the U.S. in 1996 was an estimated 264.6 million.

Source: 1997 survey released by the National Sporting Goods Association.

Index

Calendar of Upcoming Events for 1998

January

1	Rose Bowl (Pasadena, California)
1	Sugar Bowl (New Orleans, Louisiana)
2	Orange Bowl (Miami, Florida)
3–4	NFL Divisional Playoffs
4–11	U.S. Figure Skating Championships (Philadelphia, Pennsylvania)
8–18	World Swimming and Diving Championships (Perth, Australia)
11	NFL Conference Title Games
18	NHL All-Star Game (Vancouver, Canada)
19–Feb. 1	Australian Open Tennis (Melbourne, Australia)

April

1	Baseball season opens*
2 & 4	NCAA Division I Hockey Final Four (Boston, Massachusetts)
3–5	Davis Cup Tennis (1st Round)
4–11	Men's and Women's Bowling U.S. Opens (Milford, Connecticut)
9–12	Masters Golf (Augusta, Georgia)
18–19	NFL Draft* (New York, New York)
19	NBA Regular Season ends
19	NHL Regular Season ends
20	Boston Marathon (Boston, Massachusetts)
22	NHL Playoffs begin
23	NBA Playoffs begin
26	NASCAR Winston Select 500 (Talladega, Alabama)

February

1	NFL Pro Bowl (Honolulu, Hawaii)
7–22	XVIIIth Winter Olympics (Nagano, Japan)
8	NBA All-Star Game (New York, New York)
15	Daytona 500 (Daytona Beach, Florida)
16–17	Westminster Dog Show (New York, New York)

May

2	Kentucky Derby (Louisville, Kentucky)
16	Preakness Stakes (Baltimore, Maryland)
20–23	NCAA Division I Women's Golf Championships (Madison, Wisconsin)
21–29	NCAA Division I Women's Tennis Championships (Notre Dame, Indiana)
23–31	NCAA Division I Men's Tennis Championships (Athens, Georgia)
24	Indianapolis 500, (Indianapolis, Indiana)
24	NASCAR Coca-Cola 600 (Charlotte, North Carolina)
25–June 7	French Open Tennis (Paris, France)
27–30	NCAA Division I Men's Golf Championships (Albuquerque, New Mexico)
29–June 6	College World Series baseball (Omaha, Nebraska)

March

7	Iditarod Trail Sled Dog Race begins (Anchorage, Alaska)
8	NCAA Division I Men's and Women's Basketball Tournament selections announced (Kansas City, Missouri)
12	Men's NCAA Division I Basketball Tournament begins
13	Women's NCAA Division I Basketball Tournament begins
19–21	NCAA Division I Women's Swimming Championships (Minneapolis, Minnesota)
26–28	NCAA Division I Men's Swimming Championships (Auburn, Alabama)
27 & 29	Women's NCAA Final Four (Kansas City, Missouri)
28 & 30	Men's NCAA Final Four (San Antonio, Texas)
29–Apr. 5	World Figure Skating Championships (Minneapolis, Minnesota)

June

3–6	NCAA Division I Men's and Women's Outdoor Track & Field Championships (Buffalo, New York)
6	Belmont Stakes (New York)
10–July 12	World Cup Soccer (France)
18–21	U.S. Open Golf (San Francisco, California)
22–July 5	Wimbledon Tennis (Wimbledon, England)
24	NBA Draft (Vancouver, Canada)
27	NHL Draft (Buffalo, New York)

July

2–5	U.S. Women's Open Golf (Kohler, Wisconsin)
7	Baseball All-Star Game (Denver, Colorado)
11–Aug. 2	Tour de France Cycling
16–19	British Open (Royal Birkdale, Southport, Lancashire, England)
17–19	Davis Cup Tennis (2nd Round)
18–Aug. 2	Goodwill Games (New York)
23–26	U. S. Senior Open Golf (Pacific Palisades, California)
25–26	Fed Cup Tennis (1st Round)

October

2	NHL Regular Season opens*
3	Ironman Triathlon (Kailua-Kona, Hawaii)
17	Baseball World Series begins*
30	NBA Regular Season opens*

August

1	Brickyard 400 (Indianapolis, Indiana)
6–8	BASS Masters Classic Fishing (Greensboro, North Carolina)
8	All-American Soap Box Derby (Akron, Ohio)
11–16	U. S. Women's Amateur golf (Ann Arbor, Michigan)
13–16	PGA Championship Golf (Seattle, Washington)
19–22	U.S. Gymnastics Championships (Indianapolis, Indiana)
24–29	Little League World Series Baseball (Williamsport, Pennsylvania)
24–30	U. S. Men's Amateur Golf (Rochester, New York)
30	NASCAR Southern 500 (Darlington, South Carolina)
31	Triathlon World Championships (Lausanne, Switzerland)
31–Sept. 13	U.S. Open Tennis (New York, New York)

November

1	New York Marathon (New York City)
7	Breeders' Cup (Louisville, Kentucky)
21	College Football: Auburn at Alabama, Florida at Florida State, Michigan at Ohio State, Southern Cal at UCLA, Washington at Washington State
28–29	Fed Cup Tennis Final

September

6	NFL Regular Season begins
19–20	Fed Cup Tennis Semifinals
25–27	Davis Cup Tennis Semifinals
27	Baseball Regular Season ends*
29	Baseball Playoffs begin*

December

4–6	Davis Cup Tennis Final
4–6	NCAA Division I Women's Soccer Final Four (Greensboro, North Carolina)
5	College Football: Army vs. Navy (Philadelphia, Pennsylvania)
5	Big 12 Football Title Game (St. Louis, Missouri)
5	Southeastern Conference Football Title Game (Atlanta, Georgia)
11–13	President's Cup Match Golf (Royal Melbourne, Black Rock, Victoria, Australia)
11–13	NCAA Division I Men's Soccer Final Four (Richmond, Virginia)
19	NCAA Division I-AA Football Title Game (Chattanooga, Tennessee)
28	NFL Regular Season ends

*Tentative date.

Acknowledgments

My thanks to Steve Lewers for his direct involvement in getting this book off the ground, and to the Monagan clan for their encouragement and frequent diversions. Compiling the lists in this album of athletics records would not have been possible without the assistance of old friends and reliable sources and the information provided by the following individuals, organizations, and publications:

Nat Andriani, Howard Bass, Bruce Bennett, Gerry Brown, Rick Campbell, Pete Cava, Andre Christopher, Jeff Davis, Paul Dergarabedian, Eric Duhatschek, Benny Ercolani, Nancy Ferber, Debbie Goodsite, Leslie Hammond, Dave Herscher, Gary Johnson, Dan Kasen, Paul Kennedy, Bob Kirlin, Terry Lyons, Peter Matthews, Carolyn McMahon, David Moore, Kevin Murphy, Chuck Pagano, Adam Polgreen, Phil Pritchard, Heidi Schaffner, Howie Schwab, Vito Stellino, and Paul Witteman.

Exhibitor Relations Co. Inc., Federation Internationale de Football Association (FIFA), International Olympic Committee (IOC), International Tennis Federation (ITF), Ladies Professional Golfers Association (LPGA), Major League Baseball (MLB), National Association of Stock Car Auto Racing (NASCAR), National Basketball Association (NBA), National Collegiate Athletic Association (NCAA), National Football League (NFL), National Hockey League (NHL), National Sporting Goods Association, New York Racing Association (NYRA), Professional Golfers Association of America, PGA Tour, The Royal and Ancient Golf Club of St. Andrews, U.S. Golf Association (USGA), U.S. Olympic Committee (USOC), U.S. Soccer, U.S. Swimming, Inc., U.S. Tennis Association (USTA), and USA Track & Field.

Newspapers, magazines, and newsletters: *The Boston Globe, FIFA News, Financial World, Forbes Magazine, The Hockey News, NBA News, The NCAA News, The New York Times, Sports Illustrated,* and *USA Today.*

Annuals (1997): *American Racing Manual, ATP Tour Player Guide, Breeders' Cup Statistics, CART Media Guide and Record Book, WTA Tour Player Guide, Davis Cup Media Guide, European Tour Media Guide, Fed Cup Media Guide, Indianapolis 500 Media Guide, International Track & Field Annual, Kentucky Derby Media Guide, Laurel and Pimlico Media Guide, LPGA Guide, Marlboro Grand Prix Guide, NASCAR Winston Cup Series Media Guide, NCAA College Basketball Records Book, NCAA Final Four Records Book, NCAA Women's College Basketball Records Book, NCAA College Football Records Book, NFL Record & Fact Book, NHL Guide and Record Book, NYRA Yearbook & Media Guide, PGA Tour Guide, Senior PGA Tour Guide, The Sporting News Baseball Register, The Sporting News Major League Baseball Fact Book, The Sporting News NBA Guide, The Sporting News NBA Register, The Sporting News NFL Guide, The Sporting News NFL Register, The Sporting News NHL Guide, The Sporting News NHL Register, Stats Pro Football Handbook,* and *U.S. Soccer Media Guide.*

Books: *A Who's Who of Sports Champions* (1995), *All-Time Greats of British and Irish Sport* (1995), *The Baseball Encyclopedia* (1995), *The Boxing Hall of Fame Register and Record Book* (1997), *Bud Collins' Tennis Encyclopedia* (1997), *The Complete Book of the Summer Olympics* (1996), *The Complete Book of the Winter Olympics* (1994), *The Encyclopedia of World Cup Soccer* (1994), *The Golden Book of the Olympic Games* (1992), *The Guinness Book of Golf Records, Facts and Champions* (1987), *The Guinness International Who's Who of Sport* (1993), *The History of the PGA Tour* (1989), *The Hockey Encyclopedia* (1983), *Indy: 75 Years of Racing's Greatest Spectacle* (1991), *Information Please Sports Almanac* (1990–97), *Inside Sports College Basketball* (1997), *The NBA Basketball Encyclopedia* (1994), *The Official Guide of the PGA Championships* (1995), *The Official NFL Encyclopedia* (1986), *The Pro Football Chronicle* (1990), *The Ring Record Book and Boxing Encyclopedia* (1985), *The Sporting News Complete Super Bowl Book* (1995), *The Story of the World Cup* (1994), *Total Baseball* (1995), *USGA Record Books* (1895–90), *World Book Encyclopedia* (1988), and *World Book Yearbook* (1954–97).

Picture Credits

UPI/Corbis-Bettman: pages 8, 10–12, 14–18, 22, 24, 28–31, 35–36, 39, 41, 42, 46, 49–51, 55, 59–71, 74, 77, 80–83, 86–87, 93, 95, 100–3, 105, 108–113, 122, 133, 136, 137, 139–146, 158, 160–164, 166, 167, 172, 174, 175, 177, 178, 182, 185–188, 192, 196, 200, 204, 208

Reuters/Corbis-Bettmann: pages 20, 32, 47, 53, 54, 58, 79, 85, 96, 107, 169–171, 173, 174, 176, 179–181, 183

Corbis/Bettmann: Back cover (top, middle, and bottom right); part-title page; title page (top left); copyright page; pages 9, 99 (bottom), 118, 151, 154, 156, 164, 165, 184, 214

Underwood & Underwood/Corbis-Bettmann: page 26

Agence France Presse/Corbis-Bettmann: page 150

AP/Wide World Photos: Front cover; back cover (top right); title page (bottom left and right, top right); pages 7, 13, 33, 34, 38, 44, 57, 73, 89, 92, 99 (top), 114, 115, 128, 135, 138, 148, 149, 153, 178, 183, 189–191, 199, 203, 206, 209, 210, 212, 213

Michigan State University Sports Information Dept.: page 41

Northeastern University Sports Information Dept.: page 90

University of Arizona Sports Information Dept.: page 91

University of Kentucky Sports Information Dept.: page 91

NBA Properties: page 113

Doug MacLellan/Hockey Hall of Fame: page 116

Hockey Hall of Fame: page 119, 121

Imperial Oil Turofsky/Hockey Hall of Fame: page 131

Bruce Bennett Studios: page 121, 126, 127, 129, 130, 132